# TRANSNATIONAL LITIGATION IN UNITED STATES COURTS

By

## HAROLD HONGJU KOH

Dean and
Gerard C. & Bernice Latrobe Smith Professor of International Law
Yale Law School

## CONCEPTS AND INSIGHTS SERIES

FOUNDATION PRESS
75TH ANNIVERSARY

This publication was created to provide you with accurate and authoritative information concerning the subject matter covered; however, this publication was not necessarily prepared by persons licensed to practice law in a particular jurisdiction. The publisher is not engaged in rendering legal or other professional advice and this publication is not a substitute for the advice of an attorney. If you require legal or other expert advice, you should seek the services of a competent attorney or other professional.

Nothing contained herein is intended or written to be used for the purposes of 1) avoiding penalties imposed under the federal Internal Revenue Code, or 2) promoting, marketing or recommending to another party any transaction or matter addressed herein.

© 2008 By THOMSON REUTERS/FOUNDATION PRESS
395 Hudson Street
New York, NY 10014
Phone Toll Free 1–877–888–1330
Fax (212) 367–6799
foundation–press.com

Printed in the United States of America

**ISBN** 978–1–58778–735–5

 TEXT IS PRINTED ON 10% POST CONSUMER RECYCLED PAPER

*For*
*Emily Jennings Youngyon Koh*
*and*
*William Hagan Wonlim Koh*

*

# PREFACE

This book sketches the emerging process of transnational civil litigation in United States courts. International and foreign issues have commanded the attention of American courts since the beginning of the Republic, but the last thirty years have seen a growing torrent of such cases. The last few decades have produced courses in many law schools, as well as a stream of casebooks, treatises, and bar association panels detailing the doctrines emerging from such litigation. But this book attempts a simpler task: to identify the key themes that animate those doctrines. In so doing, this book attempts neither to be comprehensive nor deep. Instead, its goal is to give an audience first thinking about these issues an intelligible overview of the thematic content of this exciting, fast-moving legal field and an intuitive understanding of how the current doctrinal framework evolved.

This volume grew out of a series of lectures first presented at the private international law section of the Hague Academy of International Law, and subsequently published as *International Business Transactions in United States Courts* in Volume 261 of the *Recueil des Cours* in 1996 (Martinus Nijhoff Publishers). Those lectures, which have been significantly updated for this volume, in turn arose from two and one-half decades of teaching law students various transnational litigation subjects at the Yale Law School, and before that, at the George Washington University National Law Center. Most of all, these lectures have been informed by my own transnational litigation experience, gained from five different perspectives. I first enjoyed the privilege of grappling with these issues as a law clerk to two legendary judges, Judge Malcolm Richard Wilkey of the United States Court of Appeals for the D.C. Circuit and Justice Harry A. Blackmun of the United States Supreme Court. In the years that followed, I was immersed in these issues as a private practitioner in Washington, D.C.; as a government lawyer and policymaker working in the Justice Department's Office of Legal Counsel in the early 1980s, and later as Assistant Secretary of State for Democracy, Human Rights and Labor in the late 1990s; as a scholar and teacher offering courses in Procedure, International Business Transactions, International Human Rights, Foreign Affairs Law, and Introduction to Transnational Law at Yale Law School since 1985; and since 1990, as a human rights litigator and clinician with

Yale Law School's Allard K. Lowenstein International Human Rights Clinic, National Litigation Project.

I thank Professor Daniel Bardonnet of the Curatorium of the Hague Academy of International Law for first inviting me to deliver these lectures and to John Bloomquist and his predecessor Steven Errick at Foundation Press for helping me to see them through to publication in this form.

Every book has many authors. Behind these pages stand the many friends and family who have supported my writing and litigating over the years, and the remarkable students and colleagues at Yale who have made my life as a scholar and teacher so rewarding. I especially thank my Deans at Yale Law School, Guido Calabresi and Tony Kronman, for their unstinting support, and Nicole Hallett, Amanda Aikman, Sonia Kumar, Christopher Ashley Ford, and Mark Templeton of Yale Law School for exemplary research assistance. My longtime mentor Peter D. Trooboff, and my Yale Law School colleagues Renee DeMatteo, Gene Coakley, Camilla Tubbs, and Georganne Rogers deserve more thanks than I can express for their selfless support. I have learned endlessly from a series of able students and skilled co-teachers at the Lowenstein Clinic: including Michael Ratner, Ron Slye, Rosa Ehrenreich Brooks, Jonathan Freiman, Mary Hahn, Hope Metcalf, Ramzi Kassem, and Michael Wishnie.

As always, the greatest debt goes to the coauthors of my life: my life partner, attorney Mary-Christy Fisher, and my children, Emily Jennings Youngyon Koh and William Hagan Wonlim Koh. Because their lives have animated this book, it is to their futures that this volume is dedicated.

HAROLD HONGJU KOH
New Haven, Connecticut

# FOREWORD

# The Plan of this Book

This short volume sketches the stages and themes of transnational civil litigation in United States courts. The topic cuts across traditional law school courses in Civil Procedure, International Business Transactions, International Human Rights, Conflicts of Laws, and International Dispute Resolution.

Part One provides a general introduction to the subject of transnational litigation. Chapter I sets that subject within the broader study of transnational law and transnational legal process. Chapter II then discusses what has sometimes been called "transnational private law litigation": civil litigation that traditionally occurs within the context of a private business transaction. The chapter argues that much transnational litigation can be better understood without using the "private-public" label, by understanding that an international business transaction evolves through three stages: international business formation, international business regulation, and international business dispute-resolution. The dynamic law of business transactions tends to percolate and transform from domestic to international, from private to public and back again. Moreover, this dynamic process illuminates five key themes that run throughout transnational litigation in U.S. courts: party autonomy, national sovereignty, comity, uniformity, and the separation of powers.

Chapter III then turns to the burgeoning subject of Transnational Public Law Litigation in U.S. courts: suits brought before U.S. judges by individual and governmental litigants challenging violations of public international law, as internalized into domestic law. This Chapter suggests that several of the same factors that have given rise to the jurisprudence of international business transactions—the doctrines of separation of powers, comity and national sovereignty—have promoted a parallel impulse toward judicial diffidence in international human rights cases. Ironically, some of the U.S. judicial decisions that have had the largest impact on the development of the law of international business transactions have not been private international law cases at all, but rather, public law cases involving claims of international human rights. Several of these cases have been decided based upon trans-substantive legal principles regarding statutory construction and the interpretation of treaties. By so ruling, these public law cases have further blurred the public/private divide by generating a continuing impact upon international business disputes that may arise in the future.

The remaining Chapters then examine the tension among these core principles by studying two emerging bodies of legal doctrine that increasingly govern resolution of international business disputes in U.S. courts. The Chapters in Part Two describe what I call the *American Law of Foreign Sovereignty*. The Chapters in Part Three outline what I call the emerging *Federal Rules of Transnational Civil Procedure*.[1]

Chapters IV through VI explain how the American Law of Foreign Sovereignty embraces four related doctrines that govern how U.S. courts treat foreign sovereign entities who engage in commercial activities somehow connected to the United States. Through those commercial activities, sovereigns are drawn into U.S. courts, most often as defendants in domestic lawsuits. These doctrines include the *extraterritoriality problem*, discussed in Chapter IV, which concerns how the courts deal with foreign sovereign objections to extraterritorial application of U.S. regulatory law. Chapter IV examines how the controversial U.S. doctrine of extraterritoriality has flowed from the core principles identified in the introductory chapters, and explains how American courts have dealt with the extraterritorial application of domestic regulatory laws.

The following two Chapters then consider how the related sovereignty doctrines of act of state, foreign sovereign compulsion, and foreign sovereign immunity have affected the adjudication of commercial acts and activities of sovereign and quasi-sovereign entities. Chapter V describes the judicially created *act of state doctrine*, a doctrine of federal common law, and act-of-state's doctrinal cousin, the *foreign sovereign compulsion defense*. Chapter VI outlines the law of foreign sovereign immunity, as embodied in the U.S. Foreign Sovereign Immunities Act of 1976.[2]

What unites these doctrines is their common requirement that U.S. courts defer to foreign sovereignty: whether by deciding not to exercise jurisdiction over foreign conduct, by declining to apply an American rule of law to that conduct, or by deciding to treat the challenged act of a foreign sovereign or its agent as presumptively or conclusively valid.

---

[1] For an earlier discussion of these doctrinal clusters, see Harold Hongju Koh, *Transnational Public Law Litigation*, 100 YALE L.J. 2347, 2390-94 (1991).

[2] Foreign Sovereign Immunities Act of 1976, Pub. L. No. 94-583, 90 Stat. 2892 (1976) (codified as amended at 28 U.S.C. §§ 1602-1611 (1994)).

These doctrines take different legal and procedural forms and attach in different litigation settings. The extraterritoriality doctrine arises when courts construe the jurisdictional reach of regulatory statutes. Foreign sovereign immunity raises an issue of subject matter jurisdiction. The act of state doctrine constitutes both a rule of justiciability (admissibility) and a rule of decision, while a claim of foreign sovereign compulsion usually arises by way of affirmative defense. Yet by limiting the freedom of the courts to make determinations regarding the legality of foreign sovereign acts, each doctrine reflects common underlying concerns about national sovereignty, international comity, separation of powers, and judicial competence. Moreover, the Chapters in Part Two jointly contend that the last two decades have witnessed a marked decline in the overall deference paid by American courts to foreign sovereignty.

The Chapters in Part Three turn from these public law issues of foreign sovereignty to the variegated procedural doctrines that U.S. courts have developed to address transnational commercial litigation in cases involving both public and private entities. In domestic civil cases, the United States federal trial courts have, since 1938, operated according to a uniform set of written rules known as the Federal Rules of Civil Procedure. Yet over the last half-century, concerns about the uniformity and predictability of transnational procedural law have also led American courts to adapt to the international commercial setting pre-existing *procedural* doctrines of subject matter jurisdiction,[3] personal jurisdiction,[4] attachment,[5] service of process,[6] venue,[7] choice of law,[8] discovery,[9] and the recognition and enforcement of foreign judgments, decrees, and arbitral awards.[10]

---

[3] *See, e.g.*, Hartford Fire Insurance Co. v. California, 509 U.S. 764 (1993); United States v. Aluminum Co. of America, 148 F.2d 416 (2d Cir. 1945) (explaining scope of subject matter jurisdiction under the antitrust laws).

[4] *See, e.g.*, Asahi Metal Indus. Co. v. Superior Court, 480 U.S. 102 (1987); Helicopteros Nacionales de Colombia, S.A. v. Hall, 466 U.S. 408 (1984); Paulson Investment Co. v. Norbay Securities, Inc., 603 F. Supp. 615 (D. Or. 1984) (using national contacts test for personal jurisdiction under securities statute).

[5] *See, e.g.*, Reading and Bates Corp. v. National Iranian Oil Co., 478 F. Supp. 724 (S.D.N.Y. 1979).

[6] See, e.g., Volkswagenwerk Aktiengesellschaft v. Schlunk, 486 U.S. 694 (1988).

[7] As Chapter VIII explains, this doctrine has been subdivided into those cases concerning forum-selection clauses, *see, e.g.*, M/S Bremen v. Zapata Off-Shore Co., 407 U.S. 1 (1972), and those concerning *forum non conveniens, see, e.g.*, Piper Aircraft Co. v. Reyno, 454 U.S. 235 (1981); In re Union Carbide Corp. Gas Plant Disaster at Bhopal, India in December, 1984, 634 F. Supp. 842 (S.D.N.Y. 1986), *aff'd in part*, 809 F.2d 195 (2d Cir. 1987).

[8] As we shall see below in Chapter V, the act of state doctrine serves as a kind of federal choice-of-law principle.

[9] *See, e.g.*, Societe Nationale Industrielle Aerospatiale v. United States District Court, 482 U.S. 522 (1987).

[10] Mitsubishi Motors Corp. v. Soler Chrysler-Plymouth, Inc., 473 U.S. 614 (1985) (analyzing

The rules that have emerged from these cases increasingly constitute *de facto* Federal Rules of *Transnational* Civil Procedure.[11] These rules, developed originally in domestic commercial cases, are what the late Robert Cover called "trans-substantive" rules, inasmuch as they apply equally to cases involving different subject matters--contracts, torts, property, corporations--as well as to cases involving both private and public parties. By and large, these rules remain unwritten, for U.S. courts have evolved them on a case-by-case basis, with only occasional direction from the Supreme Court. Because of their rarity, Supreme Court rulings in this area have tended to have unusually long reverberations.[13] At this point, these transnational rules remain largely uncodified in either statute or formal rules. Moreover, because they concern the procedural power of the federal courts to promote national uniformity, they tend to represent not state law but rather, rules of federal common law.[14] Recently, some of these court-made rules have even acquired such prominence as to provoke changes in the formally promulgated Federal Rules of Civil Procedure.

Many first-term courses in Procedure, including my own, now include topics in Transnational Procedure, including transnational civil litigation and the ALI/UNIDROIT Principles and Rules of Transnational Rules of Civil Procedure, which represent cross-cutting transnational procedural rules on jurisdiction, venue, service of process, the taking of evidence, and the recognition of judgments. The American Law Institute and UNIDROIT have recently completed a project to enumerate a uniform set of procedural rules for transnational cases, expressly designed "to apply in ordinary national courts, replacing domestic procedural rules whenever the plaintiff and defendant are nationals of different states or whenever property in one state is subject to claims ... asserted by a party from another state."[15]

---

enforcement of foreign arbitration clause); Parsons and Whittemore Overseas Co. v. Societe Generale de L'Industrie du Papier (RAKTA), 508 F.2d 969 (2d Cir. 1974) (addressing enforcement of foreign arbitration award); Hilton v. Guyot, 159 U.S. 113 (1895) (discussing enforcement of foreign judgments).

[11] *See* Koh, *supra* note 1, at 2390.

[12] *See* Robert M. Cover, *For James Wm. Moore: Some Reflections on a Reading of the Rules*, 84 YALE L.J. 718, 718 (1975).

[13] Cf. Antonin Scalia, *Vermont Yankee: The APA, the D.C. Circuit, and the Supreme Court*, 1978 S. CT. REV. 345 (making a similar claim with respect to Supreme Court rulings in the area of administrative law).

[14] Roger Transgrud, *The Federal Common Law of Personal Jurisdiction*, 57 GEO. WASH. L. REV. 849 (1989) (describing how such rules have arguably evolved in the realm of personal jurisdiction).

[15] *See* Geoffrey C. Hazard, Jr. and Michele Taruffo, *Transnational Rules of Civil Procedure*: *Rules and Commentary*, 30 CORNELL INT'L L.J. 493, 493-94 (1997). *See generally* AMERICAN LAW INSTITUTE & UNIDROIT, PRINCIPLES AND RULES OF TRANSNATIONAL CIVIL PROCEDURE (2005).

Chapters VII through XII describe and criticize these procedural rules. I will suggest that much of the law the Supreme Court has made in this area, in just a handful of transnational cases, is badly reasoned or wrongly decided. Thus, Chapter VII addresses topics surrounding Jurisdiction to Adjudicate. Chapter VIII discusses the procedural rules and Supreme Court decisions that govern venue: forum non conveniens and forum-selection clauses.[16]

Chapters IX and X address Service of Process and Taking of Evidence, again focusing on the leading Supreme Court decisions.[17] Chapters XI and XII conclude by examining the law by which American courts recognize and enforce Foreign Judgments, Decrees, and Arbitral Agreements and Awards by American courts. Each Chapter will explore what these cases reveal about the interplay among the core judicial concerns identified above: about separation of powers, comity, and desires to promote uniformity of procedural rules and deference to party autonomy and national sovereignty. Where possible, these Chapters compare and contrast how the U.S. judicial system has treated a particular legal issue in international business transactions with the parallel course taken by other municipal courts.

In Chapter XIII, this book closes by asking: "Does the U.S. Supreme Court have a discernable jurisprudence of transnational litigation?" I conclude that at present, there are not one, but two competing schools of jurisprudence emerging in the current Court: a "transnationalist" jurisprudence, which sees U.S. courts as playing a key role in integrating U.S. law into an emerging transnational legal system; and a "nationalist jurisprudence," which sees the U.S. judicial role largely as preserving the autonomy of U.S. law from that global system.

---

[16] Asahi Metal Indus. Co. v. Superior Court, 480 U.S. 102 (1987); Piper Aircraft Co. v. Reyno, 454 U.S. 235 (1981); M/S Bremen v. Zapata Off-Shore Co., 407 U.S. 1 (1972).
[17] Volkswagenwerk Aktiengesellschaft v. Schlunk, 486 U.S. 694 (1988); Societe Nationale Industrielle Aerospatiale v. United States District Court, 482 U.S. 522 (1987).

\*

# TABLE OF CONTENTS

## PART FOUR: THE FUTURE OF TRANSNATIONAL LITIGATION

\*

# TRANSNATIONAL LITIGATION IN UNITED STATES COURTS

\*

# PART ONE

## INTRODUCTION TO TRANSNATIONAL LITIGATION

## CHAPTER I

### TRANSNATIONAL LITIGATION AS PART OF TRANSNATIONAL LAW

Many of the topics embraced in these pages were once grouped under the general heading of "private international law," the law governing relations between private persons in different countries, in contrast to "public international law," the law governing relations among nation-states. Today, I would argue, the topic is better captured by the term "transnational litigation," which in turn falls under the broader rubric of "transnational law."

U.S. Supreme Court Justice Joseph Story is usually credited with coining the phrase "private international law," declaring in his famous 1834 *Commentaries on the Conflict of Laws*, "[t]his branch of public law may be fitly denominated private international law, since it is chiefly seen and felt in its application to the common business of private persons, and rarely rises to the dignity of national negotiations, or national controversies."[1] Thus, traditional courses in private international law have usually embraced the subjects that American lawyers now study under the general heading of "conflicts of laws": such topics as choice of law; status, capacity, and nationality of persons; application of these principles to contracts, property, torts, and family law; proof of and application of foreign law; domicile and residence rules; enforcement of foreign judgments and arbitral awards; and the rules regarding jurisdiction and judgments of domestic courts.[2]

In the modern era, this traditional subject of "private international law" has largely ceased to exist as an independent subject. Instead, the content of private international law has gradually

---

1. JOSEPH STORY, COMMENTARIES ON THE CONFLICT OF LAWS, FOREIGN AND DOMESTIC, IN REGARD TO CONTRACTS, RIGHTS AND REMEDIES, AND ESPECIALLY IN REGARD TO MARRIAGES, DIVORCES, WILLS, SUCCESSIONS, AND JUDGMENTS 9 (Boston, Hilliard, Gray, and Company 1st ed. 1834).

2. *See generally* J.J. FAWCETT & J. CARRUTHERS, CHESHIRE, NORTH AND FAWCETT: PRIVATE INTERNATIONAL LAW (14th ed. 2008) (reviewing these topics).

overlapped and merged into what some now call the law of "international economic relations,"[3] and others term "the law of international business transactions."[4] Transactions in this modern era may still be conducted between private entities, but hardly fit Story's description as "rarely ris[ing] to the dignity of national negotiations, or national controversies." To the contrary, such transactions are now just as likely to be "public-private" in nature—i.e., transacted between private parties and governmental or quasi-governmental entities—or even "public-public"—i.e., international business transactions conducted between commercial entities of two or more sovereign governments. Indeed, one noted scholar has speculated that the law of international economic relations may now comprise as much as ninety percent of the subject traditionally known as *"public* international law."[5]

Although the phrase "private international law" continues to hold sway in Europe and Asia, in the United States, where the phrase originated, the term has been in decline at least since 1956. In his Storrs Lectures that year, delivered at Yale Law School, then-judge of the International Court of Justice Philip Jessup coined the term "transnational law" to embrace "all law which regulates actions or events that transcend national frontiers," including "[b]oth public and private international law ... [plus] other rules which do not wholly fit into such standard categories."[6]

In 1960, Harvard Law Professors Milton Katz and Kingman Brewster (later President of Yale University) adapted that concept while developing a pioneering casebook on the law of international transactions and relations.[7] Their casebook became an important part of what became the Harvard "International Legal Process School" of international law. At about the same time, their Har-

3. *See, e.g.,* JOHN H. JACKSON, WILLIAM DAVEY, AND ALAN O. SYKES, LEGAL PROBLEMS OF INTERNATIONAL ECONOMIC RELATIONS: CASES, MATERIALS AND TEXT (4th ed. 2001).

4. *See, e.g.,* RALPH H. FOLSOM ET AL., INTERNATIONAL BUSINESS TRANSACTIONS: A PROBLEM-ORIENTED COURSEBOOK (9th ed. 2006).

5. John H. Jackson, *International Economic Law: Reflections on the "Boiler Room" of International Relations,* 10 AM. U. J. INT'L L. AND POL'Y 595, 596 (1995) (emphasis in original).

6. PHILIP C. JESSUP, TRANSNATIONAL LAW 2 (1956).

7. MILTON KATZ & KINGMAN BREWSTER, JR., THE LAW OF INTERNATIONAL TRANSAC-

TIONS AND RELATIONS: CASES AND MATERIALS (1960). Kingman Brewster's intellectual approach derived from his work with his future Harvard Law colleagues Milton Katz and Roger Fisher at the General Counsel's Office at the Marshall Plan in Paris. As Brewster's biographer notes, "The Marshall Plan demonstrated process-oriented thinking in action. Brewster, Fisher, and Katz were not planners.... Their work was process: how do you make this happen? How do you get this working?" GEOFFREY KABASERVICE, THE GUARDIANS: KINGMAN BREWSTER, HIS CIRCLE, AND THE RISE OF THE LIBERAL ESTABLISHMENT 115 (2004) (quotation marks omitted).

vard colleague, former State Department Legal Adviser Abram Chayes, joined by his former deputies Thomas Ehrlich and Andreas Lowenfeld, published a series of case studies entitled *International Legal Process*, which drew explicitly upon Henry Hart and Albert Sacks's famous domestic materials on "The Legal Process" to illustrate the role of law in the process of policy decisions in the international realm.[8] Chayes and his colleagues deliberately cut across the categories of international legal studies as they are sometimes conceived—"public international law," "international organizations," "legal problems of international business," and the like, asking "How and how far do law, lawyers and legal institutions operate to affect the course of international affairs? What is the legal process by which interests are adjusted and decisions are reached on the international scene?"[9] In his 1979 Hague Lectures, Professor Lowenfeld built further upon those questions, breaking down the traditional separation between public and private international law by focusing on those aspects of transnational law that he dubbed "Public Law in the International Arena": areas in which public and private interests as well as the interests of sovereign states collide.[10] Just a few years earlier, in revising the Brewster/Katz casebook, Henry Steiner and Detlev Vagts expressly mixed public and private, domestic and international, to reconceptualize the law of international business transactions as a distinctive breed of "Transnational Legal Problems."[11]

Transnational law figured prominently not just at Harvard, but also in the pioneering work of Yale's "New Haven School of International Law," whose founding fathers were Yale law professor Myres McDougal and political scientist Harold Lasswell.[12]

8. *Compare* ABRAM CHAYES, THOMAS EHRLICH & ANDREAS LOWENFELD, INTERNATIONAL LEGAL PROCESS at xi (1968) *with* WILLIAM N. ESKRIDGE, JR. & PHILLIP P. FRICKEY, AN HISTORICAL AND CRITICAL INTRODUCTION TO HENRY M. HART, JR. & ALBERT M. SACKS, *THE LEGAL PROCESS* at ciii n.232, cxiv n.286, cxxxii n.346 (1994) (describing Chayes's and Ehrlich's schooling in Legal Process thought).

9. CHAYES, ET AL., *supra* note 8, at xi.

10. Andreas F. Lowenfeld, *Public Law in the International Arena: Conflict of Laws, International Law, and Some Suggestions for their Interaction*, 163 RECUEIL DES COURS 311 (1979).

11. HENRY J. STEINER & DETLEV F. VAGTS, TRANSNATIONAL LEGAL PROBLEMS: MATERIALS AND TEXT (1968) (now HENRY

STEINER, DETLEV F. VAGTS & HAROLD HONGJU KOH, TRANSNATIONAL LEGAL PROBLEMS: MATERIALS AND TEXT (4th ed. 1994)). The international business transactions materials in that book were later spun off into a separate volume. *See* DETLEV F. VAGTS, WILLIAM S. DODGE & HAROLD HONGJU KOH, TRANSNATIONAL BUSINESS PROBLEMS (4th ed. 2008).

12. For representative works within this vast literature, see, for example, HAROLD D. LASSWELL & MYRES S. McDOUGAL, JURISPRUDENCE FOR A FREE SOCIETY: STUDIES IN LAW, SCIENCE AND POLICY (1992) [hereinafter LASSWELL & McDOUGAL, JURISPRUDENCE FOR A FREE SOCIETY]; MYRES S. McDOUGAL ET AL., HUMAN RIGHTS AND WORLD PUBLIC ORDER (1980); MYRES S. McDOUGAL & W. MICHAEL REISMAN, INTERNATIONAL LAW ESSAYS (1981). For jurispru-

During the same Cold War era, along with a cohort of able colla-
borators, they elaborated the claims of policy science in an ex-
traordinarily broad array of fields of public international law.[13]
Like Harvard's International Legal Process School, McDougal and
Lasswell's New Haven School viewed international law through
the lens of process. Yale Law School was the intellectual home of
legal realism, and the New Haven School became, in effect, the
school of international law for legal realists. The New Haven
School criticized both legal formalism and legal positivism in international law, seeking instead to develop "a functional critique
of international law in terms of social ends ... that shall conceive of the legal order as a process and not as a condition." The
New Haven School consistently argued that international law is
not just a body of rules, but a process of authoritative decision-
making, within which "our chief interest is in the legal process,
by which we mean the making of authoritative and controlling
decisions."[14] By treating international law as more than just a
body of rules, the New Haven School committed itself not simply
to a study of bare process, but more fundamentally, to an examination of a process of authoritative decision-making dedicated to
promoting a set of normative values.

dential histories of the New Haven
School, *see generally* Richard A. Falk,
*Casting the Spell: The New Haven
School of International Law*, 104 YALE
L.J. 1991, 1997 (1995); NEIL DUXBURY,
PATTERNS OF AMERICAN JURISPRUDENCE 191–
203 (1995); Symposium, *McDougal's Jurisprudence: Utility, Influence, Controversy*, 79 AM. SOC'Y INT'L L. PROC. 266
(1985) [hereinafter Symposium, *McDougal's Jurisprudence*].

**13.** McDougal and Lasswell's colla-
borators included their successor Mi-
chael Reisman, *see, e.g.*, W. MICHAEL
REISMAN, NULLITY AND REVISION: THE REVIEW
AND ENFORCEMENT OF INTERNATIONAL JUDG-
MENTS AND AWARDS (1971); W. Michael
Reisman, *International Lawmaking: A
Process of Communication*, 75 AM. SOC'Y
INT'L L. PROC. 101, 107, 113 (1981); for-
mer Attorney General and Undersecre-
tary of State Nicholas DeB. Katzenbach,
*see, e.g.*, MORTON A. KAPLAN & NICHOLAS
DeB. KATZENBACH, THE POLITICAL FOUNDA-
TIONS OF INTERNATIONAL LAW 356 (1961); as
well as scholars of such diverse political
orientation as Richard Falk of Princeton
University, *see, e.g.*, RICHARD A. FALK, THE
STATUS OF LAW IN INTERNATIONAL SOCIETY
642–59 (1970); President Rosalyn Hig-

gins of the International Court of Justice (formerly Professor of International
Law at the London School of Econom-
ics), *see, e.g.*, ROSALYN HIGGINS, PROBLEMS
AND PROCESS 267 (1994); John Norton
Moore of the University of Virginia, *see,
e.g.*, John Norton Moore, *Prolegomenon
to the Jurisprudence of Myres McDougal
and Harold Lasswell*, 54 VA. L. REV. 662
(1968); and Burns Weston of the University of Iowa, *see, e.g.*, BURNS H. WESTON
ET AL., INTERNATIONAL LAW AND WORLD OR-
DER (1980); Burns H. Weston, *Nuclear
Weapons and International Law: Prolegomenon to General Illegality*, 4 N.Y.L.
SCH. J. INT'L & COMP. L. 227 (1983).

**14.** Myres S. McDougal & Harold D.
Lasswell, *The Identification and Ap-
praisal of Diverse Systems of Public Order*, 53 AM. J. INT'L L. 1, 9 (1959). In
1981, Michael Reisman argued that the
New Haven School viewed international
law as a "process of communication,"
which sees the legal process as compris-
ing three communicative streams, "policy content, authority signal and control
intention." W. Michael Reisman, *International Lawmaking: A Process of Communication*, 75 AM. SOC'Y INT'L L. PROC.
101, 113 (1981).

Schools of thought arise inevitably from both their political and academic times. We now live in a different political era than when the New Haven School was founded: in a "post-post-Cold War" world, after the fall not just of the Berlin Wall, but also of the Twin Towers, and in an age of globalization populated by myriad transnational actors—not just nation-states, but also multinational corporations, intergovernmental organizations, and non-state actors who are capable of serving as both transnational decision-makers and as potential transnational threats. We also live in a different academic era, where law is pervaded by interdisciplinary studies, the pursuit of scholarship is regularly mixed with clinical activities, and our legal curriculum increasingly blends public and private law.

As a student trained in Harvard's International Legal Process thinking and as a Yale professor who has spent several decades as a "fellow traveler" of the New Haven School of International Law, I have focused my own work on Philip Jessup's concept of transnational law as a hybrid of domestic and international law that has assumed increasing significance in our 21st century lives. Through the late twentieth century, most American law school curricula were artificially shoehorned into a two-by-two matrix, with one axis describing the dichotomy between domestic and international law; and the other axis dividing public from private law. First-year law students began primarily with courses in private-domestic law, such as torts, contracts, or property, then progressed to domestic-public subjects such as constitutional and criminal law. In their advanced courses, they might study public international law (the use of force or United Nations law) or private international law subjects such as Conflict of Laws and International Business Transactions, but those subjects were treated primarily at the level of contractual private-ordering, with relatively little attention paid to public law issues.

Today, however, everyone recognizes that the 20th century legal "Matrix" was a construct that no longer fits the modern legal realities of 21st century legal education. In recent years, the idea that most modern global disputes are resolved under transnational legal rules and through a transnational legal process has become a key claim of an emerging school of international legal theory now called the " 'New' New Haven School of International Law."[15] Building on the idea of transnational legal process, these international law scholars highlight the role of legal pluralism—multiple

---

**15.** *See generally* Symposium: The "New" New Haven School: International Law–Past, Present, and Future, 32 YALE J. INT'L L. 301–582 (2007); Harold Hongju Koh, *Is There a "New" New Haven School of International Law?*, 32 YALE J. INT'L L. 559 (2007), from which this discussion derives.

communities for law development, interpretation and enforcement—in creating transnational law in the absence of a single global "Leviathan."[16] "New" New Haven School theorists see "dialectical legal interactions" among these law-declaring fora—particularly through dialogue among courts around the world[17]—as helping to refine the scope of the international legal obligations of nations, corporations, nonstate actors, and individuals.

To this day, the best summary of the extant doctrines of transnational law remains the American Law Institute's Restatement (Third) of Foreign Relations Law, completed more than two decades ago.[18] One might think of transnational law as law that is neither purely domestic nor purely international, but rather, a hybrid of the two. Consider, for example, the metric system or the internet business concept of "dot.com." Are these domestic or international concepts? Of course, the intuitive answer is neither. Both are hybrids, purely transnational ideas.

Perhaps the best operational definition of transnational law, using computer-age imagery, is: (1) law that is "downloaded" from international to domestic law: For example, an international law concept that is domesticated or internalized into municipal law, such as the international human rights norm against disappearance, now recognized as domestic law in most municipal systems; (2) law that is "uploaded, then downloaded": for example, a rule that originates in a domestic legal system, such as the guarantee of a free trial under the concept of due process of law in Western legal systems, which then becomes part of international law, as in the Universal Declaration of Human Rights and the International Covenant on Civil and Political Rights, and from there becomes internalized into nearly every legal system in the world; and (3) law that is borrowed or "horizontally transplanted" from one national system to another: for example, the "unclean hands" doctrine, which migrated from the British law of equity to many other legal systems.

To understand how transnational law works, one should distinguish between what I call "transnational legal substance" and "transnational legal process." By transnational legal substance, I

---

**16.** Paul Schiff Berman, *A Pluralist Approach to International Law*, 32 YALE J. INT'L L. 307, 311 (2007).

**17.** Berman, *supra* note 16, at 321 (emphasis added); *see also* Robert B. Ahdieh, *Between Dialogue and Decree: International Review of National Courts*, 79 N.Y.U. L. REV. 2029 (2004); Melissa

A. Waters, *Normativity in the "New" Schools: Assessing the Legitimacy of International Legal Norms Created by Domestic Courts*, 32 YALE J. INT'L L. 455 (2007).

**18.** *See, e.g.*, RESTATEMENT (THIRD) OF THE FOREIGN RELATIONS LAW OF THE UNITED

mean the substantive rules that determine the legal rights and duties of transnational actors operating within a global setting. Those rules may be derived from private arrangements, such as contracts; from state and local laws that specify and empower corporate activity; from federal statutes and executive orders; from international treaties as well as federal common law rules derived from customary international law; and from the United States Constitution. Transnational legal substance is now taught in a broad array of substantive law school courses that can no longer be treated as either purely domestic or international, public or private: for example, Comparative Law, Immigration and Refugee Law, International Business Transactions, International Commercial Law, International Trade Law, Foreign Relations Law, National Security Law, Counterterrorism Law, Law of Cyberspace, Law and Development, Environmental Law, and the Law of Transnational Crimes. In each of these legal areas, global standards have become fully recognized, integrated, and internalized into domestic legal systems.

Transnational legal substance has recently brought a focus on globalization into the traditional First Term Curriculum, within the basic courses of Procedure, Torts, Constitutional Law, and Contracts. In the first-year law school curriculum, one can now imagine a course in contracts that includes, alongside traditional domestic doctrine, a discussion of *Transnational Contracts*: for example, oil development agreements between multinational oil companies and developing nations, or contracts governed by the U.N. Convention on Contracts for the International Sale of Goods. Similarly, a torts course could now add a discussion of *Transnational Torts*, both mass disasters such as the Bhopal tragedy and civil litigation of crimes against humanity and "torts in violation of the law of nations" under the Alien Tort Claims Act.[19] The basic criminal law course could be modified to include a module on such *Transnational Crimes* as terrorism, drug trafficking, trafficking in persons, and international criminal litigation in domestic courts, such as the famous *Pinochet* case.[20] Property courses can now include modules on *Transnational Property*—for example, the World Trade Organization (WTO) rules on protection of intellectual property—and there is already a rich body of teaching materials on *Comparative Constitutional Law*.[21]

STATES (1987) [hereinafter Restatement (Third)].

**19.** 28 U.S.C. § 1350 (2008); *see also* Sosa v. Alvarez–Machain, 542 U.S. 692 (2004) (stating test for what kinds of torts are actionable under this statute).

**20.** *See generally*, REED BRODY, THE PINOCHET PAPERS: THE CASE OF AUGUSTO PINOCHET IN SPAIN AND BRITAIN (2000).

**21.** *See generally* VICKI C. JACKSON & MARK TUSHNET, COMPARATIVE CONSTITUTIONAL LAW (2d ed. 2006).

By "Transnational Legal Process," I refer to the trans-substantive process in each of these issue areas whereby states and other transnational private actors use the blend of domestic and international legal process to internalize international legal norms into substantive domestic law.[22] Again using computer imagery, if transnational legal substance represents the programs being downloaded, transnational legal process is the *mechanism* through which that process of downloading occurs. As I have argued elsewhere, key agents in promoting this process of internalization include transnational norm entrepreneurs, governmental norm sponsors, transnational issue networks, and interpretive communities.[23] In this story, one of these agents triggers an interaction at the international level, works together with other agents of internalization to force an interpretation of the international legal norm in an interpretive forum, and then continues to work with those agents to persuade a resisting nation-state to internalize that interpretation into domestic law. Through repeated cycles of "interaction-interpretation-internalization," interpretations of applicable global norms are eventually internalized into states' domestic legal systems.

To take just one illustration of how transnational legal substance and process interact, consider the ancient law merchant (*"lex mercatoria"*). Originally developed as a form of business regulation among merchants in the Mediterranean, English merchants brought the customs, principles, and rules of *lex mercatoria* to England where they became incorporated into the English common law.[24] From there, this body of law migrated to the New World to become part of American common law.[25] Through the enactment

---

**22.** *See generally* Harold Hongju Koh, *The 1994 Roscoe Pound Lecture: Transnational Legal Process*, 75 NEB. L. REV. 181 (1996); Harold Hongju Koh, *Why Do Nations Obey International Law?*, 106 YALE L.J. 2599 (1997); OONA HATHAWAY & HAROLD HONGJU KOH, FOUNDATIONS OF INTERNATIONAL LAW AND POLITICS 173–204 (2006).

**23.** Transnational legal process highlights the interactions among both private citizens, whom I call "transnational norm entrepreneurs," and governmental officials, whom I call "governmental norm sponsors." The interaction among transnational norm entrepreneurs and governmental norm sponsors creates transnational networks and law-declaring fora, which create new rules of international law that are construed by interpretive communities. Through the work of these "agents of internalization," these international law rules trickle down from the international level and become domesticated into national law. *See generally* Harold Hongju Koh, *The 1998 Frankel Lecture: Bringing International Law Home*, 35 HOUS. L. REV. 623 (1998).

**24.** *See* Harold J. Berman & Colin Kaufman, *The Law of International Commercial Transactions (Lex Mercatoria)*, 19 HARV. INT'L L.J. 221, 224–29 (1978).

**25.** *See* Swift v. Tyson, 41 U.S. (16 Pet.) 1 (1842) (clarifying that the bill of exchange rules derived from *lex mercatoria* constituted part of the "general common law" to be interpreted by federal courts sitting in diversity jurisdiction).

of the Uniform Commercial Code, which sought to codify existing mercantile custom in forty nine states and the District of Columbia, *lex mercatoria* entered state statutory law. It then became treaty law as part of the United Nations Convention on Contracts for International Sale of Goods, which entered into force for the United States on January 1, 1988.[26] Thus, the transnational legal process story of *lex mercatoria* shows that it was domesticated through an historical process whereby it began as transnational custom, mutated into domestic common law, was transplanted to another national system, was codified into domestic statutory law, and finally, was uploaded into international treaty law, which is also federal law in the United States.

---

**26.** United Nations Convention on Contracts for the International Sale of Goods, Apr. 11, 1980, 1489 U.N.T.S. 3 [hereinafter CISG]. By operation of the Supremacy Clause, the CISG overrides the UCC with respect to contracts for the sale of goods between parties whose places of business are in different contracting states.

# CHAPTER II

## Transnational Private Law Litigation

Much of today's transnational civil litigation takes place within the setting of international business transactions, which has traditionally been treated as transnational private law litigation. Yet the modern law of international business transactions now straddles the public and private. It embraces not just private international law, traditionally understood, but all private and public law, at the level of contract, national law, regional law, and global law, that governs the movement of goods, services, workers, and money (in the form of both debt and equity) across national borders.

### A. The Stages of International Business Transactions

This point becomes clearer when one realizes that the law of international business transactions today falls into three discernable phases: the law of *international business formation*, the law of *international business regulation*, and the law of *international business dispute-resolution*, into which transnational civil litigation falls.

The law of International Business Formation (or the "law of dealmaking") refers to the law governing the formation, ordering, and planning of transnational commercial arrangements among individuals, business entities, and state commercial enterprises. The law of International Business Regulation encompasses the law governing the regulation of those business relationships by home and host governments and intergovernmental organizations—for example, taxation, banking regulation, securities regulation, regulation of import and export trade, competition, immigration, insolvency, and intellectual property (or regulation of innovation, as one might call it). The law of International Dispute Resolution includes the law governing the resolution of international business *disputes* through civil litigation in municipal courts or through dispute resolution before international arbitral or judicial tribunals.

So defined, the law of international business transactions sweeps much too broadly to be covered in a monograph of this length.[1] To cover the topic comprehensively, in the *formation* stage

---

1. For an effort to cover these issues comprehensively in a casebook setting, see Detlev F. Vagts, William S. Dodge & Harold Hongju Koh, Transnational Business Problems (4th ed. 2008).

we would need to study the law governing the numerous forms of doing business internationally—mergers and acquisitions, branches, subsidiaries, development agreements, joint ventures, licensings, agency and distributorship arrangements—as well as the law governing various available modes of financing international transactions: loans, letters of credit and the like.[2] To adequately study the subject of international business *regulation*, we would have to study the law of import and export controls, securities regulation, intellectual property law, antitrust, bankruptcy, taxation and general jurisdictional principles regarding extraterritorial application of domestic law. To understand better just the processes of international commercial dispute resolution, we would need to examine the various procedural issues arising in international judicial tribunals, such as chambers of the International Court of Justice (e.g., standing, exhaustion, provisional remedies, jurisdiction, etc.); international arbitral tribunals, whether standing (e.g., the Iran–U.S. Claims Tribunal in the Hague, ICSID (the International Convention on the Settlement of Investment Disputes), the Inter–American Arbitration Commission) or *ad hoc* (e.g., International Chamber of Commerce, American Arbitration Association, London Court of Arbitration, Stockholm and Japanese Chamber of Commerce, the United Nations Commission on International Trade Law (UNCITRAL)); not to mention litigation before all manner of domestic courts.[3]

While this range of issues is daunting, on reflection, the subject's breadth is hardly surprising. For if one were asked to describe a parallel curriculum of *"domestic* business transactions" for a modern law school, one would necessarily include all subjects governing the formation of business arrangements among domestic individuals and business entities—e.g., contracts, property, torts, corporations, partnership and agency law—not to mention the laws of banking, credit and financing; all subjects regarding the regulation of those private business relationships by governments—namely, taxation, bankruptcy, banking regulation, securities regulation, regulation of trade and competition, immigration, and intellectual property; and all subjects regarding the resolution of business disputes, for example, civil procedure, arbitration and alternative methods of dispute resolution, plus the principles of conflict of laws

---

**2.** *See, e.g.*, HAL S. SCOTT AND PHILIP A. WELLONS, INTERNATIONAL FINANCE: TRANSACTIONS, POLICY, AND REGULATION (13th ed. 2007).

**3.** For an admirable survey of these dispute-resolution mechanisms, see Detlev F. Vagts, *Dispute–Resolution Mechanisms in International Business*, 203 RECUEIL DES COURS 9 (1987–III).

that apply in the domestic arena. In short, the preferred curriculum for a hypothetical "domestic business transactions" course would cover virtually the entire span of a modern legal education (which in the United States, for example, is taught to graduate students over a period of three years by a legion of professors). A proper course on international business transactions would not only embrace each and every one of these subjects, but would also necessarily address the core principles of public international law, comparative law and procedure, not to mention the law of international organizations and such supra-national regional entities as the European Union!

To make this enormously broad topic manageable, this book takes as its focus the basic principles of civil litigation by which international business disputes are generally resolved by the courts of the United States, the country and legal system with which I am most familiar. Such an approach inevitably raises two objections. First, if one is interested in transnational law, why discuss international business *disputes*, rather than the broader general topic of international business transactions? In the same way as doctors tend to learn most about the healthy human body through the study of pathology, lawyers tend to learn most about the principles that advance a well-functioning international commercial system by studying the principles used to resolve disputes.

Furthermore, unlike the modern law of dispute resolution, the modern law of international business formation and regulation proves less susceptible to concise presentation simply because the global system has not yet evolved a fully—or even predominantly—international law of commercial transactions and financing—i.e., a modern *lex mercatoria*.[4] The ancient *lex mercatoria* comprised transnational private law based not on any single national law, but on the mercantile customs generally accepted by trading nations.[5] By contrast, most of the modern law governing international business formation remains national or even sub-national in character.

**4.** *See* Keith Highet, *The Enigma of Lex Mercatoria*, 63 TULANE L. REV. 613, 627 (1989) ([T]he modern *"lex mercatoria* is not at all a precise body of law or principles, with clearly definable limits and parameters. It is impossible to conceive of a draftsman inserting a reference to *lex mercatoria* into an agreement with any sense of confidence that the reference will cover anything more than the very essential rules of reason."). For efforts to describe such a modern body of rules, see, for example, BERTHOLD GOLDMAN, FRONTIERES DU DROIT ET "LEX MERCATORIA," ARCH. DE PHILOSPHIE DU DROIT (1964); Emmanuel Gaillard, *L'application de regles transnationales (lex mercatoria)*, Working Group II, International Council for International Arbitration, XII the International Arbitration Congress (Nov. 1994).

**5.** *See* Harold J. Berman and Colin Kaufman, *The Law of International Commercial Transactions (Lex Mercatoria)*, 19 HARV. INT'L L.J. 221, 224–29 (1978).

To the extent that a transnational law of formation and financing has evolved that runs across national borders, it has largely been codified in the plethora of treaties and conventions that has resulted from the work of UNCITRAL (United Nations Commission on International Trade Law), UNIDROIT (International Institute for the Unification of Private Law), and the Hague Conference on Private International Law. Examples include the U.N. Convention on Contracts for the International Sale of Goods and the attendant conventions on limitation periods, bills of exchange and promissory notes; the UNCITRAL guidelines on international construction projects; the UNIDROIT conventions on agency in the international sale of goods, international financial leasing, and international factoring; the International Chamber of Commerce INCOTERMS (International Commercial Terms created by the ICC); the conventions and law regarding carriage of goods by sea, bills of lading, marine and cargo insurance; and the law of letters of credit, particularly the Uniform Customs and Practices for Documentary Credits.

The international law of *business regulation* seems equally unruly.[6] Gradually, substantive consensus appears to be emerging regarding universal regulatory principles in such diverse areas as international taxation, maritime, air travel, telecommunications, trade, antitrust, and securities.[7] Particularly in the North American setting, a similar consensus appears to be emerging with regard to regulation of international insolvency.[8] Yet the regulatory law of the European Union changes by the moment with each successive directive that issues from Brussels. With the collapse of the Communist bloc in Eastern Europe and the rapid internationalization of the securities markets, laws regulating export restrictions and securities laws remain fundamentally in flux. Similarly, the demise of the CoCom (Coordinating Committee) and the rise of the Wassenaar Arrangement have readjusted the global system of export

---

**6.** For an admirable effort to outline the broad contours of that regulatory law, see Peter Muchlinski, Multinational Enterprises and the Law (1995).

**7.** The American Law Institute attempted to restate some of these general regulatory principles in its Restatement (Third) of the Foreign Relations Law of the United States (1986) [hereafter Restatement (Third)]. Thus, principles governing conflicts of jurisdiction, for example, are discussed in §§ 401–403 of the Restatement (Third); tax rules are covered in §§ 411–413; jurisdictional rules

of antitrust and securities are set forth in §§ 415–416; export control rules are described in § 812 and import rules in §§ 801–811; and the background rules of international monetary law are addressed in the rest of Part VIII.

**8.** *See, e.g.*, American Law Institute, Transnational Insolvency Project: Principles of Cooperation Among the NAFTA Countries (1993–2003); American Law Institute/International Insolvency Institute, Principles of Cooperation (2006), *available at* www.ali.org.

controls,[9] even while the Uruguay and Doha Rounds of World Trade Organization negotiations and the North American Free Trade Agreement (NAFTA) have rethought the core institutions and ground rules of international trade. Rather than try to capture the current state of this law in a snapshot that will be almost immediately overtaken by events, it seems more prudent to focus in this volume on the more manageable subject of international business dispute-resolution through transnational litigation.

Finally, why focus on the national courts, as opposed to other international commercial dispute-resolution fora? Of course, private international lawyers must consciously choose between resolving international commercial disputes through litigation in national courts and other dispute-resolution mechanisms, particularly international commercial arbitral and judicial fora. But the work of international judicial tribunals is regularly addressed in Public International Law courses[10] and the subject of international commercial arbitration has also recently been subjected to several treatise-length treatments.[11] Moreover, in the field of international business dispute resolution, much of the cutting-edge doctrinal developments continue to be pioneered, not in these fora, but by national courts.

Why the courts of the United States? Like the rulers of ancient China, modern American international lawyers are notorious for their parochialism. They continue to view their country as a kind of "Middle Kingdom"—the center of the universe—even while many leading indicia of economic and political power shift elsewhere. Yet for this century and last, the United States has been and remains the world's leading commercial power. Even more important, the United States today remains the leading center of international

---

**9.** The "CoCom," an acronym for Coordinating Committee for Multilateral Export Controls, was an organization of seventeen member states, principally in Western Europe plus the United States, Canada, Japan, and Turkey, established in 1947 to coordinate an embargo on the export of Western products to Eastern Bloc countries. The organization functioned for nearly half a century until 1994. Two years later, a successor regime, the Wassenaar Arrangement on Export Controls for Conventional Arms and Dual–Use Goods and Technologies was created with a Secretariat in Vienna among forty participating states to coordinate export trade of munitions and dual-use goods.

**10.** *See, e.g.*, LOUIS HENKIN, INTERNATIONAL LAW: POLITICS AND VALUES 57–60 (1995) (based on 1989 Hague Academy General Course); OSCAR SCHACHTER, INTERNATIONAL LAW IN THEORY AND PRACTICE 202–35 (1991) (based on 1982 Hague Academy General Course); Thomas M. Franck, *Fairness in the International Legal and Institutional System*, 240 RECUEIL DES COURS (1993–III) at 302–341 (based on 1993 Hague Academy General Course).

**11.** *See, e.g.*, GARY B. BORN, INTERNATIONAL COMMERCIAL ARBITRATION: COMMENTARY AND MATERIALS (2d ed. 2008); JOSEPH LOOKOFSKY, TRANSNATIONAL LITIGATION AND COMMERCIAL ARBITRATION: A COMPARATIVE ANALYSIS OF AMERICAN, EUROPEAN, AND INTERNATIONAL LAW (1993); *see also* Vagts, *supra* note 3, at 62–70, 80–84.

commercial and financial litigation. This trend is hardly historical accident. Lord Denning, Master of the Rolls, once wrote, "[a]s a moth is drawn to the light, so is a litigant drawn to the United States."[12] By so saying, Denning was referring to the magnetic attraction that commercial plaintiffs feel toward the distinctively pro-plaintiff features of the United States' civil justice system: contingency fees, broad pretrial discovery, flexible class action rules, treble damages in private antitrust cases, large jury awards, the availability of punitive damages, products liability rules, and the "American rule" on attorney's fees, whereby parties generally bear their own fees and costs, rather than routinely shift them to the losing party. These same factors also help explain why the vast bulk of the international commercial dispute resolution in the United States has tended to transpire not through arbitration, but through lawsuits in the national courts. Generous rules allowing the removal of U.S. cases from state to federal courts,[13] broad statutes granting federal causes of action and exclusive federal court jurisdiction in such regulatory areas as antitrust and securities,[14] and a liberal set of Federal Rules of Civil Procedure have further promoted the concentration of these transnational commercial cases into the U.S. *federal* courts, rather than into the courts of the fifty states. In deciding these cases, the U.S. federal courts—led by the U.S. Supreme Court—have thus begun to develop a substantial and discernible national jurisprudence of transnational litigation, whose principles have only recently begun to be understood by international lawyers of other nations.

This book treats transnational litigation in U.S. courts as a unified subject that overlaps public and private international law. Concluding and regulating international business transactions and resolving the resulting disputes represent just three of the many transnational legal problems confronted by a transnational legal system of overlapping national and international institutions and rules. For that reason, describing the details of particular rules, which are certain to change soon, should have lower priority for those interested in this field than acquiring a sound understanding of how international business transactions evolve through a transnational legal process that is marked by stages of formation, regulation, and dispute-resolution.

**12.** *Smith Kline and French Laboratories Ltd. v. Bloch*, [1983] 1 W.L.R. 730, 733.

**13.** *See, e.g.*, 28 U.S.C. § 1441 (1992).

**14.** See, e.g., 28 U.S.C. § 1337 (1992) (antitrust), 15 U.S.C. § 77v (1992) (securities).

In each stage of this transnational legal process, different themes arise. During the formation stage, the recurrent theme is conflict and accommodation of the *interests and cultures* of the contracting parties to the deal. To accommodate this conflict of cultures, the best legal solutions available tend to be the careful drafting of contracts, insurance agreements, national investment codes, bilateral investment treaties, etc. During the regulation stage, the repeated problem is extraterritoriality, an issue that has appeared in the realms of antitrust, securities, export controls, and taking of evidence. The recurring theme is the conflict and accommodation of the competing *regulatory philosophies* of the nations with concurrent jurisdiction to regulate the business arrangement. Once again, the legal solutions to this conflict vary; they range from unilateral forbearance by one nation's regulators, to formal and informal bilateral, regional and multilateral accords or treaties. During the dispute-resolution stage, the recurrent theme is conflict and accommodation among the *dispute-settlement procedures* followed by international judicial, arbitral, and domestic tribunals. The legal solutions that bring about accommodation once again include unilateral restraint by particular courts; bilateral arrangements (both private and public forum-selection clauses or agreements regarding judicial assistance); and regional and multilateral accords (for example, the Hague Service and Evidence Conventions discussed in Chapters IX and X).

## B. The Percolation and Transformation of Business Transactions

Business transactions are rarely static. Often, these three phases—of business formation, regulation, and dispute-resolution—combine into a dynamic process of "percolation and transformation" of business transactions from domestic to international, from private to public and back again. Witness, for example, the 1979 seizure of American hostages in Iran. To an unschooled observer, the case initially seemed to raise only issues of traditional "public" international law. Yet in fact, the story began with the formation and financing of thousands of ostensibly "private" business agreements between multinational corporations and the Shah's government, negotiated against the backdrop of numerous "public" bilateral and multilateral treaty commitments between Iran and the United States. After the American hostages were seized, the U.S. government imposed extensive national and transnational regulations upon these preexisting deals: a trade embargo, an extraterritorial assets freeze, and ultimately, an international agreement (the Algiers Accords) that secured the release of the hostages by unfreezing Iranian assets and transferring all claims to arbitration

16

before a newly minted Iran–United States Claims Tribunal in the Hague. Injured American claimants then raced to resolve their disputes in three fora: before the Tribunal, the International Court of Justice, and American courts.[15] The U.S. Supreme Court upheld the Algiers Accords against domestic constitutional challenge and legitimated a new process of private/public commercial arbitration before a new arbitration tribunal.[16] In short, what ostensibly began as a series of domestic "private business deals" entered between U.S. multinational enterprises and a developing-country government evolved, percolated upward, and transformed into a watershed public international political dispute, which was eventually resolved at an intergovernmental level in a manner that created a new dispute-resolution forum and new rules of transnational law.

The Iranian Hostages case is but one prominent example of this process of percolation and transformation in action. In a world where business arrangements are increasingly struck between private parties and governments, where economic sanctions are increasingly used for political ends, and where private parties can sue public entities in a variety of fora, the line between the public and the private in transnational litigation inevitably becomes hazy. For that reason, the chapters that follow discuss a number of ostensibly "public" international law cases before the U.S. Supreme Court, which have stated interpretive principles that now govern all forms of transnational litigation before U.S. courts.[17]

## C.    Five Themes of Transnational Litigation

The topic of international civil litigation in U.S. courts has stimulated numerous excellent and extensive treatises and casebooks.[18] Although an increasingly large number of law professors

---

**15.** *See, e.g.,* Dames and Moore v. Iran, Award No. 97–54–3, Dec. 20, 1983, Iranian Assets Lit. Rep. 7, 727 (Jan. 13, 1984); Case Concerning United States Diplomatic and Consular Staff in Tehran (United States v. Iran), [1980] I.C.J. Rep. 3; Dames and Moore v. Regan, 453 U.S. 654 (1981).

**16.** *See* Dames and Moore v. Regan, 453 U.S. 654 (1981).

**17.** *See, e.g.,* Sale v. Haitian Centers Council, Inc., 509 U.S. 155 (1993) (imposing territorial limit on application of Article 33 of 1951 U.N. Refugee Convention); Saudi Arabia v. Nelson, 507 U.S. 349 (1993) (finding plaintiff's claim of extraterritorial torture insufficiently connected to foreign sovereign's com-

mercial activity to lift foreign sovereign immunity); United States v. Alvarez–Machain, 504 U.S. 655 (1992) (permitting extraterritorial abduction of Mexican drug suspect).

**18.** Some leading works include GARY B. BORN ET AL., INTERNATIONAL CIVIL LITIGATION IN UNITED STATES COURTS (4th ed. 2007); ANDREAS F. LOWENFELD, INTERNATIONAL LITIGATION AND ARBITRATION (2d ed. 2002); RALPH G. STEINHARDT, INTERNATIONAL CIVIL LITIGATION: CASES AND MATERIALS ON THE RISE OF INTERMESTIC LAW (2002); THOMAS E. CARBONNEAU, CASES AND MATERIALS ON INTERNATIONAL LITIGATION AND ARBITRATION (2005); RUSSELL WEINTRAUB, INTERNATIONAL LITIGATION AND ARBITRATION: PRACTICE AND PLANNING (2d ed. 1997).

teach the subject and many attorneys practice it, most simply assume that the subject embraces a variegated collection of unrelated business and regulatory topics that lack any doctrinal or theoretical core. Like Churchill's famous pudding, the subject seems to "have no theme."[19] These volumes suggest little or no identifiable philosophy that governs what role domestic and international law should play in shaping and guiding the making and breaking of private transnational arrangements.

I argue instead that a discernible jurisprudence *is* emerging with respect to Transnational Litigation in U.S. Courts. That jurisprudence, reflected principally in key recent decisions of the U.S. Supreme Court, encompasses five core themes, which for shorthand purposes, I will call: *Party Autonomy, National Sovereignty, Comity, Uniformity*, and the *Separation of Powers*.

By *Party Autonomy*, I mean the principle that the national courts should respect, and not disrupt, the wishes of two commercial parties who have contracted for a particular business result. As former Chief Justice Warren Burger wrote for the Supreme Court in *M/S Bremen v. Zapata Off-Shore Co.*, when a business choice is "made in an arm's length negotiation by experienced and sophisticated businessmen, and absent some compelling and countervailing reason (such as fraud, undue influence, or overweening bargaining power), that agreement should be honored by the parties and enforced by the courts."[20] In essence, this judicial presumption favoring party autonomy reflects a belief that domestic principles governing sanctity of contract should be extended to arrangements made across national borders. Absent proof of coercion, adhesion or fraud, the autonomy principle suggests, the private ordering mechanisms that comprise the law of international business formation should be left undisturbed and the parties' contractual will respected.

The second principle, *National Sovereignty*, is an analogous concept used to describe not the autonomy of private parties, but of *nation-states*. As Professor Louis Henkin noted, "[s]overeignty is essentially an internal concept, the locus of ultimate authority in a society, rooted in its origins in the authority of sovereign princes."[21]

---

**19.** Once when presented with dessert, Winston Churchill famously turned to his wife and said, "Take this pudding away—it has no theme!" Christopher Soames, Memories of Churchill: A Speech to the International Churchill Societies at the Savoy Hotel, London (Sept. 25, 1986), *available at* http://

www.winstonchurchill.org/i4a/pages/index.cfm?pageid=735.

**20.** 407 U.S. 1, 12 (1972).

**21.** Louis Henkin, *President's Column*, Am. Soc'y Int'l L. Newsl., March–May 1993, at 6. Under expansive notions of national sovereignty, the rules and institutions of the international legal

Under the United Nations Charter, the concept of national sovereignty reflects the notion of "domestic jurisdiction," or a nation's internal autonomy over its internal matters.[22] In the international business arena, the principle of national sovereignty denotes the freedom of nation-states or state trading companies to consent to business arrangements with one another or with private parties, to defend their political independence and territorial integrity, to enforce their own laws within their own territory, and to avoid being judged in and by the national courts of other countries.

These first two principles, party autonomy and national sovereignty, require courts to give deference to existing arrangements that have been concluded under either contractual or sovereign veils. A third and related principle, *Comity*, flows from the respect that one sovereign is obliged to give to the sovereign acts of a co-equal nation-state. Derived from the Roman law concept of *comitas*, the concept was developed by the 17th–century Dutch scholar, Ulrich Huber, as a mode of resolving conflicts among the various Dutch provinces.[23] The British courts endorsed the concept as early as 1760, and Justice Joseph Story's *Commentaries on the Conflict of Laws* accepted the idea into American judicial and scholarly usage.[24] As the U.S. Supreme Court defined it in 1895, comity is

> neither a matter of absolute obligation, on the one hand, nor of mere courtesy and good will, upon the other ... [, but] the recognition which one nation allows within its territory to the legislative, executive or judicial acts of another nation, having due regard both to international duty and convenience, and to the rights of its own citizens or of other persons who are under the protection of its laws.[25]

Over time, American courts have increasingly read the comity doctrine as a reason why they should refrain from independent determination of cases under the law of nations.[26] In the most

system itself can be thought of as a positivist social contract created among states who are exercising their individual rights of national sovereignty.

**22.**  U.N. Charter art. 2, para. 7.

**23.**  *See* Kurt H. Nadelmann, *Introduction to Hessel E. Yntema, The Comity Doctrine*, 65 MICH. L. REV. 1, 1–2 (1966); D.J. Llewelyn Davies, *The Influence of Huber's de Conflictu Legum on English Private International Law*, 18 BRIT. Y.B. INT'L L. 49, 52 (1937); Harold G. Maier, *Extraterritorial Jurisdiction at a Crossroads: An Intersection Between Public*

*and Private International Law*, 76 AM. J. INT'L L. 280, 281–82 & n.4 (1982).

**24.**  *See* Robinson v. Bland, 2 Bur. 1077, 1 W. Bl. 234, 259 (1760); JOSEPH STORY, COMMENTARIES ON THE CONFLICT OF LAWS, FOREIGN AND DOMESTIC, IN REGARD TO CONTRACTS, RIGHTS AND REMEDIES, AND ESPECIALLY IN REGARD TO MARRIAGES, DIVORCES, WILLS, SUCCESSIONS, AND JUDGMENTS §§ 28–38 (1st ed. 1834).

**25.**  Hilton v. Guyot, 159 U.S. 113, 163–64 (1895).

**26.**  For a historical review, see Joel R. Paul, *Comity in International Law*, 32 HARV. INT'L L.J. 1 (1991).

extreme cases, the courts have applied the doctrine not simply to defer to, but also to recognize and enforce domestically, the decisions of foreign sovereigns and courts. As we shall see, in the late 19th and early 20th century, the Supreme Court gave comity special operational force when it embraced the Act of State doctrine, reasoning that "the courts of one country will not sit in judgment on the acts of the government of another, done within its own territory."[27]

The final two factors, *Uniformity* and *Separation of Powers*, arise from the United States' peculiar status as a federal nation: a subject now of major interest as well to the member states of the emerging European Union. This federal status raises questions regarding both the *vertical* and *horizontal* distributions of lawmaking authority within a federal system. The U.S. Constitution effects a vertical distribution of lawmaking authority, for it simultaneously renders federal law supreme over the law of individual states, even while placing limits upon the power of the federal government to invade both individual rights and rights reserved to the several states.[28] Yet at the same time, the first three articles of the Constitution effect a *horizontal* distribution of lawmaking authority by expressly distributing decision-making authority *within* the national government, among the Executive, Legislative, and the Judicial branches of government.[29]

As businesses have begun increasingly to extend their transnational activity across national borders, U.S. courts have increasingly stressed the need for *uniformity* in governing substantive and procedural rules. A foreign company or government, the uniformity principle suggests, should not be required to face a different set of rules depending in which of the fifty states it chooses to operate. As the Supreme Court declared in *Banco Nacional de Cuba v. Sabbatino,*

---

**27.** Underhill v. Hernandez, 168 U.S. 250, 252 (1897) ("Every sovereign state is bound to respect the independence of every other sovereign state...."); *accord* Ricaud v. American Metal Co., 246 U.S. 304, 310 (1918) ("[T]he act within its own boundaries of one sovereign state cannot become the subject of re-examination and modification in the courts of another."); Oetjen v. Central Leather Co., 246 U.S. 297, 303–04 (1918) (stating that the Act of State doctrine "rests at last upon the highest considerations of international comity and expediency"). For further discussion of these cases, see Chapter V, *infra.*

**28.** *See* U.S. Const. art. VI (supremacy clause); U.S. Const. amends. I–IX (civil and political rights); U.S. Const. amend. X (reserving undelegated power to the states).

**29.** *See* U.S. Const. art. I (federal legislative power); U.S. Const. art. II (federal executive power); U.S. Const. art. III (federal judicial power).

[i]f federal authority, in this instance this Court, orders the field of judicial competence in this area for the federal courts, and the state courts are left free to formulate their own rules, the purposes behind the [act of state] doctrine could be as effectively undermined as if there had been no federal pronouncement on the subject . . . . . [W]e are constrained to make it clear that an issue concerned with a basic choice regarding the competence and function of the Judiciary and the National Executive in ordering our relationships with other members of the international community must be treated exclusively as an aspect of federal law.[30]

Finally, *Separation of Powers*, the bedrock principle undergirding the American system of divided federal government, operates as a horizontal concept requiring federal courts to defer to executive determinations about international matters within the unique scope of executive authority. Particularly in this century, the Supreme Court has increasingly deferred to claimed presidential authority and expertise in foreign affairs.[31] In so doing, the Court has regularly required not only the states and private parties, but the lower courts and Congress as well, to defer to executive determinations so as to preserve "one voice" in our external affairs.[32] At times, the Court has transformed the separation-of-powers principle into an even more extreme institutional conclusion: That courts are not just constitutionally disabled, but *functionally incompetent* not just to find facts in international cases, but also to make the very legal determinations regarding international and foreign affairs law that they had been making since the Republic began. As Justice Robert Jackson wrote for the U.S. Supreme Court in *Chicago and Southern Air Lines, Inc. v. Waterman Steamship Corp.*, "the very nature of executive decisions as to foreign policy is political, not judicial. . . . They are decisions of a kind for which the Judiciary has neither aptitude, facilities nor responsibility and have long been held to belong in the domain of political power not subject to judicial intrusion or inquiry."[33] Yet, as I will suggest, such a claim of "judicial incompetence" must be treated with considerable skepticism. For insofar as courts can successfully invoke this rationale—based upon their alleged unfamiliarity and

---

**30.** Banco Nacional de Cuba v. Sabatino, 376 U.S. 398, 424–25 (1964).

**31.** For a description of this pattern of judicial deference, see HAROLD HONGJU KOH, THE NATIONAL SECURITY CONSTITUTION: SHARING POWER AFTER THE IRAN-CONTRA AFFAIR 134–52 (1990).

**32.** *See generally* Ralph Steinhardt, *Human Rights Litigation and the 'One*

*Voice' Orthodoxy in Foreign Affairs,* in WORLD JUSTICE?: U.S. COURTS AND INTERNATIONAL HUMAN RIGHTS 23 (Mark Gibney ed., 1991) (discussing the evolution of the "one voice" phraseology).

**33.** 333 U.S. 103, 111 (1948).

inexperience with international cases—to limit their involvement in transnational cases, the claim of judicial incompetence will eventually become a self-fulfilling prophecy.

From these core principles flow the basic assumptions that have governed the way U.S. courts have ruled in international business cases during the last four decades of this century. From the principles of party autonomy and national sovereignty have flowed a rhetorical commitment to the sanctity of both private contract and public treaty. From the principles of national sovereignty and international comity have flowed judicial limits upon the extraterritorial assertion of national jurisdiction in prescribing regulations affecting international business activities. From the principle of uniformity has flowed the impetus to prescribe uniform procedural rules for both federal and state courts in international business cases. From the principle of separation of powers has flowed a persistent emphasis by the courts on the need for judicial deference to the judgments of the U.S. President, executive branch and federal regulatory authorities with respect to transnational matters that touch on foreign affairs.

These jurisprudential principles explain and tie together many of the rulings regarding transnational litigation that have issued from U.S. courts in recent years. Yet not infrequently, these same principles have come into conflict with one another. In one breath, for example, the Court has exalted party autonomy, upholding the rights of contracting parties to select overseas fora for their disputes with the broad statement that "[w]e cannot have trade and commerce in world markets and international waters exclusively on our terms, governed by our laws and resolved in our courts."[34] Yet in another breath, the Court has effectively required that certain international commercial acts must be governed by our law and resolved in our courts, by denying that either separation of powers or comity require a U.S. court to refrain from deciding the legality of a foreign actor's extraterritorial commercial conduct.[35]

As we shall see, the recurring clash between transnationalist and nationalist thinking causes persistent tension between two jurisprudential factions within the U.S. Supreme Court, which explains much of the inconsistent decision-making on the Court regarding transnational litigation matters.

---

**34.** M/S Bremen v. Zapata Off–Shore Co., 407 U.S. 1, 9 (1972).

**35.** Hartford Fire Insurance Co. v. California, 509 U.S. 764 (1993) (citations omitted). The majority reasoned that comity did not bar adjudication, so long as the foreign defendants were not com-pelled by foreign law to act abroad "in some fashion prohibited by the law of the United States . . . or claim that their compliance with the laws of both countries is otherwise impossible." *Id.* at 799. For further discussion, see Chapter IV, *infra.*

# CHAPTER III

## TRANSNATIONAL PUBLIC LAW LITIGATION

Although transnational civil litigation has traditionally been associated with private and business law issues, the last quarter of the twentieth century witnessed the burgeoning of a counterpart phenomenon I have called "transnational public law litigation": suits brought in U.S. courts by individual and governmental litigants challenging violations of public international law.[1] These suits include international human rights suits brought by aliens against foreign and United States governments and officials in U.S. federal court under the Alien Tort Claims Act,[2] as well as actions by foreign governments against individual, American government, and corporate defendants.

Before turning in the remainder of this book to issues common to all transnational litigation, private and public, this chapter sketches first, the phenomenon of transnational public law litigation; second, the evolution of the practice of transnational public law litigation in United States courts from the beginning of the Republic to the present; and third, some current issues facing transnational public law litigants.

## A.   What Is Transnational Public Law Litigation?

Like its domestic counterpart (christened several decades ago by Abram Chayes), transnational public law litigation seeks to vindicate public rights and values through judicial remedies.[3] In both settings, parties bring "public actions," asking courts to

---

1.   This chapter derives from Harold Hongju Koh, *Transnational Public Law Litigation*, 100 YALE L.J. 2347 (1991); and Harold Hongju Koh, Filártiga v. Peña–Irala: *Judicial Internalization into Domestic Law of the Customary International Law Norm Against Torture*, in LAURA DICKINSON, MARK JANIS & JOHN NOYES, INTERNATIONAL LAW STORIES 45 (2007) [hereinafter Koh, *Filártiga Story*]. *See also* Harold Hongju Koh, *Civil Remedies for Uncivil Wrongs: Combatting Terrorism Through Transnational Public Law Litigation*, 22 TEX. INT'L L.J. 169, 193–201 (1987) (previously noting the existence of transnational public law litigation).

2.   28 U.S.C. § 1350 (2008).

3.   *Cf.* Abram Chayes, *The Role of the Judge in Public Law Litigation*, 89 HARV. L. REV. 1281 (1976) [hereinafter Chayes, *Public Law Litigation*]; Abram Chayes, *The Supreme Court, 1981 Term—Foreword: Public Law Litigation and the Burger Court*, 96 HARV. L. REV. 4 (1982). Not coincidentally, Professor Chayes was also the architect of a prominent example of transnational public law litigation, Nicaragua's suit against the United States in the International Court of Justice. *See* Abram Chayes, *Nicaragua, the United States and the World Court*, 85 COLUM. L. REV. 1445 (1985) [hereinafter Chayes, *Nicaragua*].

23

declare and explicate public norms, often with the goal of provoking institutional reform. Much as domestic public law litigants have pursued *Bivens* and Section 1983 litigation in federal courts seeking redress, deterrence, and reform of state and federal institutions through judicial enunciation of constitutional norms,[4] transnational public law litigants have pursued both "transnational tort" cases, seeking redress and deterrence for egregious civil wrongs, and "institutional reform" cases seeking revision of national governmental policies that violate rules of international conduct.

What makes transnational public law litigation unique is its melding of two conventional modes of litigation that had traditionally been considered distinct. In traditional domestic litigation, private individuals bring private claims against one another based on national law before competent domestic judicial fora, seeking both enunciation of norms and damages relief in the form of a retrospective judgment.[5] In traditional international litigation, nation-states bring public claims against one another based on treaty or customary international law before international tribunals of limited competence. Although state litigants ostensibly seek judgments from such tribunals, their objective is usually the enunciation of a public international norm that will stimulate "relief" in the form of a negotiated political settlement.[6]

Transnational public law litigation merges these two classical modes of litigation. Private individuals, government officials, and nation-states sue one another directly, and are sued directly, in a variety of judicial fora, most prominently, domestic courts. In these

---

**4.** Bivens v. Six Unknown Named Agents of the Federal Bureau of Narcotics, 403 U.S. 388 (1971); 42 U.S.C. § 1983 (1988). *Compare* Theodore Eisenberg & Stephen C. Yeazell, *The Ordinary and the Extraordinary in Institutional Litigation*, 93 HARV. L. REV. 465 (1980) with Chayes, *Nicaragua, supra* note 3, at 1479–80 (comparing the World Court's *Nicaragua* decision with *Brown v. Board of Educ.*, 347 U.S. 483 (1954)).

**5.** For the classic description of this "private law" paradigm of domestic adjudication, see Lon L. Fuller, *The Forms and Limits of Adjudication*, 92 HARV. L. REV. 353 (1978). *But cf.* Chayes, *Public Law Litigation, supra* note 3 (presenting counter-model of domestic public law litigation); Owen M. Fiss, *The Social and Political Foundations of Adjudication*, 6 LAW & HUM. BEHAV. 121 (1982) (contrasting private and public models of domestic adjudication).

**6.** Perhaps the archetype of this form of international litigation is an application before the International Court of Justice (ICJ) seeking an advisory opinion pursuant to Article 96 of the United Nations Charter. U.N. Charter, art. 96. Such an opinion does not purport to be a binding judgment; rather, it enunciates public international norms in a way that gives some litigants a greater claim of right in subsequent settlement negotiations. *See* Military and Paramilitary Activities (Nicaragua v. United States), 1986 I.C.J. 14, 172 (June 27) (separate opinion of Judge Lachs) (the World Court's "real function, whatever the character of the dispute, is 'to facilitate, so far as is compatible with its Statute, a direct and friendly settlement.'") (citation omitted), *reprinted in* 25 I.L.M. 1023, 1102 (1986).

fora, these actors invoke claims of right based not solely on domestic or international law, but rather, on a body of transnational law that blends the two. Moreover, contrary to "dualist" views of international jurisprudence, which see international law as binding only upon nations in their relations with one another, individual plaintiffs engaged in this mode of litigation usually claim rights arising directly from this body of transnational law.[7]

As in traditional domestic litigation, transnational public lawsuits focus retrospectively upon achieving compensation and redress for individual victims. But as in traditional international law litigation, the transnational public law plaintiff pursues a prospective aim as well: to provoke judicial articulation of a *norm* of transnational law, with an eye toward using that declaration to promote a political settlement in which both governmental and nongovernmental entities will participate. Thus, as I have elsewhere suggested, transnational public lawsuits exhibit five distinctive features:

> (1) a *transnational party structure*, in which states and non-state entities equally participate; (2) a *transnational claim structure*, in which violations of domestic and international, private and public law are all alleged in a single action; (3) a *prospective focus*, fixed as much upon obtaining judicial declaration of transnational norms as upon resolving past disputes; (4) the litigants' strategic awareness of the *transportability of those norms* to other domestic and international fora for use in judicial interpretation or political bargaining; and (5) a subsequent process of *institutional dialogue* among various domestic and international, judicial and political fora to achieve ultimate settlement.[8]

In the past three decades, transnational public law litigants have turned to United States courts to pursue an array of goals. All tort judgments, whether domestic or transnational, promote *compensation* of the victims; *denial of safe haven* to the defendant in the judgment-rendering forum;[9] *deterrence* of others who might

---

**7.** International law scholars have long distinguished between "monism"— the school of international jurisprudence that views international and domestic law as together constituting a unified legal system—and "dualism," the school that "view[s] international law as a discrete legal system" that "is for nations" only and "operates wholly on an inter-nation plane." Louis Henkin, *The Constitution and United States Sovereignty:* *A Century of* Chinese Exclusion *and Its Progeny*, 100 HARV. L. REV. 853, 864 (1987); *see also* Joseph G. Starke, *Monism and Dualism in the Theory of International Law*, 1936 BRIT. Y.B. INT'L L. 66.

**8.** Koh, *Transnational Public Law Litigation, supra* note 1, at 2371 (internal citations omitted).

**9.** Ironically, when Alfredo Stroessner, author of the reign of torture in Paraguay, where the *Filártiga* case tran-

contemplate similar conduct; and *enunciation of legal norms* opposing the conduct for which the defendant has been found liable. Transnational "institutional reform litigants"—like their domestic counterparts—often seek not only these aims, but also a broader political objective of *revision of illegal governmental policies*. Although transnational public law plaintiffs routinely request retrospective damages or even prospective injunctive relief, their broader strategic goals are often served by a declaratory or default judgment announcing that a transnational norm has been violated. Even a judgment that the plaintiff cannot enforce against the defendant in the rendering forum can empower the plaintiff by creating a bargaining chip for use in other political fora.

Thus, transnational public law litigation in domestic courts eschews both the traditional party structure and the normative sources of classical international law litigation. At the same time, however, such litigation implicates the same complex balance of public values—particularly concerns about comity, separation of powers, and judicial competence—that all transnational litigation cases tend to raise. In the end, like all litigation, transnational public law litigation is a development whose success should be measured not by favorable judgments, but by practical results: the norms declared, the political pressure generated, the illegal government practices abated, and the innocent lives saved.

# B. A Brief History of Transnational Public Law Litigation

## 1. Early History

Transnational public law litigation in the United States began during the early days of the American Republic. Cognizant of the Roman concept of *jus gentium*, a law "common to all men," Blackstone described the law of nations as "a system of rules, deducible by natural reason, and established by universal consent among the civilized inhabitants of the world ... to insure the observance of justice and good faith, in that intercourse which must frequently occur between two or more independent states, *and the*

---

spired, finally died in exile in Brazil, his obituary reported that Stroessner had written to an American diplomat, asking whether he could come to the United States for gallbladder surgery. The diplomat "advised the general to stay away, warning that he could become the target for a lawsuit [in the United States] by Paraguayans," presumably invoking the *Filártiga* precedent. Diana Jean Schemo, *Gen. Alfredo Stroessner, Ruled Paraguay Through Fear for 35 Years, Dies in Exile at 93*, N.Y. Times, Aug. 17, 2006, at B7.

*individuals belonging to each.*"[10] Thus, the law of nations embraced private as well as public, domestic as well as international transactions. It encompassed not simply the law governing public relations among states (the so-called "law of states")—for example, rules relating to passports and ambassadors—but also ostensibly private law, such as the "law maritime" (affecting prizes, shipwrecks, admiralty, and the like) and the "law merchant" (*lex mercatoria*), a transnational private law based not on any single national law but on mercantile customs generally accepted by trading nations.

As England became the preeminent global power, the law of nations was domesticated first into English common law, then applied to the American colonies, and subsequently incorporated into United States law.[11] With American independence, the law of nations became part of the common law of the United States. In John Jay's words, "the United States had, by taking a place among the nations of the earth, become amenable to the law of nations."[12] The Continental Congress resolved to send a diplomatic letter stating that the United States would cause "the law of nations to be most strictly observed." The Federalist Papers made extensive mention of the law of nations' role in United States courts.[13] And in the Constitution itself, Article I, Section 8, Clause 10 expressly gave Congress the power to define and punish "Piracies ... committed on the high Seas, and Offences against the Law of Nations," while Article III extended the judicial power of the United States to cases

---

**10.**  4 W. Blackstone, Commentaries 66 (emphasis added). Centuries before Jeremy Bentham coined the "horizontal" term "international law" in 1789, jurists had recognized the existence of a *jus gentium*, a "law of nations," which bound individuals no less than states. *See The Four Commentaries of Gaius on the Institutes of the Civil Law*, 1 The Civil Law 81 (S. Scott ed. 1973). Sixteenth and seventeenth century legal scholars, such as Grotius, did not distinguish municipal from international law, instead viewing the law of nations as a universal law binding upon all mankind. *See* David M. Kennedy, *Primitive Legal Scholarship*, 27 Harv. Int'l L.J. 1, 8 (1986) (discussing works of Vitoria, Suarez, Gentili and Grotius).

**11.**  For discussion of international law in English common law, see Triquet v. Bath, 97 Eng. Rep. 936 (K.B. 1764) (Mansfield, J.). For discussion of how international law became United States law, see generally Edwin M. Dickinson,

*The Law of Nations as Part of the National Law of the United States (pt. 1)*, 101 U. Pa. L. Rev. 26, 26–27 (1952); Louis Henkin, *International Law as Law in the United States*, 82 Mich. L. Rev. 1555 (1984).

**12.**  Chisholm v. Georgia, 2 U.S. (2 Dall.) 419, 474 (1793). *See also* Ware v. Hylton, 3 U.S. (3 Dall.) 199, 281 (1796) ("When the United States declared their independence, they were bound to receive the law of nations, in its modern state of purity and refinement."). *See generally* Stewart Jay, *The Status of the Law of Nations in Early American Law*, 42 Vand. L. Rev. 819, 824–28 (1989).

**13.**  14 Journals of the Continental Congress 635 (W. Ford ed., 1909); The Federalist No. 3, at 14, 15, 16 (John Jay); No. 42, at 271–73 (James Madison); No. 53, at 351 (James Madison); No. 80, at 517 (Alexander Hamilton); No. 83, at 548–49 (Alexander Hamilton) (Modern Library ed. 1937).

arising under treaties, and a large class of international cases—those affecting Ambassadors, public Ministers and consuls, admiralty and maritime cases, and cases involving foreign parties.

In the early Republic, all three branches quickly recognized the applicability of the law of nations in American courts. Executive officials such as Thomas Jefferson heralded the law of nations as "an integral part ... of the laws of the land."[14] Congress immediately enacted as part of the First Judiciary Act the Alien Tort Claims Act (ATCA), which gave the district courts jurisdiction "of all causes where an alien sues for a tort only in violation of the law of nations or a treaty of the United States."[15] As Professor White has recounted, "[t]he Framers' Constitution anticipated that international disputes would regularly come before the United States courts, and that the decisions in those cases could rest on principles of international law, without any necessary reference to the common law or to constitutional doctrines."[16] American courts regularly decided cases under the law of nations, particularly those involving piracies and prize jurisdiction (captures of enemy ships as prizes of war), and applied and clarified international law principles in cases concerning offenses against the law of nations, acquisition and control of territory, boundary disputes, questions of nationali-

**14.** *See* Letter from Thomas Jefferson, Secretary of State, to M. Genet, French Minister (June 5, 1793), *quoted in* 1 J. MOORE, DIGEST OF INTERNATIONAL LAW 10 (1906); *see also* 1 Op. Atty. Gen. 9 (1792) (opinion of Attorney General Randolph) ("The law of nations, though not specially adopted by the constitution, or any municipal act, is essentially a part of the law of the land."); *id.* at 40 (1797) (opinion of Attorney General Lee).

**15.** *See* Judiciary Act of 1789, ch. 20, § 9(b), 1 Stat. 73, 77 (codified as amended at 28 U.S.C. § 1350 (2000)). Shortly thereafter, Congress also passed statutes criminalizing piracy and assaults upon ambassadors. *See* Act of Apr. 30, 1790, ch. 9, § 8, 1 Stat. 112, 113–14; Act of Apr. 30, 1790, ch. 9, § 28, 1 Stat. 112, 118. The ATCA originally provided, in language subsequently omitted from later amendments, that federal district courts "shall also have cognizance, *concurrent with the courts of the several States, or the circuit courts, as the case may be,* of all causes where an alien sues for a tort only in violation of the law of nations or a treaty of the United States." Act of Sept. 24, 1789, ch. 20,

§ 9(b) (emphasis added). For legislative history of the Alien Tort Statute, *see generally* William R. Casto, *The Federal Courts' Protective Jurisdiction Over Torts Committed in Violation of the Law of Nations*, 18 CONN. L. REV. 467 (1986); Anne–Marie Burley, *The Alien Tort Statute and the Judiciary Act of 1789: A Badge of Honor*, 83 AM. J. INT'L L. 461 (1989).

**16.** G. Edward White, *The Marshall Court and International Law: The Piracy Cases*, 83 AM. J. INT'L L. 727, 727 (1989); *see also* Henkin, *supra* note 7, at 868 ("[E]arly United States courts and legislators regarded customary international law and treaty obligations as part of the domestic legal system. International law *was* domestic law.") (emphasis in original); RESTATEMENT (THIRD) OF THE FOREIGN RELATIONS LAW OF THE UNITED STATES § 111 introductory note ("From the beginning, the law of nations, later referred to as international law, was considered to be incorporated into the law of the United States without the need for any action by Congress or the President, and the courts, State and federal, have applied it and given it effect as the courts of England had done.").

ty, foreign sovereign immunity, and principles of war and neutrality.[17]

Gradually, components of the law of nations—the laws maritime and merchant, for example—became domesticated into America's "general common law." Federal courts sitting in admiralty jurisdiction began to apply to domestic watercourses a general maritime law derived from international law, which was deemed subject to congressional modification.[18] Throughout the early nineteenth century, American courts regularly construed and applied the unwritten law of nations as part of the "general common law," particularly to resolve commercial disputes, without regard to whether it should be characterized as federal or state. In 1842, Justice Story's classic decision in *Swift v. Tyson* applied the law merchant as general common law, announcing "[t]he law respecting negotiable instruments may be truly declared ... to be in a great measure, not the law of a single country only, but of the commercial world."[19] Equally important, nineteenth-century American courts routinely applied the law of nations to decide issues that would today be considered human rights claims.[20] Thus, at the turn of the century, Justice Gray could twice proclaim that:

> International law, in its widest and most comprehensive sense—*including not only questions of right between nations, governed by what has been appropriately called the law of nations; but also questions arising under what is usually called private international law*, or the conflict of laws, and concerning the rights of persons within the territory and dominion of one nation, by reason of acts, private or public, done within the dominions of another nation—is part of our law, and *must be ascertained and administered by the courts of justice, as often*

17.  *See, e.g.*, United States v. Smith, 18 U.S. (5 Wheat.) 153, 155 (1820) (piracy); Thirty Hogsheads of Sugar v. Boyle, 13 U.S. (9 Cranch) 191, 198 (1815) (prize jurisdiction); Respublica v. De Longchamps, 1 U.S. (1 Dall.) 111, 116 (Pa.O. & T. 1784) (attacks upon ambassador); United States v. Percheman, 32 U.S. (7 Pet.) 51, 86–87 (1833) (acquisition and control of territory); Iowa v. Illinois, 147 U.S. 1, 8–11 (1893) (boundary disputes); Shanks v. Dupont, 28 U.S. (3 Pet.) 242, 248 (1829) (question of nationality); The Schooner Exchange v. McFaddon, 11 U.S. (7 Cranch) 116, 125 (1812) (foreign sovereign immunity); The Peterhoff, 72 U.S. (5 Wall.) 28, 54–56 (1867) (principles of war and neutrality).

18.  *See* The Rapid, 12 U.S. (8 Cranch) 155, 162 (1814) ("The law of prize is part of the law of nations.... [I]t was the law of England before the revolution, and therefore constitutes a part of the admiralty and maritime jurisdiction conferred on this Court in pursuance of the Constitution.").

19.  41 U.S. (16 Pet.) 1, 19 (1842).

20.  *See, e.g.*, United States v. Percheman, 32 U.S. (7 Pet.) 51, 86–87 (1833) (protecting vested rights in private property against successor sovereign); United States v. The Schooner La Jeune Eugenie, 26 F. Cas. 832, 846 (1822) (finding slave trade an offense against the universal law of society).

*as such questions are presented in litigation between man and man, duly submitted to their determination.*[21]

When "there is no written law upon the subject," he made clear, echoing *Marbury v. Madison*,[22] "the duty still rests upon the judicial tribunals of ascertaining and declaring what the law is, whenever it becomes necessary to do so, in order to determine the rights of parties to suits regularly brought before them."[23] Justice Gray's language thus suggests that the famous law-declaring duty of *Marbury v. Madison* applies to international law, as well as domestic law, cases.

Over the first half of the twentieth century, the scope of the law of nations applied in American courts substantially narrowed. By overruling *Swift* in 1938, *Erie R.R. Co. v. Tompkins* interred the general common law, raising fears that the law of nations might be subordinated into state, not federal, law.[24] The laws merchant and maritime were assimilated into domestic law and the public/private distinction seized prominence, as conflict of laws was "privatized" and treated as a body of primarily domestic legal principles governing disputes with foreign interests or persons.[25] As the century proceeded, the courts increasingly invoked the concerns of comity, separation of powers, and judicial incompetence to mitigate their duty to declare the law of nations.

After World War II, the American civil rights movement pressed international human rights norms into service in its war against racial discrimination. American civil liberties groups filed suits in both state and federal courts, citing the human rights provisions of the United Nations Charter and the Universal Declaration of Human Rights to challenge racial discrimination in education, transportation, employment, housing, and land ownership.[26] But the courts soon fashioned the doctrine of "non-self-executing treaties" to prevent individuals from directly enforcing the new

---

**21.** Hilton v. Guyot, 159 U.S. 113 (1895). Five years later, Justice Gray repeated his words from *Hilton* almost verbatim in the famous prize case, The Paquete Habana, 175 U.S. 677, 700 (1900) ("International law is part of our law, and must be ascertained and administered by the courts of justice of appropriate jurisdiction as often as questions of right depending upon it are duly presented for their determination.").

**22.** 5 U.S. (1 Cranch) 137, 177 (1803) ("It is emphatically the province and duty of the judicial department to say what the law is.").

**23.** Hilton v. Guyot, 159 U.S. 113 (1895).

**24.** 304 U.S. 64 (1938). *See, e.g.*, Phillip Jessup, *The Doctrine of Erie Railroad v. Tompkins Applied to International Law*, 33 Am. J. Int'l L. 740 (1939).

**25.** *See* Joel Paul, *The Isolation of Private International Law*, 7 Wis. Int'l L.J. 149, 155–164 (1988).

**26.** *See generally* cases cited in Bert Lockwood, *The United Nations Charter and United States Civil Rights Litigation: 1946–1955*, 69 Iowa L. Rev. 901 (1984).

positive law,[27] and the act of state doctrine, which authorized the courts to decline to apply international law to review the validity of the act of a recognized foreign sovereign fully executed within its own territory.[28]

By diminishing the role of the courts as declarers of international law, the Supreme Court's leading act of state decision, *Banco Nacional de Cuba v. Sabbatino*, discouraged the courts "from playing important creative roles in determining common international standards," instead encouraging them to become "apologists for national policies determined by political aims of government."[29] *Sabbatino* was decided at a time when activist courts were being urged to retrench, and to embrace "the passive virtues" in their domestic constitutional decisions.[30] The courts read the case as a general directive to stay out of foreign affairs adjudication and to withdraw from public international norm-enunciation for several decades.

This judicial paralysis reached its peak during the Indochina war, when American courts consistently turned away challenges to that conflict's domestic and international legality.[31] A generation of lawyers and judges reached maturity unaware of America's rich judicial history of applying international law. Indeed, before 1980, the federal courts cited the ATCA as a basis for federal court jurisdiction in only two known cases, a 1795 maritime seizure dispute[32] and a 1961 child custody dispute.[33]

---

**27.** *See, e.g.*, Sei Fujii v. State, 38 Cal.2d 718, 242 P.2d 617 (1952); Pauling v. McElroy, 278 F.2d 252 (D.C. Cir. 1960) (individual may not invoke Charter to enjoin detonation of test nuclear weapons in Marshall Islands); Vlissidis v. Anadell, 262 F.2d 398 (7th Cir. 1959) (alien may not resist deportation on ground that UN Charter superseded racist provisions of immigration laws). Ironically, before the California Supreme Court's decision in *Sei Fujii*, four Justices of the United States Supreme Court had joined concurring opinions suggesting that the California Alien Land Law—the statute at issue in *Sei Fujii*—violated the United States' obligations under the United Nations Charter. *See* Oyama v. California, 332 U.S. 633, 647, 650 (1948) (Black, joined by Douglas, JJ. and Murphy, joined by Rutledge, JJ., concurring).

**28.** *See* Banco Nacional de Cuba v. Sabbatino, 376 U.S. 398 (1964) (discussed in Chapter V, *infra*).

**29.** MORTON KAPLAN & NICHOLAS KATZENBACH, THE POLITICAL FOUNDATIONS OF INTERNATIONAL LAW 270 (1961).

**30.** *See* Alexander Bickel, *The Supreme Court, 1960 Term Foreword: The Passive Virtues*, 75 HARV. L. REV. 40, 51 (1961).

**31.** For analyses of the unconstitutionality and international illegality of various aspects of the Indochina conflict, see generally John Hart Ely, *The American War in Indochina, Part II: The Unconstitutionality of the War They Didn't Tell Us About*, 42 STAN. L. REV. 1093 (1990).

**32.** Bolchos v. Darrel, 3 F. Cas. 810 (D.S.C. 1795).

**33.** Adra v. Clift, 195 F.Supp. 857 (D. Md. 1961), *overruled by* Taveras v. Taveraz, 477 F.3d 767 (6th Cir. 2007).

As the 1970s closed, however, two complementary trends engendered a new generation of transnational public law cases in United States judicial fora: first, the well-chronicled rise of *domestic* public law litigation as an instrument of social change through judicial creation of an American law of "constitutional torts," and second, the explosion of *transnational commercial* litigation in United States courts. As nations increasingly entered the marketplace, and the United States adopted the doctrine of restrictive sovereign immunity in the Foreign Sovereign Immunities Act, federal courts became increasingly obliged to adjudicate commercial suits brought by individuals and private entities against foreign governments.[34] These transnational suits not only returned domestic courts to the business of adjudicating international law, but also stimulated a reawakening of the bench's and bar's interest in the black-letter doctrine of international and foreign relations law.

The persistent question then arose: "if contracts, why not torture?" If American courts could subject the commercial conduct of foreign sovereigns to legal scrutiny without offending comity, why should comity immunize that same sovereign from judicial examination of its egregious public conduct? These precedents also cast doubt upon *Sabbatino*'s separation-of-powers conclusion that the lawfulness of foreign governmental acts is a quasi-political question, which courts may not constitutionally decide. If a court could hold a foreign sovereign defendant in violation of a commercial contract without usurping the executive function, why couldn't it hold the same defendant in violation of a human rights treaty, or a clearly-defined *jus cogens* norm against torture? Finally, these commercial rulings dispelled the self-fulfilling belief—increasingly accepted since Vietnam—that domestic courts somehow inherently lack the competence to manage or decide complex international law cases. If private litigants could conduct massive overseas discovery and adduce probative facts regarding a foreign state's commercial conduct, what rendered them incompetent to do the same with regard to a foreign state's heinous treatment of its own citizens? If a court could evaluate the "reasonableness" of the extraterritorial assertion of American regulatory laws or find a foreigner's minimum contacts with a forum sufficient to satisfy "due process," why couldn't the same court construe far less ambiguous terms in a human rights treaty?

**34.** Foreign Sovereign Immunities Act of 1976, 28 U.S.C. §§ 1330, 1602–1611 (2008).

## 2.  *Filártiga v. Peña–Irala*

Answering these questions, in 1980, the U.S. Court of Appeals for the Second Circuit breathed new life into the ATCA by deciding *Filártiga v. Peña–Irala*.[35] *Filártiga* inaugurated the era of human rights litigation in which we now live. Supported by an important government amicus brief pressing the Carter Administration's human rights policy,[36] *Filártiga* held that the ATCA conferred district court jurisdiction over a suit by Paraguayans versus a Paraguayan official who had tortured their relative to death in Paraguay, while acting under color of governmental authority.

Judge Irving Kaufman's opinion for the Second Circuit held that torture constitutes an actionable violation of the law of nations, sufficient to confer subject matter jurisdiction on the federal court under the ATCA.[37] The opinion relied on an array of international agreements, declarations, and state policy and practice as evidence that the law of nations prohibits torture.[38] The court further held that federal jurisdiction over such offenses is consistent with Article III of the Constitution because international law has long been recognized as "part of our law."[39] Accordingly, the court deemed it unnecessary to determine whether the ATCA itself provided the cause of action for the Filártigas' claims and whether the ATCA should be treated as an exercise of Congress's power to define and punish offenses against the laws of nations.[40] The ATCA, it explained, should be understood not to grant new rights to aliens,

---

**35.**  630 F.2d 876 (2d Cir. 1980). Filártiga's story has been told in many places, including Koh, *Filártiga Story*, *supra* note 1; a 1991 movie entitled ONE MAN'S WAR (Home Box Office 1991), directed by Sergio Toledo and starring Anthony Hopkins; in a 2004 book by RICHARD ALAN WHITE, BREAKING SILENCE: THE CASE THAT CHANGED THE FACE OF HUMAN RIGHTS (2004); and in documentary form in WILLIAM J. ACEVES, THE ANATOMY OF TORTURE: A DOCUMENTARY HISTORY OF FILÁRTIGA V. PEÑA–IRALA (2007). For two book-length treatments of the doctrines spawned by *Filártiga*, see, e.g., BETH STEPHENS & MICHAEL RATNER, INTERNATIONAL HUMAN RIGHTS LITIGATION IN U.S. COURTS (1996); THE ALIEN TORT CLAIMS ACT: AN ANALYTICAL ANTHOLOGY (Ralph G. Steinhardt & Anthony D'Amato eds., 1999).

**36.**  The Carter Administration argued that "Section 1350 encompasses the law of nations as that body of law may evolve," not as the law of nations

may have existed in 1789, when the statute was first enacted. International law, the Administration recognized, "now embraces the obligation of a state to respect the fundamental human rights of its citizens" and freedom from torture now ranks among the fundamental human rights protected by international law, and is therefore cognizable as a tort "in violation of the law of nations" for the purposes of the ATCA. Memorandum for the United States as Amicus Curiae, Filártiga v. Peña–Irala, 630 F.2d 876 (2d Cir. 1980), *reprinted in* 19 I.L.M. 585 (1980) [hereinafter *U.S. Filártiga Memorandum*]. For the story of how the Carter Administration's amicus brief came to be written, see generally Koh, *Filártiga Story*, *supra* note 1.

**37.**  Filártiga v. Peña–Irala, 630 F.2d 876 (2d Cir. 1980).

**38.**  *Id.* at 880–85.

**39.**  *Id.* at 887.

**40.**  U.S. CONST. art. I, § 8, cl. 10.

but to allow individuals to come to federal court to enforce "the rights already recognized by international law."[41]

*Filártiga* convincingly rebutted the comity, separation-of-powers, and incompetence objections to domestic judicial decision of human rights cases. The court showed no disrespect to Paraguay by trying Peña–Irala because his acts were illegal even under Paraguayan law.[42] "[F]or purposes of civil liability," the court declared, "the torturer has become—like the pirate and slave trader before him—*hostis humani generis*, an enemy of all mankind."[43] By so saying, the Second Circuit reaffirmed the Nuremburg ideal: that torture (like genocide) is never a legitimate instrument of state power. Under the court's reasoning, official torturers may not invoke comity nor cloak themselves in state sovereignty to avoid individual responsibility to their victims before a court of law. Nor, the *Filártiga* court held, must such cases invariably be dismissed under the doctrine of separation of powers. Even if the Executive Branch had not supported adjudication, the court found, the core issue in the case was quintessentially legal: whether the victims had a right to be free from torture that was actionable in federal court. Resolution of that question required only standard judicial determinations: construction of the Alien Tort Claims Act and human rights treaties. The court concluded that because the customary international law norm against torture was definable, obligatory, and universal, it constituted an actionable "tort in violation of the law of nations" for purposes of the ATCA.

On remand, U.S. District Judge Eugene Nickerson awarded the Filártigas a judgment of nearly $10.4 million, comprising compensatory damages based on Paraguayan law and punitive damages based on U.S. cases and international law.[44] By so holding, *Filártiga*'s ruling on remand created a federal common law remedy against torture, which fell squarely within the Supreme Court's prior recognition that issues "in ordering our relationships with other members of the international community must be treated exclusively as an aspect of federal law," made by the federal courts, binding on the states, but subject to legislative revision.[45] By the time that ruling issued, however, Peña–Irala had already been

**41.** *Filártiga*, 630 F.2d at 887.

**42.** *See U.S. Filártiga Memorandum, supra* note 36, at 605.

**43.** 630 F.2d at 890.

**44.** Filártiga v. Peña–Irala, 577 F.Supp. 860, 864–67 (E.D.N.Y. 1984).

**45.** Banco Nacional de Cuba v. Sabatino, 376 U.S. 398, 425 (1964). For elaboration, see Harold Hongju Koh, *Is International Law Really State Law?*, 111 HARV. L. REV. 1824 (1998).

deported, and to this day, the Filártigas have yet to recover any part of their judgment.[46]

## 3.  After Filártiga

*Filártiga* was one of those cases, described by Justice Frankfurter, that do not simply revise old precedents, but spawn entirely new ways of looking at the law.[47] The case triggered a wave of academic scholarship and more than a quarter-century of human rights litigation in U.S. courts.[48] *Filártiga* created a judicial channel for human rights activism in U.S. courts during an era in which other avenues of human rights change often appeared blocked. In the same way that *Brown v. Board of Education*[49] enabled a generation of public lawyers to devote themselves to the judicial pursuit of civil rights, *Filártiga* empowered U.S. human rights activists and legal scholars of the late twentieth century to employ domestic litigation to promote human rights norms.

In the two decades that followed, the lower federal courts elaborated on *Filártiga*'s holding that when an act represents a violation of a definable, specific, universal, and obligatory norm of international law, an alien can sue under the ATCA and be awarded civil damages for the tort. *Filártiga* came to provide the governing framework for ATCA litigation not only in the Second Circuit, but also in the First,[50] Fifth,[51] Ninth,[52] and Eleventh[53] Circuits. These lower federal decisions held that not only torture, but also extrajudicial killing,[54] disappearance,[55] arbitrary detention,[56] geno-

---

**46.** Even while deciding the civil liability of Peña–Irala, the Second Circuit declined to extend the stay of his deportation order, and the Supreme Court denied certiorari on that ruling, leading to Peña-Irala's eventual deportation back to Paraguay. Filártiga v. Peña-Irala, 442 U.S. 901 (1979). Apparently, the default judgment has never been collected. *See* R. H. Hodges, Letter to the Editor, N.Y. TIMES, Mar. 26, 1986, at A34.

**47.** Guaranty Trust Co. v. York, 326 U.S. 99, 101 (1945) (discussing Erie R.R Co. v. Tompkins, 304 U.S. 64 (1938)).

**48.** One scholar has calculated that as of July 1, 2006, *Filártiga* had been cited in some 1100 law review articles and 180 published decisions in the United States. ACEVES, *supra* note 35, at 77.

**49.** 347 U.S. 483 (1954).

**50.** *See, e.g.*, Xuncax v. Gramajo, 886 F.Supp. 162 (D. Mass. 1995).

**51.** Beanal v. Freeport–McMoRan, Inc., 969 F.Supp. 362 (E.D. La. 1997), *aff'd by* 197 F.3d 161 (5th Cir. 1999).

**52.** *See* In re Estate of Marcos, Human Rights Litig., 25 F.3d 1467, 1475 (9th Cir. 1994) ("We thus join the Second Circuit in concluding that the Alien Tort Act, 28 U.S.C. § 1350, creates a cause of action for violations of specific, universal and obligatory international human rights standards which confer fundamental rights upon all people vis-à-vis their own governments.") (internal quotation marks omitted).

**53.** *See, e.g.*, Abebe–Jira v. Negewo, 72 F.3d 844 (11th Cir. 1996) (adopting *Filártiga* approach to claims of torture and cruel, inhuman, or degrading treatment).

**54.** *See, e.g.*, Xuncax v. Gramajo, 886 F.Supp. 162, 184–85 (D. Mass. 1995).

**55.** *See, e.g.*, Forti v. Suarez–Mason, 694 F.Supp. 707, 711 (N.D. Cal. 1988).

**56.** *Xuncax*, 886 F.Supp. at 184.

cide,[57] and other kinds of gross violations[58] also fit within the category of offenses against "specific, definable, universal, and obligatory norms ..." In the Torture Victim Protection Act of 1992, Congress not only reaffirmed the ATCA, but enacted a modern statute that specifically created a federal cause of action on behalf of citizens and aliens alike for torture and summary execution.[59] The federal courts have since held not only that non-state actors can be sued for certain human rights violations,[60] but also that multinational corporations can be sued under the Alien Tort Statute so long as it can be proved that they knowingly committed or collaborated in the commission of crimes against humanity.[61]

These cases culminated on the last day of the U.S. Supreme Court's 2003 Term. Twenty-four years after *Filártiga*, in *Sosa v. Alvarez–Machain*,[62] six Justices of the Supreme Court—Justices Souter, Stevens, O'Connor, Kennedy, Ginsberg, and Breyer—reaffirmed *Filártiga*'s core insight: that when there is a norm of international character accepted by the civilized world, and defined with a specificity comparable to recognized paradigms, an alien can sue for violations of that norm in a federal court under the Alien Tort Claims Act.[63]

Justice Souter, writing for the Court, adopted a "modified-*Filártiga*" approach to the ATCA. He explained that although the ATCA was a jurisdictional statute, and not an invitation "to mold substantive law,"[64] neither does it require an explicit statutory or treaty-based cause of action. Rather, the history and intent behind the ATCA indicated that the First Congress expected the statute to

---

**57.** *See, e.g.,* Kadic v. Karadzic, 70 F.3d 232, 241–42 (2d Cir. 1995).

**58.** For a partial list of unsuccessful claims, see Derek P. Jinks, *The Federal Common Law of Universal, Obligatory, and Definable Human Rights Norms*, 4 ILSA J. INT'L & COMP. L. 465, 471–72 (1998) (collecting cases in text and footnotes).

**59.** 28 U.S.C. § 1350a (2008).The TVPA allows citizen and alien alike to sue for torture or summary execution against any official acting under U.S. or foreign law, so long as the plaintiff exhausts remedies and sues within the ten-year statute of limitations. According to the House Report, "[t]he TVPA would establish an unambiguous and modern basis for a cause of action that has been successfully maintained under

an existing law, section 1350 of the Judiciary Act of 1789...." H.R. Rep. No. 367, 102d Cong., 1st Sess., pt. 1 (1991). Significantly, the House Report referred to *Filártiga* with approval, affirmed the importance of ATCA, and indicated that it "should not be replaced." *Id. See also* S. Rep. No. 249, 102d Cong., 1st Sess. (1991) (virtually identical language in Senate report).

**60.** *See, e.g.,* Kadic v. Karadzic, 70 F.3d 232 (2d Cir. 1995).

**61.** *See generally* Presbyterian Church of Sudan v. Talisman Energy, Inc., 244 F.Supp.2d 289 (S.D.N.Y. 2003) (reviewing cases).

**62.** 542 U.S. 692 (2004).

**63.** *Id.* at 728–31.

**64.** *Id.* at 713.

have practical effect from the moment it was enacted, and to enable actions arising directly from customary international law.[65] *Sosa* thus held that courts could infer a private cause of action for certain torts in violation of the laws of nations "as an element of common law,"[66] consistent with its reading of the history and intent behind the ATCA.

*Sosa* directed courts considering claims under the ATCA to ask three questions. First, a court must assess whether the asserted claim constitutes a violation of the "present-day law of nations," not the law of nations as it existed in 1789. To do so, the Court affirmed the approach laid out by Chief Justice Marshall over a century ago:

> [W]here there is no treaty, and no controlling executive or legislative act or judicial decision, resort must be had to the customs and usages of civilized nations; and, as evidence of these, to the works of jurists and commentators, who by years of labor, research and experience, have made themselves peculiarly well acquainted with the subjects of which they treat.[67]

Second, the Court must determine whether the asserted violation of the law of nations is "accepted by the civilized world and defined with specificity comparable to the features of the eighteenth-century paradigms we have recognized" as existing at the time of enactment of the ATCA.[68] Those historical paradigms were the three offenses identified by Blackstone: piracy, violations of safe conduct, and offenses against ambassadors.[69] More generally, these offenses fell within the category of "rules binding individuals for the benefit of other individuals overlapped with the norms of state relationships."[70] When enacting the ATCA, the Founders were thinking of these violations of the laws of nations, "admitting of a judicial remedy and at the same time threatening serious consequences in international affairs."[71]

---

65. *Id.* at 719.

66. *Id.* at 725; *see also id.* at 715 (describing a "sphere in which these rules binding individuals for the benefit of other individuals overlapped with the norms of state relationships," creating a "narrow set of violations of the law of nations, admitting of a judicial remedy and at the same time threatening serious consequences in international affairs").

67. The Paquete Habana, 175 U.S. 677, 700 (1900) (quoted in *Sosa*, 542 U.S. at 734).

68. 542 U.S. at 725; *see also id.* at 732 ("Whatever the ultimate criteria for accepting a cause of action subject to jurisdiction under § 1350, we are persuaded that federal courts should not recognize private claims under federal common law for violations of any international law norm with less definite content and acceptance among civilized nations than the historical paradigms familiar when § 1350 was enacted.").

69. *Id.* at 715.

70. *Id.*

71. *Id.*

Third and finally, *Sosa* warned that any inquiry into whether an ATCA claim is judicially enforceable must account for the "collateral consequences" of recognizing such an action,[72] particularly the foreign policy implications of permitting a judicial remedy for such a claim.[73] Applying this test to the facts before it, the *Sosa* Court rejected Alvarez–Machain's claim that the law of nations prevented his arbitrary arrest and detention, "defined as officially sanctioned action exceeding positive authorization to detain" under any domestic law.[74] The Court noted that although a survey of national constitutions revealed that many countries prohibit arbitrary detention, the consensus about this prohibition was "at a high level of generality."[75] In effect, the Court concluded that Alvarez–Machain's claim of temporary arbitrary arrest did not rise to the level of specificity or acceptance of the acknowledged human rights prohibition against prolonged arbitrary detention.

Significantly, in so holding, the *Sosa* Court effectively rejected three narrower theories of the ATCA that had been asserted throughout the post-*Filártiga* ATCA litigation in the lower courts. The first was the idea that courts should not hear these cases because, by their nature, they raise non-justiciable political questions, a theory first offered by Judge Roger Robb of the D.C. Circuit in 1984.[76] But if courts are simply construing an enacted statute, the Alien Tort Claims Act, and the words being interpreted are the words "torts in violation of law of nations," it is hard to see why construing those words should not be a quintessentially judicial task.

The *Sosa* Court also rejected a second, originalist position, which was first taken by Judge Bork in his concurring opinion in the *Tel–Oren* case in 1984.[77] Judge Bork asserted that courts were

**72.** *Id.* at 732–33. Specifically, the Court identified five reasons that counsel "caution" in recognizing a private right of action to adjudicate new violations of the law of nations: (1) that the prevailing conception of the common law has changed since 1789; (2) post-*Erie* reluctance to involve courts in generating federal common law rules of decision; (3) the general preference for leaving the creation of a private right of action to the legislature; (4) potential disruption of U.S. foreign policy; and (5) the lack of legislative encouragement of "judicial creativity" in this field. *Id.* at 725–29.

**73.** *Id.* at 727–28 ("[M]any attempts by federal courts to craft remedies for the violation of new norms of international law would raise risks of adverse foreign policy consequences.").

**74.** *Sosa*, 542 U.S. at 736.

**75.** *Id.* at 736 n.27.

**76.** Tel–Oren v. Libyan Arab Republic, 726 F.2d 774, 823 (D.C. Cir. 1984) (Robb, J., concurring).

**77.** 726 F.2d at 775 (Bork, J., concurring). For a discussion of the relationship between the ATCA and the common law, see William S. Dodge, *The Historical Origins of the Alien Tort Statute: A Response to the Originalists*, 19

wrong to infer a private cause of action for violations of the law of
nations directly from the ATCA, federal common law, or international law itself.[78] He acknowledged that certain kinds of claims
could be heard in these ATCA cases, but he argued that this could
only happen if the claims had existed in the eighteenth century,
when the statute was first enacted. Contrary to modern views of
dynamic statutory interpretation,[79] Judge Bork essentially asserted
that the list of "law of nations" claims cognizable in ATCA cases
should be frozen in time and limited to piracy, attacks on diplomats, and violations of safe conduct. Under Judge Bork's view, a
victim of genocide would have no recovery for genocidal acts, even
though customary international law had long since evolved to
recognize both an individual human right to be free from genocide
and the universal jurisdiction and obligation of all nations to
punish it.[80]

Third and finally, *Sosa* refused to adopt a view of the ATCA
expressed by two law professors, Curtis Bradley and Jack Goldsmith, and also pressed by some of the briefs in the *Sosa* case:
namely, that the courts should recognize no cause of action unless
the political branches expressly consent by enacting such claims
into positive law.[81] Under this theory, if there is no implementing
act by the national political branches, then international law either
has no status in U.S. law, or must be construed as some species of
state law. As I have argued elsewhere, it makes little sense to argue
that customary international law is really state law.[82] Professors
Bradley and Goldsmith assert that the canonical case of *Erie R.R.
Co. v. Tompkins*[83] supports their conclusion, but as every first-year
law student knows, the Supreme Court's landmark decision in *Erie*
rested on the constitutional argument that in exercising general
federal common lawmaking power, the federal courts had "invaded
rights which . . . are reserved by the Constitution to the several
States."[84] But no such constitutional problem exists when federal
courts determine rules of customary international law, because
"[f]ederal judicial determination of most questions of customary

HASTINGS INT'L & COMP. L. REV. 221, 231–
37 (1996).

**78.** *See* Tel–Oren v. Libyan Arab Republic, 726 F.2d 774, 798–823 (D.C. Cir.
1984) (Bork, J., concurring);

**79.** *See generally* WILLIAM N. ESK-
RIDGE, JR., DYNAMIC STATUTORY INTERPRETA-
TION (1994).

**80.** *See* RESTATEMENT (THIRD) OF THE
FOREIGN RELATIONS LAW OF THE UNITED
STATES § 702 cmt. d & reporters' note 3

(1986); *id.* § 404 cmt. d; *id.* § 907 cmt. a
(1986).

**81.** Curtis A. Bradley & Jack L.
Goldsmith, *Customary International
Law as Federal Common Law: A Cri-
tique of the Modern Position*, 110 HARV.
L. REV. 815 (1997).

**82.** Harold Hongju Koh, *Is International Law Really State Law?*, 111 HARV.
L. REV. 1824 (1998).

**83.** 304 U.S. 64, 79 (1938).

**84.** *Id.* at 78.

international law transpires not in a zone of core state concerns, such as state tort law, but in a foreign affairs area in which the Tenth Amendment has reserved little or no power to the states."[85]

Even after *Sosa* rejected the claim that customary international law lacks status as federal common law in U.S. law, academic critics of *Filártiga* sought to reassert that claim, but were quickly rebutted.[86] Writing about the *Sosa* decision, one distinguished federal courts expert, Judge William Fletcher of the Ninth Circuit, concluded:

> [From] *Sosa*, [w]e now know two things that perhaps we did not know before. First, we know—because the Supreme Court has told us—that there is a federal common law of international human rights based on customary international law.... Second, we also know—though *not* because the Court has told us—that the federal common law of customary international law is federal law in both the jurisdiction-conferring and the supremacy-clause senses. I am somewhat surprised, given the lead-up to *Sosa*, that the Court did not discuss the subject matter jurisdiction problem that has haunted the ATS almost from the beginning. But despite its lack of discussion, the Court's decision necessarily implies that the federal common law of customary international law is jurisdiction-conferring. [T]he only basis for the federal court to hear an alien versus alien suit under the ATS is the federal nature of the substantive claim.[87]

## C. Current Issues in Transnational Public Law Litigation

The several years since *Sosa* give no sign that the Supreme Court's adoption of the modified *Filártiga* test has opened the floodgates of ATCA litigation. Since *Sosa*, most of the pending ATCA cases have nevertheless been dismissed on cautionary grounds.[88] Still, in *Sosa*, the Supreme Court effectively conceded

**85.** Koh, *supra* note 82, at 1831–32.

**86.** *Compare* Curtis A. Bradley, Jack L. Goldsmith & David H. Moore, Sosa, *Customary International Law, and the Continuing Relevance of* Erie, 120 HARV. L. REV. 869 (2007) (reasserting Bradley and Goldsmith position after *Sosa*) *with* William S. Dodge, *Customary International Law and the Question of Legitimacy*, 120 HARV. L. REV. F. 19 (2007), *available at* http://www.harvardlaw review.org/forum/issues/120/feb07/dodge. pdf (rebutting that position).

**87.** William A. Fletcher, Essay, *International Human Rights in American Courts*, 93 VA. L. REV. in BRIEF 1, 7 (2007), *available at* http://virginialawre view.org/inbrief.php?s=inbrief&p= 2007/03/22/fletcher.

**88.** Since *Sosa*, as of May 2007, there have been thirteen ATCA cases decided by the courts of appeals and thirty-six by the district courts, most of which have been dismissed. Nine of the thirteen court of appeals decisions dismissed all ATCA claims presented: five

that transnational litigation, which had originated in the context of private commercial suits in U.S. courts against foreign governments, had properly migrated into the realm of certain human rights suits against the United States and foreign governments and officials.

Upon examination, transnational public law litigation represents only the judicial face of the broader procedural phenomenon that I call "Transnational Legal Process":

> the transubstantive process whereby states and other transnational private actors use the blend of domestic and international legal process to internalize international legal norms into domestic law.[89] Through repeated cycles of "interaction-interpretation-internalization," interpretations of applicable global norms are eventually internalized into states' domestic legal systems.

A transnational legal process approach helps to explain *how* international law matters, in three key senses. First, it helps to explain how transnational law functions in a *dynamic* way to constrain state behavior. In a second, *normative* sense, it illustrates how law and legal process help to create norms and construct national interests. Transnational Legal Process scholars see international norms as filtering through legal process mechanisms to play a critical role in reformulating national interests and reconstituting national interests. Third, as one scholar put it, the goal of transnational legal process is *constitutive*: "not simply to change behavior, but to change minds."[90]

Transnational public law litigation illustrates all three faces of transnational legal process: first, the "vertical" dimension, by which international norms infiltrate domestic law through "trickle-

---

on political question grounds; two for failure to state a substantive claim; one on sovereign immunity grounds against U.S. officials; and a final case was dismissed based on statutory preemption. Similarly, of the district court cases, twenty-eight of the thirty-six cases were dismissals or motions for summary judgment against the plaintiff: three on political question grounds; sixteen for failure to state a claim (including for non-recognition of corporate or secondary liability); four were for sovereign immunity (against U.S. officials); three were on procedural grounds (e.g., statute of limitations, *forum non conveniens*); one was dismissed on state secrets grounds; and one on motion for summary judgment

before trial. *See* Kimberly Gahan, Litigating the Law of Nations: An Analysis of Post–*Sosa* Alien Tort Claims Act Developments and Strategies for Future Claims (Apr. 30, 2007) (unpublished paper, on file with the author).

**89.** *See generally* Harold Hongju Koh, *The 1994 Roscoe Pound Lecture: Transnational Legal Process*, 75 NEB. L. REV. 181 (1996); Harold Hongju Koh, *Why Do Nations Obey International Law?*, 106 YALE L.J. 2599 (1997).

**90.** Melissa A. Waters, *Normativity in the "New" Schools: Assessing the Legitimacy of International Legal Norms Created by Domestic Courts*, 32 YALE J. INT'L L. 463, 470 (2007).

down lawmaking;"[91] second, the "horizontal" dimension by which such norms are transplanted from one country to another; and third, the "bottom-up dimension," whereby norms are "uploaded" from national into international legal institutions.[92]

In submissions to the United Nations, the U.S. government has called *Filártiga* a "pivotal decision" demonstrating the nation's commitment to protecting human rights, and cited the line of ATCA cases as a model for redressing human rights violations.[93] In turn, an array of United Nations bodies—including the U.N. Secretariat,[94] the U.N. Commission and Sub–Commission on Human Rights[95] and various human rights Special Rapporteurs[96]—have all

---

**91.** Sarah H. Cleveland, *Norm Internalization and U.S. Economic Sanctions*, 26 Yale J. Int'l L 1 (2001).

**92.** Janet Koven Levit, *A Bottom–Up Approach to International Lawmaking: The Tale of Three Trade Finance Instruments*, 30 Yale J. Int'l L. 125 (2005); Janet Koven Levit, *Bottom–Up International Lawmaking: Reflections on the New Haven School of International Law*, 32 Yale J. Int'l L. 399 (2007). The discussion that follows derives from the Brief for International Jurists Mary Robinson et al. as Amici Curiae Supporting Respondent, *Sosa v. Alvarez–Machain*, 542 U.S. 692 (2004), for which the author served as counsel of record.

**93.** In 1995, the United States government reported to the U.N. Commission on Human Rights that the ATCA "represents an early effort by the United States Government to provide a remedy to individuals whose rights have been violated under international law." *See* The Secretary–General, Addendum, *Question of the Human Rights of All Persons Subjected to Any Form of Detention or Imprisonment*, ¶¶ 13, 15, U.N. Doc. E/CN.4/1996/29/Add.2 (Jan. 18, 1996); *see also* Comm. Against Torture, *Consideration of Reports Submitted by States Parties Under Article 19 of the Convention: Initial Report of the United States of America*, ¶¶ 4–8, U.N. Doc. CAT/C/SR.424 (Feb. 9, 2001). Several years later, in a report to the U.N. Committee Against Torture, the U.S. government again emphasized the importance of the ATCA, repeating key language from its 1996 report:

U.S. law provides statutory rights of action for civil damages for acts of

torture occurring outside the United States. One statutory basis for such suits, the Alien Tort Claims Act of 1789, codified at 28 U.S.C. § 1350, represents an early effort to provide a judicial remedy to individuals whose rights had been violated under international law.

Comm. Against Torture, Addendum, *Consideration of Reports Submitted by States Parties Under Article 19 of the Convention: Report of the United States of America*, ¶ 277, U.N. Doc. CAT/C/28/Add.5 (Feb. 9, 2000). The U.S. government also characterized the decision in *Filártiga* as "pivotal" and described its subsequent extension to other human rights claims. *Id.* at ¶ 280 (citing In Re Estate of Ferdinand E. Marcos, 25 F.3d 1467 (9th Cir. 1994) and Kadic v. Karazdic, 70 F.3d 232 (2d Cir. 1995)).

**94.** The Division for Social Policy and Development of the United Nations Secretariat relied on *Filártiga* to conclude that "[t]he domestic enforceability of customary international law is manifest in the case of *Filártiga v. Peña–Irala*.... [D]omestic court[s] may discover international legal principles by consulting executive, legislative and judicial precedents, international agreements, the recorded expertise of jurists and commentators, and other similar sources." Division for Social Policy and Development of the United Nations Secretariat, *Compilation of International Norms and Standards Relating to Disability*, §§ 1.2, 1.4 (draft July 2002).

**95.** In 1993, the UN Sub–Commission on Human Rights relied on *Filártiga* for developing appropriate standards

---

**96.** See note 96 on page 43.

incorporated the principles expressed in *Filártiga* into different areas of human rights law. Regional[97] and treaty bodies[98] have also cited *Filártiga* and its progeny in the process of developing international legal norms prohibiting torture, genocide, and other serious violations of international law. And both the International Court of Justice[99] and the International Criminal Tribunal for the former Yugoslavia ("ICTY")[100] have drawn guidance from the *Filártiga* jurisprudence.

for determining whether conditions of imprisonment fall below fundamental human rights guarantees. *See* Hum. Rts. Comm., *The Administration of Justice and the Human Rights of Detainees,* ¶ 69, U.N. Doc. E/CN.4/Sub.2/1993/21 (June 25, 1993).

**96.** The Special Rapporteur appointed by the Commission on Human Rights to elaborate "the right to restitution, compensation and rehabilitation for victims of gross violations of human rights and fundamental freedoms" relied upon the ATCA as a leading example for states to "provide remedies for violations occurring outside their territory." The High Commissioner for Human Rights, Note, *The Right to a Remedy and Reparation for Victims of Violations of International Human Rights and Humanitarian Law,* ¶ 114, U.N. Doc. E/CN.4/2003/63 (Dec. 27, 2003). Similarly, the Special Rapporteur on Contemporary Forms of Slavery lauded the ATCA as "a potential forum for redress" in cases in which foreign fora have proven inadequate. Special Rapporteur on Contemporary Forms of Slavery, *Contemporary Forms of Slavery: Systematic Rape, Sexual Slavery, and Slavery–Like Practices During Armed Conflict,* ¶ 52, U.N. Doc. 4/Sub.2/1998/13 (June 22, 1998). Another Special Rapporteur cited the ATCA as an example of "effective remedies" for gross violations of international law, recognizing that ATCA is limited in its "appli[cation] to customary international law norms, such as the prohibition of slavery, genocide, torture, crimes against humanity and war crimes." The Secretary–General, *The Right to Food,* ¶ 40 & n.32, U.N. Doc. A/58/330 (Aug. 28, 2003) (reporting the findings of the Special Rapporteur on the Right to Food on the potential of the Alien Tort Claims Act as a method of redress for violations of human rights by transnational corporations, and citing U.S. cases following *Filártiga*).

**97.** The Inter–American Commission on Human Rights has held that the ATCA, as interpreted in *Filártiga*, constitutes an adequate and effective domestic remedy for international human rights violations. Kenneth Walker v. United States, Case P12.049, Report No. 62/03, Inter–Am. C.H.R., OEA/Ser.L/V/II.118 doc. 70 rev ¶¶ 47, 47 n.18 (2003), *available at* http://www.cidh.org/annualrep/2003eng/usa.p12049.htm.

**98.** The Human Rights Committee of the ICCPR has followed *Filártiga* in urging that under Article 2.3 of that treaty, civil remedies must be available for all individuals, including non-citizens, within the territory of a state party. *See, e.g.,* Human Rts. Comm., Bakhtiyari v. Australia: *Communication No. 1069/2002,* ¶ 12, U.N. Doc. CCPR/C/79/D/1069/2002 (Nov. 6, 2003).

**99.** In Case Concerning the Arrest Warrant of 11 April 2000 (D.R.C. v. Belgium), 2002 I.C.J. 3 (Feb. 14), the U.S., British, and Dutch Judges filed a joint concurring opinion which addressed the appropriate scope of universal criminal jurisdiction, inter alia, by highlighting ATCA jurisprudence, and describing it as conforming to global trends of extending civil jurisdiction over extraterritorial conduct in appropriate cases. *Id.* at ¶¶ 47–48 (Joint Separate Opinion of Higgins, Kooijmans and Buergenthal, JJ.).

**100.** In the first case prosecuted at the ICTY, the international judges relied on that Second Circuit's post-*Filártiga* decision in Kadic v. Karadzic, 70 F.3d 232 (2d Cir. 1995), to determine that crimes against humanity do not require an element of state action. Prosecutor v. Tadic, No. IT–94–1–T, Judgment, ¶ 655,

Similarly, foreign domestic courts have also followed the *Filár-tiga* approach in selectively incorporating fundamental norms of international law into domestic law. In the *Pinochet* case, for example, the British House of Lords cited *Filártiga* for the proposition that only a select group of customary international norms are justiciable in national courts—including torture.[101] The English Court of Appeal echoed these sentiments, discussing approvingly *Filártiga*'s characterization of torturers as *"hostis humani generis."*[102] Other democratic countries have engaged in remedial efforts parallel to the ATCA, recognizing that their international responsibilities require them to exercise jurisdiction over serious violations committed outside their territory, by their nationals as well as foreign nationals.[103] In recognition of these responsibilities, many states now indirectly provide civil remedies for serious violations of international law, even when they are committed abroad, by allowing victims to append civil claims to criminal prosecutions.[104]

reprinted in 36 I.L.M. 908, 945 (1997) (citing *Kadic*, 70 F.3d at 232). In another significant case before the ICTY, the judges relied on *Filártiga* in determining the status of the prohibition against torture during wartime. Prosecutor v. Furundzija, No. IT–95–17/1–T, Judgment, ¶ 147, *reprinted in* 38 I.L.M. 317, 348 (1998) ("There exists today universal revulsion against torture: as a USA Court put it in *Filártiga v. Peña–Irala*, 'the torturer has become, like the pirate and the slave trader before him, *hostis humani generis*, an enemy of all mankind.' ") (quoting *Filártiga*, 630 F.2d at 876). In the *Kunarac* case, the ICTY Trial Chamber cited both *Filártiga* and *Karadzic* to conclude that an international criminal tribunal could convict a defendant of war crimes for committing torture during an armed conflict, even if that defendant is not a government official or acting in concert with a government official. Prosecutor v. Kunarac, IT–96–23–T, Judgment, ¶ 470 (Feb. 22, 2001), *available at* http://www.un.org/icty/kunarac/trialc2/judgement/kun-tj010 222e.pdf.

**101.** *See* Regina v. Bow Street Metropolitan Stipendiary Magistrate and Others, Ex parte Pinochet Ugarte (No. 3), [2000] 1 A.C. 147, 159 (H.L.).

**102.** Al–Adsani v. Government of Kuwait, (1994) 100 I.L.R. 465, (1996) 107 I.L.R. 536 (Eng. C.A. 1996).

**103.** The National Commission on Human Rights in India, for example, highlighted *Filártiga*'s importance in the development of national judicial remedies for violations of fundamental human rights. *See* National Commission on Human Rights, Sardar Patel Bhawan, Case No. 1/97/NHRC, ¶ 23 (Aug. 4, 1997). In particular, the Commission noted the effect of these developments on Indian law: "In India great strides have since been made in the field of evolving legal standards for remedial, reparatory, punitive and exemplary damages for violation of human rights." *Id*. at ¶ 24.

**104.** *See, e.g.,* C. PR. PÉN. arts. 689, 689–2 to –10 (France) (extraterritorial jurisdiction for crimes of torture, terrorism, and others); *id*. at arts. 2–3 (authorizing victims to join criminal prosecution as *partie civile*); International Crimes Act of 2003, arts. 2–8, 10, 21 (Netherlands) (extraterritorial jurisdiction for genocide, war crimes, torture, and crimes against humanity); Wetboek van Strafrecht [Criminal Code], art. 36(f) (The Netherlands) (authorizing victims to append civil claims to criminal prosecution); Wetboek van Strafvordering [Code of Criminal Procedure], art. 51a (The Netherlands); Poinikas Kodikas [Criminal Code], art. 8 (Greece) (extraterritorial jurisdiction for many serious international offenses); Kodikas Poinikas Dikonomias [Code of Criminal

Throughout Latin America, the *Filártiga* case and its progeny have fortified a movement of human rights activists who are now bringing the leaders of Operation Condor to justice in their home countries. And foreign legal scholars have increasingly looked to American transnational public law litigation in urging greater judicial internalization of human rights norms in other domestic legal systems.[105]

In sum, the *Filártiga* doctrine has promoted a useful and growing partnership among the work of U.S. courts, international tribunals, and human rights organs. By so doing, *Filártiga* illustrates a key claim of the "New New Haven School of International Law": that dialectical legal interactions among various law-declaring fora—particularly through transnational judicial dialogue—can help to refine the scope of international legal obligations.[106]

At this writing, the two main issues in transnational public law litigation are: first, precisely what constitutes a *Sosa* ATCA violation, namely a violation of "norms of international character accepted by the civilized world and defined with specificity compara-

---

Procedure], arts. 63–70, 82–88 108, 137D, 468, 480, 488 (Greece) (authorizing victims to append civil claims to criminal cases); Völkerstrafgesetzbuch [Code of Crimes Against International Law of 2002] (F.R.G.) (criminalizing war crimes, crimes against humanity and war crimes); *id.* § 1 ("This Act shall apply to all criminal offences against international law designated under this Act, to serious criminal offences designated therein even when the offence was committed abroad and bears no relation to Germany."); Strafprozeïordnung [StPO] [Code of Criminal Procedure], §§ 403–406c (F.R.G.) (authorizing victims to append civil claims to criminal cases); Codice penale [Penal Code] art. 10 (Italy) (extraterritorial criminal jurisdiction over torture); Law No. 498 of 3 November 1988 (Italy) (same); Codice di Procedura Penale [Criminal Procedure Code] Arts. 74, 90, 101, 394, 396 (Italy) (enabling victims to bring civil claims for compensation and restitution within criminal proceedings); Organic Law of the Judicial Power of 1985, art. 23.4 (Spain) (extraterritorial criminal jurisdiction for serious violations of international law including torture, crimes against humanity, war crimes, genocide, and international terrorism); Ley de Enjuiciamiento Criminal [L.E. Crim.] [Law of Criminal Proceedings] art. 112 (Spain) (providing that any criminal complaint filed by a victim is also a civil claim unless the claimant expressly states otherwise).

**105.** *See, e.g.,* Eyal Benvenisti, *The Influence of International Human Rights Law on the Israeli Legal System: Present and Future,* 28 Isr. L. Rev. 136 (1994); Eyal Benvenisti, *Judges and Foreign Affairs: A Comment on the Institut de Droit International's Resolution on "The Activities of National Courts and the International Relations of their State,"* 5 Eur. J. Int'l L. 423 (1994); Gennady M. Danilenko, *The New Russian Constitution and International Law,* 88 Am. J. Int'l L. 451 (1994); Henry G. Schermers, *The Role of Domestic Courts in Effectuating International Law,* 3 Leiden J. Int'l L. 77 (1990); and Eric Stein, *International Law in Internal Law: Toward Internationalization of Central–Eastern European Constitutions?,* 88 Am. J. Int'l L. 427 (1994).

**106.** *See generally* Harold Hongju Koh, *Is There a "New" New Haven School of International Law?,* 32 Yale J. Int'l L. 559 (2007); Melissa A. Waters, *supra* note 90; Robert B. Ahdieh, *Between Dialogue and Decree: International Review of National Courts,* 79 N.Y.U. L. Rev. 2029 (2004).

ble to recognized paradigms" such as torture or genocide? The second question is whether and to what extent corporations can be held liable for "torts in violation of the law of nations" under the ATCA. Some have argued that there is currently an ATCA litigation "crisis" brewing regarding its applicability to corporations.[107] Although the Supreme Court has yet to address the corporate responsibility issue on the merits, the situation hardly seems to have risen to crisis proportions. For if states and individuals can be held liable for torts in violation of international law, then there seems no reason why corporations should not also be held liable, for the simple reason that both states and individuals *act through* corporations. Given that reality, what legal sense would it make to let state and individuals immunize themselves from liability for gross violations through the mere artifice of corporate formation?

As history and precedent make clear, corporations can be held liable in two ways, particularly when they are involved in *jus cogens* violations.[108] First, corporations can be held liable as agents of the state committing what Andrew Clapham calls "complicity offenses," namely, acting under color of state law or in concert with state actors.[109] Second, it has always been true that private actors, including corporations, can be held liable under international law if they commit certain "transnational offenses"—namely, heinous offenses that can be committed by either a public or a private entity. For example, if a corporation committed piracy or slave trade or fostered an attack on an ambassador, it would be considered *hostes humani generis* (enemies of all mankind) even if it acted in a purely private capacity. Even Judge Bork acknowledged this point in his concurring opinion in *Tel–Oren v. Libyan Arab Republic*.[110] Indeed, it was on this basis that the Nuremberg Tribunal held

**107.** *See, e.g.,* GARY HUFBAUER & NICHOLAS K. MITROKOSTAS, AWAKENING MONSTER: THE ALIEN TORT STATUTE OF 1789 (2003).

**108.** For an excellent review, see Steven R. Ratner, *Corporations and Human Rights: A Theory of Legal Responsibility,* 111 YALE L.J. 443 (2001). *See generally* Harold Hongju Koh, *Separating Myth from Reality About Corporate Responsibility Litigation,* 7 J. INT'L ECON. L. 263 (2004), from which the following discussion derives.

**109.** Andrew Clapham, *On Complicity, in* LE DROIT PÉNAL À L'ÉPREUVE DE L'INTERNATIONALISATION 241 (M M. Henzelin and R. Roth, eds., 2002).

**110.** 726 F.2d 774, 798, 813–14 (D.C. Cir. 1984) (Bork, J., concurring) ("What kinds of alien tort actions, then, might the Congress of 1789 have meant to bring into federal courts? According to Blackstone, a writer certainly familiar to colonial lawyers, 'the principal offences against the law of nations, animadverted on as such by the municipal laws of England, [were] of three kinds; 1. Violation of safe-conducts; 2. Infringement of the rights of ambassadors; and 3. Piracy.' ... One might suppose that these were the kinds of offenses for which Congress wished to provide tort jurisdiction for suits by aliens in order to avoid conflicts with other nations.") (citations omitted). *See also id.* at 794–95 (Edwards, J., concurring) (finding that there are a "handful of crimes," including slave trading, "to which the law of nations attributes *individual liability,*"

private German industrialists—Flick, I.G. Farben and Krupp—criminally liable for their support of and participation in the Holocaust, finding that the Nuremberg Charter permitted prosecution of a private group or organization and stating that the action of the company and its representatives "under these circumstances cannot be differentiated from acts of plunder or pillage committed by officers ... or ... officials of the Third Reich."[111] Moreover, under Article 4 of Genocide Convention, a private corporation can commit or aid and abet in genocide, for example, by producing lethal toxic gas for use in a concentration camp.[112] The same goes for Common Article 3 of the Geneva Conventions, which binds all parties to an armed conflict, including those who may be non-state actors.[113]

Corporations can have specific intent to commit crimes. After all, under many U.S. federal laws, such as the antitrust statutes[114] or the Racketeer Influenced Corrupt Organizations (RICO) statutes,[115] corporations have long been held criminally liable for their specific intent to commit a crime. Nor does it make sense to argue that international law may impose criminal liability on corporations, but not civil liability. Indeed, Congress passed two statutes—the Alien Tort Claims Act and the Torture Victim Protection Act (TVPA)—precisely to provide civil remedies for international law violations.[116] These statutes constitute a form of domestic legislative internalization of an international norm. Finally, even if for some reason international law did not impose civil liability directly, there is nothing to prevent domestic law (e.g. the ATCA) from supple-

---

such that state action is not required for ATS liability).

**111.** United States v. Krauch, 8 CCL No. 10 Trials, at 1081, 1140 (1952) (U.S. Mil. Trib. VI 1948). In three cases decided by American courts sitting in occupied Germany under Control Council Law No. 10—United States v. Flick, United States v. Krauch (the *I.G. Farben Case*), and United States v. Krupp—leading German industrialists were prosecuted for crimes against peace (i.e., initiating World War II), war crimes, and crimes against humanity. *See* 1 Trials of War Criminals Before the Nuremberg Military Tribunals, at xvi (photo. reprint 1998), vols. 6–9 (1950–1953) (1949). These trials led to convictions of the industrialists not only for slave labor, but also, in the case of *Flick*, for financial contributions to the SS.

**112.** Convention on the Prevention and Punishment of the Crime of Genocide art. 4, Dec. 9, 1948 78 U.N.T.S. 277 (entered into force Jan. 12, 1951) ("Persons committing genocide or any of the other acts enumerated in article III shall be punished, whether they are constitutionally responsible rulers, public officials or private individuals."). *Cf.* The Zyklon B Case: Trial of Bruno Tesch and Two Others, 1 Law Reports of Trials of War Criminals 93 (1997) (Brit. Mil. Ct. 1946) (holding individuals liable for producing and supplying lethal gas to concentration camp).

**113.** *See, e.g.*, Geneva Conventions Relative to the Laws of War, art. 3, 6 U.S.T. 3316, 75 U.N.T.S. 135.

**114.** 50 U.S.C. §§ 1–2 (2000).

**115.** 18 U.S.C. §§ 1961 *et seq.* (2000).

**116.** 28 U.S.C. §§ 1350, 1350a.

menting international criminal law remedies with civil remedies arising out of domestic law.[117] Indeed, in *Kadic v. Karadzic* and its progeny, the Second Circuit and other circuits have held that the ATCA provides domestic civil remedies against non-state actors who violate international law.[118]

Moreover, corporations can probably be held liable not just for direct, transnational offenses—which can be committed by private or public actors—but also for their indirect offenses in complicity with gross human rights abuses. Thus, like any aider and abettor, corporations can be held liable for the small class of cases that arise out of a claim of violation of obligatory, definable, and universal norms of international law (direct offenses) as well as for their complicity in a public actor's violation of international law. Indeed, it was precisely the theory of the recent Holocaust Assets deal that private companies, banks, and officials were part of a common plan or conspiracy to commit war crimes or crimes against humanity.[119]

To constitute a "complicity offense," the corporate conduct must meet a very high threshold. As the International Criminal Tribunal for the Former Yugoslavia ("ICTY") specified in the *Tadic* case, the assistance must be direct and substantial,[120] and as the Tribunal noted in the *Furundzija* case in December 1998, the corporate conduct must constitute "practical assistance, encourage-

---

**117.** *See, e.g.*, RESTATEMENT (THIRD) OF THE FOREIGN RELATIONS LAW OF THE UNITED STATES § 404 cmt. b (1987) ("[I]nternational law does not preclude the application of non-criminal law on [the] basis [of universal interests], for example, by providing a remedy in tort or restitution for victims of piracy.").

**118.** 70 F.3d 232, 239 (2d Cir. 1995) ("[C]ertain acts violate the law of nations whether undertaken by those acting under the auspices of a state or as private individuals."). *See also* Doe I v. Unocal, 395 F.3d 932, 946 (9th Cir. 2002) ("Thus, under *Kadic*, even crimes like rape, torture, and summary execution, which by themselves require state action for ATCA liability to attach, do *not* require state action when committed in furtherance of other crimes like slave trading, genocide or war crimes, which by themselves do not require state action for ATCA liability to attach. We agree with this view and apply it below to Plaintiffs' various ATCA claims.").

**119.** *See generally* STUART E. EIZENSTAT, IMPERFECT JUSTICE: LOOTED ASSETS, SLAVE LABOR, AND THE UNFINISHED BUSINESS OF WORLD WAR II (2003) (describing the evolution of the Holocaust Assets Deal).

**120.** *See* Prosecutor v. Tadic, Case No. IT–94–I–T, Judgment, ¶ 674 (May 7, 1997), *available at* http://www.un.org/icty/tadic/trialc2/judgement/index.htm ("The most relevant sources for such a determination are the Nuremberg war crimes trials, which resulted in several convictions for complicitous conduct. While the judgments generally failed to discuss in detail the criteria upon which guilt was determined, a clear pattern does emerge upon an examination of the relevant cases. First, there is a requirement of intent, which involves awareness of the act of participation coupled with a conscious decision to participate by planning, instigating, ordering, committing, or otherwise aiding and abetting in the commission of a crime. Second, the prosecution must prove that there was participation in that the conduct of the accused contributed to the commission of the illegal act.").

---

ment, or moral support which has a substantial effect on the perpetration of a crime."[121]

The International Law Commission's rules of state responsibility suggest that complicity constitutes provision of "aid or assistance to another ... facilitating the commission of the wrongful act by the latter".[122] Similarly, Article 7(1) of the ICTY Statute[123] and Article 25 of the Rome Statute of the International Criminal Court hold private citizens criminally liable for committing crimes jointly with or through another person.[124]

Taken together, all of this suggests that private corporations could be held liable in transnational public law litigation either for direct human rights violations or for acts in complicity with state human rights violations. At this writing, less than two dozen human rights cases have been filed against corporations, and of these, only three or four have survived a motion to dismiss, and no suit has yet been fully adjudicated in the plaintiffs' favor.[125]

As we shall see in the forthcoming chapters, under current law, the reason why seems clear. For corporate defendants subjected to transnational public law litigation, the ultimate solution lies in what I call in the chapters that follow the "Federal Rules of Transnational Procedure." Those chapters note currently very high, multiple procedural barriers to recovery under the ATCA; to be actionable, the acts committed by a private corporation:

>   *a.*   must be brought in a proper forum with personal jurisdiction and venue;
>
>   *b.*   must not be barred by statute of limitations;

**121.** *See* Prosecutor v. Furundzija, Case No. IT–95–17/1, Judgment, ¶ 249 (Dec. 10, 1998), *available at* http://www.un.org/icty/furundzija/trialc2/judgement/index.htm ("[T]he legal ingredients of aiding and abetting in international criminal law ... consists of practical assistance, encouragement, or moral support which has a substantial effect on the perpetration of the crime.").

**122.** International Law Commission, *Second Report on State Responsibility*, ¶ 159, U.N. Doc. A/CN.4/498/Add.1 (Apr. 1, 1999) (prepared by James Crawford).

**123.** Statute of the International Tribunal for the Prosecution of Persons Responsible for Serious Violations of International Humanitarian Law Committed in the Territory of the Former Yugo-

slavia Since 1991, U.N. Doc. S/RES/827, art. 7(1) ("A person who planned, instigated, ordered, committed, or otherwise aided and abetted in the planning, preparation or execution of a crime [under this Statute] shall be individually responsible for the crime.").

**124.** *Rome Statute of the International Criminal Court*, art. 25(3), U.N. Doc. A/CONF.183/9, 39 ILM 999 (July 17, 1998) ("[A] person shall be criminally responsible ... if that person ... aids, abets, or otherwise assists in its commission or attempted commission.").

**125.** The cases to date are summarized in the appendices to GARY HUF-BAUER & NICHOLAS K. MITROKOSTAS, AWAKENING MONSTER: THE ALIEN TORT STATUTE OF 1789 (2003).

   *c.* must state a claim upon which relief can be granted, which means alleging either a transnational offense that either a state or private individual could commit, for example, a violation of an obligatory, definable, and universal norm of international law, or an act of actionable complicity in violation of international law in the sense of practical assistance, encouragement, or moral support which has a substantial effect on the perpetration of a state crime; and

   *d.* must be proven, not just pleaded, with the plaintiff carrying a significant burden of proving the link between cause and effect.

These are hard standards to prove, which means that a successful ATCA plaintiff needs to show much, much more than simply that the multinational enterprise has chosen to invest in a "troublesome country." Small wonder then, that the courts have thus far dismissed most of the transnational public law cases brought against corporations for lack of subject matter jurisdiction, *forum non conveniens* and the like.

In short, despite the hyperbole, it is hard to see where the corporate responsibility litigation "crisis" lies, when no court has rendered any final judgment against any U.S. company under the ATCA. The policy solution would therefore not seem to be legislation to revise the ATCA, as some corporations have advocated, but rather, shrewd litigation to weed out insubstantial ATCA claims, letting the relatively few meritorious ones that run the procedural gauntlet go to judgment, as was the case in *Filártiga* itself.

# PART TWO
## THE AMERICAN LAW OF FOREIGN SOVEREIGNTY
## CHAPTER IV
### THE EXTRATERRITORIALITY PROBLEM

The chapters so far have suggested that within the decisions of the U.S. Supreme Court, one may discern five core jurisprudential principles regarding International Business Transactions: Party Autonomy, National Sovereignty, International Comity, Uniformity, and the Separation of Powers.

*Party Autonomy* refers to the principle that the court should respect, and not disrupt, the wishes of two parties who have contracted for a particular business result. *National sovereignty* refers to the parallel freedom of nation-states, or their trading companies, to consent to business arrangements with private parties, to enforce their own laws within their own territory, to defend their political independence and territorial integrity, and to avoid being judged in the national courts of other countries. *Comity* describes the respect and "recognition which one nation allows within its territory to the legislative, executive, or judicial acts of another nation, having due regard both to international duty and convenience, and to the rights of its own citizens, or of other persons who are under the protection of its laws."[1] *Uniformity* refers to the perceived need for uniform rules to govern international business proceedings in the federal courts of all fifty of the United States. Finally, *Separation of Powers* refers to the constitutional principle of divided federal government that leads the federal courts to defer to the discretion of the United States President and executive branch when they act upon international business matters that touch upon foreign affairs.

How have these five principles together shaped the doctrine of extraterritorial application of United States law?

## A. Types of Conflicts

At the outset, it is worth asking why the topic of extraterritoriality, or transnational reach of governmental regulation, has

---

1. Hilton v. Guyot, 159 U.S. 113, 164 (1895).

achieved such public prominence. First, a multinational enterprise's business interests, by definition, are not confined to a single nation's borders. Multinational enterprises engage in a huge array of business activities in myriad countries, with borders becoming increasingly irrelevant to their strategic plans. By the same token, nation-states pursue regulatory interests that are also not coterminous with their borders. Nation-states have interests in regulating not only those private activities that occur within their territory, but also the activities of their nationals when they are abroad, as well as an interest in regulating foreign commercial activities that may cause detrimental effects within their territory. A third contributing factor has been the rise of global regulation. In such areas as export controls, foreign payments, and intellectual property, for example, foreign policy or national security interests have motivated nation-states to seek to regulate entire classes of private business activities that previously had been largely unregulated.

These factors have all contributed to the broad rise of economic interdependence among nations and business. For as businesses and nation-states have increasingly reached out overseas, and as the level of global regulation has increased, it has become inevitable that national differences in regulatory philosophies arising from cultural differences, historical path-dependence, and differences in regulatory philosophies and regulatory schemes will lead to conflicts of regulatory jurisdiction. As noted earlier, the legal solution to such conflicts range from unilateral forbearance by one nation's regulators, to formal and informal bilateral, regional, and multilateral accords or treaties. The central issue posed for the courts of aggressive regulating countries such as the United States is how, within the scope of judicial authority, to provoke such legal solutions. On the one hand, a nation's courts may mandate unilateral forbearance by local regulators; on the other hand, they may tolerate inter-jurisdictional regulatory clash, leaving it to the politicians to work out the necessary political resolutions.[2]

Against this background, it should become clear that as a legal term, "extraterritoriality" should carry no necessary negative or pejorative connotation.[3] It is well established that international law recognizes five distinct bases for the exercise of national jurisdic-

---

**2.** As we shall see later in this chapter, the two leading approaches applied by the U.S. courts, in the *Timberlane* and *Laker* cases, choose the forbearance and toleration approaches, respectively, to regulatory conflict.

**3.** Europeans tend to prefer the term "extraterritoriality," usually accompa-

nied by a shake of the head and a pointing of fingers, while Americans prefer the more neutral phrase "Conflicts of Regulatory Jurisdiction" (usually without mentioning which nation created the jurisdictional conflict in the first place).

tion.[4] First and foremost, of course, all nations exercise jurisdiction based on *territoriality*, but also, to a lesser extent on four other grounds as well: most prominently, *nationality*, but on occasion, via the *protective principle*—when a regulating state exercises jurisdiction based on acts by non-nationals against the security of the state;[5] *passive personality*—when a regulating state exercises jurisdiction based on acts against the country's nationals;[6] and *universal jurisdiction*—when a regulating state exercises jurisdiction based on acts that constitute universal crimes, such as piracy, torture, genocide, or slave trade.[7] Given that public international law permits states to exercise jurisdiction based on five alternative grounds, only one of which is explicitly territorial, no presumption of illegitimacy should automatically arise simply because a nation applies its domestic law extraterritorially. Extraterritoriality connotes only that a nation is purporting to regulate based on some prescriptive ground other than strict territoriality.

Similarly, it should be clear that a particular instance of extraterritorial application of U.S. law need not necessarily create a political or legal problem, unless two conditions are simultaneously met. The first is *multiple regulation*: when the United States and another nation are seeking to regulate the same private conduct. The second is *conflicting regulation*: when the two nations seeking to regulate are in fact pursuing regulatory philosophies that clash with one another. If both conditions exist, then extraterritorial assertion of U.S. jurisdiction would both encroach upon the national sovereignty of the other state and offend the principle of comity, by causing, not avoiding, ill-will with the other nation. On the other hand, if only one nation seeks to regulate the conduct or if two nations regulate the same conduct, but with essentially the same goal in mind, then neither sovereignty nor comity concerns should validly arise.

*Environmental Defense Fund v. Massey*, a case decided by the U.S. Court of Appeals for the D.C. Circuit, well illustrates the first requirement of multiple regulation.[8] In that case, the National Science Foundation (NSF), a U.S. governmental entity, made plans to incinerate food wastes in Antarctica, in an open landfill near McMurdo Station. Not only is Antarctica not a sovereign state, it also lacks any government, any permanent population, nor has any

---

4. For an exhaustive treatment of this subject, see the first part of Part IV of the American Law Institute's RESTATEMENT (THIRD) OF THE FOREIGN RELATIONS LAW OF THE UNITED STATES §§ 401–04 & reporters' notes (1987) [hereinafter RESTATEMENT (THIRD)].

5. *Id.* § 402, cmt. f.

6. *Id.* § 402, cmt. g.

7. *Id.* § 404.

8. Environmental Defense Fund v. Massey, 986 F.2d 528 (D.C. Cir. 1993).

single nation laid claim to sovereignty over it.[9] An environmental group filed suit alleging that the NSF had violated U.S. domestic environmental laws by failing to prepare an environmental impact statement before conducting the Antarctica incineration, which the plaintiffs alleged would produce highly toxic pollutants. The U.S. government responded that the environmental law did not apply extraterritorially, but the appeals court rejected that claim, reasoning that Antarctica is a continent without a sovereign, and that no other sovereign had expressed an interest in the matter. Accordingly, the Court reasoned, application of the U.S. law within the territory of Antarctica, although undeniably extraterritorial, "would not conflict with the primary purpose underlying this venerable rule of interpretation—to avoid ill-will and conflict between nations arising out of one nation's encroachments upon another's sovereignty."[10]

The second condition—that regulations be not just multiple, but conflicting—can be seen in the United States' 1980 decision to freeze Iraqi and Kuwaiti assets following Saddam Hussein's invasion of Kuwait. Previous extraterritorial asset freezes by the U.S. directed against Iran and Libya had created political conflicts, because the U.S. government had attempted to freeze accounts in Paris and London extraterritorially, even while the French and British government authorities had chosen not to freeze those same accounts.[11] But in the Iraq case, no similar extraterritoriality "problem" arose. Although there was multiple regulation, competing regulatory philosophies did not conflict, because participating nations had reached a multilateral agreement to achieve the same goal through U.N. Security Council sanctions.

Thus, rather than automatically condemning extraterritorially, one should seek more carefully to distinguish among three types of conflicts of jurisdiction. The first are "nonconflicts," or cases in which one nation attempts to regulate certain conduct extraterrito-

---

**9.** *See* Antarctica Treaty, Dec. 1, 1959, 12 U.S.T. 794, 402 U.N.T.S. 71.

**10.** *Massey*, 986 F.2d at 534 (quoting State Department official).

**11.** During the Iranian Hostages Crisis of 1979–80, President Carter tried to freeze Eurodollar accounts in French and English banks held by "persons subject to the jurisdiction" of the United States, a term construed to include not just branches, but also subsidiaries of American companies that might prove to be nationals of the other country under local company law. In 1986, President Reagan repeated the process in response to Libya's acts of state-sponsored terrorism. In Libyan Arab Foreign Bank v. Bankers Trust Co., [1989] Q.B. 728, a U.K. court ordered the U.K. branch of a U.S. bank to make payment to a Libyan bank despite a U.S. law prohibiting payment, characterizing the transaction as one governed by British, not U.S. law. *Id.* at 728. For discussion of these events, see Peter Smedresman & Andreas Lowenfeld, *Eurodollars, Multinational Banks, and National Law*, 64 N.Y.U. L. Rev. 733, 746–61 (1989).

rially, but no other nation exhibits an interest in or attempts to regulate the same conduct: for example, regulation on the high seas or in a no-man's land such as Antarctica. Second, "soft conflicts" occur when two nations do seek to regulate the same conduct, but exhibit no substantial differences in regulatory philosophy, instead disagreeing only about choice of regulatory techniques or methods, differences of regulatory approach that can generally be accommodated through negotiation, agreement, or memoranda of understanding.[12] "Hard conflicts"—the third, most intractable, type of conflict—arise when two nations not only seek to regulate the same conduct, but do so with decidedly different regulatory philosophies. This occurs, for example, with respect to taking of evidence or competition policy, where the United States stands virtually alone in embracing policies of broad pretrial discovery and treble damages in private antitrust actions. Given that the regulatory conflicts in these cases are sharp and direct, such regulatory differences cannot be easily negotiated away through bilateral negotiations.

In his 1979 Hague Lectures, Professor Andreas Lowenfeld offered what has become a familiar tripartite breakdown of types of national jurisdiction.[13] That tripartite categorization—now enshrined through Lowenfeld's efforts as Associate Reporter into Section 401 of the American Law Institute's *Restatement (Third) on the Foreign Relations Law of the United States*—distinguishes among a nation-state's *Jurisdiction to Prescribe*, or to make generally applicable laws, particularly through legislation; its *Jurisdiction to Enforce*, or to compel compliance with law, particularly through executive action; and its *Jurisdiction to Adjudicate*, or to subject someone to judicial process, particularly through the courts.[14]

---

**12.** Take, for example, the rules regarding service of process. As we shall see in Chapter IX, virtually all nations recognize that the defendant should be given notice of a lawsuit through delivery to that defendant of legal documents announcing that the suit has begun. But precisely what constitutes effective service—for example, leaving the documents with the concierge of a hotel, as opposed to service directly by hand—may differ from country to country. Such a soft procedural conflict usually reflects historical tradition and path-dependence more than deep-rooted national policy. Thus, in many cases, the conflict can be resolved by two or more nations by negotiation, agreement, and memoranda of understanding. But with respect to such matters as antitrust policy, by contrast, the United States and other nations tend to disagree not simply about technique, but about the *substance* of the policy to be followed. Unlike soft conflicts, such hard regulatory differences are far less easily negotiated away.

**13.** Andreas Lowenfeld, *Public Law in the International Arena: Conflict of Laws, International Law, and Some Suggestions for their Interaction*, 163 RECUEIL DES COURS 311, 326–27 (1979).

**14.** RESTATEMENT (THIRD), *supra* footnote 4, at § 401.

Not surprisingly, the hardest conflict arises when a regulated entity confronts a situation of conflicting orders. Conflicting orders typically arise when U.S. government regulators attempt to exercise nationality-based enforcement jurisdiction over entities doing business within the territory of another country, which is concurrently exercising territorial enforcement jurisdiction to compel from those entities the opposite result.

Perhaps the most famous recent example arose in 1982, when in response to continued Soviet repression in Poland, the Reagan Administration sought to apply U.S. export control laws extraterritorially over French and British subsidiaries of American corporations who had assumed contractual obligations to send products to the Soviet Pipeline.[15] The incident well illustrated the pattern of percolation and transformation from private to public described in Chapter II. The Reagan administration applied the pipeline regulations, *inter alia*, to shipments planned by Dresser France, a French subsidiary of a U.S. company (reasoning that foreign subsidiaries of a U.S. company are subject to U.S. nationality-based jurisdiction as U.S.-controlled companies) and to John Brown Engineering, a British company that planned to make products with component parts received from American companies. Both France and the United Kingdom protested the legality of the pipeline regulation, and invoked their blocking statutes, leaving the regulated entities caught between "a Reagan and a hard place."[16] Thus, governmental efforts to regulate a large network of ostensibly "private" export contracts between Western oil equipment suppliers and Eastern European buyers percolated up to the intergovernmental level, and transformed into a public international incident. That episode raged until the Reagan administration ultimately backed down, and withdrew its administrative sanctions before their validity could be finally resolved by U.S. courts.

The episode also fostered a classic struggle among the jurisprudential principles identified above. As a foreign policy matter, the

**15.** Amendments to the Export Administration Act of 1979 expanded the power of the executive branch to prohibit exports from any country of goods or technology exported by foreign subsidiaries of U.S. corporations. The Reagan administration then invoked those amendments to issue the pipeline regulations, which in turn barred foreign subsidiaries of U.S. corporations from helping to build the Trans–Siberia pipeline. For discussion of the incident, see John Ellicott, *Extraterritorial Trade Controls—Law, Policy, and Business, in* PRIVATE INVESTORS ABROAD—PROBLEMS AND SOLUTIONS IN INTERNATIONAL BUSINESS 1 (1983).

**16.** *See* European Communities, *Comments on the U.S. Regulations Concerning Trade with the U.S.S.R.*, reprinted in 21 INT'L LEG. MATS. 891 (1982); United Kingdom, *Statement and Order Concerning the American Export Embargo with Regard to the Soviet Gas Pipeline*, reprinted in 21 INT'L LEG. MATS. 851 (1982).

United States executive branch sought to enforce *uniformity* of application of its export control laws upon all American companies doing business with the Pipeline, wherever located, and when challenged, asked a U.S. court to defer to those efforts as a matter of *separation of powers*.[17] At the same time, the European jurisdictions complained that the extraterritorial application of the regulations had invaded their *national sovereignty* and offended principles of *comity*, while the regulated businesses complained that the U.S. government had violated the *party autonomy* and sanctity of their existing commercial contracts.

The U.S. case raising this issue terminated before reaching the U.S. Supreme Court. But in the *Sensor Nederland* case,[18] the District Court in The Hague ruled that jurisdictional principles of international law did not permit those sanctions to be applied extraterritorially to bar an export to a French buyer of goods originating outside the United States by a Dutch subsidiary of an American company. The Dutch court decided that under a bilateral treaty of Friendship Commerce and Navigation between the U.S. and the Netherlands, the Dutch seller lay beyond the reach of U.S. nationality-based jurisdiction. Not being bound by either American notions of separation of powers or uniformity of American regulation, the Dutch court chose to uphold the contractual autonomy of the parties.[19] While conceding that the United States law might appropriately be applied "to American citizens who, wishing to evade the American embargo, to that end set up a non-American corporation outside the United States,"[20] absent such a nationality link, the court suggested, U.S. regulation of the transaction would offend comity and national sovereignty, hence "rais[ing] the question of whether the jurisdiction rule that brings about such [extraterritorial] effects is compatible with international law."[21]

## B.  Prescriptive Jurisdiction and the Effects Doctrine

The types of conflicts-of-jurisdiction that most frequently come before the United States courts are cases in which private parties claim that extraterritorial business activities of foreign companies

---

**17.**  *See, e.g.*, Dresser Indus. v. Baldridge, 549 F.Supp. 108 (D.D.C. 1982).

**18.**  Compagnie Europeene des Petroles S.A. v. Sensor Nederland B.V., District Court, The Hague, 1982, Rechtspraak van de Week 167, *reprinted in* 22 Int'l Leg. Mats. 66 (1983).

**19.**  The Court's order directed the Dutch company to deliver the goods ordered promptly, in the contractually agreed upon manner. *Id.*

**20.**  22 Int'l Leg. Mats. 66, 73 (1983).

**21.**  22 Int'l Leg. Mats. at 71 (1983).

have effects upon United States national interests, thereby falling within the *prescriptive jurisdiction* of an Act of Congress. If the U.S. court agrees, then the challenge to the legality of those activities under the extraterritorially-applied federal statute falls within the limited *subject matter jurisdiction* of the United States federal courts. These cases, which have arisen most prominently in the area of antitrust or competition policy, have caused severe political problems because they have pitted the *de facto* territoriality of the European jurisdiction against the *de jure* "objective territoriality" of the United States, which has regulated admittedly extraterritorial activities based on their "direct, substantial, and reasonably foreseeable effects on U.S. territory or commerce."[22]

The "effects doctrine" originated in the famous 1909 Supreme Court decision in *American Banana Co. v. United Fruit Co.*[23] In that case, American Banana brought a private action against United Fruit seeking treble damages and charging violation of U.S. antitrust laws for acts that were allegedly committed in Costa Rica and Panama. Justice Oliver Wendell Holmes, writing for the Court, found it "surprising to hear it argued that [the acts causing the damage] were governed by the act of Congress."[24] He went on to suggest that the Court should presume that all American legislation is *prima facie* territorial in scope, and with little additional analysis, found it "entirely plain" that what the defendant had done in Central America was not covered by the statute.[25]

*American Banana* came to stand for three principles. The first, soon to be discarded, was that the U.S. Sherman Act stops at the water's edge. Second, Justice Holmes did not deny that Congress could regulate extraterritorial conduct, he simply held that it had not expressly exercised the power to do so. Thus, although he concluded that the extraterritorial business activities of foreign companies fell outside the scope of the statute, he left open the possibility that those acts might still lie within the prescriptive jurisdiction of a Congress that intended to regulate overseas conduct.

The third notion, which the current Supreme Court has greatly emphasized, is the judicial *presumption against extraterritoriality* in the interpretation of regulatory statutes. "[I]n case of doubt,"

**22.** With regard to extraterritorial regulation, President Reagan's Assistant Attorney General of the Antitrust Division, William Baxter, was once heard to say "If we regulate it, we don't consider it extraterritorial." For further discussion of the subject matter jurisdiction of the federal courts, see Chapter VII, *infra*.

**23.** 213 U.S. 347 (1909).

**24.** *Id.* at 355.

**25.** *Id.* at 357.

Holmes suggested, the Court should adopt "a construction of any statute as intended to be confined in its operation and effect to the territorial limits over which the lawmaker has general and legitimate power."[26] On closer examination, that presumption, later enshrined in *Foley Bros. v. Filardo*,[27] draws upon three separate rationales: conflict-of-laws, comity, and a public international law respect for national sovereignty. In *American Banana*, Holmes first reasoned that for the Sherman Act to regulate extraterritorial conduct would violate "the general and almost universal rule [of conflict of laws] that the character of an act as lawful or unlawful must be determined wholly by the law of the country where the act is done."[28] Holmes secondly reasoned, citing an 1870 opinion of the English Exchequer Chamber[29] that

> For another jurisdiction . . . to treat [a private party] according to its own notions . . . would be an interference with the authority of another sovereign, contrary to the *comity* of nations, which the other state concerned justly might resent.[30]

Holmes' third rationale suggested that extension of U.S. regulatory law to extraterritorial conduct would offend sovereignty, thus violating public international law. This violated a principle of statutory construction stated by Chief Justice John Marshall in a charming 1804 case, *The Schooner Charming Betsy*: "[A]n act of Congress ought never to be construed to violate the law of nations if any other possible construction remains."[31] As later explicated in Justice Story's opinion in *The Appolon*,[32] this canon flows from a general presumption that the extraterritorial assertion of U.S. jurisdiction would be "at variance with the independence and sovereignty of foreign nations."[33]

In fact, in the decades following *American Banana*, all three rationales for this presumption against extraterritoriality—comity, public international law, and conflicts—were significantly relaxed. In 1927, the Permanent Court of International Justice decided the

---

**26.** *Id.*

**27.** 336 U.S. 281 (1949).

**28.** 213 U.S. at 356.

**29.** Phillips v. Eyre, 6 L.R. 4, Q.B. 225, 239; L.R. 6, Q.B. 1, 28 (Exch. Div. 1870) ("[T]he civil liability arising out of a wrong derives its birth from the law of the place, and its character is determined by that law.").

**30.** 213 U.S. at 356 (emphasis added).

**31.** Murray v. The Schooner Charming Betsy, 6 U.S. (2 Cranch) 64, 118 (1804). For a detailed analysis of this principle, see Ralph Steinhardt, *The Role of International Law as a Canon of Domestic Statutory Construction*, 43 VAND. L. REV. 1103 (1990). For a modern application, see United States v. Palestine Liberation Organization, 695 F.Supp. 1456, 1465 (S.D.N.Y. 1988).

**32.** 22 U.S. (9 Wheat.) 362 (1824).

**33.** *Id.* at 370.

famous *S.S. Lotus* case,[34] which raised the question whether France or Turkey could apply its criminal laws to the conduct of a French national on a French ship that had collided with a Turkish ship on the high seas. The Court refused to lay down a general rule of public international law that states could not extend the application of their laws and the jurisdiction of their courts to persons, property and acts outside their territory, instead suggesting that the same incident might be subject to the concurrent jurisdiction of the two nations. "The territoriality of criminal law," the Court said, "therefore, is not an absolute principle of international law and by no means coincides with territorial sovereignty."[35] It followed, the Court suggested, that territorial exercise of jurisdiction was not strictly mandated by principles of comity. In the decades following the *Lotus* Case, U.S. conflicts law similarly witnessed the abandonment of strict territoriality with respect to the analysis of both conflict of laws,[36] and judicial jurisdiction.[37]

The watershed moment arrived with the 1945 case of *United States v. Aluminum Co. Of America (Alcoa)*,[38] a U.S. government enforcement action under section one of the Sherman Act. The U.S. Government claimed that Alcoa had conspired to participate in a Swiss-based cartel of aluminum producers fixing production quotas.[39] Judge Learned Hand's opinion found that "settled law" allowed any state "to impose liabilities even upon persons not within its allegiance for conduct outside its borders that has [negative] consequences within its borders"[40]—a test of "harmful domestic effects."

*Alcoa* triggered the modern era of extraterritoriality, which has been characterized by the migration and recurrence of the extraterritoriality problem from one regulatory area to another. This era has had four distinctive features. First, virtually all of these cases have involved the *United States* extending its regulatory arm beyond American territory into foreign territory, thereby provoking the other nation's ire. Only occasionally in the past few years has the so-called "reverse-ET problem" arisen, in which the European

**34.** Judgment 9, 1927, P.C.I.J., series A, No. 10 at 19–20.

**35.** *Id.* at 19–20.

**36.** For discussion of these trends, see generally RESTATEMENT (SECOND) OF CONFLICT OF LAWS § 6 (1969) (most significant relationship analysis); Friedrich K. Juenger, *American and European Conflicts Laws*, 30 AM. J. COMP. L. 117, 121–25 (1982); Gary B. Born, *A Reappraisal of the Extraterritorial Reach of U.S.* *Law*, 24 LAW & POL'Y INT'L BUS. 1, 27 (1992).

**37.** International Shoe Co. v. Washington, 326 U.S. 310 (1945). *See* Chapter VII, *infra*.

**38.** 148 F.2d 416 (2d Cir. 1945).

**39.** Oddly, the Second Circuit heard the case on a certificate of reference from the U.S. Supreme Court, because that Court lacked a quorum of justices. *See id.* at 421.

**40.** 148 F.2d at 443.

Union seeks to extend its jurisdiction into U.S. territory.[41] Second, although some conflicts have been instigated by U.S. government agencies and others by private lawyers, the latter cases have proven far more severe, because fewer government-to-government channels exist to mitigate such conflicts. Third, most of the cases have been settled politically, through diplomatic protests, negotiations, and memoranda of understanding, usually leaving no clear judicial articulation of the legally mandated rules of conduct. Fourth, and not surprisingly, although the non-American judicial decisions on the subject have been hostile to American jurisdiction, virtually all of the American decisions have favored it, leaving considerable confusion about what, if any, the agreed-upon international rules of conduct are. In *Alcoa*, Judge Hand had created a two-step test: The United States government could regulate extraterritorial conduct if the plaintiff could show both the defendants' *intent to affect* and an *actual effect* upon U.S. commerce.[42] Yet during the next several decades, the U.S. courts minimized Hand's requirement of a showing of anti-competitive intent, upholding extraterritorial jurisdiction in hundreds of foreign trade cases, based on *de minimis* domestic effects.[43]

Emboldened by this judicial deference, during the 1950s and 60s, aggressive U.S. government enforcement began under the "effects doctrine" directed at the shipping,[44] aeronautics,[45] watchmaking,[46] synthetic fibers,[47] lampmaking,[48] and petroleum indus-

---

**41.** *See, e.g.*, the Vredeling Directive, 21 INT'L LEG. MATS. 422 (1982), which would have required multinational corporations with a parent or subsidiary in the European Union to disclose at least once a year a picture of the activities of its intercorporate affiliates located abroad.

**42.** *Id.* at 444.

**43.** "Following Alcoa, the assertion of jurisdiction was almost uniformly upheld as the lower courts put less and less emphasis on the question of intent and required only trivial effects in the United States to assert jurisdiction over anti-competitive conduct anywhere in the world." Spencer Weber Waller, *Antitrust and American Business Abroad Today*, 44 DEPAUL L. REV. 1251, 1260–61 (1995); *see also* WILBUR FUGATE & LEE H. SIMOWITZ, FOREIGN COMMERCE AND THE ANTITRUST LAWS app. b at 498 (2d ed. 1973) (noting that in 248 cases filed in the 28 years after *Alcoa*, none were dismissed for lack of jurisdiction).

**44.** In the 1960s, the U.S. Federal Maritime Commission undertook a campaign to secure information from shipping lines operating to and from U.S. concerning allegedly anticompetitive shipping conferences. *See, e.g.*, Montship Lines, Ltd. v. Federal Maritime Board, 295 F.2d 147 (D.C. Cir. 1961); Federal Maritime Commission v. DeSmedt, 366 F.2d 464 (2d Cir.), *cert. denied*, 385 U.S. 974 (1966). This led to a round of narrow blocking statutes in the United Kingdom, West Germany, France, and Norway.

**45.** *See, e.g.*, Civil Aeronautics Board v. Deutsche Lufthansa Aktiengesellschaft, 591 F.2d 951 (D.C. Cir. 1979).

**46.** In the *Swiss Watchmakers* case, the Justice Department alleged that four U.S. and five Swiss watchmakers had made a complex web of industry-wide agreements to prevent growth of watch industry outside Switzerland. After the U.S. court issued an equity decree, the

---

**47–48.** See note 47–48 on page 62.

tries.[49] These early confrontations were generally resolved through unilateral forbearance by the U.S. actor, after diplomatic protest by the foreign party, refusal of a foreign court to cooperate with a contested order, or diplomatic negotiations leading to a bargained-for settlement. Several of these confrontations gave rise to governmental orders, and later blocking statutes, in which European jurisdictions ordered their nationals not to comply with any measure or decision of other states regarding regulation or competition.[50]

By the mid–1970s these disputes shifted from the government-to-government level to private litigants, who sought to secure information about an alleged worldwide uranium producers' cartel in anticipation of proving jurisdiction and a direct effect on the United States.[51] In response, Australia, Canada, France, the U.K., and South Africa issued a new wave of specific or general blocking statutes designed expressly to counter private litigation or investigations emanating from the United States.[52] With the globalization of the securities markets, the effects doctrine then spread into the securities field with a line of decisions by the U.S. Court of Appeals for the Second Circuit.[53] As carried forward to the present day,

Swiss government protested. Intergovernmental negotiations eventually led to a modification of the original judgment, under which no defendant was prohibited or required to do any act in Switzerland inconsistent with Swiss law. *See* United States v. Watchmakers of Switzerland Information Center, Inc., 1963 Trade Reg. Rep. (CCH) ¶ 70,600 (S.D.N.Y. 1962); 1965 Trade Reg. Rep. (CCH) ¶ 71,352 (S.D.N.Y. 1965).

**47.** In the famous case of *United States v. Imperial Chem. Indus.*, 105 F.Supp. 215 (S.D.N.Y. 1952), the U.S. government alleged a worldwide cartel to control production and distribution of nylon, a product covered by both U.S. and foreign patents. Although the U.S. district court ordered ICI to reconvey its foreign patent, the British court refused to give effect to the U.S. judgment because the patent was English in character and beyond the jurisdiction of U.S. courts. *See* British Nylon Spinners Ltd. v. Imperial Chemical Industries, Ltd., ch. 37 (1954), 3 All E.R. 88, p. 975.

**48.** *See* United States v. General Electric Co., 82 F.Supp. 753 (D.N.J. 1949), in which the federal court found a world wide lamp cartel to exist, and fashioned a worldwide decree designed

to eliminate it. When the Netherlands protested this invasion of its patent system, the U.S. District Court retreated, and chose not to hold the Dutch company in contempt.

**49.** *See* In re Investigation of World Arrangements with Relation to the Production, Transportation, Ref. and Distribution of Petroleum, 13 F.R.D. 280 (D.D.C. 1952).

**50.** The Canadian Province of Ontario enacted the first such statute in response to a U.S. federal court order in 1947, which was soon followed by blocking statutes enacted by the United Kingdom, the Netherlands, France, Italy, and of the Canadian provinces. For a comprehensive listing of such statutes, see RESTATEMENT (THIRD) § 442, reporter's note 4.

**51.** *See* In re Uranium Antitrust Litigation, 617 F.2d 1248 (7th Cir. 1980).

**52.** For a comprehensive listing of such statutes, see RESTATEMENT (THIRD) § 442, reporter's note 4.

**53.** The U.S. securities laws, enacted principally in 1933 and 1934, apply to securities sold in interstate and foreign commerce and govern registration, antifraud and disclosure provisions. The an-

these decisions generally recognized the United States' broad right to assert legislative jurisdiction over extraterritorial conduct, coupled with significant discretion in the enforcing agency to refuse to exercise that right in the appropriate circumstances.[54]

By the early 1960s, in *Continental Ore Co. v. Union Carbide and Carbon Corp.*, the Supreme Court all but overruled *American Banana*'s "water's edge" approach.[55] But what remained unclear was what limiting principle, if any, the U.S. courts would place on the extraterritorial exercise of U.S. jurisdiction. In 1976, the United States Court of Appeals for the Ninth Circuit announced that principle in *Timberlane Lumber Co. v. Bank of America*,[56] which introduced interest-balancing to comity analysis in international

tifraud provisions have been most frequently applied to protect securities markets of the United States from fraud in transactions that affect U.S. markets. The main decisions in these cases have been made not by the Supreme Court, but by the Second Circuit, in a series of decisions by the renowned Judge Henry Friendly. Schoenbaum v. Firstbrook, 405 F.2d 200 (2d Cir. 1968), *cert. denied*, 395 U.S. 906 (1969), applied the effects doctrine from antitrust law to a dispute between two Canadian companies over Canadian purchases of stock with nonpublic information. The court found jurisdiction proper even if the harmful conduct occurred entirely outside the United States, so long as the foreign security was registered and traded in the United States and the action injured U.S. investors. In 1972, in Leasco Data Processing Equip. Corp. v. Maxwell, 468 F.2d 1326 (2d Cir. 1972), the court held that when a nonresident makes abundant misrepresentations in the United States, such conduct amounts to a significant U.S. effect. In Bersch v. Drexel Firestone, Inc., 519 F.2d 974 (2d Cir. 1975), *cert. denied*, 423 U.S. 1018 (1975), Judge Friendly ruled that a court may refuse to exercise jurisdiction if conduct is merely preparatory, predominantly foreign, and effects are generalized.

**54.** In Consolidated Gold Fields PLC v. Minorco, 871 F.2d 252 (2d Cir. 1989), for example, the Second Circuit generously interpreted the extraterritorial reach of the antifraud provisions of the Williams Act, extending its prior decisions in *Schoenbaum* and *Bersch* to

reach a Luxembourg corporation's attempted hostile cash-for-stock tender offer for the stock of a U.K. company. Significantly, Minorco, the raider, seemed to have deliberately structured its $4.9 billion transaction to avoid U.S. securities laws. Americans represented only 2.5% of the shareholders with 5.3 million shares in the target, Gold Fields. Minorco sent offering documents not directly into the United States, but rather, to British nominees of American shareholders. Because the British nominees were required by law to forward the tender offer documents to shareholders and American Depositary Receipt banks in the United States, the Second Circuit held that this predominantly foreign transaction had substantial effects within the United States. This ruling brought the takeover under the prescriptive jurisdiction of the securities law and helped to contribute to the eventual dropping of the takeover attempt by Minorco. *See* Jill Fisch, *Imprudent Power: Reconsidering U.S. Regulation of Foreign Tender Offers*, 87 Nw. U. L. Rev. 523, 541–46 (1993).

**55.** 370 U.S. 690, 705 (1962). The U.S. Supreme Court recently characterized *Continental Ore* as having "substantially overruled" *American Banana*. *See* W.S. Kirkpatrick and Co. v. Environmental Tectonics Corp., 493 U.S. 400, 407 (1990).

**56.** 549 F.2d 597 (9th Cir. 1976), *cert. denied*, 472 U.S. 1032 (1985). *See also* Timberlane Lumber Co. v. Bank of America, 749 F.2d 1378, 1383–84 (9th Cir. 1984).

antitrust cases. The court applied a three-part analysis in deciding whether the U.S. antitrust laws applied to foreign conduct abroad:

[1] [T]he antitrust laws require in the first instance that there be some effect, actual or intended, on American foreign commerce before the federal courts may legitimately exercise subject matter jurisdiction under those statutes. [2] Second, a greater showing of burden or restraint may be necessary to demonstrate that the effect is sufficiently large to present a cognizable injury to the plaintiffs and therefore, a civil violation of the antitrust laws ... [3] Third, there is the additional question which is unique to the international setting of whether the interests of, and links to, the United States ... are sufficiently strong, vis-à-vis those of other nations, to justify an assertion of extraterritorial authority.[57]

To analyze the third factor, the court prescribed a seven-factor interest-balancing test,[58] which it deemed a "jurisdictional rule of reason" required by "a regard for comity and the prerogatives of other nations."[59] By so stating the inquiry, *Timberlane* restructured judicial consideration of the extraterritoriality question in a way that balanced the competing jurisprudential concerns described above. In effect, *Timberlane* directed courts adjudicating challenges to extraterritorial application of U.S. regulatory law to foreign business activity to address three deeper questions, which I shall call the questions of domestic authority, legislative intent, and legal constraint:

1. The question of *domestic authority* asks:

Does the governmental institution whose action has been challenged have constitutional or statutory *authority* to exercise regulatory authority over the international economic activity in question?

---

**57.** 549 F.2d at 613.

**58.** *Id.* at 613–14. These factors derived from (the future Yale President) KINGMAN BREWSTER, ANTITRUST AND AMERICAN BUSINESS ABROAD 446 (1958). They included: (1) the degree of conflict with foreign law or policy, (2) the nationality or allegiance of the parties and the locations or principal place of business of corporations, (3) the extent to which enforcement by either state can be expected to achieve compliance, (4) the relative significance of effects on the United States as compared with those elsewhere, (5) the extent to which there is explicit purpose to harm or affect American commerce, (6) the foreseeability of such effect, and (7) the relative importance to the violations charged of conduct within the United States, as compared with conduct abroad. *See generally* Waller, *supra* note 43 (discussing Brewster's influence on antitrust law). As noted earlier, President Brewster began his scholarly career as a member of the Harvard International Legal Process School. *See* Chap. I, note 7.

**59.** 549 F.2d at 612.

2.   The question of *legislative intent* asks:

Given the presumption against extraterritoriality, has Congress made clear its *intent* that the governmental institution may exercise its authority extraterritorially against the conduct at issue here?

3.   The question of *legal constraint* asks:

Do international law or comity impose a *legal constraint* upon that institution's extraterritorial exercise of power?

On analysis, the authority question really reflects concerns regarding separation of powers and uniformity of regulation. Article I, Section 8, Clause 3 of the United States Constitution (the foreign commerce clause) gives Congress authority under U.S. law to issue uniform rules regulating private economic activity abroad. By first asking whether the extraterritorial conduct has *some* effect on the United States, *Timberlane* effectively ensured that the courts would have subject matter jurisdiction to hear a case within the scope of Congress's domestic authority to regulate foreign commerce power. By secondly asking whether the anti-competitive effect on U.S. commerce is not just trivial, but reasonably direct and substantial, *Timberlane* effectively ensured that parties would not be able to invoke the limited jurisdiction of the courts unless they had stated a claim upon which relief could be granted under the antitrust laws.

The intent question reflects deference both to party autonomy and national sovereignty. For if Congress does not make explicit its intent to regulate a private business arrangement occurring overseas, that arrangement should presumptively be left alone, both in the interests of sanctity of contract, and to avoid extending U.S. sovereignty into the territorial sovereignty of another nation. But if Congress makes its intent to act extraterritorially clear, the statute controls as domestic law, and a U.S. court is bound to enforce it, leaving the U.S. executive branch to deal with whatever international consequences might arise.

The constraint question blends concerns about comity, international law, and the sovereignty of foreign nations. For the interest-balancing test clarified that it is not in the interests of the United States, other nations, or the international system as a whole for the U.S. to apply its antitrust laws to the full extent arguably permitted by the statutory language or the Constitution. By following *Timberlane*'s analysis, a U.S. court could factor in these concerns and apply interest-balancing as a kind of judicial "brake" to determine when U.S. law will not be applied extraterritorially even in cases where U.S. prescriptive jurisdiction might reach so far.

In the ensuing years, the *Timberlane* standard won broad acceptance with the American judiciary, academy, Executive Branch, Congress, and even other nations. With variations, the Ninth Circuit's test was adopted by most other federal courts of appeals.[60] Section 403 of the American Law Institute's *Restatement (Third)* effectively adopted both halves of the *Timberlane* test—effects and interest-balancing—in determining when a nation's exercise of prescriptive jurisdiction is or is not "reasonable." The ALI's interest-balancing test differs from *Timberlane* in two important respects: First, it treats comity as an inherent limit on the prescriptive, legislative jurisdiction of Congress, not on the adjudicative jurisdiction of the federal courts; and second, it adds to the list of relevant factors the extent to which the regulation in question is consistent with, and important to, the "international system."[61] By so saying, the ALI made explicit that the principle of comity should act as a workable analytic device to balance not just foreign versus United States' interests, but also the broader needs of the international system.

*Timberlane* also influenced the U.S. Department of Justice, whose 1988 and 1995 *Antitrust Enforcement Guidelines for International Operations* specifically contemplates extraterritorial prosecution of U.S. antitrust laws, subject to a comity-based balancing test that excludes the international system concerns.[62] And in 1982, Congress amended the Sherman Act with the Foreign Trade Antitrust Improvements Act,[63] which made clear that Congress does intend U.S. antitrust law to apply to monopolistic conduct in foreign markets that cause a "direct, substantial, and reasonably

---

**60.** *See, e.g.*, Mannington Mills, Inc. v. Congoleum Corp., 595 F.2d 1287, 1297 (3d Cir. 1979); Montreal Trading Ltd. v. Amax Inc., 661 F.2d 864, 869 (10th Cir. 1981), *cert. denied*, 455 U.S. 1001 (1982); O.N.E. Shipping Ltd. v. Flota Mercante Grancolombiana, S.A., 830 F.2d 449, 451–53 (2d Cir. 1987); In re Uranium Antitrust Litig., 617 F.2d 1248, 1255–56 (7th Cir. 1980).

**61.** *See* RESTATEMENT (THIRD) § 403 (2)(e)–(f). The Associate Reporter for these *Restatement (Third)* sections was Professor Andreas Lowenfeld of NYU, who as noted previously, was also a member of the Harvard International Legal Process School of International Law. *See* Chap. I, notes 8 & 10 and accompanying text.

**62.** *See* U.S. Department of Justice, *Antitrust Enforcement Guidelines for International Operatives*, 55 ATRR SPECIAL SUPP. 32 (Nov. 17, 1988); U.S. Dept. of Justice and Federal Trade Commission, *Antitrust Enforcement Guidelines for International Operations* § 3.1 (1995) [hereafter 1995 *U.S. Antitrust Guidelines*]. An April 1992 revision made it even clearer that the U.S. government is prepared to apply the antitrust laws extraterritorially to challenge the anticompetitive conduct abroad of foreign companies or cartels whose behavior affects U.S. commerce by restricting or otherwise interfering with the ability of U.S. exporters to compete in an overseas market. *See* U.S. Department of Justice, Justice Department Will Challenge Foreign Restraints on U.S. Exports Under Antitrust Laws (Apr. 3, 1992), *reprinted in* 4 TRADE REG. REP. (CCH) ¶ 13,108 (Apr. 14, 1992).

**63.** 15 U.S.C. § 6(a) (1982).

foreseeable effect" on U.S. domestic or import commerce or export commerce engaged in by U.S. domestic business.[64]

In recent years, the U.S. position on extraterritoriality has even won a striking measure of international acceptance. Since the *Grosfillex* case,[65] the European Commission has asserted Community jurisdiction based on substantial, intended, and direct anticompetitive effects of extraterritorial action. In the *Dyestuffs*[66] and *Wood Pulp*[67] cases, the European Court of Justice carefully avoided invoking the effects doctrine, but nevertheless asserted jurisdiction based on the principle of "objective territoriality," which permits states to exercise jurisdiction over extraterritorial conduct if the consummating act is done within the Community. In *Wood Pulp*, wood purchasers outside the European Community allegedly infringed Article 85 of the Treaty of Rome through horizontal price-fixing. When the Advocate General urged application of the "effects test," the Court suggested that if an anticompetitive agreement is "implemented" through contracts made with purchasers within the European Community, it violates Community Law.[68] By this "implementation approach," the Court has effectively extended the competition provisions of Articles 85 and 86 of the Treaty of Rome to apply extraterritorially to extra-Community conduct.[69] According to commentators, the effects doctrine is now considered a valid basis of jurisdiction in countries ranging from Argentina, China, Cuba, Denmark, France,[70] Germany,[71] Italy, Japan,[72] Mexico, Sweden and Switzerland.[73]

---

**64.** By so saying, however, Congress only set the jurisdictional threshold. It said nothing about the applicability or nonapplicability of comity considerations once this jurisdictional threshold has been met. *See* Hartford Fire Insurance v. California, 509 U.S. 764, 798 (1993).

**65.** *See* Grosfillex–Fillistorf, 1964 J.O. (58) 915, 3 C.M.L.R. 237 (1964).

**66.** Case 48/69, Imperial Chemical Indus., Ltd. v. Commission, 1972 E.C.R. 619, 3 C.M.L.R. 557 (1972).

**67.** Case 89/85, Ahlstrom v. Commission, 1988 E.C.R. 5193, 1988 C.M.L.R. 901 (1988) (The Wood Pulp Case).

**68.** *Id.* at 5243.

**69.** 1988 E.C.R. at 5215. For further discussion of *Dyestuffs* and *Wood Pulp*, see Dieter Lange & John Sandage, *The Wood Pulp Decision and Its implication for the Scope of EC Competition Law*, 26 COMMON MKT L. REV. 137 (1989); Roger Alford, *The Extraterritorial Application*

of *Antitrust Laws: The United States and European Community Approaches*, 33 VA. J. INT'L L. 1, 27–37 (1992).

**70.** Berthold Goldman, *Les Champs D'Application Territoriale des lois sur las Concurrence*, 128 RECUEIL DES COURS 631, 669 (1969) (France).

**71.** In Germany, for example, Section 98(2) of the Law Against Restraints on Competition says that the law "shall apply to all restraints on competition that have effects within the territory in which this law applies." Gesetz Gegen Wettbeuerbsbeschräenkungen, 1957 Bundesgesetzblatt [BGBI] 1081 (July 7). *See also* David J. Gerber, *The Extraterritorial Application of the German Antitrust Laws*, 77 AM. J. INT'L L. 756 (853).

**72.** *See* HIROSHI IYORI & AKINDRI UESUGI, THE ANTIMONOPOLY LAWS OF JAPAN 44–50 (1983) (noting provisions of Monopoly Act against anticompetitive behavior and Japanese analogues to the U.S. "Rule of Reason" test).

**73.** *See generally* David I. Gerber, *Beyond Balancing: International Law*

Outside the United States, the use of comity as a constraint upon the effects doctrine has also found some, but more grudging, acceptance. In the European Union, the Court gave the international comity approach relatively short shrift in the *Wood Pulp* case.[74] But publicists are noting a growing use of the American *Restatement's (Third)* "reasonableness" approach, often citing Judge Fitzmaurice's separate opinion in the *Barcelona Traction* case, which states that international law obligates every state to "exercise moderation and restraint as to the extent of [its] jurisdiction . . . in cases having a foreign element."[75]

Even as *Timberlane* won broad acceptance in the United States, it faced a significant challenge from the U.S. Court of Appeals for the D.C. Circuit, with its 1984 decision in *Laker Airways v. Sabena, Belgian World Airlines*.[76] In that case, the liquidator of Sir Freddie Laker's defunct Skytrain air service brought an antitrust suit in the United States District Court for the District of Columbia against competing American and foreign airlines, alleging that defendants had engaged in predatory pricing designed to destroy Laker's low-fare transatlantic service. The foreign defendants countersued in the United Kingdom's High Court of Justice and obtained an injunction and a series of restraining orders against Laker's interference in their English proceedings. Laker in turn secured a protective injunction from the United States district court, preventing the foreign defendants from acting abroad to interfere with the district court's jurisdiction over Laker's suit.

In an opinion by Judge Malcolm Richard Wilkey, the D.C. Circuit affirmed, concluding that the district court was entitled to issue the injunction both to preserve its rights to exercise U.S. antitrust jurisdiction as well as to prevent evasion of public policies important to the United States.[77] The D.C. Circuit found a hard,

*Restraints on the Reach of National Laws*, 10 YALE J. INT'L L. 185, 201–02 (1984); Michael Akehurst, *Jurisdiction in International Law*, 46 BRIT. Y.B. INTL L. 145, 153–54, 181 n.4 (1972) (collecting citations to the laws of these countries).

**74.** *Wood Pulp*, 1988 E.C.R. at 5244.

**75.** Case Concerning the Barcelona Traction, Light and Power Co. (Belgium v. Spain), 1970 I.C.J. 3, 105 (Feb. 5) (separate opinion of Judge Fitzmaurice).

For commentary, see, for example, Karl Meesen, *Antitrust Jurisdiction Under Customary International Law*, 78 AM. J. INT'L L. 783 (1984); Alford, *supra* note 69, at 15–16; David Massey, *How the American Law Institute Influences Customary Law: The Reasonableness Requirement of the Restatement of Foreign Relations Law*, 22 YALE J. INT'L L. 419 (1997).

**76.** 731 F.2d 909 (D.C. Cir. 1984).

**77.** *Id.* at 927–33.

irreconcilable conflict to exist between the British and U.S. policies and attitudes toward the underlying antitrust cause of action as well as toward the jurisdictional issues. But significantly, in addressing that conflict, the court declined to follow the Ninth Circuit's interest-balancing approach from *Timberlane*. Judge Wilkey conceded that "in the interest of amicable relations, we might be tempted to defuse unilaterally the confrontation by jettisoning our jurisdiction," but reasoned that domestic courts cannot resolve hard conflicts of international jurisdiction by attempting to weigh and balance two nations' competing regulatory interests, for such determination are "essentially ... political."[78] Unlike *Timberlane*, which emphasized comity and international law rationales for interest balancing, *Laker* rested heavily on separation of powers reasoning. In attacking interest-balancing, Judge Wilkey wrote:

> Judges are not politicians. The courts are not organs of political compromise.... [B]oth institutional limitations on the judicial process and Constitutional restrictions on the exercise of judicial power make it unacceptable for the Judiciary to seize the political initiative and determine that legitimate application of American laws must evaporate when challenged by a foreign jurisdiction.[79]

Ultimately, *Laker*, like most extraterritoriality disputes, ended before it reached the Supreme Court.[80] But in the 1980s and 1990s, the debate between the comity-based approach typified by *Timberlane* and the separation-of-powers approach of *Laker* raged in both non-judicial and judicial fora.

In the 1980s, further hard conflicts arose in the assets freezes effected by the United States government in response to the Iranian Hostages Crisis and Libyan terrorist activities,[81] as well as with regard to the extraterritorial export controls imposed in the Soviet Pipeline case discussed earlier. In each of these cases, the dispute

**78.** *Id.* at 953.

**79.** *Id.* at 953–54. Judge Wilkey also rejected international comity as a basis for requiring dismissal of the injunction, "finding in effect that he who seeks comity, must do comity and that the British had done no such thing." Harold G. Maier, *Resolving Extraterritorial Conflicts, or "There and Back Again,"* 25 VA J. INT'L L. 7, 33 n. 38 (1984).

**80.** In the end, the British House of Lords effectively acceded to U.S. jurisdiction, ultimately allowing Laker's appeal. The Lords discharged the injunction against Laker's prosecution of the United States litigation, reasoning that only the United States courts were competent to decide the merits of the antitrust claims. *See* British Airways Bd. v. Laker Airways Ltd., [1984] 3 W.L.R. 413 (H.L.) In response, the United States district court issued another injunction prohibiting British interference in the litigation, which the parties ultimately settled. Laker Airways Ltd. v. Pan American World Airways, 596 F.Supp. 202 (D.D.C. 1984).

**81.** *See* Smedresman and Lowenfeld, *supra* note 11.

was precipitated by the U.S. decision to construe generously the term "person subject to the jurisdiction of the United States" to include foreign subsidiaries of U.S. companies operating abroad.[82]

Extraterritoriality again surged into public prominence in March 1996, with President Clinton's signature into law of the so-called Helms–Burton Act, in response to the Cuban shootdown of two civilian aircraft in international airspace.[83] Like the earlier Soviet Pipeline incident, the case is a prime example of "transnational legal process," the process by which private and public issues intertwine in the transnational arena, and percolate up to provoke the development and internalization of new norms of international law.[84] Title III of the Act grants any U.S. national with a claim for property confiscated by Cuba since 1959 to bring suit in U.S. courts against any person who "traffics" in such property. By so saying, the provision went even beyond the extraterritorial reach of the Soviet Pipeline regulations, for it effectively sought to regulate the conduct of wholly foreign companies who are not subsidiaries or even licensees of U.S. companies. The European Union quickly objected to the Act, and Canada and Mexico both requested consultations with the United States under the terms of the NAFTA.[85] The European Union, United Kingdom, Canada, and Mexico all adopted laws forbidding their nations from complying with Helms–Burton, and permitting their nations to clawback awards against them under the Act by filing countersuits in their own courts.[86] In

---

**82.** Indeed, the first celebrated incident of this nature was the famous *Fruehauf* case of the mid–1960s, in which the U.S. attempted to apply its export control regulations to a 70% French-owned subsidiary of an American company that was awarded a contract to supply trucks for export from France to the People's Republic of China. When the U.S. Treasury Department learned of the contract, it instructed the U.S. parent to order its subsidiary to cancel the contract or face U.S. penalties. When the American parent agreed, the French directors of the subsidiary successfully petitioned a French court to appoint a temporary administrator for the subsidiary to carry out the contract. After the appointment was upheld on appeal, the United States backed down. *See* Cours d'appel [CA] [regional courts of appeal] Paris, Societe Fruehauf Corp. v. Massardy, [1965] Gaz. Pal. 86, *reprinted in* 5 INT'L LEG. MATS. 476 (1966); [1968] D. Jur. 147 (1965), discussed in

STEINER, VAGTS AND KOH, TRANSNATIONAL LEGAL PROBLEMS 993 (4th ed. 1994).

**83.** Cuban Liberty and Democracy Solidarity Act of 1996, Pub. L. No. 104–114, 110 Stat. 785 (Mar. 12, 1996) (codified at 22 U.S.C. §§ 6021–91).

**84.** *See generally* Harold Hongju Koh, *Transnational Legal Process*, 75 NEB. L. REV. 181 (1996); Harold Hongju Koh, *Why Do Nations Obey International Law?*, 106 YALE L.J. 2599 (1997); William Dodge, *The Helms–Burton Act and Transnational Legal Process*, 20 HASTINGS INT'L AND COMP. L.Q. 713 (1997).

**85.** *See* European Union, *Demarches Protesting the Cuban Liberty and Democratic Solidarity (Libertad) Act (Mar. 5 and 13, 1996)*, 35 INT'L LEG. MATS. 397 (1996); *Sanctions: NAFTA Designates Confer on Complaint Against Helms–Burton Under Chapter 20*, 13 INT'L TRADE REP. (BNA) 27 (July 3, 1996).

**86.** *See* U.K. Protection of Trading Interests Act 1980 as revised by Statuto-

response, President Clinton suspended Title III's right of action on several successive occasions, so long as the allies were continuing in their efforts to promote a transition to democracy in Cuba.[87]

The European Union pressed the claim that the Act violated the GATT before the World Trade Organization, which impaneled a panel to hear the complaint. But on the eve of the hearing, the matter was temporarily resolved by political accommodation, as the United States and the EU concluded a memorandum of understanding under which the EU would temporarily suspend its case, pending negotiations of bilateral and multilateral agreements to prevent companies from investing in illegally expropriated assets.[88] After a year, the panel lost its jurisdiction over the matter, and the EU chose not to pursue the matter further before the WTO. The European Union then introduced a Council Regulation binding all member states, declaring the extraterritorial provisions of the Helms–Burton Act to be unenforceable within the European Union, permitting recovery of any damages imposed under the Act, and applying sanctions against any U.S. companies and their executives who made Title III complaints.[89] The Helms–Burton incident simply confirms the practical point made earlier: that in the end, hard conflicts between regulatory philosophies can only be definitively resolved through political accommodations of those competing philosophies. The process is usually one of challenge, response, unilateral forbearance, and eventually negotiated settlement via bilateral, regional or multilateral accords, which in turn generate new substantive norms of international law.

## C. Legislative Intent and the Hardened Presumption Against Extraterritoriality

In the early 1990s, the extraterritoriality issue also returned to the United States Supreme Court, arising five times in four years

ry Instrument 1992 No. 2449, (US Cuban Assets Control Regulations) Order 1992 (which pre-existed Helms–Burton); Foreign Extraterritorial Measures Act of Canada, Bill C–54, *available at* http://www2.parl.gc.ca/HousePublications/Publication.aspx?pub=bill&doc=C–54&parl=35&ses=2&language=E; Law of Protection of Commerce and Investments from Foreign Policies that Contravene International Law of Mexico, Official Journal of the Federation (Oct. 23, 1996). *See generally* Canadian, European Union, and Mexican Responses to the U.S. Helms–Burton Act, 36 INT'L LEG. MATS. 111 (1997).

**87.** Dodge, *supra* note 84, at 719.

**88.** *Id.* at 720.

**89.** Council Regulation 2271/96, Protecting Against the Effects of the Extra–Territorial Application of Legislation Adopted by a Third Country, and Actions Based Thereon or Resulting Therefrom, 1996 O.J. (L 309), *available at* http://eur-lex.europa.eu/LexUriServ/LexUriServ.do?uri=CELEX:31996R2271:EN:HTML.

with regard to foreign sovereign immunity,[90] employment discrimination,[91] environmental law,[92] federal torts,[93] and immigration and refugee law.[94] In nearly every case, the issue became one of domestic statutory interpretation, focusing on the second question of intent, described above. In these cases, the Supreme Court has applied the presumption against extraterritoriality with increasing rigidity, exalting that presumption into virtually a "clear-statement" principle. The pattern began in 1989 in *Argentine Republic v. Amerada Hess Shipping Corp.*[95] There, the Court applied the presumption against extraterritoriality to plaintiffs' claim that the noncommercial tort exception of the Foreign Sovereign Immunities Act—which waives foreign sovereign immunity against tort damages suits for causing injury in waters "subject to the jurisdiction of the United States—"[96] could reach the high seas. The Court rejected that claim, concluding that foreign sovereign immunity is not waived for noncommercial torts that occur on the high seas.[97] In *EEOC v. Arabian American Oil Co. (Aramco)*[98] the Court refused to apply a federal civil rights law, Title VII of the Civil Rights Act of 1964, to a U.S. company that had allegedly discriminated against a U.S. citizen who worked as its employee in Saudi Arabia. The statute in question applied to all U.S. employers except those who employ aliens "outside any state"—language which suggested that the law did therefore apply to employers who employ *citizens* outside any state. Nevertheless, the Court, speaking through Chief Justice Rehnquist, ruled that "unless there is 'affirmative intention of the Congress clearly expressed,' we must presume [Congress] 'is primarily concerned with domestic conditions.' "[99] The Court held that the presumption acts as a tool of statutory construction that "serves to protect against unintended clashes between our laws and those of other nations which could result in international discord."[100] By so saying, the Court suggested that the presumption

**90.** Argentine Republic v. Amerada Hess Shipping Corp., 488 U.S. 428 (1989).

**91.** EEOC v. Arabian American Oil Co., 499 U.S. 244 (1991).

**92.** Lujan v. Defenders of Wildlife, 504 U.S. 555 (1992) (dismissing for lack of standing). *See also id.* at n. 4 (1992) (Stevens, J., concurring in judgment) (relying on presumption against extraterritoriality).

**93.** Smith v. United States, 507 U.S. 197 (1993) (declining to apply statutory waiver of immunity in Federal Tort Claims Act to Antarctica).

**94.** Sale v. Haitian Centers Council, 509 U.S. 155 (1993).

**95.** 488 U.S. 428 (1989).

**96.** 28 U.S.C. § 1605(a)(5) (1994).

**97.** *See* 488 U.S. at 440.

**98.** 499 U.S. 244 (1991).

**99.** *Id.* at 248 (citation omitted).

**100.** *Id.* (citing McCulloch v. Sociedad Nacional de Marineros de Honduras, 372 U.S. 10, 20–22 (1963)). In *Aramco* the United States agreed that comity is the driving force behind the presumption. *See* Brief of the EEOC at 25–26, EEOC v. Arabian American Oil Co., 499

was specifically designed to protect international comity and national sovereignty.

One year later, in *Lujan v. Defenders of Wildlife*,[101] the Court denied standing to environmental groups to challenge government funding of activities where no immediate and particularized injury to the group members could be shown. Justice Stevens' concurring opinion argued on comity grounds that the presumption against extraterritoriality should be invoked to bar application of an environmental statute to the activities of private litigants within another sovereign state.[102]

If the presumption against extraterritoriality rests principally on comity, logic would suggest that the presumption should *not* apply either on the high seas or elsewhere where extraterritorial assertion of U.S. law would not infringe upon the rights of another sovereign. But in two odd decisions the following term, the Court applied the presumption first to Antarctica, and second to the high seas, both areas governed exclusively by international law. In *Smith v. United States*,[103] the spouse of an American contractor killed in Antarctica sought to sue the United States under the Federal Tort Claims Act, which waives the United States' sovereign immunity, except for certain claims, including any claim arising in a foreign country. The plaintiff argued that Antarctica was not a foreign country, and hence that her suit was not barred. But again citing the presumption against extraterritoriality—which the Court found to be "rooted in a number of considerations, not the least of which is the common sense notion that Congress generally legislates with domestic concerns in mind"[104]—the Court held that the FTCA's waiver did not apply in Antarctica.

Three months later, the Court decided *Sale v. Haitian Centers Council*,[105] in which Haitian refugees challenged the Clinton and Bush Administration's policy of interdicting and returning fleeing Haitians on the high seas. The plaintiffs invoked the absolute prohibition against summary return ("refoulement") found in both Article 33 of the 1951 Refugee Convention and the implementing provisions of the Immigration and Nationality Act, which directed,

U.S. 244 (1991) (urging extraterritorial application because "Title VII is unlikely to generate serious conflicts with the laws of individual foreign states.").

**101.** 504 U.S. 555 (1992).

**102.** *Id.* at 585–89 and n. 4 (1992).

**103.** 507 U.S. 197 (1993).

**104.** *Id.* at 204 n.5.

**105.** 509 U.S. 155 (1993). I should disclose that I was counsel of record for the plaintiffs in *Haitian Centers Council*. For more detailed criticism of the Court's opinion, see Harold Hongju Koh, *The Haiti Paradigm in United States Human Rights Policy*, 103 YALE L.J. 2391 (1994).

without geographic limit, that "The Attorney General *shall not* deport or *return any alien*" to a country where he faces persecution.[106] The Court rejected their claim, suggesting in dictum that the presumption against extraterritoriality has "special" force when courts construe "statutory provisions that may involve foreign and military affairs for which the President has unique responsibility."[107]

In dissent, Justice Blackmun argued that "the presumption that Congress did not intend to legislate extraterritorially has *less* force—perhaps, indeed, no force at all—when a statute on its face relates to foreign affairs."[108] He noted that the presumption is meant to operate only where there is "unexpressed congressional intent,"[109] and that here, there was no real ambiguity regarding the statute's reach, given that the immigration provision in question expressly barred the "return ... [of] any alien," without apparent geographic limit.[110] As the dissent noted, the Court applied the presumption mechanically, without regard for the various rationales that underlie it. For the statutory presumption against extraterritoriality was designed primarily to avoid judicial interpretations of a statute that infringe upon the rights of another sovereign, and thus should have had no force or relevance on the high seas, where no possibility existed for conflicts with other jurisdictions.[111] Nor did it make sense to presume that Congress had legislated with exclusively territorial intent when enacting a law governing a distinctively international subject matter—the transborder move-

---

**106.** *See* 509 U.S. at 158 n.1.

**107.** *Id.* at 188.

**108.** *Id.* at 206–07(Blackmun, J., dissenting) (emphasis in original).

**109.** Foley Bros., Inc. v. Filardo, 336 U.S. 281, 285 (1949).

**110.** The Executive Order under which the interdiction occurred authorized the Coast Guard "[t]o return" Haitian vessels and their passengers to Haiti. But oddly, the Court construed this legal prohibition against the "return" of aliens as inapplicable to the U.S. government's return of the Haitians. Nor did Justice Stevens adequately explain why the plain meaning of the French word "refouler," in Article 33 of the Refugee Convention, did not equally bar the return, when French newspapers were contemporaneously reporting that "Les Etats–Unis ont decide de *refouler* di-

rectement les refugies recueillis par la garde cotiere." *Le bourbier haitien*, LE MONDE, June 1, 1992, cited at 509 U.S. at 192.

**111.** Significantly, in both the Antarctica and the Haitian cases, the U.S. government modified its position from the *Aramco* case. *See* Brief of United States at 23–25, Smith v. United States, 507 U.S. 197 (1993) (now asserting that the presumption against extraterritoriality is applied generally and forecloses application of U.S. law even where comity is of no concern); Brief of United States at 27, McNary v. Haitian Centers Council, 498 U.S. 479 (1991) (arguing that the "Presumption bars application of federal statutes to the high seas as well as foreign countries."). The Court nevertheless accepted the Government's revised position in both instances, without even noting the inconsistency.

ment of refugees—that enforced an international human rights obligation embodied in a multilateral convention.

Whether or not the Court properly applied the presumption against extraterritorial application of the INA, it clearly should not have applied it to presume that the United States' obligations under Article 33 of the *Refugee Convention* are territorial.[112] A presumption that treaty parties contract solely for domestic effect, if generally applied, would permit the United States to commit genocide or torture on the high seas, notwithstanding the universal, peremptory prohibitions of the Genocide and Torture Conventions. It made no sense to presume that Congress enacted universal human rights obligations governing transborder activities with an exclusively territorial focus.

More fundamentally, by applying this inapposite canon of statutory construction, the Court not only ignored its duty to construe statutes so as to save them from infirmity under international law,[113] but even construed the statute in such a way that it deliberately *offended* the spirit of the treaty the statute was meant to execute. Equally bizarre, the Court invoked the presumption in a case where the executive branch had itself cited the statute as the basis for its authority to act extraterritorially.[114] If petitioners were correct that the statute's presumption against extraterritorial application operated to deny the Haitians protection on the high seas, *a fortiori*, it also should have operated to deny the President extraterritorial *authority* to stop the Haitians outside U.S. waters.

Why did the Court strain to apply the presumption in a case where it so clearly did not apply? By suggesting that the presumption against extraterritoriality has "special" force when courts construe "statutory provisions that may involve foreign and military affairs for which the President has unique responsibility,"[115] the Court clearly signaled that its decision was driven not by comity, but by *separation of powers*. The Court clearly sought in the Haitian case to defer to executive authority in foreign affairs.[116] The

---

**112.** *See id.* at 183 (claiming that "a treaty cannot impose uncontemplated extraterritorial obligation on those who ratify it through no more than a general humanitarian intent.").

**113.** *See id.* at 207 (Blackmun, J., dissenting).

**114.** The Government cited two sections of the Immigration and Nationality Act as authority for their actions in reaching well beyond the territory of the United States to seize Haitians and force them back to the land they are fleeing. *See id.* at 160 (Executive Order citing §§ 212(f) and 215(a) of the Immigration and Nationality Act). But neither statutory provision specifically authorized the President to act beyond United States borders.

**115.** Sale v. Haitian Ctrs. Council, 509 U.S. 155, 187 (1993).

**116.** Significantly, the Court had foreshadowed its ruling in the *Haitian* case for the previous two years, when

point was confirmed just one week later, when the Court finally returned to the extraterritoriality question, but this time in the context of international antitrust. Curiously, just one week after rigidly applying the presumption in the Haitian case, the Court *permitted* extraterritorial application of the Sherman Act to foreign conduct, without citing any of these extraterritoriality cases or otherwise explaining how the presumption against extraterritoriality had been overcome.[117]

## D. *Hartford Fire Insurance*

Unlike the presumption against extraterritoriality cases, which have turned on the question of legislative intent, the *Hartford Fire Insurance* case turned on the third question described above: whether international law or comity imposed an *independent legal constraint* upon the ability of Congress or the courts to engage in extraterritorial exercises of governmental power. In the *Hartford Fire Insurance* case, the Court addressed that issue in the international antitrust context, the first such case to reach the Court in more than thirty years. Persons who had bought commercial liability insurance in the United States sued certain U.K. reinsurance companies doing business at the reinsurance market at Lloyds of London. Three of their many claims were that defendants had violated the United States antitrust laws by agreeing to restrict the scope of reinsurance and reinsurers' reinsurance being offered in the United Kingdom.[118] Thus, as in *Timberlane*, the question was whether U.S. antitrust law reached extraterritorially to punish the conduct of foreign participants in a foreign market, acting legally in that market under a scheme of regulation approved by the foreign sovereign. All parties conceded that the U.S. interest in a relatively open international reinsurance market was in tension with the long-standing British interest in maintaining a relatively closed self-regulating English reinsurance submarket.

Significantly, the debate between the majority and dissent turned on whether the intent question or the constraint question was at issue. All parties conceded that the Congress had the authority to regulate the London defendants' conduct if they wanted to, and that the Foreign Trade Antitrust Improvements Act of

the full Court had voted against the Haitians no less than seven times on various preliminary rulings. *See* Koh, *supra* note 105, at 2413–14.

117.  *See* Hartford Fire Insurance Co. v. California, 509 U.S. 764 (1993).

118.  The defendants were accused of jointly refusing to offer reinsurance for insurance of certain high-risk commercial liabilities.

1982[119] prohibited conduct that had a direct, substantial, and reasonably foreseeable effect on U.S. domestic or import trade.

Applying the seven *Timberlane* factors, the trial court declined to exercise jurisdiction against the U.K. reinsurers under the principles of international law and comity stated in *Timberlane*. The trial judge concluded that such enforcement "would lead to significant conflict with English law and policy"—the first *Timberlane* factor—and further concluded that this conflict was *not* outweighed by other factors in the comity analysis, hence giving sufficient reason to decline the exercise of jurisdiction.[120] The U.S. Court of Appeals for the Ninth Circuit reversed the trial court's comity-based dismissal, reinstating the London claims.[121] Also applying *Timberlane* analysis, the appeals court agreed that there was a significant conflict between U.S. antitrust law and long-standing English law and policy favoring self-regulation by English reinsurers. It went on to conclude, however, that given the direct, substantial, and reasonably foreseeable effects on U.S. commerce, which conferred jurisdiction over the claim under the Foreign Trade Antitrust Improvements Act of 1982, it is only in an unusual case that comity considerations would require a court to abstain from exercising that jurisdiction.[122] Finding no such unusual circumstances here, the Court decided that one factor, a direct conflict with foreign law—standing alone—was insufficient to overcome the presumption of U.S. jurisdiction created by the words of the statute.[123]

A closely divided Supreme Court affirmed the Court of Appeals' result, but not its reasoning. Justice Souter, speaking for five Justices on this issue, agreed that the District Court had improperly concluded that the principle of international comity barred it from exercising Sherman Act jurisdiction over the three London reinsurance claims. Applying the effects test, the Court first held that "[a]lthough the proposition was perhaps not always free from doubt, it is well established by now that the Sherman Act applies to foreign conduct that was meant to produce and did in fact produce some substantial effect in the United States."[124] The Court decided that Congress had intended to exercise prescriptive jurisdiction over the claims alleged here: "that the London reinsurers engaged

**119.** 15 U.S.C. § 6a (1984).
**120.** 723 F.Supp. 464, 489–90 (N.D. Cal. 1989).
**121.** 938 F.2d 919 (9th Cir. 1991).
**122.** *Id.* at 931.
**123.** *Id.* at 933.
**124.** 509 U.S. at 795–96. As Professor Kramer has noted, no prior Supreme

Court case had ever, in fact, applied the Sherman Act extraterritorially based on effects alone. *See* Larry Kramer, *Extraterritorial Application of American Law After the Insurance Antitrust Case: A Reply to Professors Lowenfeld and Trimble*, 89 Am. J. Int'l L. 750 (1995).

in unlawful conspiracies to affect the market for insurance in the United States and that their conduct in fact produced substantial effect."[125]

In a curious move, the Court assumed without deciding that a court may decline to exercise jurisdiction over foreign conduct based on grounds of international comity. By so assuming, the Court failed to clarify whether and to what extent comity is an appropriate factor in deciding whether to exercise antitrust jurisdiction. The five-Justice majority went on evaluate the only *Timberlane* factor that the Court of Appeals had balanced in defendants' favor: the claim of a conflict between domestic and foreign law. Justice Souter agreed that defendants' conduct was lawful in United Kingdom, but held that this was not enough to create a direct conflict with U.S. law. Essentially, Justice Souter applied a "foreign sovereign compulsion" test: Did British law *require* the defendants to act in some fashion prohibited by the law of the United States? Finding that defendants had made no claim that their compliance with the laws of both countries would be otherwise impossible, the Court affirmed the reinstatement of plaintiffs' claims.

In a four-Justice dissent (joined by Justices O'Connor, Kennedy, and Thomas), Justice Scalia argued that the three London claims should have been dismissed. Significantly, he rested on congressional intent, arguing that Congress had never intended to reach defendants' conduct in the first place. He first argued that the presumption against extraterritoriality had been overcome, but then invoked the *Charming Betsy* presumption to argue that an assertion of prescriptive jurisdiction by Congress over defendants would be unreasonable, in violation of international law, and hence that Congress could not have intended to regulate it. The dissent called "breathtakingly broad" the Court's conclusion that no true conflict between U.S. and British law existed, and argued that the conclusion "will bring the Sherman Act and other laws into sharp and unnecessary conflict with the legitimate interests of other countries—particularly our closest trading partners."[126] Applying conflict-of-laws reasoning, Justice Scalia denied the majority's assertion that no conflict exists between U.S. and U.K. law. "[T]here is clearly a conflict in this litigation" even though British law did not compel defendants to violate U.S. law, he argued, because "applicable foreign and domestic law provide different substantive rules of decision to govern the parties' dispute...."[127]

**125.** 509 U.S. at 796.

**126.** 509 U.S. at 820 (Scalia, J., dissenting).

**127.** *Id.* at 822.

## E.  Whither Extraterritoriality?

Where do the Supreme Court's latest decisions leave the American law of extraterritoriality? Curiously, the Court has moved simultaneously in opposite directions. In cases where Congress has made its intent to legislate extraterritorially plain, the Court has made it exceedingly difficult for foreign defendants to seek dismissal based on comity.[128] *Hartford Fire Insurance* requires defendants to establish not simply that the conduct that the U.S. declares illegal was legal at home, but that their home country actually *compelled* them to act in the manner that violates U.S. law. Since this threshold showing will be tremendously difficult to meet, the *Timberlane* balance has now been tipped almost conclusively in favor of U.S. law, regardless of how attenuated the connection between the foreign conduct and the United States may be.

The *Hartford Fire Insurance* Court's treatment of an issue that has puzzled courts and dogged international business lawyers for decades is stunningly brief and elliptical. It leaves unclear a gaping issue: whether the Court has rejected the *Restatement*'s approach to interest-balancing, or whether it merely refused to apply that approach to the facts of that case. As a result, the lower courts are left with little guidance as to the third "constraint" question highlighted above: is *Timberlane* still good law?[129] And is reasonableness a principle of international law or comity that independently constrains the unilateral exercise of U.S. jurisdiction? Indeed, the Court's analysis even leaves unclear whether the ultimate question of extraterritorial reach is one of discretion or jurisdiction.[130] Apart from the issue of conflict, the *Hartford Fire Insurance*

---

**128.** In addition to the Helms–Burton Act, discussed *supra*, Congress enacted the Iran–Libya Sanctions Act of 1996, Pub. L. No. 104–172, §§ 5–6, 110 Stat. 1541, 1543–45, which allows for the imposition of U.S. trade sanctions against anyone in the world who makes certain investments in Iran and Libya; the Cuban Democracy Act of 1992, 106 Stat. 2575 (1992) (codified at 22 U.S.C. §§ 6001–10 (1992)) which led to mandatory enforcement of U.S. embargo policy against Canadian and other foreign companies whose sole jurisdictional contact with the U.S. was their ownership by American parent companies; and the War Crimes Act of 1996, Pub. L. No. 104–192, § 2401(a)(b), 110 Stat. 2104, which allows for imposition of criminal penalties against anyone committing certain war crimes anywhere in the world, if a U.S. national is either the perpetrator or the victim of the crime.

**129.** Significantly, the Ninth Circuit has read *Hartford Fire Insurance* as overruling its holding on what constitutes a conflict, but "not question[ing] the propriety of [*Timberlane's*] jurisdictional rule of reason or the seven comity factors." Metro Indus., Inc. v. Sammi Corp., 82 F.3d 839, 846 n.5 (9th Cir. 1996).

**130.** *See* 509 U.S. at 764 (Souter, J.) (expressly leaving unclear whether a U.S. Court may ever decline to exercise Sherman Act jurisdiction, or whether it may employ comity analysis to decide there is no jurisdiction in the first instance).

majority concluded that it did not need to address "other considerations that might inform a decision to refrain from the exercise of jurisdiction on grounds of international comity."[131] But the Court left unclear whether it was saying that the only relevant comity factor *in that case* was conflict with foreign law (a conflict which the Court said did not exist) or whether the Court was more broadly rejecting balancing of comity interests in *any* case where there is no true conflict. Because the latter would be a much more dramatic result for the Court to have reached *sub silentio*, I am inclined to doubt that it meant to rule so broadly. Indeed, the shallowness of the majority's reasoning, the close split among the Justices, and the force of Justice Scalia's dissent all suggest that the Court may be ready to hear another case on the issue fairly soon.[132]

How does *Hartford Fire Insurance* affect the current balance among the five core principles I have outlined? Three conclusions can quickly be drawn. First, the case significantly weakens international defenses based on national sovereignty, comity, and party autonomy, giving Congress even broader freedom to regulate liberally under the effects doctrine. The Court has now adopted an exceedingly narrow view of foreign regulatory sovereignty, whereby the freedom of the United Kingdom to regulate its own national companies within its own territory in no way exempts those companies from complying with United States law *unless* the United Kingdom has taken such a strong sovereign stand that it has, in

---

**131.** *Id.* at 799.

**132.** More than a decade after *Hartford Fire*, in F. Hoffmann–La Roche Ltd. v. Empagran, 542 U.S. 155 (2004), foreign and domestic vitamin purchasers sued foreign and domestic vitamin manufacturers and distributors, alleging a price-fixing conspiracy in violation of the Sherman Act. The Supreme Court asked whether U.S. courts had jurisdiction under the Foreign Trade Antitrust Improvements Act (FTAIA), 15 U.S.C. § 6a (2008), over lawsuits by foreigners for antitrust injuries sustained abroad that are independent of domestically sustained injuries. The Court answered that question in the negative, declining jurisdiction where price-fixing conduct significantly and adversely affects both customers outside and within the United States, "but the adverse foreign effect is independent of any adverse domestic effect." 542 U.S. at 164. Citing *Hartford Fire*, the Court stated that "application of our antitrust laws to foreign anticompetitive conduct is nonetheless reasonable, and hence consistent with principles of prescriptive comity, insofar as they reflect a legislative effort to redress *domestic* antitrust injury that foreign anticompetitive conduct has caused." *Id.* at 165 (emphasis added). But "[w]here foreign anticompetitive conduct plays a significant role and where foreign injury is independent of domestic effects," prescriptive comity cuts against jurisdiction. *Id.* The Court did not decide whether U.S. jurisdiction might exist because of foreign harm which is inextricably linked or bound up with foreign and domestic harms, and remanded that issue to the D.C. Circuit, which found that no such factual link existed. Empagran S.A. v. F. Hoffman–LaRoche Ltd., 417 F.3d 1267 (D.C. Cir. 2005), *cert. denied*, 126 S.Ct. 1043 (2006). In effect, *Empagran* recognizes a new comity limitation on prescriptive jurisdiction based on the murky notion of "independent adverse foreign effect," a concept that the lower courts will now need to elaborate.

effect, ordered the company to violate U.S. law. Moreover, the Court has linked this diminished view of sovereignty with a dismissive view of *comity*, implying that United States courts need not give respect to "the legislative, executive, or judicial acts of another nation," unless those acts clearly embody the national sovereignty of the other country in the form of a clear prohibition.[133] Second, the Court gives short shrift to the principle of *party autonomy*. The Court gives U.S. government regulators broad freedom to regulate even in a case where two parties have contracted outside the U.S. for a particular business result if a court deems their contract to have a direct, substantial and reasonably foreseeable anticompetitive effect within the United States.

Third, and ironically, the Court's recent decisions exalting the presumption against extraterritoriality dramatically limit the extraterritorial application of United States law in any case in which Congress' intent to apply that law abroad is not crystal clear. The only unifying feature of these cases seems to be that the individuals claiming extraterritorial rights—civil rights plaintiffs, environmental plaintiffs, and refugees—end up losing. The Antarctica and Haitian cases make it clear that the Court no longer rests the presumption on international comity—the desire to avoid conflict with the laws of other nations. Instead, the Court increasingly relies on the parochial thought that, in this day and age, the national legislature of the world's leading superpower generally legislates with only domestic conditions in mind.[134] Yet if this is the rationale, the presumption against extraterritoriality is clearly obsolete and ought to be eliminated. As several commentators have persuasively argued, the presumption no longer accurately reflects public international law, conflicts or contemporary business or regulatory reality.[135] As the Haitian and Antarctica cases show, the Court now applies the presumption with little regard for its original policy rationale and to circumstances where it clearly does not apply. In the next breath, however, the Court does not even mention it in a case (e.g., *Hartford Fire Insurance*) where it might well have serious bearing.[136] One need not adopt a presumption

---

**133.** Hilton v. Guyot, 159 U.S. 113, 164 (1895).

**134.** *See Aramco*, 499 U.S. at 248 ("[U]nless there is the affirmative intention of the Congress clearly expressed, we must presume it is primarily concerned with domestic conditions.") (citations omitted).

**135.** *See* Born, *supra* note 36, at 59–99 (arguing that the territoriality presumption no longer reflects principles of

private or public international law or the full range of congressional concerns). *See also* Larry Kramer, *Vestiges of Beale: Extraterritorial Application of American Law*, 1991 SUP. CT. REV. 179, 184; Jonathan Turley, *When in Rome: Multinational Misconduct and the Presumption Against Extraterritoriality*, 84 NW. U.L. REV. 598 (1990).

**136.** *See Hartford Fire Insurance*, 509 U.S. at 814 (Scalia, J., dissenting) (noting that absent precedent, "it would

*favoring* extraterritoriality, as several of these commentators have urged, to recognize that a territorial presumption has clearly outlived its day. If a prime purpose for the presumption is to promote consistency of statutes with international law, then the *Charming Betsy* presumption alone more directly serves that purpose.[137] If, instead, the presumption aims to promote the separation of powers, it does so in a most peculiar way: by allowing courts to impose territorial limits that Congress and the President have not specified in the language of the statutes themselves.[138] In the hands of the Supreme Court, the presumption has too often become yet another tool of judicial deference. It remains to be seen whether the Court would seriously apply the presumption in a case where the U.S. government is seeking actively to enforce U.S. market-protecting laws against foreign business activity.[139]

In the meantime, however, it seems clear that the two remaining principles of decision, *uniformity* and *separation of powers*, have carried the day. The Court clearly seeks uniform rules to govern international business proceedings in the federal courts of all fifty states with regard to foreign anti-competitive conduct. In a world of multiple sovereigns, where multinational corporations constantly do business across national lines, the Court is suggesting that corporations should plan and direct their conduct on the assumption that if they affect the U.S. economy they will be potentially subject to U.S. regulatory laws. Moreover, *Hartford Fire Insurance* arguably brings the U.S. and E.U. approaches to comity closer together, for in both jurisdictions, the Court has accepted the notion that comity bars jurisdiction primarily in those cases where the foreign law has directly required the anti-competitive conduct.[140]

be worth considering whether that presumption controls the outcome" in the antitrust context).

**137.** *See* note 31, *supra.*

**138.** Thus, shortly after the Court applied the presumption in *Aramco,* Congress moved quickly to overrule it by statute. *See* Civil Rights Act of 1991, Pub. L. No. 102–166, 105 Stat. 1071 (codified at 42 U.S.C. § 2000e(f))

**139.** Significantly, in the Supreme Court's opinion in *Empagran, supra* note 132, Justice Breyer suggested a comity-based presumption against extraterritorial statutory application of antitrust law, noting that "if America's antitrust policies could not win their own way in the international marketplace for such ideas, Congress, we must assume,

would not have tried to impose them, in an act of legal imperialism, through legislative fiat." 542 U.S. 155, 169 (2004). In that case, however, the Court construed the so-called "domestic-injury exception" to the FTAIA, and found no statutory jurisdiction over an independent adverse foreign harm. The Court noted, "Congress sought to *release* domestic (and foreign) anticompetitive conduct from Sherman Act constraints when that conduct causes foreign harm. Congress, of course, did make an exception where that conduct also causes domestic harm," which the *Empagran* Court found to be lacking on the record before it. *Id.* at 166 (emphasis in original).

**140.** *See* Roger Alford, *The Extraterritorial Application of Antitrust Laws: A*

An even more dominant theme, however, is *separation of powers*, and judicial deference to executive discretion. The majority's conclusion in the *Hartford Fire Insurance* case closely tracked the Government's brief and supported the Justice Department's antitrust enforcement interests.[141] Similarly, the Court's ruling against the Haitian refugees, in the face of both contrary domestic statute and international treaty, makes clear that this Court is prepared to defer to the executive branch's interests when they are clearly expressed and strongly urged.[142]

In short, the extraterritoriality area signals that the Supreme Court's respect for international law, comity, party autonomy, and foreign sovereignty are all waning, at the expense of its interests in rule-uniformity and separation of powers. The next two Chapters test the extent to which the same conclusion may be drawn with respect to the Court's treatment of three other faces of foreign sovereignty: the act of state doctrine, and the foreign sovereign compulsion defense, and foreign sovereign immunity.

*Postscript on Hartford* Fire Insurance Co. v. California, 34 Va. J. Int'l L. 213, 225–29 (1993) (pointing out the convergence between *Hartford Fire Insurance* and *Wood Pulp* on the point).

**141.** *Cf.* Brief for the United States as Amicus Curiae at 10, 22–29, Hartford Fire Insurance Co. v. California, 509 U.S. 764 (1993) (Nos. 91–1111, 91–1128).

**142.** *See generally* Koh, *supra* note 105, at 2420–21 (recounting recent Court precedents favoring executive discretion in foreign affairs).

# CHAPTER V

## THE ACT OF STATE DOCTRINE AND FOREIGN SOVEREIGN COMPULSION

The previous Chapter discussed the American doctrine of extraterritoriality, the first of four faces of foreign sovereignty in the United States courts. The next two Chapters address three other faces: the act of state doctrine, the foreign sovereign compulsion defense, and foreign sovereign immunity (as codified in the U.S. Foreign Sovereign Immunities Act of 1976).[1]

Each of these topics warrants a textbook of its own.[2] Thus, I will not attempt the impossible task of discussing these doctrines in detail, but will instead focus upon clarifying the relationship among them and their connection to the five core principles of international business transactions enumerated in the previous chapters.

## A. Relationships Among the Doctrines

The three doctrines share a common heritage in the English common law of act of state. In Lord Denning's 1975 explication of the 1845 House of Lords case of *Duke of Brunswick v. King of Hanover*,[3] he distinguished among "three separate doctrines" of act of state: what we would call foreign sovereign immunity, the act of state doctrine, and a third doctrine allowing, under certain circumstances, a defense to a tort action on the ground that the defendant "acted under the orders of ... a foreign government,"[4] or in our parlance, "foreign sovereign compulsion."

At the outset, we should underscore three important differences among these doctrines: procedural differences, occasions for exercise, and source of legal obligation. First, *procedural differences*: From its inception, foreign sovereign immunity has been seen as a limit upon the jurisdictional power of federal courts.

---

**1.** 28 U.S.C. §§ 1602–11 (2000).

**2.** Indeed, the subject of foreign sovereign immunity alone has been the subject of at least four entire courses of lectures at the Hague Academy of International Law in the last four decades. *See* Peter D. Trooboff, *Foreign Sovereign Immunity: Emerging Consensus on Principles*, 200 RECUEIL DES COURS 235 (1986–V); Ian Sinclair, *Law of Sovereign Immunity—Recent Developments*, 167

RECUEIL DES COURS 113 (1980); Sompong Sucharitkul, *Immunities of Foreign States Before National Authorities*, 149 RECUEIL DES COURS 89 (1976); N.C.H. Dunbar, *Controversial Aspects of Sovereign Immunity in the Case Law of Some States*, 132 RECUEIL DES COURS 197 (1971).

**3.** 2 H.L. Cas. 1 (1848).

**4.** Buttes Gas and Oil Co. v. Hammer, [1975] Q.B. 557, 573 (C.A.) (Eng.).

Thus, if the defendant is immune, the court must dismiss the case for lack of subject matter and personal jurisdiction. The act of state doctrine, by contrast, is a rule of decision which in some cases acts as a rule of abstention. If it is properly invoked by the defendant, the court must abstain from deciding a case, even if it has jurisdiction over it. Thus, the act of state doctrine functions like the "political question" doctrine in American constitutional law, or the admissibility doctrine in public international law, giving reasons why a court may decline to decide a claim over which it undeniably has jurisdiction. Foreign sovereign compulsion, which has been seen in the U.S. principally in the antitrust area, is an implied affirmative defense. U.S. courts have read this defense into their construction of the antitrust statutes as a permissible objection that defendants can raise when moving to dismiss an antitrust complaint. A larger issue, as we shall see, is whether this doctrine has broader applicability outside the antitrust context.

A second key difference among the doctrines is the *occasions* on which they may be exercised. Foreign sovereign immunity attaches only when a foreign sovereign, or its agency or instrumentality, is a defendant in a civil case. In this respect, it differs, for example, from diplomatic immunity, which attaches in civil *or* criminal litigation whenever the behavior of an individual acting in an official capacity as a representative of a foreign sovereign is called into question.[5] The act of state doctrine may be invoked either by a sovereign or by a private defendant who claims that the litigation requires the court to sit in judgment upon the governmental act of a foreign state fully executed within its own territory. The foreign sovereign compulsion defense also tends to arise in civil litigation, but where a private defendant claims that his case cannot be adjudicated without passing upon a particular kind of act of state— namely, a foreign governmental order which compelled his or her contested conduct. Thus, adapting the facts of the *Hartford Fire Insurance* case discussed in the last chapter, suppose that for some sovereign reason, the United Kingdom ordered its own reinsurance companies to agree to a scheme that raised the price of insurance in the United States. If an American company sued both the United Kingdom and the British company for antitrust violations, the

---

**5.** Diplomatic immunity is, of course, frequently invoked in U.S. courts under the doctrine of executive suggestion, codified at 22 U.S.C. § 254d (2008). *See, e.g.*, United States v. Kostadinov, 734 F.2d 905 (2d Cir. 1984) (citing to the Diplomatic Relations Act, 22 U.S.C. §§ 254a–254e (1994) (implementing Vienna Convention on Diplomatic Relations, Apr. 18, 1961, 23 U.S.T. 3227, 500 U.N.T.S. 95)); United States v. Lumumba, 578 F.Supp. 100 (S.D.N.Y. 1983); Vulcan Iron Works, Inc. v. Polish American Machinery Corp., 479 F.Supp. 1060 (S.D.N.Y. 1979).

defendants would claim that the action against the United Kingdom should be dismissed for lack of jurisdiction under the doctrine of foreign sovereign immunity, that the U.K. government order itself constitutes a nonjusticiable act of state, and that the suit against the British company should be dismissed on grounds of foreign sovereign compulsion.

A third key difference between the doctrines centers upon the *source of legal obligation.* In the United States, foreign sovereign immunity is now required by federal statute, the Foreign Sovereign Immunities Act of 1976. The act of state doctrine is not generally required by statute or international law—treaty or customary law—but has become part of the specialized federal common law that governs in both U.S. state and federal courts after the Supreme Court's 1938 decision in *Erie R.R. Co. v. Tompkins.*[6] Post–*Erie* federal common law rules operate as judge-made rules of horizontal uniformity and vertical supremacy.[7] The foreign sovereign compulsion defense also represents a kind of statutory-gap-filling federal common law, which both grows out of judicial interpretation of a particular statute, the Sherman Act,[8] and formed a well-accepted part of the legal context against which Congress acted when it adopted that Act in 1890.

Despite these important differences, each of these doctrines shares three unifying characteristics: deference, balancing, and institutional competence. First, each doctrine asks a U.S. court in a civil case to decide whether and to what extent to *defer* to foreign sovereignty: whether to exercise jurisdiction (foreign sovereign immunity), to apply a foreign rule of law (the act of state doctrine), or to recognize an affirmative defense to a particular allegation (foreign sovereign compulsion). In the act of state context, the court expresses its deference to the sovereignty of the defendant or its parent entity in one of two ways: by declining to decide the case on the merits (abstention) or by deciding the case on the merits, but treating the challenged act of the foreign sovereign as if it were presumptively or conclusively valid (e.g., applying the foreign law as the rule of decision in the case).

**6.** 304 U.S. 64 (1938) (generally requiring federal courts sitting in diversity jurisdiction to apply state law as rules of decision on substantive matters).

**7.** *See* Texas Industries, Inc. v. Radcliff Materials, Inc., 451 U.S. 630, 641 (1981) ("Against some congressional authorization to formulate substantive rules of decision, federal common law exists only in such narrow areas as those concerned with the rights and obligations of the United States, interstate and international disputes implicating conflicting rights of states or our relations with foreign nations, and admiralty cases.").

**8.** 15 U.S.C. §§ 1–7 (1992).

Second, each of these doctrines asks the court to balance among the five competing jurisprudential principles I have previously enumerated: sanctity of contract, rule-uniformity, national sovereignty, separation of powers, and international comity. For example, granting foreign sovereign immunity to a state trading company promotes comity toward that foreign nation's sovereignty. At the same time, however, recognizing a commercial activity exception to the principle of foreign sovereign immunity promotes sanctity of contract by affording private businesspeople who contract with sovereign entities the same chance of recovery from breach that they would have had if they had contracted with another private party. A commercial activity exception similarly promotes uniform treatment of commercial parties, by refusing to distinguish among sovereign and non-sovereign defendants.

The act of state doctrine serves the quite different function of protecting national sovereignty, comity, and the separation of powers, as well as the conflicts rule that the law of the territorial situs should apply to a challenged act. Foreign sovereign compulsion extends the mantle of national sovereign power beyond governmental entities to reach those private parties who have been ordered to act in a certain way by their government.

Third, each of these doctrines raises a difficult question of *institutional competence*. For each asks which institution of the U.S. federal government—Congress, the courts, or the executive branch—is best qualified to weigh these competing concerns. Should these decisions be made by Congress in a detailed statute, as has occurred in the United States and many other countries through codification of the Foreign Sovereign Immunities Act? Should courts elaborate these principles, largely without legislative guidance, through federal common law rulemaking, as has occurred with act of state doctrine and foreign sovereign compulsion defense? Or should these decisions be made on an *ad hoc* political basis via executive suggestion in individual cases, as has occurred, for example, in the case of the doctrine of head-of-state immunity.[9]

9. In the United States, head-of-state immunity is a customary international law defense that has been incorporated into federal common law, and which has generally been asserted by the U.S. Executive Branch on a case-by-case basis. *See, e.g.*, In re Doe, 860 F.2d 40 (2d Cir. 1988); In re Grand Jury Proceedings, Doe No. 700, 817 F.2d 1108 (4th Cir. 1987); United States v. Noriega, 746 F.Supp. 1506 (S.D. Fla. 1990); Estate of Domingo v. Republic of the Philippines, 694 F.Supp. 782 (W.D. Wash. 1988). Although some former sovereign defendants have asserted an ex-head of state immunity, that doctrine has not generally taken hold, particularly when the new legitimate government (which presumably possesses the sovereign prerogative) and has waived the ex-head of state's residual immunity. *See, e.g.*, In re Grand Jury Proceedings, 817 F.2d 1108 (4th Cir. 1987), *cert. denied*, 484 U.S. 890 (1987); Paul v. Avril, 812 F.Supp. 207

Against this background, three noticeable trends have emerged from the recent Supreme Court decisions in these areas. First, as in the area of extraterritoriality, there appears to be a general *decline in the deference* shown by U.S. courts to foreign sovereignty—a weakening across the board of each of these protective doctrines. Second, as in the extraterritoriality cases, when balancing competing concerns, the U.S. courts have tended increasingly to emphasize separation of powers and uniformity of rules over comity and party autonomy concerns. Third, with regard to institutional competence questions, a split appears to be emerging between the academy and the practicing bar. On the one hand, an academic consensus is growing that all of these areas are ripe for codification. Yet in practice, these areas seem increasingly to be dominated by common law rules being generated by the many federal courts working in this field.

## B.   The Act of State Doctrine

With these trends in mind, let us turn first to the act of state doctrine, which in the United States, has lived through three eras: first, the years before 1964, and the Supreme Court's decision in *Banco Nacional de Cuba v. Sabbatino*;[10] second, the period from 1964–1990, and the Court's unanimous ruling in *W.S. Kirkpatrick and Co. v. Environmental Tectonics Corp.*,[11] and third, the era from 1990 to the present. Each of these eras has seen a different judicial balancing of the jurisprudential concerns identified above.

### 1.   Before 1964: Comity and Conflicts Analysis

Before its 1964 decision in *Sabbatino*, the Supreme Court treated the act of state doctrine principally as a conflict-of-laws principle deriving from concerns about international comity and national sovereignty. In *Underhill v. Hernandez*,[12] the Court declared that "[e]very sovereign state is bound to respect the independence of every other sovereign state," thus mandating that "the courts of one country will not sit in judgment on the acts of the

(S.D. Fla. 1993). *See generally* Peter Evan Bass, Note, *Ex–Head of State Immunity: A Proposed Statutory Tool of Foreign Policy*, 97 YALE L.J. 299, 301 n.10 (1987) (reviewing head of state immunity cases since 1952). There is also some uncertainty as to whether the Executive Branch may legitimately assert common law head of state immunity to immunize a foreign leader who is accused of a *jus cogens* violation. *See, e.g.,* Ye v. Jiang Zemin, 383 F.3d 620 (7th Cir. 2004) (supporting such an assertion).

**10.**   376 U.S. 398 (1964).

**11.**   493 U.S. 400 (1990).

**12.**   168 U.S. 250 (1897).

government of another done within its own territory."[13] In 1918, the Supreme Court repeated that the doctrine "rests at last upon the highest considerations of international comity and expediency."[14]

Under this conflict of laws rationale, U.S. courts applied the doctrine primarily to protect *foreign* governments from embarrassment by recognizing and enforcing those foreign state laws as rules of decision in U.S. courts. As Justice Clarke wrote in *Ricaud v. American Metal Co., Ltd.*, "[t]o accept [an act of state as] a ruling authority and to decide accordingly is not a surrender or abandonment of jurisdiction, but is an exercise of it."[15] In an important sense, the act of state doctrine simply reinforced traditional notions of territoriality-based sovereignty in conflict of laws. When a foreign government committed a taking of property (the traditional factual predicate in these cases), the U.S. court would apply the law of the state of situs—the place where the property was located—as the rule of decision in the case.

Thus, until the early part of the 20th century, the act of state doctrine operated primarily within the realm of private international law, as it continues to do under the contract-oriented act of state doctrine that still functions in the United Kingdom, the commonwealth countries, and some civil law jurisdictions.[16] After the Supreme Court's 1938 decision in *Erie R.R. Co. v. Tompkins*, however, it remained unclear whether the act of state doctrine was to be considered a rule of federal law, or law that would vary from state to state in each of the fifty states of the Union. Nor was it clear what role executive suggestion—i.e., suggestions by executive branch officials that the doctrine should or should not apply in particular cases—should play in the doctrine's exercise.

Both issues arose in the *Bernstein* litigation,[17] which raged for nearly a decade before the New York federal courts. Arnold Bern-

---

**13.** *Id.* at 252.

**14.** Oetjen v. Central Leather Co., 246 U.S. 297, 303–04 (1918).

**15.** 246 U.S. 304, 309 (1918).

**16.** In English law, the classic case remains Luther v. James Sagor and Co., [1921] 3 K.B. 532 (C.A.) (Eng.).Various civil law countries have also applied the rule, while usually making exceptions for foreign acts that are contrary to public order. *See, e.g., Ropit* case, Cour de Cassation (France), [1929] *Recueil General Des Lois et Des Arrets* (Sirey) Part I, 217; Eugen Dietrich Graue, *Germany: Recognition of Foreign Expropriations*, 3

Am. J. Comp. L. 93 (1954); Martin Domke, *Indonesian Nationalization Measures Before Foreign Courts*, 54 Am. J. Int'l L. 305 (1960) (excerpting Dutch cases). *See generally* Restatement (Third) of the Foreign Relations Law of the United States § 444, reporters' note 12; *Sabbatino*, 376 U.S. at 422 (1964) (collecting common law and civil law precedents).

**17.** Bernstein v. Van Heyghen Freres Societe Anonyme, 163 F.2d 246 (2d Cir. 1947); Bernstein v. N.V. Nederlandsche–Amerikaansche Stoomvaart–Maatschappij, 173 F.2d 71 (2d Cir. 1949); 210 F.2d 375 (1954) (per curiam).

stein, a German Jew who alleged that he had been imprisoned by the Nazis and forced under duress to transfer his property to a German corporation, sued for the proceeds of the New York property in a New York state court. When the defendant removed the case to federal court, the Second Circuit, in an opinion by Judge Learned Hand, initially dismissed, applying the act of state doctrine. In 1949, Jack Tate, the Acting Legal Adviser of the State Department (later Associate Dean of Yale Law School), sent a letter to the plaintiff's attorneys that came to be known by the generic term "Bernstein Letter": a U.S. Government communication to the court expressing opposition to application of the act of state doctrine, and the government's intention "to relieve American courts from any restraint upon the exercise of their jurisdiction to pass upon the validity of acts of Nazi officials."[18] Based upon this "supervening expression of Executive Policy," the Second Circuit amended its mandate and permitted the district court to conduct the trial notwithstanding the act of state doctrine.[19]

## 2. *1964–90: Separation of Powers*

The precise precedent established by the *Bernstein* case remained unclear. For the Court suggested that had the Nazi regime come into a U.S. court seeking enforcement of an expropriatory order, the court would have been free to refuse enforcement of the order for reasons of public policy.[20] That reasoning was put to the test after the Cuban revolution of the late 1950s, however, when Castro's government engaged in widespread expropriations of private property, seizing millions of dollars and breaching numerous private contracts. Like the Iranian Hostages Crisis discussed in Chapter II, the Cuban expropriations represented the quintessential seminal public event, whereby a unilateral governmental action works its way down to the private domestic level, affects foreign businesses and wreaks havoc among a broad network of private business arrangements, creating disputes that then percolate back up to the intergovernmental level and transform into incidents that generate and internalize new rules of public international law.[21]

**18.** Bernstein v. N.V. Nederlandsche–Amerikaansche Stoomvaart–Maatschappij, 173 F.2d 71 (2d Cir. 1949); 210 F.2d 375 (1954) (per curiam).

**19.** 210 F.2d at 375.

**20.** *See* 163 F.2d 246, 249 ("[I]f in 1937 it had been the law of the Third Reich that any private person might seize a Jew and by threats of imprisonment or by torture force him to transfer his property, by hypothesis no court of New York would recognize such a transfer as affecting the victim's title, and if the spoilator came to New York with the property in his possession, the victim could reclaim it.").

**21.** *See* Harold Hongju Koh, *Transnational Legal Process*, 75 NEB. L. REV. 181, 183–86 (1996) (elaborating how this

In the 1964 landmark case, *Banco Nacional de Cuba v. Sabbatino*,[22] the Supreme Court recast the act of state doctrine into its modern form. Although the facts of the case are complex, stripped to its essentials, *Sabbatino* asked the simple question: who owned the sugar? Castro's government issued a decree of nationalization, executed within Cuban territory, directed against U.S.-owned property, that was not accompanied by the payment of prompt, adequate, and effective compensation. Thus, the expropriatory decree doubly offended international law, insofar as it was both discriminatory and unaccompanied by adequate compensation.[23] The national bank of Cuba sued an American representative of an expropriated sugar company for proceeds from the sale of the sugar that had been expropriated while sitting on a boat in Cuban territorial waters. The bank claimed to own the sugar by virtue of the act of state: the nationalization decree. Sabbatino, the American representative, asked the courts to hold that the act of state, the expropriatory decree, was invalid under international law.

By a surprising vote of 8–1, the United States Supreme Court rejected that request and enforced the Cuban expropriation decree. In an opinion by the second Justice Harlan, the Court said first, that the act of state doctrine was strictly compelled by neither international law nor the Constitution. In the next breath, however, the Court suggested that the act of state doctrine does have " 'constitutional' underpinnings," because it "arises out of the basic relationships between branches of government in a system of separation of powers."[24] By so saying, the Supreme Court explicitly wrested the act of state doctrine from its historic roots as a rule of deference derived from international comity and conflicts of law, and recast it into a rule based upon constitutional separation-of-powers concerns. The doctrine, the Court suggested, reflects "the

process works). Indeed, the enactment of the Helms–Burton Act, discussed in Chapter IV, shows the enduring generative power of the Cuban expropriation episode for U.S. and international law.

**22.**  376 U.S. 398 (1964).

**23.**  *Cf.* RESTATEMENT (THIRD), *supra* note 16, § 712 ("A state is responsible under international law for injury resulting from (1) a taking by the state of the property of a national of another state that (a) is not for a public purpose, or (b) is discriminatory, or (c) is not accompanied by provision for just compensation; For compensation to be just under this Subsection, it must, in the absence of exceptional circumstances, be in an amount equivalent to the value of the property taken and be paid at the time of taking ... and in a form economically usable by the foreign national....").

**24.**  376 U.S. at 423. (The doctrine "concerns the competency of dissimilar institutions to make and implement particular kinds of decisions in the area of international relations. The doctrine as formulated in past decisions expresses the strong sense of the Judicial Branch that its engagement in the task of passing on the validity of foreign acts of state may hinder rather than further this country's pursuit of goals both for itself and for the community of nations as a whole....").

strong sense of the Judicial Branch that its engagement in the task of passing on the validity of foreign acts of state may hinder" the conduct of foreign affairs.[25] At the same time, the Court took a major step toward uniformity, by federalizing the act of state doctrine as a rule of federal common law binding on federal and state courts alike. *Sabbatino* recognized that the need for predictability and clarity in foreign affairs favored the creation of uniform rules to govern judicial proceedings in all fifty states. Given the mischief that would ensue if each state could formulate its own act of state rule,[26] the Court concluded, any "issue concerned with a basic choice regarding the competence and function of the Judiciary and the National Executive in ordering our relationships with other members of the international community must be treated exclusively as an aspect of federal law," which "should not be left to divergent and perhaps parochial state interpretations."[27] In the ensuing decades, the Supreme Court has routinely cited *Sabbatino* for the proposition that a "few areas, involving 'uniquely federal interests,' are so committed by the Constitution and laws of the United States to federal control that state law is pre-empted and replaced, where necessary, by federal law of a content prescribed (absent explicit statutory directive) by the courts—so-called 'federal common law.' "[28] The Court has specifically found such a "distinctive federal interest" to inhere in rules, such as the act of state doctrine, that affect "the exterior relation of this whole nation with other nations and governments."[29]

That the Court rejected the doctrine's traditional comity/international law rationale becomes clearer once one recognizes that the plaintiff, the Cuban bank, came into a U.S. court to take money

---

**25.** *Id.* at 423.

**26.** *See id.* at 424 ("If . . . the state courts are left free to formulate their own [act of state] rules, the purposes behind the doctrine could be as effectively undermined as if there had been no federal pronouncement on the subject.").

**27.** *Id.* at 425. The full paragraph reads as follows:

> However, we are constrained to make it clear that an issue concerned with a basic choice regarding the competence and function of the Judiciary and the National Executive in ordering our relationships with other members of the international community must be treated exclusively as an aspect of federal law. It seems fair to assume that

the Court did not have rules like the act of state doctrine in mind when it decided *Erie R. Co. v. Tompkins*. Soon thereafter, Professor Philip C. Jessup, now a judge of the International Court of Justice, recognized the potential dangers were *Erie* extended to legal problems affecting international relations. He cautioned that rules of international law should not be left to divergent and perhaps parochial state interpretations. His basic rationale is equally applicable to the act of state doctrine.

*Id.* (citations omitted).

**28.** Boyle v. United Techs. Corp., 487 U.S. 500, 504 (1988).

**29.** *Id.* at 508 n.4 (citation omitted).

from an American citizen, relying on its own domestic governmental decree, which violated international law. In deciding that the Cuban expropriation decree validly transferred the money to the bank, the *Sabbatino* majority voted not simply to defer to a Cuban expropriatory decree, but actually to *enforce* it against an expropriated company's American owners. Yet the comity rationale that had guided previous act of state decisions would presumably have led the Court to decline to enforce a Cuban decree that itself violated comity and international law.[30] Thus, *Sabbatino* restated the act of state doctrine as an inordinately strong conflicts principle favoring the territorial state, for it precluded even the use of contrary U.S. public policy as a basis for departing from the foreign state's territorial rule of decision. As Justice White noted in his powerful dissent, the Court held that "not only are the courts powerless to question acts of state proscribed by international law ... they must render judgment and thereby validate the lawless act."[31]

---

**30.** The practical effect of *Sabbatino* was to require U.S. courts not merely to defer to, but to enforce, a foreign act of state that not only violated international law and U.S. public policy, but also would have violated the Fifth Amendment takings clause of the U.S. Constitution if it had been accomplished by the U.S. government. As Professor Myres McDougal later observed,

> The vice in *Sabbatino* was, not in that it honored the act of a foreign State, but in that *it honored the act of a State in violation of international law.* There is a genuine international law doctrine of act of state, though the majority in *Sabbatino* did not seem to know about it, which requires States to honor each other's acts ... when within their jurisdiction *and in accord with the international law of responsibility of States....* It, however, completely frustrates the basic purpose of this genuine doctrine of act of state ... if it is applied to secure the honoring of acts in violation of international law.

MYRES McDOUGAL & ROBYN JASPER, THE FOREIGN SOVEREIGN IMMUNITIES ACT OF 1976: SOME SUGGESTED AMENDMENTS, PRIVATE INVESTORS ABROAD—PROBLEMS AND SOLUTIONS IN INTERNATIONAL BUSINESS IN 1981 at 67–68 (1981) (emphasis added).

**31.** *See id.* at 439 (White, J., dissenting). Justice White's persuasive dissent

emphasized the judicial duty to decide cases in accordance with international law. His opinion appears to have been strongly influenced by the *amicus curiae* brief of the Executive Committee of the American Branch of the International Law Association, which was co-authored by White's former professor, Professor Myres McDougal of Yale Law School (who also taught Professor Lee A. Albert, Justice White's law clerk during the Court's 1963 term).

In a unpublished memorandum to the author, Professor Albert explained Justice White's dissent, which he observed being written first hand, this way:

> It was precisely [Justice White's] conviction that judges can and therefore must do their job of passing on the validity of public acts under international norms without messing up American foreign relations that led him to reject with force the paralysis of judges under the act of state doctrine. The notion that judges were not competent to apply international law when it was assuredly relevant to a decision on the merits offended him deeply. That White was alone in this position in Sabbatino did not prevent him from doing what he deemed to be his job: deciding issues and cases, even hard ones, not avoiding or evading them. Hence he had, I know, little affection for Alex Bickel's passive vir-

With respect to the issue of judicial competence to apply international law to the underlying conduct, the Court took a sliding-scale approach:

[I]t is apparent that the greater the degree of codification or consensus concerning a particular area of international law, the *more appropriate* it is for the judiciary to render decisions regarding it, since the courts can then focus on the application of an agreed principle to circumstances of fact. It is also evident that some aspects of international law touch much more sharply on national nerves than do others; the less important the implications of an issue are for our foreign relations, the weaker the justification for exclusivity in the political branches. The balance of relevant considerations may also be shifted if the government which perpetrated the challenged act of state is no longer in existence.... *Therefore, rather than laying down or reaffirming an inflexible and all encompassing rule in this case, we decide only that the Judicial Branch will not examine the validity of a taking of property within its own territory by a foreign sovereign government, extant and recognized by this country at the time of suit, in the absence of a treaty or other unambiguous agreement regarding controlling legal principles, even if the complaint alleges that the taking violates customary international law.*[32]

Given the harshness of the result for American business interests, it is hardly surprising that the rule in *Sabbatino* proved unpopular. Although eight justices voted for the result in *Sabbatino*, in retrospect, that unstable coalition came about through an odd alliance among the judicial restraint, anticolonialist and anticorporatist elements on the Court.[33] That alliance never coalesced again, and over time, three distinct coalitions on the Court emerged, none of which could alone command a Supreme Court majority. The first, led by Justice Brennan, usually joined by Justices Stewart, Marshall, and Blackmun, viewed the doctrine as a doctrine of abstention, analogous to the political question doc-

---

tues.... In White's view in Sabbatino, judges can do the job of applying international law, just as in other cases he thought that law enforcement and other government officials would do their jobs responsibly. This assumption of regularity was not invariable and Justice White's willingness to assume good faith was not indiscriminate, to be sure. Nonetheless on many occasions this attitude separated him from other members of the Court.

Letter from Lee A. Albert to author on Reflections on a Clerkship with Justice Byron White (Oct. 30, 2003).

**32.** *Id.* at 428 (emphasis added).

**33.** Among the majority, Justices Harlan (who wrote the opinion) and Stewart ranked as the major proponents of judicial restraint; Justices Black, Douglas, Clark, Brennan, Goldberg, and Chief Justice Warren arguably fell within the anticolonial, anticorporatist camp.

trine.[34] Another coalition, led by Justice White, the sole dissenter in *Sabbatino*, and eventually joined by Chief Justice Burger, Justice Powell, and Justice Rehnquist, pushed for adoption of multiple exceptions to the basic rule. Justice Douglas (and his successor Justice Stevens) tended to adopt a maverick posture unallied with the other coalitions. Thus, for more than a quarter century after *Sabbatino*, no act of state opinion could command a Court majority.

Instead, by 1990, through elaboration by both the lower courts and splintered Supreme Court decisions, the basic rule of nonreviewability had come to develop seven distinct exceptions. These exceptions are implicit in the following general statement of the rule:

> [1]   Subject to a statute, [2] treaty or unambiguous agreement regarding controlling legal principle, neither state nor federal courts in the United States may examine the validity of [3] a public act [4] of a recognized foreign sovereign [5] fully executed within that state's own territory [6] raised in an affirmative claim [7] absent a communication from the Executive Branch, commonly called a *Bernstein letter*, urging the court to make such an adjudication.[35]

To state the rule in this form is to identify its seven exceptions: for statutes; treaties and controlling legal principles; commercial acts; unrecognized states; extraterritorial acts; counterclaims; and cases involving *Bernstein* letters, i.e., Executive Branch communications urging adjudication. Each of these seven exceptions has claimed differing degrees of support from various appellate courts and Supreme Court justices.[36] Like the exceptions to the hearsay rule in evidence law, which permit the admissibility of "trustworthy hearsay," each exception reflects a *de facto* judicial determination that

---

**34.** See, e.g., First National City Bank v. Banco Nacional de Cuba, 406 U.S. 759, 785–90 (1972) (Brennan, J., dissenting); Alfred Dunhill of London, Inc. v. Republic of Cuba, 425 U.S. 682, 726–28 (1976) (Marshall, J., dissenting).

**35.** Not only does the statement in text closely track the Supreme Court's holding in *Sabbatino*, quoted in text accompanying note 32, above, it also closely resembles Section 442 of the American Law Institute's *Restatement (Third)*, *supra* note 16, which similarly declares that, subject to modification by an act of Congress:

> In the absence of a treaty or other unambiguous agreement regarding controlling legal principles, courts in

the United States will generally refrain from examining the validity of a taking by a foreign state of property within its own territory, or from sitting in judgment on other acts of a governmental character done by a foreign state within its own territory and applicable there.

**36.** For detailed discussions of the exceptions, see GARY BORN, INTERNATIONAL CIVIL LITIGATION IN UNITED STATES COURTS 685–744 (3d ed. 1996); Joseph W. Dellapenna, *Deciphering the Act of State Doctrine*, 35 VILLANOVA L. REV. 1 (1990); Michael Bazyler, *Abolishing the Act of State Doctrine*, 134 U. PA. L. REV. 325 (1986).

principles of comity, conflict-of-laws, and separation of powers would not be offended by adjudicating a foreign act of state in a case where the exception is invoked.

Take first, for example, the "statutory exception," which has allowed courts to decide the legality of acts of state if a statute allows them to do so, for example, the second Hickenlooper Amendment to Foreign Assistance Act of 1961.[37] When Congress and the President acting together have mandated it, the courts have reasoned, adjudication is appropriate, because separation-of-powers concerns evaporate, American public policy has been clearly stated for conflicts purposes, and the political branches have explicitly determined that courts may decide the legality of the foreign state even in the face of comity concerns. Similarly, the so-called "treaty or controlling legal principle" exception—which has never been adjudicated by the Supreme Court, but has been almost uniformly recognized by lower courts[38]—rests on the rationale that adjudication reinforces national sovereignty without violating separation powers. In such cases, the U.S. political branches have specified what the negotiated rule should be, the foreign state has waived comity objections by contracting for the rule, and the negotiated rule has been chosen as the rule of decision, thereby averting any conflicts concerns.[39] The third exception, for commercial acts, won four votes in the 1976 *Dunhill* case,[40] on the theory that a broad

**37.** 22 U.S.C. § 2370 (e)(2) (2000) ("[N]o court in the United States shall decline on the ground of the federal act of state doctrine to make a determination on the merits giving effect to principles of international law in a case in which a claim of title or other right to property is asserted by any party including a foreign state (or a party claiming through such state) based upon (or traced through a confiscation or other taking after January 1, 1959, by an act of that state in violation of the principles of international law. . . .")). *See also* 9 U.S.C. § 15 (1994) (holding act of state doctrine inapplicable to enforcement of certain arbitral agreements and awards).

**38.** *See, e.g.*, Kalamazoo Spice Extraction Co. v. Ethiopia, 729 F.2d 422, 425 (6th Cir. 1984) (doctrine does not apply to case in which standard clause of bilateral treaty provides the controlling legal standard regarding measure of compensation for a taking); Ramirez de Arellano v. Weinberger, 745 F.2d 1500 (D.C. Cir. 1984) (en banc), *vacated on*

*other grounds*, 471 U.S. 1113 (1985). *See generally* Note, *A Treaty Exception to the Act of State Doctrine: A Framework for Judicial Application*, 4 B.U. INT'L L.J. 201 (1986).

**39.** Similarly, the Restatement recognizes that a "controlling legal principle" might include a "claim arising out of an alleged violation of fundamental human rights—for instance, a claim on behalf of a victim of torture or genocide," and the like. *See generally* RESTATEMENT (THIRD) §§ 701–03 (enumerating such *jus cogens* norms). Such adjudication would "probably not be defeated by the act of state doctrine, since the accepted international law of human rights is well established and contemplates external scrutiny of such acts." *Id.* § 443 cmt. c.

**40.** Alfred Dunhill of London, Inc. v. Cuba, 425 U.S. 682, 708 (1976) (Justices White, Burger, Powell, and Rehnquist) ("declin[ing] to extend the act of state doctrine to acts committed by foreign sovereigns in the course of their purely commercial operations.").

international consensus exists as to the applicable rules of law regarding commercial activities, thus rendering the matter appropriate for a court to decide, and making it unlikely that a decision invalidating the foreign act would "touch sharply upon the nerves" of other members of the global community.[41] The fourth exception—which permits U.S. courts to pass upon the legality of acts of unrecognized foreign states, such as the Palestine Liberation Organization in the early 1990s[42]—builds on *Sabbatino*'s explicit suggestion that an unrecognized state has lesser comity objections to judicial process, rendering adjudication of such states acts fully consistent with separation of powers.[43]

The three remaining exceptions rest on similar reasoning. The fifth requirement—that the act of state be fully executed within the state's own territory—has been read by the lower federal courts for example, to permit adjudication of the liability of Latin American governments for breaches of sovereign debts that occur in New York.[44] The sixth, counterclaim exception, first enunciated by Justice Douglas in the *Citibank* case,[45] derives from the equitable assumption that a foreign state who comes into a U.S. court as a plaintiff seeking relief should not be able to invoke the act of state defense to avoid a counterclaim or setoff (up to the level of the initial claim). Seventh and finally, the *Citibank* case also witnessed three justices (Rehnquist, White and Burger) favoring adoption of the *Bernstein* exception, which would render the doctrine inapplicable in cases where the Executive branch has sent the court a formal communication favoring adjudication.[46] As with the other excep-

---

**41.** *Compare Dunhill*, 425 U.S. at 704, with *Sabbatino*, 376 U.S. at 428, quoted in text at note 34, *supra*.

**42.** Klinghoffer v. S.N.C. Achille Lauro, 937 F.2d 44, 47 (2d Cir. 1991) (finding Palestine Liberation Organization not to be a sovereign state for FSIA purposes).

**43.** *See Sabbatino*, 376 U.S. at 428 ("The balance of relevant considerations may also be shifted if the government which perpetrated the challenged act of state is no longer in existence ... for the political interest of this country may, as a result, be measurably altered.").

**44.** *See, e.g.*, Allied Bank Int'l v. Banco Credito Agricola de Cartago, 757 F.2d 516, 521 (2d Cir. 1985) ("The act of state doctrine is applicable to this dispute only if ... the situs of the debts was in Costa Rica.... In this case Costa Rica could not wholly extinguish the

Costa Rican banks obligation to timely pay United States dollars to Allied in New York."); *see also* Republic of Iraq v. First National City Bank, 353 F.2d 47 (2d Cir. 1965); Tchacosh Co., Ltd. v. Rockwell Int'l, 766 F.2d 1333 (9th Cir. 1985); F. & H.R. Farman–Famaian Consulting Engineers Firm v. Harza Engineering Co., 882 F.2d 281 (7th Cir. 1989); Bandes v. Harlow and Jones, Inc., 852 F.2d 661, 666–67 (2d Cir. 1988) (also relying upon the situs requirement).

**45.** First National City Bank v. Banco Nacional de Cuba, 406 U.S. 759, 771 (1972) (Douglas, J., concurring) [hereafter *Citibank*] (citing National City Bank v. Republic of China, 348 U.S. 356, 361–62 (1955)).

**46.** In *Citibank*, the situation was made more complex by the fact that the Government letter submitted in that case was a Bernstein letter limited to

tions, an "Executive Suggestion" exception (which Justices Douglas, Powell, Brennan, Stewart, Marshall, and Blackmun opposed in *Dunhill*), rests on the theory that a *Bernstein* letter signals the absence of comity or separation-of-powers objections to adjudication of the act of state. The countervailing danger, as Justice Douglas put it colorfully in *Citibank*, is that such an exception for Executive suggestion would make the Court "a mere errand boy which may choose to pick some people's chestnuts from the fire, but not others."[47]

## 3. 1990–Present: Conflicts Without Comity

Such was the state of the law when the Supreme Court finally returned to this area with its 1990 decision in *W.S. Kirkpatrick and Co. v. Environmental Tectonics Corp.*,[48] the most important act of state case decided by the Court since *Sabbatino*. *Kirkpatrick*, the first act of state case in twenty-six years to command a majority of the court, even surpassed *Sabbatino* by being unanimous. Three of the Justices sitting on the case (Scalia, O'Connor, Kennedy) were new to the Court since *Dunhill*, and hearing their first Supreme Court case on the matter. But Justice Scalia, for one, was hardly a novice on the subject, having had extensive prior experience with the act of state doctrine as a private and government lawyer.[49] *Kirkpatrick* did not involve expropriation, the classic act of state scenario, but rather, a suit by a failed American bidder against a rival American company, claiming that the defendant had obtained a Nigerian government contract based upon a suspicious payment

urging the adjudication of a counterclaim.

**47.** 406 U.S. 759, 773 (Douglas, J., concurring); *see also id.* at 791 (Brennan, J., dissenting) (arguing that *Bernstein* exception "politicizes the judiciary" and "relinquishes the [legal] function to the Executive by requiring blind adherence to its requests that foreign acts of state be reviewed").

**48.** 493 U.S. 400 (1990).

**49.** Justice Scalia, perhaps the Court's leading exponent of separation of powers and judicial deference to the Executive Branch, was formerly Assistant Attorney General for the Justice Department's Office of Legal Counsel in the Ford Administration. He argued the *Dunhill* case for the government shortly after leaving office, and as a private

attorney, favored the application of the act of state doctrine before the Ninth Circuit in International Assoc. of Machinists and Aerospace Workers v. OPEC, 649 F.2d 1354 (9th Cir. 1981). As a judge on the U.S. Court of Appeals for the D.C. Circuit in Ramirez v. Weinberger, 745 F.2d 1500, 1567 (D.C. Cir. 1984) (en banc), he joined Judge Starr's dissenting opinion favoring dismissal of that suit on act of state doctrine grounds. Given this background, one might have expected Justice Scalia to write a far different kind of opinion in *Kirkpatrick*, one deferring to the executive branch on separation of powers grounds and applying the act of state doctrine based on either the commercial act or the *Bernstein* exceptions to existing doctrine.

of about $1.7 million to a Nigerian national. The U.S. government submitted not one, but two *Bernstein*-type letters to various courts, saying that the act of state doctrine should not apply.[50]

Available to the Court were three fairly simple ways to avoid applying the act of state doctrine. First, it could have enshrined the "commercial act" exception into majority opinion, concluding that the decision to award a commercial contract to Kirkpatrick, based on a bribe designed to induce the award, constituted a commercial act by the Nigerian government that fell outside the scope of the act of state doctrine. Alternatively, the Court could have treated the U.S. Government's letters as *Bernstein* letters and simply followed the Executive branch's position, which suggested that the act of state doctrine should not bar adjudication of the case.[51] Third, the Court could have recognized a new exception to the act of state doctrine, which some lower courts had adopted: an exception that allowed adjudication in cases where the plaintiff asked the court to examine not the validity, but only the underlying motivation, of the foreign government's act.[52]

**50.** The first letter, cited in Justice Scalia's opinion, 493 U.S. at 408 n.*, was written to the district court on December 10, 1986, and questioned whether or not an act of state was actually at issue. The Court's opinion ignored a subsequent letter dated July 25, 1989, however, attached to the Solicitor General's Supreme Court brief, which in more classic *Bernstein* fashion, simply said that the Legal Adviser to the State Department saw no unacceptable risk of embarrassment to the U.S. executive branch from judicial resolution of the case.

**51.** In *Kirkpatrick*, this option was complicated by the fact that there was not one, but three, communications from the Executive Branch regarding the case. Although the original *Bernstein* letter was sent from the Acting Legal Adviser of the State Department to the plaintiffs' attorney, see 210 F.2d at 275, since then, most *Bernstein* letters have been written by the Legal Adviser of the State Department to the Solicitor General. Although the Legal Adviser wrote such a letter in *Kirkpatrick*, and the Solicitor General submitted an amicus brief to the Court stressing the commercial activity factor and the need to respect executive discretion, the Court cited neither, choosing instead to follow the recommendation of the original 1986

letter from the Legal Adviser which had questioned whether the act of state doctrine applied at all. *See* 493 U.S. at 408 n.*.

**52.** *See, e.g.*, Clayco Petroleum Corp. v. Occidental Petroleum Corp., 712 F.2d 404, 407 (9th Cir. 1983) ("In this case . . . the very existence of plaintiffs' claim depends upon establishing that the motivation for the sovereign act was bribery, thus embarrassment would result from adjudication."); Mannington Mills, Inc. v. Congoleum Corp., 595 F.2d 1287, 1294–95 (3d Cir. 1979) (allowing suit to go forward when "the crucial acts occurred as a result of a considered policy determination by a government to give effect to its political and public interests. . . ."). *But see Hunt v. Mobil Oil Corp.*, 550 F.2d 68, 77 (2d Cir. 1977) (act of state doctrine applies to prevent court from "mak[ing] inquiry into the subtle and delicate issue of the policy of a sovereign nation" because Libyan government's motivation for challenged seizure is inseparable from its validity). For further discussion of an exception when the motivation is bribery, see generally Note, Clayco Petroleum Corp. v. Occidental Petroleum Corp.: *Should There Be a Bribery Exception to the Act of State Doctrine?*, 17 CORNELL INT'L L.J. 407 (1984).

Justice Scalia, writing for the unanimous Court, took none of these routes, instead returning to first principles and reexamining the historical "evolution of the jurisprudential foundation for the act of state doctrine."[53] While acknowledging that the doctrine had previously rested on comity and international law grounds, the Court reconfirmed that the doctrine now operates "as a consequence of domestic separation of powers" concerns.[54] The Court definitively rejected the notion that the doctrine exists primarily to preserve "international comity, respect for the sovereignty of foreign nations on their own territory," noting that:

> The act of state doctrine does not establish an exception for cases and controversies that may embarrass foreign governments, but merely requires that, in the process of deciding, the acts of foreign sovereigns taken within their own jurisdictions shall be deemed valid.[55]

The Court further described the doctrine not as "some vague doctrine of abstention but as a 'principle of decision binding on federal and state court alike.' "[56] This federal common law conflict-of-laws principle applies only when the validity, not the facts, of a foreign act of state are at issue. Thus, Justice Scalia suggested, the various exceptions to the doctrine did not even come into play, because the case failed the threshold act of state test: whether "a court must decide—that is, when the outcome of the case turns upon—the effect of official action by a foreign sovereign. When that question is not in the case, neither is the act of state doctrine."[57] Here, the Court said, none of the plaintiffs' claims charged that some official act of the Nigerian government was illegal—including the legality of the disputed contract.[58] Thus, Justice Scalia concluded, the case involved no act of state at all and the act of state doctrine simply did not apply.

As a judicial opinion, *Kirkpatrick* leaves much to be desired. Like the comity analysis of *Hartford Fire Insurance*, the Court's brief and conclusory opinion, issued only seven weeks after argument, reveals little real debate or coming to terms within the Court over the jurisprudential underpinnings of the act of state doctrine.

---

**53.** 493 U.S. at 404.

**54.** *Id.*

**55.** *Id.* at 409.

**56.** *Id.* at 406, citing *Sabbatino*, 376 U.S. at 427. Justice Scalia's opinion in *Kirkpatrick* thus resembles his dissent in *Hartford Fire*, in pressing for the treatment of foreign sovereignty issues as conflict-of-laws questions.

**57.** *Id.* at 406.

**58.** 493 U.S. at 405 ("Nothing in the present suit requires the court to declare invalid, and thus ineffective as a rule of decision for the courts of this country, the official act of a foreign sovereign performed within its own territory.") (internal citation omitted).

By focusing on "the validity," rather than the legality or effect, of a foreign state's act, *Kirkpatrick* invites metaphysical hair-splitting as to when a case raises the validity, as opposed to the underlying motivation, of a foreign state's act, a distinction which has been left for the lower courts to resolve.[59] Nor is it clear how seriously to take the Court's injunction that the act of state doctrine shall not be applied to protect foreign states from embarrassment. One could easily imagine a case—for example, an American suing the Russian President for an unlawfully motivated business deal on eve of crucial arms control talks—in which this assertion would be put to the test.

At the same time, however, *Kirkpatrick* clearly inaugurates a new era in act of state jurisprudence. The decision returns the act of state doctrine to its pre–1964 conflict-of-laws roots, but now without the comity and national sovereignty rationales that undergirded those early cases. While reaffirming the doctrine's *separation-of-powers* rationale, the Court avoided the simple expediency of adopting the *Bernstein* exception and following a general practice of deference to executive suggestion. Indeed, the separation-of-powers rationale for the doctrine has so taken hold since *Sabbatino* that it has even migrated to the United Kingdom, which in 1981 decided to adopt the perspective that the act of state doctrine rests less on international law and comity, than on the inherent nature and limits of the judicial function.[60]

*Kirkpatrick* also struck a significant blow for *uniformity* by announcing a new threshold rule. Rather than simply creating another exception to the doctrine, or fitting this case within a pre-existing exception, the Court created a new threshold test for all act of state cases, which strongly limits the applicability of the doctrine as a whole. By holding that a case only involves an act of state if and only if "a court *must decide*—that is when the outcome of the case turns upon—the effect of official action by a foreign sovereign,"[61] the Court removed the possibility of an act of state defense in a case where there is governmental conduct in the background,

---

**59.** The facts of *Kirkpatrick*, for example, could have been characterized as involving the validity of the Nigerian government's decision to award a government contract motivated by a bribe.

**60.** *See* Buttes Gas and Oil Co. v. Hammer, [1982] A.C. 888, 936–38 (H.L.). For comparative analysis, see Michael Singer, *The Act of State Doctrine of the United Kingdom: An Analysis with Comparison to United States Practice*, 75 AM. J. INT'L L. 283 (1981); Peter Cane,

*Prerogative Acts, Acts of State and Justiciability*, 29 INT'L AND COMP. L.Q. 680 (1980); Hugh M. Kindred, *Acts of State and the Application of International Law in English Courts*, 1981 CAN. YBK. IN'TL L. 271. *See also* Hugh M. Kindred, *Acts of State and the Application of International Law in Canadian Courts*, 10 REV. DROIT U. SHERBROOKE 271 (1979).

**61.** 493 U.S. at 406 (emphasis in original).

but no direct challenge has been lodged against the lawfulness of that government action. By so holding, *Kirkpatrick* sharply limits the applicability of the doctrine as a defense in business suits between two private parties. Henceforth, it is no longer enough for a defendant to claim that a lawsuit should be dismissed simply because it was doing business with a foreign government. Instead, the defendant must argue that the only way he can be held liable is for the court to declare the foreign government's act illegal.[62] Thus, *Kirkpatrick* marks a victory for party autonomy as well as uniformity, for the decision makes it less likely that private companies who do business against foreign governments will enjoy special protection against their contracting parties in the U.S. courts. At the same time, however, the decision makes it more likely that parties will be free to sue contracting parties who defraud them, without the defendants seeking haven in the shield of the act of state doctrine. *Kirkpatrick* leaves open, however, for a defendant to claim that the government actually forced him to commit the challenged act, a claim that would give rise to the act of state doctrine's kindred defense: foreign sovereign compulsion.

## C. Foreign Sovereign Compulsion

The foreign sovereign compulsion defense rests on the notion that a private party who has been compelled by a foreign sovereign or by foreign law cannot be held liable for taking an action that arguably violates the U.S. antitrust laws. The doctrine lies somewhere between act of state and the comity rule in *Timberlane*.[63] For like the Act of State Doctrine, foreign sovereign compulsion is a comity-based doctrine that U.S. courts apply to defer to a particular kind of act of state, a foreign governmental command issued to a private party within the foreign state's own jurisdiction. Abstaining from adjudicating based on foreign sovereign compulsion treats the defendant's anticompetitive act as equivalent to the act of the government itself, and avoids embarrassing both the foreign government and the United States government with a ruling that the foreign state's act is illegal. From the perspective of party autonomy, the doctrine recognizes the inherent unfairness in forcing a defendant to be subjected to a hard conflict of the type described in Chapter IV, in which he is bound to violate the law of one or the other regulating countries. Alternatively, the foreign sovereign

**62.** The Court concluded that merely making the findings of "the facts necessary ... to establish that ... [an act of state] was unlawful" did not make the doctrine applicable. 493 U.S. at 406.

**63.** Timberlane Lumber Co. v. Bank of America, 549 F.2d 597 (9th Cir. 1976). *See* Chapter IV, *supra.*

compulsion defense can be viewed as an extreme form of *Timber-lane* interest-balancing, in which the Court dismisses on comity grounds out of deference to the foreign country's laws, because the defendants' proof of foreign sovereign compulsion conclusively establishes four of the *Timberlane* factors.[64]

Like the act of state doctrine, the defense applies only when the foreign government is ordering a private act within its own territory (e.g., applying mandatory product standards, forcing membership in a producer's association, etc.). Comity would not require a U.S. court to defer, for example, to a foreign order to a private actor to violate U.S. antitrust law within the United States. Nor does the defense apply when the foreign government has only encouraged the challenged conduct, rather than actually compelling it, in the sense that "a refusal to comply with the foreign government's command would give rise to the imposition of penal or other severe sanctions."[65] Nor, finally, does the defense appear to apply with full force to strictly procedural matters, such as a foreign government's blocking order with respect to production of documents.[66]

For all of this buildup, surprisingly few reported cases have actually been dismissed on grounds of foreign sovereign compulsion.[67] In the leading case, *Interamerican Refining Corp. v. Texaco*

**64.** *Id.* at 614, cited in Chapter IV, note 58, *supra*. These four factors are: (1) the degree of conflict with foreign law or policy; (2) the extent to which enforcement by either state can be expected to achieve compliance; (3) the relative significance of effects on the United States as compared with those elsewhere; and (4) the relative importance to the violations charged of conduct within the United States as compared with conduct abroad.

**65.** U.S. Dep't of Justice and Federal Trade Commission, Antitrust Enforcement Guidelines for International Operations § 3.32 (1995) [hereafter 1995 *U.S. Antitrust Guidelines*].

**66.** *See* Societe Internationale pour Participations Industrielles et Commerciales, S.A. v. Rogers, 357 U.S. 197 (1958) (in the face of conflicting procedural order, U.S. court requires party to make a good-faith attempt to secure permission to disclose documents covered by foreign secrecy laws, suggesting that failure to do so may lead to drawing

factual inferences unfavorable to the nonproducing party); RESTATEMENT (THIRD) § 442 cmt. e (distinguishing "conflicts in substantive law" from conflicts "in the litigation process, and in particular with pretrial procedures, in situations where the forum state by definition has jurisdiction over the parties and the proceedings and foreign substantive law would not ordinarily be involved. Accordingly, somewhat less deference to the law of the other state may be called for.").

**67.** In addition to the *Interamerican* case, two older district court cases apparently approved the doctrine as an antitrust defense. *See* United States v. General Electric Co., 115 F.Supp. 835, 878 (D. N.J. 1953); United States v. Imperial Chem. Indus., 105 F.Supp. 215 (S.D.N.Y. 1952). In O.N.E. Shipping Ltd. v. Flota Mercante Grancolombiana, S.A., 830 F.2d 449, 453 (2d Cir. 1987), the U.S. Court of Appeals for the Second Circuit also relied on foreign sovereign compulsion as an alternative ground of dismissal.

*Maracaibo, Inc.*,[68] the government of Venezuela prohibited oil companies from making shipments of crude oil to a company called Interamerican, forcing that company to terminate operations. The District Court dismissed the plaintiff's private antitrust action, reasoning "Commerce may exist at the will of the [foreign] government, and to impose liability for obedience to that will would eliminate for many companies the ability to transact business in foreign lands."[69]

Unlike the act of state doctrine, the foreign sovereign compulsion rule is one with which the Supreme Court has flirted, but never formally recognized. Most recently, the issue arose before the Court in the mammoth Japanese television litigation, *Matsushita Elec. Indus. Co. v. Zenith Radio Corp.*[70] There, American TV companies brought antitrust actions against seven Japanese companies and their subsidiaries, charging that defendants had engaged in predatory pricing by setting prices artificially high in the Japanese television market, permitting them to dump similar TVs in the U.S. market at minimum "check prices"—i.e., prices below fair value that were set by MITI, the Japanese Ministry for International Trade and Industry. Pretrial discovery in the case took eight years, and resulted in what was probably the longest trial court decision in American history (nearly 500 pages in length). The Japanese manufacturers claimed that their actions had been compelled by MITI, and in a letter to the Court, MITI confirmed that the challenged business rules had in fact been created under its direction and that the Japanese exporters had no alternative but to abide by this arrangement.

The Court of Appeals denied the defendants summary judgment on the foreign sovereign compulsion point, but on Supreme Court review, the Solicitor General pressed the issue, arguing that the Court should recognize the defense on grounds of both comity and separation of powers. Not surprisingly, the Government stressed separation of powers considerations over international comity concerns, arguing that sovereign compulsion should be available as a defense when the conduct at issue was in fact compelled by a foreign government. It is in such cases, the government claimed, that the imposition of liability by American courts is likely to touch most sharply on foreign concerns, and thus pose the greatest difficulties for the conduct of our foreign relations.[71]

---

**68.** 307 F.Supp. 1291 (D. Del. 1970).

**69.** 307 F.Supp. at 1297.

**70.** 475 U.S. 574 (1986).

**71.** U.S. Brief as Amicus Curiae at 8, Matsushita Elec. Indus. Co. v. Zenith Radio Corp., 475 U.S. 574 (1986) (No. 83–2004).

For similar separation of powers reasons, the Solicitor General suggested further that the foreign sovereign compulsion defense should be unavailable in an antitrust suit brought by the United States, as opposed to a private party.[72] The Supreme Court avoided the issue, instead ruling for the defendants on the substantive ground that the plaintiffs' theory of predatory pricing was speculative (a strange conclusion to reach in a case that took eight long years to bring to the eve of trial).[73] Both the majority and the dissent explicitly reserved the validity of the foreign sovereign compulsion defense for another day.[74] Nevertheless, the defense has been widely accepted both by the American Law Institute's *Restatement (Third) of Foreign Relations Law*[75] and the Justice Department's *Antitrust Enforcement Guidelines for International Operations.*[76]

It remains unclear whether the doctrine will remain limited to the antitrust area, as a judicial interpretation of the Sherman Act, or whether it should apply more generally to other regulatory areas (for example, the export control area discussed in the Soviet Pipeline case discussed in the last chapter). Perhaps the doctrine's greatest potential significance will come in the realm of international trade law, where foreign governments—particularly Japan—have regularly imposed "voluntary restraints" upon the export to the U.S. market of automobiles, steel, semiconductors, and the like. The U.S. government in these cases has generally advised the Japanese government that these arrangements enjoy antitrust immunity, so long as the Government of Japan is actually compelling its companies to comply with the specified measures, on the assumption that such advice would ultimately be vindicated by the U.S. courts.[77]

---

**72.** *Id.* at 23–24. By so arguing, the Government sought to build upon a suggestion by lower courts that the act of state doctrine should not apply to actions brought by the U.S. government, reasoning that "any governmental enforcement represents a judgment of the wisdom of bringing a proceeding, in light of the exigencies of foreign affairs. Act of state concerns are thus inapplicable since the purpose of the doctrine is to prevent the judiciary from interfering with the political branches' conduct of foreign policy." Clayco Petroleum Corp. v. Occidental Petroleum Corp., 712 F.2d 404, 409 (9th Cir. 1983); *accord* Jimenez v. Aristeguieta, 311 F.2d 547, 558 (5th Cir. 1962). If the courts should accept this argument in a future case, they would clearly be basing the foreign sovereign compulsion defense on separation of powers, rather than comity, grounds.

**73.** *Id.* at 588–93.

**74.** *Id.* at 582–83 and 605 n.5 (dissenting opinion)

**75.** *See* RESTATEMENT (THIRD) §§ 441–42 (1987).

**76.** 1995 U.S. Antitrust Guidelines § 3.32.

**77.** For a discussion of voluntary export restraints and restraint agreements, see generally JOHN JACKSON, WILLIAM DAVEY AND ALAN SYKES, LEGAL PROBLEMS OF INTERNATIONAL ECONOMIC RELATIONS: CASES, MATERIALS AND TEXT 654–56 (3d ed. 1995).

Finally, the doctrine arose almost covertly in the Supreme Court's recent ruling in the *Hartford Fire Insurance* case,[78] which is discussed at greater length in Chapter IV. As noted there, the Supreme Court majority found that federal jurisdiction "undoubtedly" existed over the plaintiffs' claims, then concluded that "the only substantial question in this case is whether there is in fact a true conflict between domestic and foreign law."[79] Justice Souter agreed that defendants' conduct was lawful in U.K., but held that "[s]ince [defendants] do not argue that British law requires them to act in some fashion prohibited by the law of the United States, or claim that their compliance with the laws of both countries is otherwise impossible, we see no conflict with British law."[80] Essentially, Justice Souter applied to the interest-balancing phase of extraterritoriality analysis a "foreign sovereign compulsion" test. Finding that defendants had made no claim that British law *required* them to act in some fashion prohibited by the law of the United States, he also found no need to refrain from adjudication based on international comity grounds.

By so ruling, *Hartford Fire Insurance* requires defendants to establish not simply that the extraterritorial conduct that the U.S. declares illegal was legal at home, but that their home country actually forced them to act in the manner that violates U.S. law. Since this threshold showing will be tremendously difficult to meet, the *Timberlane* balance has been tipped powerfully in favor of U.S. jurisdiction, regardless of how attenuated the connection between the foreign conduct and the United States may be. By so holding, *Hartford Fire Insurance* comes close to absorbing the foreign sovereign compulsion defense into general extraterritoriality analysis. For in effect, the Court suggests that no case would be dismissed on the comity factor of conflicting laws, unless it could already be dismissed under the foreign sovereign compulsion defense. In short, the majority suggests, international comity only compels respect for that extremely limited class of foreign sovereign acts that directly compel a violation of U.S. law.

By so saying, the Court significantly weakens international defenses based on national sovereignty and comity, and broadens Congress's freedom to regulate liberally under the effects doctrine. For myriad foreign regulations reflect regulatory philosophies different from the American one, and may be strongly bound up in

---

**78.** 509 U.S. 764 (1993).

**79.** *Id.* at 798, citing Justice Blackmun's separate opinion in Societe Nationale Industrielle Aerospatiale v. United States Dist. Ct., 482 U.S. 522, 555 (1987) (Blackmun, J., concurring), discussed in greater detail in Chapter X, *infra*.

**80.** 509 U.S. at 798.

national interest and heritage, although they do not order nationals to violate U.S. law. *Hartford Fire* takes a remarkably narrow view of foreign regulatory sovereignty: within British territory, the Court suggests, the United Kingdom's regulation of its own national companies in no way exempts those companies from also complying with United States law, except in those extraordinary circumstances in which the U.K. has taken an adamant sovereign stand and ordered British companies not to comply with U.S. law. Moreover, the Court links this diminished view of sovereignty with a narrow view of comity, suggesting that the United States need not give "recognition ... within the courts of its territory to the legislative, executive or judicial acts of another nation," unless those acts take the strong form of foreign sovereign compulsion.[81] Finally, the case is a victory for separation of powers, for the Court's shallow reasoning on this point closely tracked the U.S. Government's *amicus curiae* brief, which was itself a thinly disguised recycling of its foreign sovereign compulsion position in *Matsushita*.[82] At the same time, party autonomy and rule-uniformity in international business have suffered, as parties conducting international transactions must conduct business in the shadow not only of the law of the jurisdiction in which the transaction occurs, but also under the broader scrutiny of U.S. regulatory laws.

**81.** Hilton v. Guyot, 159 U.S. 113, 164 (1895).

**82.** *See* Brief for the United States as Amicus Curiae, Hartford Fire Insurance Co. v. California, 509 U.S. 764 (1993) (Nos. 91–111, 91–1128).

# CHAPTER VI

## FOREIGN SOVEREIGN IMMUNITY

Not surprisingly, the Supreme Court's most recent decisions regarding foreign sovereign immunity reveal the same trends witnessed above: declining respect for international comity and national sovereignty, and a greater focus on concerns of separation of powers, uniformity and party autonomy. As noted above, foreign sovereign immunity has served a function in American courts that is both different from, but closely related to that played by the act of state doctrine. As Justice Marshall noted in the *Dunhill* case, on the one hand,

> the doctrines of sovereign immunity and act of state ... differ fundamentally in their focus and in their operation. Sovereign immunity accords a defendant exemption from suit by virtue of its status. By contrast, the act of state doctrine exempts no one from the process of the court. Equally applicable whether a sovereign nation is a party or not, the act of state doctrine merely tells a court what law to apply to a case....[1]

On the other hand, as Justice White noted, writing for three justices in *Dunhill*, the doctrines share underlying policy concerns, inasmuch as

> the proper application of each [doctrine] involves a balancing of the injury to our foreign policy, the conduct of which is committed primarily to the Executive Branch, through judicial affronts to sovereign powers, ... against the injury to the private party, who is denied justice through judicial deference to a raw assertion of sovereignty, and a consequent injury to international trade.[2]

## A. History

Like the act of state doctrine, foreign sovereign immunity in the United States has lived through three distinct eras.[3] For present purposes, it suffices to note that the first era, of absolute foreign sovereign immunity, which dated from the beginning of the

---

1. Alfred Dunhill of London, Inc. v. Republic of Cuba, 425 U.S. 682, 725–26 (1976) (Marshall, J., dissenting).

2. *Id.* at 682 n.18 (White, J, joined by three Justices).

3. For an excellent history of the U.S. law and summary of the emerging international law principles, see Peter D. Trooboff, *Foreign State Immunity: Emerging Consensus on Principles*, 200 RECUEIL DES COURS 235 (1986).

Republic until 1952, revolved around Chief Justice John Marshall's famous declaration in *Schooner Exchange v. McFaddon*:

> The jurisdiction of the nation within its own territory is necessarily exclusive and absolute. It is susceptible of no limitation not imposed by itself.... All exceptions, therefore, to the full and complete power of a nation within its own territories must be traced up to the consent of the nation itself.[4]

After the *Schooner Exchange*, the Court dealt only sporadically with the foreign sovereign immunity question, usually by evaluating executive suggestions of immunity or non-immunity with respect to libeled ships. In 1926, the State Department declined to recognize the immunity of a merchant vessel owned by and in service of a foreign government, but the Court nevertheless continued to recognize immunity, thereby refusing to participate in a burgeoning international movement toward restrictive immunity.[5] As Professor Lowenfeld has noted: "[t]hat case rested entirely on the Supreme Court's understanding of international law and precedent, without any reference to considerations of foreign policy or the desires of the United States Government."[6]

But in *Ex Parte Peru*,[7] the Court began to shift foreign sovereign immunity toward a political rationale. There, the Court ordered the release of a Peruvian vessel, treating the State Department's certification of the vessel immunity "as a conclusive determination by the political arm of the government that the continued retention of the vessel interferes with the proper conduct of our foreign relation."[8] In words redolent of the later act of state cases, the Court declared that "courts may not so exercise their jurisdiction [over foreign sovereigns and their property] as to embarrass the executive arm of the government in conducting foreign relations."[9] Two years later, in a similar case involving a Mexican government-owned ship, the State Department took no position with respect to the vessel's asserted immunity, which led the courts to deny immunity, reasoning that absent a suggestion of immunity by the State Department, "courts may decide for themselves whether all the requisites of immunity exist."[10]

---

4.  *See, e.g.*, Schooner Exchange v. McFaddon, 11 U.S. (7 Cranch) 116, 136 (1812).

5.  Berizzi Bros. Co. v. S.S. Pesaro, 271 U.S. 562 (1926).

6.  *See* ANDREAS F. LOWENFELD, INTERNATIONAL LITIGATION AND ARBITRATION 589 (1993).

7.  318 U.S. 578 (1943).

8.  *Id.* at 589.

9.  *Id.* at 588.

10.  Republic of Mexico v. Hoffman, 324 U.S. 30, 34–35 (1945).

In May 1952, Acting U.S. Legal Advisor of the State Department Jack B. Tate (who also, curiously enough, had authored the original *Bernstein* letter) sent the Acting Attorney General the famous "Tate Letter,"[11] which by executive policy, shifted United States policy somewhat belatedly toward the emerging international doctrine of restrictive sovereign immunity. After surveying state practice, the Tate Letter suggested that only the "Soviet Union and its satellites" seemed bent on full acceptance of the absolute theory of sovereign immunity; that "the granting of sovereign immunity to foreign governments in the courts of the United States is most inconsistent with the action of Governments of the United States in subjecting itself to suit in these same courts"; and that "the widespread and increasing practice on the part of governments of engaging in commercial activities makes necessary a practice which will enable people doing business with them to have their rights determined in the court."[12] By so saying, the Tate Letter effectively acknowledged that international law and private autonomy concerns favored the move to restrictive sovereign immunity, and that comity concerns did not oblige the United States to recognize immunity for those states that did not reciprocate.

The Tate Letter itself, however, soon created uniformity problems. For to cope with the welter of requests for executive suggestions, the Department of State was forced to create a quasi-judicial process within the Department to evaluate requests for immunity.[13] It soon became apparent that, particularly in highly politicized cases, suggestions of immunity would be granted or denied based on political, not legal, imperatives.[14] By the early 1970s, the second era had become fraught with confusion, particularly over the key substantive question: where should courts draw the line between sovereign and commercial acts?[15] At the same time, procedural uncertainties abounded: regarding how to serve process upon a sovereign; when and how immunity could be waived; whether and

---

**11.** 26 DEP'T ST. BULL. 984 (1952).

**12.** *Id.* at 985.

**13.** These decisions are digested in Saddler, Vagts, and Ristau, eds., *Sovereign Immunity Decisions of the Department of State*, 1977 DIG. U.S. PRAC. INT'L L. 1017.

**14.** See, for example, Rich v. Naviera Vacuba, S.A., 295 F.2d 24 (4th Cir. 1961), in which the U.S. government suggested immunity for a Cuban freighter to avoid exacerbating differences that had arisen after the hijacking of a Cu-

ban patrol vessel to the United States. For background material on the incident, see 1 ABRAM CHAYES, THOMAS EHRLICH & ANDREAS LOWENFELD, INTERNATIONAL LEGAL PROCESS: MATERIALS FOR AN INTRODUCTORY COURSE 87–154 (1986).

**15.** Victory Transport v. Comisaria General, 336 F.2d 354, 360 (2d Cir. 1964) ("The conceptual difficulties involved in formulating a satisfactory method of differentiating between acts *jure imperii* and acts *jure gestionis* have led many commentators to declare that the distinction is unworkable.")

to what extent prejudgment attachments and post-judgment executions were available, and what sovereign assets were or were not absolutely immune from judicial process.

The success of the Vienna Conventions on consular and diplomatic immunities[16] and the conclusion of the European Convention on State Immunity (which entered into force in 1976)[17] gave impetus to the third era: the worldwide movement for codification of foreign sovereign immunity rules. Starting in the early 1970s, the Departments of State and Justice began to study a jointly-sponsored bill which eventually became the Foreign Sovereign Immunities Act of 1976 (FSIA or Act).

The FSIA's passage was motivated by the jurisprudential values discussed in earlier chapters. By codifying the emerging international law consensus regarding the restrictive theory of foreign sovereign immunity, the Act preserved comity and promoted international law by bringing the U.S. into line with the emerging international consensus. The FSIA became only one piece of a worldwide movement to codify the law of foreign sovereign immunity, which soon came to include the U.K. State Immunity Act of 1978,[18] and the state immunity laws of Singapore,[19] South Africa,[20] Pakistan,[21] Canada,[22] and Australia.[23] This codification movement still continues, at the multilateral level, with codification efforts found in the European Convention on State Immunity and an Additional Protocol that became effective in 1976 (the "European Convention"),[24] the Draft Inter–American Convention on the Jurisdictional Immunity of States,[25] the Draft Convention on State Immunity of the International Law Association,[26] and the Interna-

---

**16.**  *See* Vienna Convention on Diplomatic Relations, Apr. 18, 1961, 23 U.S.T. 3227, 500 U.N.T.S. 95; Vienna Convention on Consular Relations, Apr. 24, 1963, 21 U.S.T. 77, 596 U.N.T.S. 261.

**17.**  11 Int'l Leg. Mat. 470 (1972).

**18.**  17 Int'l Leg. Mat. 1123 (1978).

**19.**  Singapore State Immunity Act (1979), in *U.N. Materials on Jurisdictional Immunities of States and Their Property*, U.N. Doc. ST/LEG/SER.B/20 (1982).

**20.**  South Africa State Immunity Act (1979), in *U.N. Materials on Jurisdictional Immunities of States and Their Property*, U.N. Doc. ST/LEG/SER.B/20 (1982).

**21.**  Pakistan State Immunity Ordinance (1981), in *U.N. Materials on Jurisdictional Immunities of States and Their Property*, U.N. Doc. ST/

LEG/SER.B/20 (1982); *see also* Qureshi v. U.S.S.R., 1981 S.C. 377, 20 Int'l Leg. Mat. 1060 (1981) (Pakistani decision subjecting U.S.S.R. to suit based on commercial contracts notwithstanding Soviet claim of foreign sovereign immunity).

**22.**  21 Int'l Leg. Mat. 798 (1982).

**23.**  25 Int'l Leg. Mat. 715 (1986).

**24.**  The European Convention on State Immunity, Europ. T. S. No. 074 entered into force on June 11, 1976 between eight European nations, *available at* http://conventions.coe.int/Treaty/en/Treaties/Html/074.htm.

**25.**  This instrument, drafted in 1983, has never entered into force.

**26.**  *See generally* Note, *The International Law Association Draft Convention on Foreign Sovereign Immunity*, 23 Va. J. Int'l L. 635 (1983).

tional Law Commission's United Nations Convention on Jurisdictional Immunities of States and their Property, which was adopted by the General Assembly in December 2004, but is not yet in force.[27]

Yet at the same time, codification of rules clarified the separation of powers by establishing that henceforth, foreign sovereign immunity issues would be quintessentially *legal* questions, to be determined by the courts with the persuasive, but not binding, advice of the Executive Branch. Moreover, the codification era brought much-needed uniformity to foreign sovereign immunity law, as the statute announced an exclusive and uniform set of rules and procedures for adjudicating claims against foreign states and instrumentalities in U.S. courts, including service of process, pre- and post-judgment attachment, and enforcement of and execution upon foreign assets. In its current form, the statute functions as an all-purpose procedural chameleon.[28] For the statute acts as the basis for subject matter jurisdiction in the federal courts, as a long-arm statute that confers personal jurisdiction upon the federal courts and that dictates rules of service of process and venue, and as the statutory vehicle authorizing pre-judgment and post-judgment attachment of foreign state assets.

The statute begins by declaring Congress's adherence to the restrictive theory of foreign sovereign immunity.[29] The statute defines the term "foreign state" broadly, including not only the state itself, but also its political subdivisions, and its agencies or

**27.** For a report of the lengthy work of the International Law Commission on the jurisdictional immunities of states and their property, see http://untreaty.un.org/ilc/summaries/4_1.htm (June 30, 2005); Virginia Morris, *The International Law Commission's Draft Convention on the Jurisdictional Immunities of States and their Property*, 17 DEN. J. INT'L L. AND POL'Y 395 (1989); D.W. Grieg, *Forum State Jurisdiction and Sovereign Immunity Under the International Law Commission's Draft Articles*, 38 INT'L & COMP. L.Q. 243 (1989); D.W. Grieg, *Specific Exceptions to Immunity Under the International Law Commission's Draft Articles*, 38 INT'L & COMP. L.Q. 560 (1989). As of May 2007, there are 28 signatories to the Convention and 4 instruments of ratification have been deposited. The United States has not yet taken any formal position with respect to the UN Convention, but ratification by the United States seems unlikely un-til the FSIA has been amended to ensure harmonization of domestic law with this international instrument.

**28.** Under the statute, the availability of an exception to immunity confers subject matter jurisdiction, which conjoined with service of process, also confers personal jurisdiction. See Texas Trading and Milling Corp. v. Federal Republic of Nigeria, 647 F.2d 300, 307–08 (2d Cir. 1981), *cert. denied*, 454 U.S. 1148 (1982). This creates the anomaly that a defendant who waives immunity under 28 U.S.C. § 1605(a)(1) can thereby waive his objection to subject matter jurisdiction, which U.S. federal courts usually do not permit.

**29.** See 28 U.S.C. § 1602 (1994) ("[S]tates are not immune from the jurisdiction of foreign courts insofar as their commercial activities are concerned....").

"instrumentalities," a category which includes a corporation a majority of whose shares of stock are owned by a foreign state.[30]

Under the statute, a foreign state is presumed to be immune from suit unless one of the exceptions set forth in § 1605 applies. The exception of most intense interest to international business practitioners is the "commercial activity" exception to sovereign immunity, which preserves sanctity of contract and private autonomy by allowing private parties to litigate against their sovereign and quasi-sovereign partners in the same way as against their private contract partners.[31] Congress made it clear that the test of what constitutes a commercial activity "shall be determined by reference to the nature of the course of conduct or particular transaction or act, rather than by reference to its purpose."[32] By so saying, Congress intended that the courts apply a "private person" test: asking whether the activity under challenge is one in which a private person could engage. Moreover, the legislative history clarified that a regular course of commercial conduct would include "the carrying on of a commercial enterprise, such as a mineral extraction company, an airline or a state trading corporation.... [If] an activity is customarily carried on for profit, its commercial nature could readily be assumed."[33]

## B.  Supreme Court Decisions

Remarkably, although the statute has been amended several times and massively litigated before the lower courts, since 1976, it has come quite rarely before the Supreme Court.[34] The first two Supreme Court decisions construing the act did not directly address the heart of the statute, but rather promoted the statute's uniform application by upholding the statute's constitutionality and its exclusivity as a basis of federal court jurisdiction over foreign sovereigns. In *Verlinden v. Central Bank of Nigeria,*[35] a Netherlands corporation sued an instrumentality of the Nigerian government in a federal court. The defendant claimed the statute was unconstitutional because the Constitution did not envision suits between aliens in federal courts on nonfederal claims. The Court sustained

**30.**  *Id.* § 1603(b)(1)–(2).

**31.**  *Id.* § 1605(a)(2).

**32.**  *Id.* § 1603(d).

**33.**  H. Rep. No. 94–1487 (1976).

**34.**  A computer-assisted search reveals that United States courts have cited the Foreign Sovereign Immunities Act of 1976 in over two thousand cases since it became law. For comprehensive listings of lower court decisions, see Joseph Dellapenna, Suing Foreign Governments and Their Corporations (1988); Gary B. Born, International Civil Litigation in United States Courts 199–285 (3d ed. 1996). These lectures deal with the various procedural aspects of litigating against foreign sovereigns in Chapters VII–XIII, *infra.*

**35.**  461 U.S. 480 (1983).

the constitutionality of the Act on the ground that it codified the standards governing foreign sovereign immunity as substantive federal law, and thus was not merely jurisdictional, but "arose under" federal law, as was required by Article III of the U.S. Constitution.

In *Argentine Republic v. Amerada Hess Shipping Corp.*,[36] plaintiffs sought to sue the government of Argentina under a different jurisdictional provision, the Alien Tort Claims Act,[37] which (as has been described in Chapter III above) has been increasingly invoked to bring international human rights claims in United States courts.[38] The Court held, relying on the statute's plain language, that the FSIA provided the exclusive basis of federal jurisdiction against foreign sovereigns, and thus, plaintiffs were obliged to proceed against Argentina under the congressionally mandated framework of the Foreign Sovereign Immunities Act.[39]

Taken together, *Verlinden* and *Amerada Hess* struck a blow for uniformity, as the Court reaffirmed the legislative goal of "channel[ing] cases against foreign sovereigns away from the state courts and into federal courts, thereby reducing the potential for a multiplicity of conflicting results among the courts of the 50 states."[40] For international business practitioners, however, the heart of the statute has always been the commercial activity exception to the Foreign Sovereign Immunities Act, 28 U.S.C. § 1605(a)(2),[41] which lifts the immunity of the foreign state in three enumerated circumstances:

> [1] In which the action is based upon a commercial activity carried on in the United States by the foreign state; or [2] upon an act performed in the United States in connection with a commercial activity of the foreign state elsewhere; or [3] upon an act outside the territory of the United States in connection with a commercial activity of the foreign state elsewhere and that act causes a direct effect in the United States.[42]

For shorthand purposes, I will refer to "Clause One cases," which address a foreign sovereign entity's act *and* activity in the

---

**36.** 488 U.S. 428, 434 (1989).

**37.** 28 U.S.C. § 1350 (1994).

**38.** See, for example, *Filártiga v. Peña–Irala*, 630 F.2d 876 (2d Cir. 1980), and its progeny. For a discussion of this litigation, see Harold Hongju Koh, *Transnational Public Law Litigation*, 100 Yale L.J. 2347, 2358–75 (1991).

**39.** *But see Amerada Hess*, 488 U.S. at 438 (noting that the Alien Tort Statute "of course has the same effect after the passage of the FSIA as before with respect to defendants other than foreign states").

**40.** *Verlinden*, 461 U.S. at 497.

**41.** *See, e.g.*, Texas Trading and Milling Corp. v. Federal Republic of Nigeria, 647 F.2d 300, 307–08 (2d Cir. 1981), cert. denied, 454 U.S. 1148 (1982).

**42.** 28 U.S.C. § 1605(a)(2).

United States; "Clause Two cases," which address a foreign sovereign's act inside but commercial activity outside the United States; and "Clause Three cases," which address commercial acts and activities outside the United States, but which acquire their nexus to the United States by virtue of causing a direct effect in the United States. Obviously, Clause Three cases represent the most difficult exercises of U.S. judicial jurisdiction over foreign sovereigns because of two phrases: "commercial activity" and "direct effect." For although Congress defined commercial activity by reference to the nature and not the purpose of the course of the conduct, in the years following enactment of the statute, some lower courts smuggled "purpose" considerations into the statute by asking whether the foreign government's activity also served some sovereign goal.[43]

A typically confusing case arises when foreign governments—sometimes in combination with other governments—have regulated the extraction, processing and sale of natural resources. In *International Association of Machinists v. OPEC*,[44] an American labor union sued the Organization of Petroleum Exporting Countries (OPEC) and thirteen member nations for classic price-fixing. The district court initially dismissed on the ground that OPEC's actions were sovereign, not commercial, in nature[45] But on appeal, the Ninth Circuit affirmed, based not on the FSIA, but rather, on the act of state doctrine, reasoning that price-fixing was an act that could be accomplished by private parties, even if undertaken for a sovereign purpose.

The FSIA's legislative history leaves unclear the precise connection between the "direct effect" necessary to waive foreign sovereign immunity based on an external commercial act and the "substantial, direct and reasonably foreseeable effect" on U.S. domestic commerce or U.S. import commerce necessary to bring a case within the scope of the Federal Trade Antitrust Improvements Act of 1982.[46] Both kinds of contacts need to be distinguished from the constitutional "minimum contacts" test that will be discussed in Chapter VII below: the test for determining whether a foreign sovereign defendant has sufficient contacts with the United States or a state thereof to confer personal jurisdiction over him. Thus,

---

**43.** *See, e.g.*, MOL, Inc. v. Peoples Republic of Bangladesh, 736 F.2d 1326 (9th Cir. 1984) (Bangladesh's termination of a contract for trade of rhesus monkeys concerned its sovereign right to regulate imports and exports and its sovereign right to regulate its natural resources.).

**44.** 649 F.2d 1354 (9th Cir. 1981).

**45.** 477 F.Supp. 553, 567–68 (C.D. Cal. 1979).

**46.** 15 U.S.C. § 6a (1994).

significant confusion reigned regarding how these three kinds of contacts tests relate and overlap.

It was not until sixteen years after the FSIA's initial passage that the Supreme Court finally construed the heart of the statute. The leading case, *Republic of Argentina v. Weltover*,[47] was a Clause Three ("direct effect") case, in which Argentina and its central bank claimed immunity from a suit seeking to compel defendants to honor contractual obligations under bonds that defendants had unilaterally rescheduled to meet Argentina's foreign debt burden. The case raised the two core Clause Three issues: first, did Argentina's unilateral rescheduling of the debt constitute a "commercial activity," and second, did that activity have a direct effect in the United States? A unanimous Court, once again speaking through Justice Scalia, answered both questions in the affirmative.

Significantly, the Court applied an historical approach to construing the statutory definition of commercial activity, asking what was "the meaning generally attached to [the] term ['commercial'] under the restrictive theory [in 1976] at the time the statute was enacted."[48] The Court also used the *Dunhill* plurality opinion's discussion of the commercial act exception as a contemporaneous guide to the FSIA's meaning.[49] The Court first held that Argentina's participation in the bond market was something a private actor could do, and hence was commercial in nature, despite the fact that the bonds were not issued to earn a profit, nor were they capable of issuance by a private party.[50] Second, the Court decided that defendants' conduct had a direct effect in the United States. Justice Scalia rejected defendants' argument that these effects must also be substantial and foreseeable, although he did concede that the effect should be more than *de minimis*. The Court defined a direct effect as one that follows as an "immediate consequence of the defendant's activity."[51] Here,

> Respondents had designated their accounts in New York as the place of payment, and Argentina made some interest payments into those accounts before announcing that it was rescheduling the payments. Because New York was thus the place of performance for Argentina's ultimate contractual obligations, the rescheduling of those obligations had a "direct effect" in the United States.[52]

**47.** 504 U.S. 607 (1992).
**48.** *Id.* at 612–13.
**49.** *Id.* at 614.
**50.** *Id.*

**51.** *Id.* at 617.
**52.** *Id.* at 619.

A direct effect resulted because money that was supposed to have been delivered to a New York bank for deposit was not forthcoming.

By defining "commercial activity" broadly and "direct effect" liberally, the Supreme Court greatly strengthened the position of United States banks vis-à-vis foreign sovereign debtors during a debt crisis. Public debt instruments like those used by Argentina, the Court suggested, "are in almost all respects garden-variety debt instruments: They may be held by private parties; they are negotiable and may be traded on the international market ... and they promise a future stream of cash income."[53] By giving private creditors the benefit of their bargain with foreign government debtors, the Court emphasized private autonomy and uniformity and deemphasized claims that either international comity or national sovereignty mandate a deferential approach to foreign debt rescheduling. Separation-of-powers concerns also probably pushed the Court to defer to executive discretion in the *Weltover* case, as its opinion once again closely followed the position in the U.S. government's brief.

The question remains whether foreign states may enter any kinds of commercial contracts, particularly of a kind that did not exist in 1976, without exposing themselves to U.S. suits under the commercial activity exception. *Weltover*'s broad language now makes it unlikely that an intergovernmental commercial arrangement with regard to natural resources, such as price-fixing or market division arrangement of the kind alleged in *OPEC*, would enjoy any kind of sovereign immunity protection.

With respect to "direct effect," the Court's decision was similarly generous toward commercial plaintiffs. In post-*Weltover* cases raising claims of anticompetitive foreign sovereign conduct, courts must now apply three different tests for determining the degree of a foreign sovereign instrumentality's contacts with the United States: a "direct, substantial and reasonably foreseeable effects" test for determining whether prescriptive, antitrust jurisdiction exists under the Foreign Trade Antitrust Improvements Act; the FSIA's "direct effect" or "immediate consequences" test for assessing whether an exception to foreign sovereign immunity exists, thus establishing subject matter jurisdiction; and (assuming that foreign sovereigns have constitutional rights),[54] a Fifth Amendment "purposeful minimum contacts" test for determining whether the

---

**53.** *Id.* at 616.

**54.** *See generally* Lori F. Damrosch, *Foreign States and the Constitution*, 73 Va. L. Rev. 483 (1987) (suggesting that foreign states have no such rights).

direct effect alleged under the statute is also constitutionally sufficient to confer personal jurisdiction over the sovereign defendant. Although each of these bodies of doctrine has evolved separately, it remains unclear whether over time, these three tests will remain different, or whether in practice they will merge into a general authorization of suits against those who conduct commercial activities abroad with more than *de minimis* impact upon the U.S. economy.

*Weltover*'s broad reading of the commercial activity exception's "direct effect" language also highlighted the discrepancy between the statute's treatment of extraterritorial commercial and noncommercial torts. Under Clause Three, a plaintiff can sue for extraterritorial commercial wrongs, but under the "noncommercial tort" exception to the statute, immunity is waived only for noncommercial cases "in which money damages are sought against a foreign state for personal injury or death, or damage to or loss of property, *occurring in the United States* . . . ."[55] In *Amerada Hess*, the Court had applied the presumption against extraterritoriality to that provision and concluded that foreign sovereign immunity is not waived for noncommercial torts that occur on the high seas.[56] The ruling had the effect of driving tort plaintiffs toward the more territorially generous commercial activity exception, even in cases where the nexus between the injury and the commercial activity appears strained. In *Saudi Arabia v. Nelson*[57] the fourth FSIA case to come before the Supreme Court, an American employee of the Saudi Arabian royal hospital and his spouse sought damages for personal injury against the Saudi Arabian government. Nelson claimed that after he had been actively recruited for his job, he was tortured by Saudi Arabian police in retaliation for his efforts to report hazards at the hospital during the course of his employment. Barred by the territorially restricted noncommercial tort exception, Nelson avoided Clause Three of the commercial activity exception (the most territorially lenient provision) and sued instead under Clause One, which required that his claim be "based upon" a commercial activity carried on by the defendant in the United States.

The Court of Appeals for the Eleventh Circuit accepted his claim in what appeared to be a virtually fact-specific ruling.[58] But shortly after the first Gulf War, Saudi Arabia pleaded with the Bush Administration to support its petitioner to the Supreme Court.[59] When the Solicitor General sided with the Saudis, the

---

**55.** 28 U.S.C. § 1605(a)(5) (2000) (emphasis added).

**56.** *See* 488 U.S. at 440.

**57.** 507 U.S. 349 (1993).

**58.** 923 F.2d 1528 (11th Cir. 1991).

**59.** *See* Neil Lewis, *After the War: U.S. Wants Saudi Torture Suit Settled*, N.Y. Times, Apr. 23, 1991, at A11.

Supreme Court, in a five-Justice opinion by Justice Souter, granted review and reversed. The majority held first, that Nelson's claims were "connected to," but not "based upon," commercial activity in the U.S., thus failing the nexus requirement of Clause One.[60] Second, in an even more striking conclusion, the Court ruled that the allegedly tortious conduct in question—the abuse of power by the Saudi police—did not constitute commercial activity. The Court decided that the use of police to commit torture within the employment relationship was not commercial conduct, reasoning that "however monstrous such abuse undoubtedly may be, a foreign state's exercise of the power of its police has long been understood for purposes of the restrictive theory as peculiarly sovereign in nature."[61]

In my judgment, both of the Court's conclusions were not just wrong, but potentially dangerous. As both Justices White and Stevens pointed out in their separate opinions, the Nelsons' claims were clearly "based upon" the operation of a hospital—a commercial activity—and that activity did have sufficient connection to the U.S., through the Saudi recruiting activity in the U.S., to bring it within Clause One.[62] The Court instead chose to treat the complaint as based upon police activities and detention practices, which it found to be peculiarly sovereign. Yet those practices could also have been characterized as commercial, because they were allegedly conducted in retaliation for Nelson's reporting of hazards on the job, something that private employers can also do. As *amicus* human rights organizations pointed out, it was hardly unprecedented for Saudi governmental employers to threaten foreign workers with detention and torture in work-related disputes.[63] As Justice White noted, the irony of the Court's reasoning is that it would have permitted Nelson to sue if his wages had been cut in retaliation for his claims, or if he had been disciplined by private hospital employees, but perversely immunized Saudi Arabia once the royal hospital chose to bring official police in to torture him.[64]

---

**60.** 507 U.S. at 357 (1993).

**61.** *Id.* at 361.

**62.** *Id.* at 364 (White, J., joined by Blackmun, J., concurring in the judgment); *id.* at 377 (Stevens, J., dissenting). A different result might also have obtained under Article 11 of the International Law Commission Draft Convention on the Jurisdictional Immunities of States and Their Property, which bars states from invoking immunity "in a proceeding which relates to a contract of employment between the State and an individual for work performed or to be performed, in whole or in part, in the territory of that other State." *See* note 27, *supra.*

**63.** *See* Brief of Human Rights Watch as Amicus Curiae at 6, Saudi Arabia v. Nelson, 507 U.S. at 357 (1993) (No. 91–522). I should note here that I was a signatory to one of the human rights amicus rights briefs in *Nelson*.

**64.** *Id.* at 367 (White, J., concurring in the judgment) ("had the hospital retaliated against Nelson by hiring [pri-

The Court's reasoning suggests that it has yet to grasp two fundamental international human rights principles that were established at Nuremberg: that courts may pierce the veil of state sovereignty when governmental officials commit international crimes, and that "courts—both international and domestic—are peculiarly appropriate fora for the determination of official rights and responsibilities for crimes against humanity."[65]

As a human rights disappointment, *Nelson* thus joins the Haitian refugee case[66] and several other recent Supreme Court rulings disfavoring aliens and denying enhanced judicial protection for international human rights.[67] The Court's skepticism toward Nelson's case reflected its broader reluctance to apply enhanced judicial scrutiny to international human rights abuses. The real problem with *Nelson*, in my view, was that the Court saw it as a human rights case masquerading as a commercial activity case. As such, *Nelson* predictably made bad commercial law. As before, the case illustrates that comity and sovereignty concerns are on the wane, and separation of powers factors on the rise in these cases. For in granting review and ruling for Saudi Arabia, the Court followed the urging of the Bush Administration, which was in turn motivated to urge review largely by a political factor: the massive support that the Saudis had just given to the United States during the Gulf War.

*Nelson* thus further illustrates the transnational process of intertwining public and private in the international business area stressed throughout these lectures. For public intergovernmental ties between the United States and Saudi Arabia first prompted closer ties among their businesses, which led to the employment of American citizens in Saudi Arabia witnessed in both *Nelson* and the *Aramco* cases. The density and strategic importance of those busi-

---

vate] thugs to do the job, I assume the majority would consent to calling it 'commercial.' ").

**65.** *See generally* Koh, *supra* note 38, at 2359.

**66.** Sale v. Haitian Centers Council, 509 U.S. 155 (1993), discussed in Chapter IV.

**67.** In addition to the Haitian case, in recent terms, the Court has denied a criminal defendant the protection of an extradition treaty crafted to prevent his kidnapping, United States v. Alvarez–Machain, 504 U.S. 655 (1992); upheld the INS policy of arresting and detaining unaccompanied minors, Reno v. Flores, 507 U.S. 292 (1993); and vacated lower court orders directing the INS to accept legalization applications beyond the statutory deadline, Reno v. Catholic Social Servs., Inc., 509 U.S. 43 (1993). The Court has long disfavored aliens seeking entry into the United States, and in recent years has come to look skeptically upon the claims of both asylum-seekers and those, like the Haitian and Cuban refugees of the early 1990s, who sought not an affirmative right to entry, but only the negative right not to be returned to their persecutors. *See* Sale v. Haitian Centers Council, 509 U.S. 155 (1993); CABA v. Christopher, 43 F.3d 1412 (11th Cir. 1995), *cert. denied*, 116 S.Ct. 299 (1995).

ness networks helped motivate the U.S. to mobilize the multinational coalition that prompted the Gulf War after Iraq invaded Kuwait. The close public links between the countries confirmed during the Gulf War then influenced the U.S. Government's decision to support Supreme Court review in *Nelson*, which in turn spawned a new Supreme Court interpretation of the "based upon" language of the commercial activity exception to the Foreign Sovereign Immunities Act. As in other episodes recounted here, private business disputes percolated up to the intergovernmental level and transformed into public episodes, which were ultimately resolved through rule-making that has now been internalized into the domestic laws of the participant nations.

Following *Saudi Arabia v. Nelson*, the Court heard four FSIA cases in five years: concerning the FSIA's retroactivity, determination of a company's status as an "instrumentality of a foreign state," the immovable property exception, and the relationship between the FSIA and the federal procedural rule on indispensable parties. In the two most recent cases, the Court has explored technical corners of the statute: the contours of the immovable property exception and the relationship between the FSIA and the federal joinder rules.[68]

The two retroactivity cases, *Republic of Austria v. Altmann* and *Dole Food Co. v. Patrickson*, have made even clearer the Supreme Court's growing tendency to restrict foreign sovereign immunity. The first of these, *Republic of Austria v. Altmann*, turned on an unusually arresting set of facts. The uncle of Maria Bloch–Bauer Altmann, a United States citizen, owned several valuable paintings by the famous Austrian artist Gustav Klimt, which were expropriated by the Austrian government during WWII. Seeking to recover them, Altmann sued the Republic of Austria and the Austrian Art Gallery (an instrumentality of the foreign state) in an Austrian court, but prohibitively high filing fees imposed by those courts forced her to abandon those claims. She then filed suit in California federal court, invoking the FSIA's exception for expropriation of "rights in property taken in violation of international law."

---

**68.** In Permanent Mission of India to the United Nations v. City of New York, ___ U.S. ___, 127 S.Ct. 2352 (2007), the Court held that the text of FSIA, the contemporaneous materials relied upon by Congress, and the post-enactment practice all indicate that the immovable property exception, 28 U.S.C. § 1605(a)(4) (2008), confers jurisdiction upon U.S. courts to declare the validity of tax liens placed by the City of New York on property that foreign sovereigns hold to house their employees. In Republic of Philippines v. Pimentel, ___ U.S. ___, 128 S.Ct. 2180 (2008), the Court concluded that Federal Rule of Civil Procedure 19 required a federal court to dismiss an interpleader action involving a foreign country that had successfully claimed foreign sovereign immunity.

(§ 1605(a)(3)'s expropriation exception). The defendants argued that the FSIA did not apply retroactively to the date when the alleged expropriation occurred (1948). The Supreme Court rejected that claim, holding that the Act applied retroactively not only to conduct occurring before the enactment of FSIA in 1976, but also to events occurring in the *Schooner Exchange* era, before the adoption of the Tate Letter's "restrictive theory" of Foreign Sovereign Immunity in 1952.

Another *de facto* retroactivity issue arose the previous term, in *Dole Food Co. v. Patrickson*, when a group of farm workers from Central America filed a state-court suit alleging injury from chemical exposure against Dole Food Company, which subsequently impleaded the Dead Sea Companies, which formerly had been majority-owned by the state of Israel (and hence were "instrumentalities of a foreign state" for purposes of the FSIA). Dole removed the action to federal court, arguing that the federal common law of foreign relations provided federal question jurisdiction. But the Court of Appeals reversed, reasoning that the Dead Sea Companies were not instrumentalities of Israel, insofar as a corporate subsidiary could not claim "instrumentality" status where the foreign state owns a majority of the shares of a corporate parent, but not the subsidiary itself. The Court unanimously ruled that instrumentality status should be determined at the time of the filing of the complaint, and held, by a vote of 7–2, that only direct ownership satisfied the instrumentality requirement and that a foreign state must itself own a majority of a corporation's shares for that company to be deemed an instrumentality of the foreign state for FSIA purposes.[69]

Looking back over the topics covered in this Part, one sees a trend toward declining deference to foreign sovereignty recurring across the landscape of the American law of foreign sovereignty. In the act of state area, the Court has not applied the doctrine to bar litigation of a suit for more than thirty years since *Sabbatino*, and *Kirkpatrick* has furthered that trend by limiting the availability of the act of state doctrine via the Court's new threshold test. The foreign sovereign compulsion defense has been confined to a limited zone of applicability, and will probably be invoked in the near future primarily to immunize "voluntary" trade restraint agreements that have been specifically negotiated to serve the U.S. government's foreign policy interests. In the field of foreign sover-

---

**69.** 538 U.S. 468 (2003). Concurring in part and dissenting in part, Justice Breyer, joined by Justice O'Connor, argued that the statutory prerequisite of "other ownership interest ... owned by a foreign state," covers a foreign state's legal interest in a corporate subsidiary, where that interest consists of the foreign state's ownership of a corporate parent that owns the shares of the subsidiary. *Id.* at 480 (Breyer, J., concurring in part and dissenting in part).

eign immunity, the U.S. government has relatively little to fear from a long-term trend of declining immunity, as the United States owns few state trading companies and engages in far fewer governmentally orchestrated private trade practices than many other countries. Since so few of its businesses operate specifically to promote national sovereign aims, the United States has less to fear than most trading states from broad application of a "nature" rather than "purpose" test for commercial activities. As the globe's most aggressive extraterritorial regulator, the U.S. government also has the least to gain politically from judicial recognition of broadly deferential notions of comity, which could restrain discretionary U.S. regulation of all manner of extraterritorial activity, whether it be anticompetitive contracts, debt and securities trades, or the movement of refugees on the high seas.

Accordingly, the U.S. government has generally encouraged the trend toward declining sovereignty, and the U.S. Supreme Court has generally deferred to the executive branch's urgings. The resulting plethora of transnational suits in the last two decades of the 20th century served to return domestic courts to the business of adjudicating international law, from which they had largely excluded themselves since *Sabbatino*. This movement also stimulated a reawakening of the bench's and bar's interest in the black-letter doctrine of international and foreign relations law. This interest helped spark the revision of the *Restatement (Third) of Foreign Relations Law*, which has in turn prompted still more transnational adjudication. As the earlier discussion of the presumption against extraterritoriality revealed, rules of American foreign sovereignty law that were first generated in the human rights realm now migrate freely into the commercial realm and back again.[70]

---

**70.** This point can be illustrated particularly starkly with respect to the waiver exception to the FSIA. 28 U.S.C. § 1605(a)(1) permits a waiver whenever a foreign state has waived its immunity either explicitly or by implication. The "implied waiver" issue has been broadly litigated in both the commercial and the human rights context. *See, e.g.,* Maritime Int'l Nominees Establishment v. Republic of Guinea, 693 F.2d 1094 (D.C. Cir. 1982), *cert. denied*, 464 U.S. 815 (1983); Smith v. Socialist People's Libyan Arab Jamahiriya, 101 F.3d 239 (2d Cir. 1996), *cert. denied*, 520 U.S. 1204 (1997). With respect to both fields, the general rule has been that implied waivers are disfavored. Accordingly, in response to recent egregious cases of terrorism and extra-judicial killing, Congress has been motivated to enact explicit abrogations of foreign sovereign immunity for suits

> in which money damages are sought against a foreign state for personal injury or death that was caused by an act of torture, extrajudicial killing, aircraft sabotage, hostage taking, or the provision of material support or resources ... for such an act if such act or provision of material support is engaged in by an official, employee, or agent of such foreign state while acting within the scope of his or her office, employment, or agency.

28 U.S.C. § 1605(a)(7) (1996). In addition, section 1605(a)(7) imposes the requirements that: (1) the U.S. must have

The increasingly close intertwining and transformation of public and private helps to explain the most recent developments in foreign sovereign immunity law.[71] As I have recounted elsewhere, following the FSIA's enactment in the mid 1970s, transnational commercial litigation exploded in United States courts.[72] As decisions such as *Weltover* reveal, even nations acting out of strong sovereign motivation have been increasingly subjected to suit for their marketplace actions, forcing federal courts to develop techniques for adjudicating business suits brought by individuals and private entities against foreign governments. As the courts' competence and comfort level with these cases has grown, they have proven less diffident about adjudication.

Over time, it has become inevitable that the resurgence of transnational *private* law litigation would force reevaluation of the comity, separation of powers, and incompetence rationales for judicial abstention in transnational *public* law cases. As noted in Chapter III, the question began to arise: "[I]f contracts, why not torture?" If American courts could subject the commercial conduct of foreign sovereigns to legal scrutiny without offending comity, separation of powers, or exceeding their judicial competence, why should those same factors immunize those sovereigns from judicial examination of their egregious public behavior? Such thinking helps explain why transnational public law cases now regularly vie with commercial cases to generate new interpretations of the American law of foreign sovereignty, with regard to extraterritoriality,[73]

designated the foreign state as a state sponsor of terrorism pursuant to section 6(j) of the Export Administration Act of 1979; (2) the act must have occurred outside the foreign state; and (3) the claimants and victims must have been U.S. nationals at the time the acts occurred. *Id.* § 1605(a)(7)(A)–(B).

**71.** For a particularly graphic example of the intertwining of public and private, see Alejandre v. Republic of Cuba, 996 F.Supp. 1239 (S.D. Fla. 1997), where the families of four civilians shot down in international airspace won a default judgment of more than $187 million against the Cuban Air Force and Government, but failed to collect on that judgment. On appeal, the U.S. Court of Appeals for the Eleventh Circuit refused to allow the plaintiffs to garnish debts owned by American telecommunications companies against a Cuban governmental telephone service provider to satisfy the default judgment against Cuba. *See*

Alejandre v. Telefonica Larga Distancia de Puerto Rico, Inc., 183 F.3d 1277 (11th Cir. 1999). The appeals court ruled that the telephone company's property in the United States was immune from garnishment under the FSIA, because the company had separate juridical status from Cuba, and thus the debts owed to that company did not constitute commercial property owned by an instrumentality of a foreign state exempt from foreign sovereign immunity. Ironically, despite having won the default judgment by a holding of liability under the terrorism exception to the FSIA, the plaintiffs could not then collect that judgment from commercial assets that were found to be insufficiently sovereign to be vulnerable to post-judgment attachment.

**72.** *See* Koh, *supra* note 38, at 2365–66.

**73.** Sale v. Haitian Centers Council, 509 U.S. 155 (1993).

norms of treaty interpretation,[74] foreign sovereign immunity,[75] and the act of state doctrine.[76]

This link between public and private becomes even clearer when one turns to an examination of procedural rules applied in both kinds of cases. For as we shall see, procedural rules developed with regard to such doctrines as *forum non conveniens* or enforcement of judgments in a transnational commercial context can quickly migrate into the human rights context and back again. It is to these "trans-substantive" federal rules of transnational civil procedure that the next chapters now turn.

**74.** *See, e.g.*, United States v. Alvarez–Machain, 504 U.S. 655 (1992).

**75.** *See, e.g.*, Argentine Republic v. Amerada Hess Shipping Corp., 488 U.S. 428 (1998); Smith v. Socialist People's Libyan Arab Jamahiriya, 101 F.3d 239 (2d Cir. 1996), *cert. denied* 520 U.S. 1204 (1997).

**76.** Republic of the Philippines v. Marcos, 862 F.2d 1355, 1360–61 (9th Cir. 1988) (*en banc*).

*

# PART THREE
## THE FEDERAL RULES OF TRANSNATIONAL CIVIL PROCEDURE
## CHAPTER VII

### JURISDICTION TO ADJUDICATE

Thus far, this book has pursued two persistent themes: first, the link between the public and the private in the litigation of international business cases before the United States Supreme Court; and second, the growing dominance of separation of powers, uniformity, and private autonomy concerns over the themes of international comity, national sovereignty, and consistency with international law. The last three chapters demonstrated these themes particularly with respect to foreign sovereignty issues before the U.S. courts, and closed by showing how the transnational litigation of public law cases—particularly in the area of international human rights—has influenced the law governing the resolution of international business disputes.

The next six chapters will demonstrate how these themes run as well through the evolving *procedural* doctrines that govern all transnational civil suits that are conducted in United States courts: what I have called the *Federal Rules of Transnational Civil Procedure*. To test this argument, one must first understand the five phases of any transnational civil lawsuit in a U.S. Court:

1. *Jurisdiction to Adjudicate*, which divides into both jurisdiction over the subject matter ("subject matter jurisdiction") and jurisdiction over the parties to the suit ("personal jurisdiction");

2. *Venue* or Choice of Forum, which in the commercial setting divides into an *ex ante* question—have the parties previously signed a forum-selection clause choosing a forum for a prospective lawsuit, and if so, what effect should be given to it?—and an *ex post* question: if not, under what circumstances should the suit be dismissed on grounds of *forum non conveniens*, that is, because a balancing of public and private interest factors

suggest that the U.S. court is an inconvenient forum to hear the case?

3. *Service of Process*: an inquiry into whether the court has perfected its personal jurisdiction over the defendant by properly serving him with notification of the lawsuit;

4. *Taking of Evidence*, particularly in the pretrial (or discovery) phase of the suit; and finally the

5. *Recognition and Enforcement* of foreign judgments, decrees, and arbitral awards.

After reviewing the history and sources of transnational procedure, this chapter addresses the first subject, jurisdiction, and the next four chapters address venue, service of process, discovery, and recognition and enforcement of judgments and arbitral awards.[1]

## A. History and Sources of Transnational Procedure

Before describing these doctrines in greater detail, let me first sketch the working principles that provide the sources of civil procedure in American commercial litigation. In the American domestic commercial setting, highly articulated doctrines already exist to govern subject matter and personal jurisdiction, venue, service of process, pretrial discovery, and the recognition and enforcement of judgments, decrees, and arbitral awards. These procedural doctrines, which comprise the introductory American law course on Civil Procedure, derive principally from four sources: the Constitution, statutes, the Federal Rules of Civil Procedure, and judge-made common law.[2]

---

**1.** In choosing to focus in on these five procedural topics, I have deliberately excluded several other subjects, which have been covered elsewhere in far more detail than could be provided here. *See generally* Andreas Lowenfeld, *International Litigation and the Quest for Reasonableness*, 245 RECUEIL DES COURS 9 (2008). For a fine discussion of choice of law, see Lea Brilmayer, *The Role of Substantive and Choice of Law Policies in the Formation and Application of Choice of Law Rules*, 252 RECUEIL DES COURS 19 (1995). Similarly, provisional relief in transnational litigation has received excellent analysis in Lawrence Collins, *Provisional and Protective Measures in International Litigation*, 234 RECUEIL DES COURS 19 (1992). *See also* George Bermann, *Provisional Relief in Transna-*

*tional Litigation*, 35 COLUM. J. TRANSNAT'L L. 553 (1997). Nor do I address antisuit injunctions or parallel proceedings. For a useful biography, see Douglas Reichert, *Provisional Remedies in International Litigation: A Comprehensive Bibliography*, 19 INT'L LAW. 1429 (1985).

**2.** For excellent "hornbook" surveys of the field, see JAMES FLEMING JR., GEOFFREY C. HAZARD, JR. & JOHN LEUBSDORF, CIVIL PROCEDURE (4th ed. 1992); JACK FRIEDENTHAL, MARY KAY KANE & ARTHUR MILLER, CIVIL PROCEDURE (4th ed. 2005). For an introduction aimed at both a common law and civil law audience, see GEOFFREY C. HAZARD, JR. & MICHELE TARUFFO, AMERICAN CIVIL PROCEDURE: AN INTRODUCTION (1993).

The United States Constitution declares in Article III that "the federal judicial power of the United States" shall extend to the United States Supreme Court and its inferior federal courts and further delineates which cases or controversies the federal courts may permissibly hear. In the Fifth Amendment, which binds the national government, and the Fourteenth Amendment, which binds the several states, the Constitution further requires that litigants who sue in our courts may not "be deprived of life, liberty, or property, without due process of law," that is, treatment that is both substantively and procedurally fair.

Statutes of the United States, enacted by Congress and the President, comprise a second, subordinate source of federal procedural law. As we have seen, a number of statutes enacted by Congress have been specifically directed toward international business problems, with significant procedural dimensions, the most prominent being the Foreign Sovereign Immunities Act (FSIA) of 1976.

A third source of transnational procedural rules are the uniform "Federal Rules," such as the Federal Rules of Civil Procedure (hereafter indicated with capitalization), which derive their authority from the Rules Enabling Act of 1934.[3] That statute grants the Supreme Court formal authority to make uniform rules regarding practice and procedure in the federal courts, so long as those rules abridge no substantive rights. These Federal Rules issue from an elaborate process. They are drafted by a Reporter (usually an academician) supported by an Advisory Committee consisting of academics, practitioners and judges, then are passed on to the Judicial Conference of the United States, then on to the Supreme Court. The Court generally holds no hearing, proceeding, or argument, but nevertheless reviews those rules before transmitting them on to Congress, which must act affirmatively by statute to stop them from going taking effect. Federal Rules are "transsubstantive," inasmuch as they apply equally to cases involving different subject matters—contracts, torts, property, corporations—as well as to cases involving both private and public parties.[4] Although the Federal Rules of Civil Procedure were originally drafted with a predominant focus on domestic litigation, as we shall see, over time, they have increasingly adjusted to address the peculiar problems and challenges of transborder commercial litigation.

---

**3.**   28 U.S.C. § 2072 (1996).

**4.**   Robert Cover, *For James Wm. Moore: Some Reflections on a Reading of the Rules*, 84 YALE L.J. 718, 718 (1975).

Fourth, there are judge-made federal common law rules of procedure, which courts make by construing written rules in light of the Due Process clauses and by filling gaps in existing procedural law.[5] As we saw in Chapter V, the Supreme Court in *Sabbatino*[6] recognized a zone of specialized federal common law for matters affecting the foreign relations of the United States. Over time, decisions of the U.S. Supreme Court and the lower courts have, on a case-by-case basis, developed unwritten rules of federal common law to promote national uniformity, party autonomy, and international comity in international business cases. We have already examined a number of these earlier in this volume, for example, the statutory cases addressing the presumption against extraterritoriality; the *Timberlane* interest-balancing approach to comity in legislative jurisdiction, the act of state doctrine, and the foreign sovereign compulsion defense.[7] As we shall see in the chapters ahead, some of these unwritten court-made rules have recently even acquired such prominence as to provoke changes in the formal written Federal Rules of Civil Procedure, particularly with respect to Federal Rule 4, which governs notice.

Over the last three decades, these rules have been increasingly modified to deal with the unique problems of international civil litigation. In this process, a fifth body of law has proliferated to create a unique set of procedural rules for transnational cases: namely, treaties of the United States that govern transnational procedural questions. These treaties, which have resulted largely through the work of the Hague Conference on Private International Law, now include the Hague Service and Evidence Conventions, the New York Convention on the Enforcement of Arbitral Awards, and the Hague Convention on Choice of Court Agreements.[8] Moreover, the first three of these treaties have recently been construed by the Supreme Court in important interpretive decisions, which will be discussed in future chapters.[9]

---

**5.** *See generally* Stephen B. Burbank, *The Reluctant Partner: Making Procedural Law for International Civil Litigation*, 57 L. & CONTEMP. PROBS. 103, 125–27 (2008).

**6.** *Banco Nacional de Cuba v. Sabbatino*, 376 U.S. 398, 425 (1964).

**7.** *See* Louis Henkin, *International Law as Law in the United States*, 82 MICH. L. REV. 1555, 1563 n.32 (1984) (suggesting that certain judge-made rules in international relations regarding the judicial function may even "be constitutionally immune from congressional regulation").

**8.** For a description of how the Hague Conference has promoted the development of these treaties, see generally Peter Pfund, *The Progressive Development of Private International Law: The International Process and the United States Approach*, 249 RECUEIL DES COURS 21 (2008).

**9.** Volkswagenwerk Aktiengesellschaft v. Schlunk, 486 U.S. 694 (1988) (construing Hague Service Convention); Societe Nationale Industrielle Aerospat-

Several commentators have questioned whether the subject of international civil litigation possesses any thematic integrity. One commentator has concluded, for example, that although "this area of law is growing apace, it remains a definition and a category without a theory," resulting in a "seemingly random hodgepodge of doctrines and topics connected as a field only by a common 'international' or 'foreign element.' "[10] Yet I will argue that, in fact, these doctrinal areas do reflect common themes, namely the interplay among the five core judicial concerns identified in earlier chapters. These decisions particularly emphasize separation of powers and desires to promote uniformity of procedural rules and deference to party autonomy in transnational business decisions, and only to lesser extent do they focus on the countervailing themes of national sovereignty and comity. With this background, let us now turn to the topic of Jurisdiction to Adjudicate.

# B. Jurisdiction to Adjudicate

Jurisdiction to Adjudicate divides into two issues, subject matter jurisdiction and personal jurisdiction. Both concern issues of power and authority, not discretion.[11] The subject matter jurisdiction inquiry asks: do both Constitution and statutes of the United States confirm that this is the kind of case that a federal court is authorized to hear? The personal jurisdiction inquiry asks: do both the Constitution and statutes of the United States confirm that this court may constitutionally bind this defendant and his property with its judgment?

---

iale v. United States District Court, 482 U.S. 522 (1987) (construing Hague Evidence Convention); Mitsubishi v. Soler Chrysler–Plymouth, Inc. 473 U.S. 614 (1985) (construing New York Convention on Enforcement of Arbitral Awards).

**10.** Anne–Marie Slaughter Burley, *International Law and International Relations Theory: A Dual Agenda*, 87 AM. J. INT'L L. 205, 230 (1993). *See also* Stephen B. Burbank, *The World in Our Courts*, 89 MICH. L. REV. 1456, 1459 (1991) ("[I]nternational civil litigation [is] part of a process of cross-fertilization in which (1) doctrine and techniques developed in the context of domestic cases are brought to bear on problems presented in international litigation, and (2) the increasingly international dimen-

sions of litigation in our courts prompt changes in doctrine and techniques, which are then applied in domestic cases.").

**11.** In this respect, jurisdiction is distinguishable from four other issues of justiciability that often arise in a U.S. court (and which are discussed in Chapters V and VI, *supra*): should the court refuse to hear the case because it presents (1) a political, and not a legal, question; (2) an act of State by a recognized foreign sovereign fully executed within its own territory; (3) a private act compelled by the foreign government (foreign sovereign compulsion); or (4) a violation of comity, or manifest lack of respect for the prerogatives of a foreign sovereign within its own territory?

## 1. Subject Matter Jurisdiction

In transnational cases, the question of subject matter jurisdiction—the court's power to hear a particular type of cases—has tended to be uncontroversial. To the extent that such cases are heard in state court, the issue hardly arises, because such courts exercise general subject matter jurisdiction. A foremost canon of U.S. procedural law is that the federal courts are courts of limited subject matter jurisdiction.[12] Such courts may only hear those cases that fall within the "federal judicial power of the United States" pursuant to Article III of the U.S. Constitution and that Congress has authorized them to hear by a jurisdictional statute in Title 28, the judicial chapter of the United States Code.

Most transnational cases fall under one of four statutory provisions: Section 1330, which as we saw in the last chapter gives federal courts exclusive jurisdiction to hear suits brought against foreign sovereigns under the Foreign Sovereign Immunities Act;[13] section 1331, which gives federal courts jurisdiction to hear cases "arising under" so-called "federal questions": the statutes, treaties, and Constitution of the United States;[14] and section 1332, which authorizes federal courts to hear "diversity cases," or suits between citizens of different states, or between citizens of the United States and aliens, on private law matters in which the amount in controversy exceeds $75,000, an amount easily satisfied in almost any garden-variety contract or tort case.[15] In transnational public law cases, aliens have usually sued under the Alien Tort Claims Act, section 1350, which grants rights to aliens to sue for "torts only in violation of the law of nations," which the courts have deemed to be federal questions in the Article III sense.[16]

**12.** Capron v. Van Noorden, 6 U.S. (2 Cranch) 126 (1804).

**13.** 28 U.S.C. § 1330 was the basis for jurisdiction in the *Amerada Hess, Weltover,* and *Nelson* cases discussed in Chapter VI.

**14.** 28 U.S.C. § 1331 was a basis for federal jurisdiction in the antitrust and securities cases that were discussed in Chapter IV. As Justice Scalia pointed out in his dissent in *Hartford Fire Insurance,* once a defendant's alleged conduct was deemed to fall within the prescriptive territorial jurisdiction of the Sherman Act, a suit against that defendant also presumptively fell within the subject matter jurisdiction of a federal

court. *See* 509 U.S. at 812–13 (Scalia, J., dissenting).

**15.** Diversity cases made up more than 55,000 of the new cases filed in federal district courts in fiscal year 2003, representing more than 20% of the new federal cases filed during that year. Although federal diversity jurisdiction ostensibly exists to protect non-residents, proposals to reduce the workload of the federal courts by curtailing or abolishing diversity jurisdiction have been urged upon (and rejected by) Congress since the 1920s. *See* Jack Friedenthal, Mary Kay Kane & Arthur Miller, supra note 2, at 26 n.8.

**16.** 28 U.S.C. § 1350 (2008). ATCA plaintiffs usually also involve the Tor-

The only real subject matter jurisdiction barrier posed in transnational cases is the absence of diversity jurisdiction under Article III or 28 U.S.C. § 1332, when one alien seeks to sue another alien in federal court on a private cause of action.[17] But such circumstances are rare, given that in most transnational cases, the alien plaintiff who seeks a federal forum can find a federal statute to cite in his complaint.[18] Moreover, as we saw in Chapter VI, in *Verlinden v. Central Bank of Nigeria*[19], the Supreme Court held that aliens may sue foreign sovereign entities in United States, citing the Foreign Sovereign Immunities Act as their basis for Article III federal question jurisdiction.[20] Nor, historically, has there been any jurisdictional barrier to aliens bringing commercial actions against other aliens in the courts of the several states.

## 2. Personal Jurisdiction

The more difficult question, then, is personal jurisdiction: whether the court may bind the defendant and his property with its judgment? That question in turn breaks into questions of power and notice, both of which raise the constitutional question whether the court has asserted its authority in a manner that has afforded the defendant due process of law. As stated in the Supreme Court's

---

ture Victim Protection Act, 28 U.S.C. § 1350a (2008). *See generally* Filártiga v. Peña–Irala, 630 F.2d 876 (2d Cir. 1980) and its progeny, discussed in Chapter III, *supra*.

**17.** *See, e.g.*, Arai v. Tachibana, 778 F.Supp. 1535 (D. Haw. 1991) (denying federal jurisdiction in suits between aliens). In 1988, Congress amended section 1332 to authorize diversity jurisdiction in suits in which an alien is admitted to permanent residence in the United States. In Singh v. Daimler–Benz, 9 F.3d 303 (3d Cir. 1993), the Third Circuit recently held that a permanent resident alien could sue a German automobile manufacturer in a case where a U.S. citizen was also party to the action. For a discussion of the historical origins and contemporary arguments regarding alienage, as opposed to diversity, jurisdiction, see generally Kevin Johnson, *Why Alienage Jurisdiction? Historical Foundations*

*and Modern Justifications for Federal Jurisdiction Over Disputes Involving Noncitizens*, 21 YALE J. INT'L L. 1 (1996).

**18.** *See, e.g.*, 15 U.S.C. § 77v (2008) (securities); 28 U.S.C. §§ 1331 (federal questions), 1333 (admiralty, maritime and prize), 1334 (bankruptcy), 1337 (antitrust), 1338 (patent, copyright, and trademark), 1343 (civil rights), 1345–46 (cases in which the U.S. government is a plaintiff or a defendant).

**19.** 461 U.S. 480 (1983).

**20.** As Chief Justice Burger wrote in *Verlinden*, the FSIA's "jurisdictional grant is within the bounds of Article III, since every action against a foreign sovereign necessarily involves application of a body of substantive federal law, and accordingly 'arise under' federal law, within the meaning of Article III." 461 U.S. at 497. *See, e.g.*, Filártiga v. Peña–Irala, 630 F.2d 876 (2d Cir. 1980).

landmark opinion in *International Shoe Co. v. Washington*,[21] the power issue raises a question of substantive fairness. Assuming that Congress or a state legislature has attempted to exercise power over an extraterritorial defendant by enacting a "long-arm statute," do the defendant's actions vis-à-vis the forum constitute volitional "minimum contacts" between the defendant and the forum State, "such that the exercise of jurisdiction does not offend traditional notions of fair play and substantive justice"[22] embodied in the Due Process Clauses of the Fifth Amendment (with regard to the federal court's action) and the Fourteenth Amendment (with regard to the state court's action)? The notice question, to which we will return toward the end of this chapter, raises a subsequent issue of procedural fairness: even assuming that judicial power exists over a defendant, has the plaintiff perfected that power by following proper procedures specified in state, federal, statutory, or treaty law to give the defendant reasonable notice and opportunity to be heard before a judgment is entered?

The Supreme Court's treatment of the power question in international business cases reflects a century-long constitutional evolution from rigid test based on *territoriality* to a more flexible standard based on fairness measured by "contacts." The original concept, stated in the famous case of *Pennoyer v. Neff*,[23] understood that a state court lacked authority to exercise power over a defendant unless he was physically present in the forum's territory at the time the lawsuit began. This territoriality principle, which *Pennoyer* explicitly derived from rules of public law, was designed to protect comity and sovereignty, by ensuring that one state did not improvidently extend its judicial arm into the territory of another.[24] Moreover, *Pennoyer* expressly linked the common-law territorial principle of personal adjudication to two constitutional concepts: the procedural concept of due process and the structural concept of full faith and credit. Justice Field, writing for the Court, reasoned that a judgment rendered against someone who was present in the territory was both substantively fair to the individual and deserving of enforcement—via the interstate comity mandat-

21. 326 U.S. 310 (1945).
22. *Id.* at 316 (citations omitted).
23. 95 U.S. (5 Otto) 714 (1877).
24. *See id.* at 722 (Field, J.) (*Pennoyer*'s territorial rule "would seem to follow from two well-established principles of public law respecting the jurisdiction of an independent State over persons and property.... One of these principles is, that every State possesses exclusive jurisdiction and sovereignty over persons and property within its territory.... The other principle of public law referred to follows from the one mentioned; that is, that no State can exercise direct jurisdiction and authority over persons and property without its territory.").

ed by the Full Faith and Credit Clause of the Constitution—in all other states of the United States.

Ironically, *Pennoyer*'s notion of physical presence was antiquated even when written. As Professor Juenger has noted, "a quarter of a century before *Pennoyer*, tradition-bound England had enacted the Common Law Procedure Act, which permitted service abroad and thereby authorized the very 'extraterritoriality' Justice Field condemned."[25] As national business activities of corporations proliferated, U.S. courts were inevitably forced to develop a set of proxies for a defendant's physical presence in the forum to reach parties outside the forum. In *Blackmer v. United States*,[26] for example, the Supreme Court upheld a subpoena served upon a nonresident American citizen in France, reasoning that American citizenship could serve as a proxy for territorial presence under such circumstances.[27] Over time, other such proxies as domicile,[28] place of incorporation, registration to do business or actually "doing business" in the forum,[29] acts within the forum by an alter ego or agent (from which the courts implied consent),[30] and the presence of the defendant's tangible and intangible property within the forum all came to serve as bases for judgments issued by various states against extraterritorial defendants. These judgments were in turn given full faith and credit in other states of the U.S. as consistent with constitutional guarantees of due process.

It soon became apparent that all of these proxy criteria were at best placeholders for a more fundamental notion of fairness. In its famous 1945 decision in *International Shoe Co. v. Washington*,[31] the Supreme Court redefined the constitutional standard of power into whether the defendant has sufficiently volitional "minimum contacts" with the forum as to render it fair to subject him to suit

---

**25.** Friedrich Juenger, *Judicial Jurisdiction in the United States and the European Communities: A Comparison*, 82 MICH. L. REV. 1195, 1197 (1984).

**26.** 284 U.S. 421 (1932).

**27.** Upon discovery of the Teapot Dome scandal in 1923, Blackmer, one of the Americans involved fled to France. To compel his testimony in the subsequent criminal proceedings, Congress passed a law authorizing the federal district courts to compel the attendance of American witnesses abroad in connection with domestic criminal proceedings. When Blackmer failed to respond to a subpoena, he was held in contempt. The Supreme Court affirmed, reasoning that "[t]he jurisdiction of the United States over its absent citizen, so far as the binding effect of its legislation is concerned, is a jurisdiction in personam, as he is personally bound to take notice of the laws that are applicable to him and to obey them." 284 U.S. 421, 438 (1932).

**28.** *See, e.g.*, Milliken v. Meyer, 311 U.S. 457, 462–63 (1940).

**29.** *See, e.g.*, Philadelphia and Reading Ry. Co. v. McKibbin, 243 U.S. 264, 265 (1917).

**30.** *See, e.g.*, Saint Clair v. Cox, 106 U.S. 350, 356 (1882); Hargrave v. Fibreboard Corp., 710 F.2d 1154 (5th Cir. 1983).

**31.** 326 U.S. 310 (1945).

there for his business activities. Over time, the Court has massaged that standard into a two-part inquiry regarding: first, *purposeful availment*: whether the defendant's voluntary contacts with the forum sufficiently resemble consent as to authorize the forum's exercise of sovereignty over him; and second, *reasonableness*, whether, after balancing the interests of the plaintiff, defendant, and the state, it is reasonable to subject the defendant to suit there. The Court recently stated the test this way:

> Once it has been decided that a defendant purposefully established minimum contacts within the forum State, these contacts may be considered in light of other factors to determine whether the assertion of personal jurisdiction would comport with fair play and substantial justice.... Thus courts in appropriate case[s] may evaluate the burden on the defendant, the forum State's interest in adjudicating the dispute, the plaintiff's interest in obtaining convenient and effective relief, the interstate judicial system's interest in obtaining the most efficient resolution of controversies, and the shared interest of the several States in furthering substantive social policies....
> [W]here a defendant who purposefully has directed his activities at forum residents seeks to defeat jurisdiction, he must present a compelling case that the presence of some other considerations would render jurisdiction unreasonable.[32]

This two-tiered analysis of judicial power based on purposeful contacts and a discretionary balancing of conveniences carries overtones of *Timberlane's* bifurcation of prescriptive jurisdiction into effects and comity based on interest-balancing. Yet as Justice Scalia pointed out in *Weltover*, the two standards differ, inasmuch as the power prong of the personal jurisdiction test requires only minimum contacts, while the *Timberlane* test for subject matter and prescriptive jurisdiction requires reasonably foreseeable, direct, and substantial effects.[33]

---

**32.** *See* Burger King Corp. v. Rudzewicz, 471 U.S. 462, 478 (1985) (citations and quotation marks omitted).

**33.** In *Weltover*, discussed in Chapter VI, the Court held that under the FSIA's commercial activity exception, a court could hold a foreign sovereign defendant liable for refusal to repay on a bond because that act had a direct effect in the United States. The Court rejected the notion that the commercial activity exception "contains any unexpressed requirement of 'substantiality' or 'foreseeability.'" 504 U.S. at 618. Moreover, the Court found that "[b]y issuing negotiable debt instruments denominated in United States dollars and payable in New York and by appointing a financial agent in that city, Argentina purposefully avail[ed] itself of the privilege of conducting activities within the United States." *Id.* at 619–20 (citations and quotation marks omitted). This rendered consistent with the Due Process clause of the Fifth Amendment an assertion of personal jurisdiction over Argentina via the statutory exception. But significantly, the Court did not go on to balance

In 1977, in *Shaffer v. Heitner*, the Court invalidated *Pennoyer*'s approval of asserting *in rem* or *quasi in rem* jurisdiction over a nonresident based solely on the presence of his property within the territory.[34] The Court declared that henceforth, "all assertions of state-court jurisdiction must be evaluated according to the standards set forth in *International Shoe* and its progeny."[35] "To the extent that [*Pennoyer* and its progeny] are inconsistent with this standard," the Court said, "those cases are overruled."[36] But whether the post-*International Shoe* standards should give greater emphasis to contacts or convenience has remained subject to extensive debate.

On examination, by focusing first on implied consent, the purposeful availment requirement reflects concerns about party autonomy and the limits of state sovereignty. By contrast, the second stage—the reasonableness requirement—seeks to balance concerns about fairness to the individuals affected with comity toward other states of the Union and the interstate judicial system, which also have interests in the dispute. Both requirements have been easily satisfied in cases where the defendant voluntarily makes a general appearance to defend, or in transnational contract cases, where the defendant has signed a forum-selection clause previously agreeing to be sued somewhere in United States. Out of deference to party autonomy, the courts have concluded that such a signature ensures both purposeful availment and the reasonableness of exercising power over him.[37] But more difficult cases have arisen when a transnational business commits acts or produces a product that ultimately causes a tort in a jurisdiction in which it does not do business. In such cases, one coalition of Justices, led until recently by Justice White, has emphasized state power over defendant's convenience, asserting that

> [e]ven if the defendant would suffer minimal or no inconvenience from being forced to litigate before the tribunals of another State; even if the forum State has a strong interest in applying its law to the controversy; even if the forum State is the most convenient location for litigation, the Due Process Clause, acting as an instrument of interstate federalism, may

conveniences and analyze the *reasonableness* of asserting personal jurisdiction over Argentina. Most likely, the Court simply assumed the reasonableness of taking jurisdiction, in effect reading Argentina's commercial acts as amounting to implied consent to suit on those acts in the United States.

**34.** 433 U.S. 186 (1977).

**35.** *Id.* at 212.

**36.** *Id.* at 212 n.39.

**37.** *See, e.g.,* Burger King Corp. v. Rudzewicz, 471 U.S. 462 (1985); M/S

sometimes act to divest the State of its power to render a valid judgment.[38]

A second coalition, which (until their retirement) included Justices Brennan, Marshall and Blackmun, emphasized convenience over state sovereignty. This group argued that

> [t]he clear focus in *International Shoe* was on fairness and reasonableness ... The Court specifically declined to establish a mechanical test based on the quantum of contacts between a State and the defendant.... The existence of contacts, so long as there were some, was merely one way of giving content to the determination of fairness and reasonableness.[39]

## a.  COMPARATIVE JUDICIAL JURISDICTION

At this point, it becomes useful to compare the U.S. law of judicial jurisdiction with the emerging federal law of the European Union. The comparison once again reveals the intermingling of public and private. For although public international law has historically dealt with the question of jurisdiction to adjudicate only in government-initiated actions, as transnational private civil litigation has increasingly extended judicial jurisdiction extraterritorially, the issues of comity, sovereignty, and separation of powers discussed earlier in the context of prescriptive jurisdiction have again recurred.[40]

In the same way as the common law has treated physical presence as the touchstone of its jurisdictional tradition, the civil law tradition has traditionally followed the rule of *actor sequitur forum rei*, i.e., that the plaintiff follows the defendant to the forum of the defendant's domicile.[41] The rule has varied, however, with "differences among civil-law countries [being] as great as differences between given civil-law and common-law countries."[42] Thus, jurisdictional law has focused in the Netherlands, France, and

Bremen v. Zapata Off–Shore Co., 407 U.S. 1 (1972).

**38.**  World–Wide Volkswagen Corp. v. Woodson, 444 U.S. 286, 294 (1980).

**39.**  *Id.* at 307 (Brennan, J., dissenting).

**40.**  For a discussion of judicial jurisdiction under international law in the nineteenth century, see Gary Born, *Reflections on Judicial Jurisdiction in International Cases*, 17 GA. J. INT'L AND COMP. L. 1 (1987). For discussions of the modern state of the subject, see RESTATEMENT (THIRD) OF THE FOREIGN RELATIONS LAW OF THE UNITED STATES §§ 421–23

(1986); Andrew Strauss, *Beyond National Law: The Neglected Role of the International Law of Personal Jurisdiction in Domestic Courts*, 36 HARV. INT'L L.J. 373 (1995).

**41.**  *See* Gerhard Walter and Rikke Dalsgaard, *The Civil Law Approach*, in TRANSNATIONAL TORT LITIGATION: JURISDICTIONAL PRINCIPLES 41, 42 (Campbell McLachlan & Peter Edward Nygh, eds., 1996).

**42.**  Henry de Vries and Andreas Lowenfeld, *Jurisdiction in Personal Actions—A Comparison of Civil Law Views*, 44 IOWA L. REV. 306, 344 (1959).

Switzerland upon the defendant's domicile,[43] in Germany upon the defendant's domicile and property, and in France on the plaintiff's nationality.[44] As in the United States, each of these state rules has raised concerns regarding jurisdictional chauvinism. For example, section 23 of the German Civil Code authorizes *in personam* jurisdiction over any nonresident defendant who owns assets in Germany; going beyond even *Pennoyer*, it requires no prior attachment[45]— nor that the size of the judgment be limited to the value of the property.[46] Article 14 of the French Civil Code enables French plaintiffs to sue anyone in French courts based on the *plaintiffs'* nationality, without regard to whether the defendants or the dispute has any connection to France.[47] Moreover, most continental European countries do not recognize the Anglo–American doctrine of *forum non conveniens*, thus limiting the discretion of their courts to decline jurisdiction over suits that are brought in plainly inconvenient fora or with the prime goal of harassing the defendant.[48]

Although the architects of the European Communities saw the need to reconcile these competing rules and to curb unreasonable assertions of member-state jurisdiction, the drafters of the Treaty of Rome could not agree upon precise analogs to due process and full faith and credit. The Treaty of Rome's most pertinent provision, Article 220, instead urged members states to negotiate "with a view to securing for the benefits of their nationals ... the

---

**43.** *See, e.g.*, Article 59 of the Swiss Federal Constitution, which states that ordinarily a personal action against a Swiss domiciliary can only be brought in the canton in which the defendant is domiciled. Fleiner–Giacometti, *Schweizerisches Bundesstaatsrecht* 861 (1949, reprinted 1969).

**44.** *See* Juenger, *supra* note 25, at 1204.

**45.** Germany, Code of Civil Procedure (Zivilprozessordnung) § 23 ("Actions pertaining to property against a person having no domicile in the interior may be brought before a court in whose district property of the defendant is situated, or the subject of the action is situated."); de Vries & Lowenfeld, *supra* note 42 at 332–34.

**46.** Apparently, under a parallel provision of Austrian law, an Austrian court took jurisdiction in a paternity suit over the French Olympic skier, Jean–Claude Killy, based on the fact that when departing from Austria, he had left a piece of underwear behind!

*See* RUDOLF SCHLESINGER, HANS BAADE, MIRJAN DAMASKA AND PETER HERZOG, COMPARATIVE LAW: CASES, TEXT, MATERIALS 395 n.87a (5th ed. 1988).

**47.** *See also* de Vries and Lowenfeld, *supra* note 42, at 316–30.

**48.** For a decision explicitly declining to introduce *forum non conveniens* into German law, see L.G. Muenchen I, decision of Nov. 25, 1982, 4 IPRax 318 (1984), *aff'd*, O.L.G. Muenchen, decision of June 22, 1983, 4 IPRax 319 (1984). *See generally* P. Schlosser, *Report on the Convention on the Association of the Kingdom of Denmark, Ireland and the United Kingdom of Great Britain and Northern Ireland to the Convention on Jurisdiction and the Enforcement of Judgments in Civil and Commercial Matters and to the Protocol on its Interpretation by the Court of Justice*, 22 O.J. EUR. COMM. (No. C 59) 71, 97 (Mar. 5, 1979); Richard Fentiman, *Jurisdiction, Discretion and the Brussels Convention*, 26 CORNELL INT'L L.J. 59 (1993). For further discussion, see Chapter VIII, regarding Venue.

simplification of formalities governing the reciprocal recognition and enforcement of judgments...."[49] The Committee of Experts appointed under this article then used its mandate to create a detailed Brussels Convention on Jurisdiction and Recognition of Judgments in Civil and Commercial Matters.[50] The Brussels Convention was soon closely emulated by the Lugano Convention, the analog for the European Free Trade Area (EFTA) states.[51]

Professor Juenger has succinctly summarized the Brussels Convention's key elements as follows:

1.   The courts at the defendant's domicile (or, in the case of an enterprise, its principal place of business) have general jurisdiction;

2.   Enterprises that maintain a branch or other establishment in a member state can be sued there on causes of action arising out of these local operations;

3.   Limited personal jurisdiction is provided for contract and tort actions;

4.   There is exclusive local jurisdiction in actions concerning real property, the internal affairs of corporations and other associations, and rights recorded in public registers.

5.   Certain classes of plaintiffs, *i.e.* consumers, policyholders and support claimants, are accorded the jurisdictional privilege to litigate in the member state in which they are domiciled;

6.   Special rules liberally authorize joining and impleading parties not otherwise subject to the jurisdiction of the court in which the principal action is pending;

7.   By means of forum-selection clauses the parties can stipulate to the jurisdiction of member state courts.[52]

**49.** Treaty Establishing the European Economic Community, Mar. 25, 1957, 298 U.N.T.S. 11 (entered into force Jan. 1, 1958).

**50.** Sept. 27, 1968, 15 O.J. Eur. Comm. (No. L 299) 32 (entered into force Feb. 1, 1973), *reprinted in* 29 INT'L LEG. MATS. 1417 (Dec. 31, 1972) [hereafter *Brussels Convention*]. For a current version, see EC 33 O.J.C. 189, 28 July 1990.

**51.** Sept. 16, 1988, EC O.J. Eur. Comm. (No. L 319) 9, Nov. 25, 1988 (entered into force Feb. 1, 1973), reprinted in 28 INT'L LEG. MATS. 620 (1989)

[hereafter *Lugano Convention*]. The Lugano Convention is a modified version of the Brussels Convention, designed specifically to bridge differences between the EC countries and the EFTA group (Austria, Finland, Iceland, Norway, Sweden, and Switzerland). For a review and analysis of the relationships between the Brussels and Lugan Conventions, see Elizabeth M. McCaffrey, *The Lugano and San Sebastion Conventions: General Effects*, 11 CIV. JUST. Q. 12 (1992).

**52.** *See* Juenger, *supra* note 25, at 1204 (citations omitted).

The Brussels Convention sets forth a limited list of criteria (the "white list") which EU members and their states may use as the basis for extraterritorial jurisdiction.[53] Only such judgments as are rendered on a permitted basis by a given EU member state's national court will be recognized and enforced in another member state according to the "full faith and credit" clause in Title III of the Brussels scheme.[54] Moreover, decisions based on a "black list" of "exorbitant" bases of jurisdiction set forth in Article 3 of the Convention—such as Article 14 of the French Civil Code and Section 23 of the German Civil Code—cannot be enforced against EU domiciliaries.[55]

Thus, the European judicial system now bears certain resemblances to the American jurisdictional system, inasmuch as both permit their member entities to legislate long-arm statutes based on domicile and corporate seat. As in the U.S. after *Shaffer v. Heitner*, the Brussels Convention has largely abolished jurisdiction *in rem*, in the sense of permitting an action to be started against a nonresident based purely on the presence of his property within the forum.[56] Both U.S. law and the Brussels Convention permit jurisdiction based on voluntary appearance or when there is written evidence of express agreement to consent to jurisdiction.[57] Finally, the Brussels Convention also permits its member nations to legislate long-arm statutes based on *forum contractus*, the place of performance of the obligation in question or in the courts of the place where the breach of contract occurred.[58]

In a classic 1966 article, Professors Arthur von Mehren and Donald Trautman suggested a distinction between "general jurisdiction"—when a defendant has sufficient contact with a forum to legitimate the assertion of jurisdiction over him for all matters—and "specific jurisdiction"—when a defendant's contacts suffice to warrant asserting jurisdiction over him only for matters related to that activity with the forum.[59] Applied to the Brussels Convention, this analysis suggests that a defendant's domicile or principal place of business confers "general jurisdiction" upon the jurisdiction of domicile, which allows the defendant to be sued there even on

**53.** *See* Brussels Convention, art. 5.

**54.** *See* Brussels Convention, arts. 25–49.

**55.** *See id.* art. 3 (list of exorbitant jurisdictions).

**56.** *But see id.* art. 5(7) (cargo and freight jurisdiction), 16(1) (immovable property).

**57.** *See* JOSEPH LOOKOFSKY, TRANSNATIONAL LITIGATION AND COMMERCIAL ARBITRA-

TION: A COMPARATIVE ANALYSIS OF AMERICAN, EUROPEAN, AND INTERNATIONAL LAW 23 (1993).

**58.** *Id.* at 33–62.

**59.** Arthur T. von Mehren and Donald T. Trautman, *Jurisdiction to Adjudicate: A Suggested Analysis*, 79 HARV. L. REV. 1121 (1966).

claims unrelated to the contact with the forum.[60] Other kinds of contacts, particularly contractual ones, give rise to specific jurisdiction under both the Brussels Convention and U.S. law.[61]

## b. THREE HARD CASES

With this background, let us consider three areas in which the U.S. and EC approaches diverge: the degree of affiliation between the defendant and the forum necessary to confer broad jurisdiction on the forum to decide both related and unrelated claims against the defendant (so-called "general jurisdiction"); second, the assertion of "specific jurisdiction" over defendants for certain extraterritorial acts that cause tortious injury in the forum; and third, so-called "tag jurisdiction," the assertion of personal jurisdiction over a non-domiciliary based solely on his transient presence in the forum.

### i. General Jurisdiction

In the half-century since *International Shoe*, the U.S. courts have addressed all three hard cases in the international setting. During that time, the Supreme Court has also heard a number of personal jurisdiction cases involving alien civil defendants.[62] In the first, *Perkins v. Benguet Consolidated Mining Co.*,[63] a nonresident American plaintiff sued a Philippine corporation in Ohio state court on two causes of action conducted by the defendant outside the state. During the Japanese occupation of the Philippines, the corporation had conducted business activities in Ohio. The Court deemed those activities, which included "directors' meetings, business correspondence, banking, stock transfers, payment of salaries, purchasing of machinery, etc." to be "continuous and systematic," thus rendering "fair and reasonable" the exercise of specific jurisdiction over claims related to those in-state activities. With respect to a case involving an unrelated contact, however, the Court found

**60.** *See* Brussels Convention arts. 2, 53.

**61.** *Compare* Burger King Corp. v. Rudzewicz, 471 U.S. 462 (1985), *with* Brussels Convention art. 5(1).

**62.** Perkins v. Benguet Consolidated Mining Co., 342 U.S. 437 (1952); Insurance Corp. Of Ireland, Ltd. v. Compagnie Des Bauxites De Guinee, 456 U.S. 694 (1982); Helicopteros Nacionales de Colombia v. Hall, 466 U.S. 408 (1984); Asahi Metal Indus. Co. v. Superior Court of California, 480 U.S. 102 (1987).

**63.** 342 U.S. 437 (1952) ("The answer to the question whether the state courts of Ohio are open to a proceeding *in personam* against an amply notified foreign corporation to enforce a cause of action not arising in Ohio and not related to the business or activities of the corporation in that State, rests entirely upon the law of Ohio, unless the due process clause of the Fourteenth Amendment compels a decision either way.").

that it would not violate "federal due process for Ohio either to take or decline jurisdiction of the corporation, in this proceeding."[64] This ruling left the Ohio courts free to rule for the plaintiff on remand.

Thirty years later, in *Insurance Corp. of Ireland, Ltd. v. Compagnie des Bauxites de Guinee*,[65] a Delaware corporation, headquartered in and 49% owned by the Republic of Guinea, sued several foreign insurance companies for failure to pay on an insurance policy. The foreign defendants made a special appearance to contest personal jurisdiction and refused to comply with court-ordered discovery, by which the plaintiff sought to establish essential jurisdictional facts. In upholding the sanction, the Supreme Court held that defendants had consented to adjudication of at least the jurisdictional issue, and that the lower court thus had power to obligate them to abide by its discovery rules, laid down to govern determination of the issue.

*Perkins* and *Insurance Corp. of Ireland* delineated the spectrum along which a court could constitutionally exercise personal jurisdiction over a foreign corporation. When the defendant has continuous and systematic contacts with the forum, as in *Perkins*, a court may constitutionally exercise general jurisdiction over it based even on unrelated claims. Yet as *Insurance Corp.* showed, even if a defendant corporation's only contact with the forum is its appearance to contest jurisdiction, the court has specific jurisdiction to award sanctions against it in relation with that appearance. The question remained, however: just where should one draw the line between the contacts sufficient to confer general and specific jurisdiction?

In *Helicopteros Nacionales de Colombia v. Hall*,[66] the Court sought to answer that question, for the first time accepting Professors von Mehren and Trautman's distinction between general and specific jurisdiction.[67] In *Helicopteros*, a helicopter purchased from Bell Helicopter in Texas by a Colombian helicopter company, Helicol, crashed in Peru while transporting American workers to an oil construction project. The Colombian company had no place of business or license in Texas, but had numerous contacts with it: it had sent its chief executive officer to Houston for a contract negotiation; it had accepted into a New York bank account checks drawn on a Houston bank; it had purchased helicopter equipment

---

**64.** *Id*. at 440.

**65.** 456 U.S. 694 (1982).

**66.** 466 U.S. 408 (1984).

**67.** *Id*. at 414 n.8.

and training session from Bell; and it had sent personnel to Bell's Texas facilities.

In an opinion by Justice Blackmun, the Court found that Texas lacked power to assert *in personam* jurisdiction over Helicol because it lacked the continuous and systematic contacts with Texas necessary to support general jurisdiction on a tortious cause of action not related to its contract with the Texas company. Justice Blackmun reasoned that some of the contacts were nonvolitional, that the money transfer was of negligible significance, and that the repeated travel of the company's chief executive officer to Texas did not constitute continuous and systematic activity. Nor was the mere purchase of services (training) along with a package of goods (the helicopter) sufficient to satisfy the standard for general jurisdiction.

*Helicopteros* came as a surprise, for the Court could just have easily have tabulated the numerous contacts between the defendant company and the state and found them to be sufficiently "continuous and systematic" as to meet the *Perkins* standard. That the Justices took a different course suggests that the ruling really rested on separation of powers and deference to executive prerogatives in foreign affairs. Looking back, we can see that *Perkins* arose in the aftermath of World War II. By declining to find jurisdiction inconsistent with due process, the Court freed the plaintiffs to sue locally a foreign company that had done business with the Japanese, and then had apparently used Ohio as a haven to reap profits from its Philippine business even during the Japanese wartime occupation. *Helicopteros*, by contrast, arose during a major flurry of U.S. concern over a growing international trade deficit. The Solicitor General submitted an *amicus curiae* brief citing congressional testimony by the United States Trade Representative regarding the causes of that deficit.[68] The Government's brief argued that extending general state-court jurisdiction over any foreigner who bought a package of high-technology goods and training from the United States would put the United States at a competitive trade disadvantage vis-à-vis other countries whose courts do not exercise their jurisdiction so expansively.[69] By so saying, the federal government charged the Texas court, whose decision was under review, with

**68.** *See* Brief for the United States as Amicus Curiae, Helicopteros Nacionales de Colombia v. Hall, 466 U.S. 408 (1984).

**69.** *See id.* at 6 ("In this case we ask the Court to recognize that the realities of today's sophisticated marketing practices, particularly for 'high technology' products, frequently make employee training and related services an essential part of a purchase agreement. Thus, it is not uncommon for foreign firms desiring to buy high technology products to send their operational and maintenance employees to the United States to receive such training.... The issue is substantial because of the critical importance of foreign trade to our national

erecting trade barriers that the federal executive branch had expressly sought to reduce.[70]

If the helicopter had crashed in an EU country, not Peru, it seems likely that the Brussels Convention would have mandated the same outcome as *Helicopteros*. For in matters of tort, Article 5(3) of the Brussels Convention permits suit only "in the courts for the place where the harmful event occurred" and thus would have excluded the action. But suppose the plaintiffs had sued the helicopter manufacturer as well as the operator, and the manufacturer were a European company domiciled somewhere else in EU. In that case, the Brussels Convention would have permitted the plaintiff to proceed against both defendants without regard to the level of contacts of the nondomiciliary defendant.[71]

### ii.  Extraterritorial Jurisdiction over Foreign Tortfeasors

The Court's most important recent jurisdictional decision for international business transactions came in *Asahi Metal Indus. Co. v. Superior Court of California*.[72] There, a Chinese tire company sued a Japanese valve manufacturer for indemnity in California state court, based on a single, related contact: a tire that blew up in a California motorcycle accident. In a splintered decision, four Justices found the necessary power over the defendant lacking.[73]

economy. A foreign firm that finds itself subject to suit in a state court on an unrelated cause of action merely because it has sent employees to that state to learn how to operate and maintain equipment purchasers may well find it more expedient to do its foreign trading with firms in other countries.").

**70.** *See id.* at 6 ("The Executive Branch and Congress have, in recent years, taken important steps to remove obstacles and potential obstacles to the competitive standing of American firms in world markets. Those efforts would be severely undercut if they were met with the imposition of new barriers such as that imposed by the decision below."); *id.* at 1–2 ("[F]oreign corporations might be dissuaded from purchasing American products if the mere purchases of products in the U.S. as part of the purchase agreement is sufficient to subject foreign businesses to the jurisdiction of American courts for causes of action totally unrelated to their purchases. Such a result would be detri-

mental to the government's efforts to promote the export of American products.").

**71.** *Cf.* Brussels Convention, art. 6(1) ("A person domiciled in a Contracting State may also be sued: (1) where he is one of a number of defendants, in the courts for *the place where any one of them is domiciled*.") (emphasis added).

**72.** 480 U.S. 102 (1987).

**73.** In a part of her opinion joined by Justices Rehnquist, Powell, and Scalia Justice O'Connor reached the further conclusion that defendant had not purposefully availed—i.e., *de facto* consented to subject itself to suit in California—simply by placing its product into the stream of commerce that ultimately ended up in California:

The placement of a product into the stream of commerce, without more, is not an act of the defendant purposefully directed toward the forum state. Additional conduct of the defendant may indicate an intent or purpose to

Eight Justices found the exercise of jurisdiction unreasonable.[74] Justice O'Connor's opinion reached both conclusions, resting on two grounds: invasion of personal autonomy and separation of powers. With respect to the first, she noted that the foreign defendant had to travel to California and subject itself to "the unique burdens placed upon one who must defend oneself in a foreign legal system should have significant weight in assessing the reasonableness of stretching the long arm of personal jurisdiction over national borders."[75] Invoking separation of powers, she further added, "In every case, ... the Federal interest in Government's foreign relations policies, will be best served by a careful inquiry into the reasonableness of the assertion of jurisdiction in the particular case, and an unwillingness to find serious burdens on an alien defendant outweighed by minimal interests on the part of the plaintiff or the forum state."[76] By recognizing the growing *internationalization* of American commerce, *Asahi* paralleled prior decisions recognizing the growing nationalization of American commerce.[77] In evaluating the reasonableness of asserting jurisdiction, the Court for the first time mentioned "the international context," urging a *Timberlane*-type "inquiry into the reasonableness of the assertion of jurisdiction in the particular case," including a weighing not just of the interests of the parties and the forum state, but also "the procedural and substantive interests of other nations in a state court's assertion of jurisdiction over an alien defendant," and "the Federal interest in Government's Foreign relations policies."[78]

serve the market in the forum State: for example, designing the product for the market; advertising, establishing channels, or marketing through a distributor.

*Id.* at 104 (O'Connor, J.).

Thus, the Court set the stage for a "stream of commerce plus" test for what constitutes a defendant's purposeful availment of the right to do business in the forum. *Id.* at 102.

**74.** Justice Brennan, White, Marshall, Blackmun and Stevens all agreed that the exercise of adjudicatory jurisdiction over Asahi was unreasonable, joining the opinion of Justices O'Connor, Rehnquist and Powell on this point. In an echo of his later opinion in *Weltover*, Justice Scalia joined only the part of Justice O'Connor's opinion that found power lacking, and therefore expressed no opinion on reasonableness.

**75.** *Id.* at 114.

**76.** *Id.* at 115.

**77.** *Cf.* McGee v. International Life Ins. Co., 355 U.S. 220, 222–23 (1957) ("In part this is attributable to the fundamental transformation of our national economy over the years. Today many commercial transactions touch two or more States and may involve parties separated by the full continent. With this increasing nationalization of commerce has come a great increase in the amount of business conducted by mail across state lines. At the same time modern transportation and communication have made it much less burdensome for a party sued to defend himself in a State where he engages in economic activity.").

**78.** *Id.* at 115.

*Asahi*'s focus upon the national interest in judicial jurisdiction was also flagged by a footnote in that case suggesting

> we have no occasion here to determine whether Congress could, consistent with the Due Process Clause of the Fifth Amendment, authorize *federal court* personal jurisdiction over alien defendants based on the aggregate of national contacts, rather than on the contacts between the defendant and the [particular] State in which the federal court sits.[79]

By this statement, the Court was again expressing concerns about uniformity—can a U.S. citizen sue a foreign defendant who seeks to avoid personal jurisdiction by carefully avoiding developing minimum contacts with any single federal jurisdiction? If so, such a defendant would enjoy *de facto* immunity from suit in the U.S., even on federal claims such as antitrust and securities, which invoke national, rather than purely local, regulatory interests.[80] Among academics, whether a federal court may exert personal jurisdiction over an alien defendant based on a theory of "national contacts" has been hotly contested.[81] This debate finally prompted the Federal Rule-makers to address the question by promulgating the new Fed. R. Civ. P. 4(k)(2). That provision, to which we will turn in Chapter IX, when we look at service of process, addresses the national contacts issue by authorizing the exercise of territorial jurisdiction over the person of any defendant against whom is made a claim under any federal law, even if that person "is not subject to the courts of general jurisdiction of any state."

Arguably, the Brussels Convention would have mandated the same outcome as in *Asahi*. In matters of tort, Article 5(3) of the Brussels Convention permits suit "in the courts for the place where the harmful event occurred," a term analogous to the traditional

---

**79.** *Id.* at 113 n.* (emphasis added). *See also* Omni Capital Int'l v. Rudolf Wolf and Co. Ltd., 484 U.S. 97, 102 n.5 (1987) (also reserving the national contacts issue for later decision).

**80.** If the "national contacts" test were in fact unconstitutional, this would raise a possible inconsistency with the extraterritorial application of Clause Three of the FSIA's commercial activity exception. As we saw in *Weltover*, discussed in Chapter VI, a claim may be made under that exception for any commercial act and activity outside the U.S. that has a direct effect inside the U.S. One could imagine a case in which a foreign sovereign's act had a direct ef-

fect on the United States as a whole, but less-than-minimum contacts with any given state. Absent a "national contacts" standard, it could be argued that applying the exception to those facts would constitute an unconstitutional extension of the "direct effects" long-arm.

**81.** *See, e.g.*, Graham Lilly, *Jurisdiction Over Domestic and Alien Defendants*, 69 Va. L. Rev. 85 (1983); Robert Casad, *Personal Jurisdiction in Federal Question Cases*, 70 Tex. L. Rev. 1589 (1992); Roger Transgrud, *The Federal Common Law of Personal Jurisdiction*, 57 Geo Wash. L. Rev. 849, 850 (1989).

concept of *forum delicti commissi*.[82] In *Handelswekerij G.J. Bier B.V. v. Mines de Potasse*,[83] the European Court of Justice held that the "place where the harmful event occurred" means both the place where the damage occurred and the place of the event giving rise to it, a strongly pro-plaintiff rule for defective product cases. This rule would have allowed the plaintiff motorcyclist in *Asahi* to sue in California, the place of the injury.[84] What would muddy the waters is the factual curiosity that in *Asahi*, the injured rider of the motorcycle settled his case after impleading the Chinese inner tube manufacturer, which in turn sought indemnity by cross-complaint against the Japanese valve company. Thus, by the time the *Asahi* case reached the U.S. Supreme Court, the case had become a truly transnational conflict: a Chinese inner tube manufacturer suing a Japanese valve manufacturer for indemnity before a California state court for a sale made in Taiwan on a Japanese goods shipment of a product that later exploded in California. Since Article 5 of the Brussels Convention allows tort suits only against persons domiciled in the EU Contracting States (which *Asahi*, by analogy, was not), it seem unlikely that the ECJ would have sustained an indemnity action under the Convention brought between two non-domiciliary companies based solely on the local location of the ultimate tort.

### iii. Transient Jurisdiction

Where U.S. law and EU law quite distinctively diverge is in the third area, transient or "tag" jurisdiction.[85] Under the U.S. law of territorial presence, a court may acquire general jurisdiction over a foreigner who is only transitorily present in the forum, by virtue of personal service of process on his person, even on a cause of action unrelated to his presence in the forum. In *Grace v. MacArthur*,[86] a famous federal case, the court sustained jurisdiction when the defendant was served while in the act of passing high over Arkansas on a commercial air flight from Tennessee to Texas.

**82.** *Id.*, art. 5(3). *See also* Germany, Code of Civil Procedure (Zivilprozessordnung) § 32; French Civil Code art. 59 (12).

**83.** Case 21/76 [1976] ECR 1735, [1977] 1 CMLR 284.

**84.** *See* LOOKOFSKY, *supra* note 57, at 237 ("California is the *forum delicti*: that is, at least, the place where plaintiff's injury was sustained. Under the Brussels Convention, the inquiry would stop there.").

**85.** For discussion of this form of jurisdiction, see Earl Maltz, *Sovereign Authority, Fairness, and Personal Jurisdiction: The Case of the Doctrine of Transient Jurisdiction*, 66 WASH. U. L. Q. 671 (1988); Harold G. Maier and Thomas McCoy, *A Unifying Theory for Judicial Jurisdiction and Choice of Law*, 39 AM. J. COMP. L. 249, 271–80 (1991).

**86.** 170 F.Supp. 442 (E.D. Ark. 1959).

Under the Brussels Convention, transient jurisdiction over another EU domiciliary based solely on territorial service of process would be deemed "exorbitant". Indeed, Article 3 of the Brussels Convention bars application of the most closely analogous EU national rules—in the United Kingdom and Denmark—to bar application of tag jurisdiction over domiciliaries of the EC. Moreover, the *Restatement (Third)* opines that "Jurisdiction based on service of process on one only transitorily present in state is no longer acceptable under international law if that is the only basis for jurisdiction and the action in question is unrelated to that state."[87]

But in the 1990 case of *Burnham v. Superior Court of California*,[88] all nine Justices upheld this remnant of territorial presence, invoking radically varying grounds. In an opinion for four Justices on most issues, Justice Scalia upheld the exercise of general jurisdiction over a defendant, based solely on transient presence, by relying on historically accepted concepts of territorial sovereignty.[89] Justice Brennan's concurring opinion for four others made the more plausible argument that, after *Shaffer v. Heitner*,[90] all exercises of state court jurisdiction must be evaluated under the *International Shoe* standard, and that assertion of jurisdiction here was reasonable and fair under the circumstances presented there.[91] Justices White and Stevens agreed in one-paragraph opinions that contained little real analysis.[92]

*Burnham* did not involve a foreign defendant, but critics quickly saw its incompatibility with the Brussels Convention's rules against exorbitant jurisdiction.[93] In the years following, the Court has not granted plenary review to a case holding that the *Burnham* rule should apply, where a foreign domiciliary was served while transitorily present in the U.S.

---

**87.** RESTATEMENT (THIRD) § 421, reporters' note 5.

**88.** 495 U.S. 604 (1990).

**89.** *Id.* at 619 ("jurisdiction based on physical presence alone constitutes due process because it is one of the continuing traditions of our legal system that define the due process standard of 'traditional notions of fair play and substantial justice.' ").

**90.** 433 U.S. 186 (1977).

**91.** 495 U.S. at 629–30 (Brennan, J., concurring in the judgment).

**92.** Justice White simply asserted that the rule "has been and is so widely accepted throughout this country that I could not possibly strike it down." *Id.* at 628. Justice Stevens agreed for the historical reasons given by Justice Scalia, the fairness considerations given by Justice Brennan, and "the commonsense displayed by Justice White." *Id.* at 640.

**93.** For critical commentary, see Peter Hay, *Transient Jurisdiction, Especially Over International Defendants: Critical Comments on* Burnham v. Superior Court of California, 1990 U. ILL. L. REV. 593; Patrick Borchers, *The Death of the Constitutional Law of Personal Jurisdiction: From Pennoyer to Burnham and Back Again*, 24 U.C. DAVIS L. REV. 19 (1990); Russell Weintraub, *An Objective Basis for Rejecting Transient Jurisdiction*, 22 RUTGERS L.J. 611, 626 (1991).

Whether tag jurisdiction will be invalidated on grounds of unreasonableness with respect to a foreigner now seems as likely to arise in an international human rights suit in a U.S. court, as in a transnational business case. In *Kadic v. Karadzic*,[94] for example, a class of Bosnian victims (some of them residing in America) sued Radovan Karadzic, the leader of the Bosnian Serb state of Srpska under the Alien Tort Claims Act[95] and other statutes, seeking compensation for atrocities committed in the former Yugoslavia, including rape, murder, forced prostitution, and impregnation, acts of torture, genocide, extrajudicial killing, war crimes, and other crimes against humanity. Karadzic was served with process by hand while visiting New York, in a New York hotel located outside the United Nations headquarters district.[96] The district judge dismissed for lack of subject matter jurisdiction, and on appeal, the Second Circuit reversed, finding both subject matter and personal jurisdiction. In so saying, the Second Circuit followed an *amicus curiae* memorandum co-signed by the Solicitor General and the Legal Adviser of the State Department supporting plaintiffs' jurisdictional position. The appellate court unanimously held, citing *Burnham*, that personal service upon Karadzic "comports with the requirements of due process for the assertion of personal jurisdiction," and that "if [plaintiffs] personally served Karadzic with the summons and complaint while he was in New York but outside of the U.N. headquarters district ... he is subject to the personal jurisdiction of the District Court."[97] Moreover, the appeals court rejected Karadzic's claims that he was entitled to immunity from service of process based on the U.N.–U.S. Headquarters Agreement and claimed federal common law immunity. The Supreme Court then denied *certiorari*, rendering the Second Circuit's ruling on the issue the controlling law of the case.[98]

**94.** 70 F.3d 232 (2d Cir. 1995), *cert. denied*, 518 U.S. 1005 (1996).

**95.** 28 U.S.C. § 1350 (2008).

**96.** I should disclose that I was co-counsel for the class action plaintiffs in Doe v. Karadzic (No. 93 Civ. 878 (PKL) (S.D.N.Y. 1997)), one of the two cases decided on the Second Circuit's appeal. Kadic v. Karadzic (No. 93 Civ. 81163 (PKL) (S.D.N.Y. 1997)), a parallel proceeding, that did not contain class allegations, was brought in the same court on behalf of several Bosnian women and two Bosnian women victims' organizations.

**97.** 70 F.3d at 232, 248.

**98.** 518 U.S. 1005 (1996). On remand, in February 1997, after a magistrate judge ordered Karadzic to apply for a visa from the State Department in order to attend a deposition in New York City, Karadzic faxed a personally signed letter saying that he had instructed his attorney not to participate further in the proceedings before the court. Ironically, the penultimate paragraph of his letter argued that the court's exercise of jurisdiction over him would impair the future effectiveness of the United Nations, whose War Crimes Tribunal Karadzic had flouted for many years. Karadzic thus failed to "plead or otherwise defend" a civil action over which a federal court has proper juris-

Some have suggested that defendants such as Karadzic could invoke language in Justice O'Connor's opinion in *Asahi*, which warned that "[t]he unique burdens placed upon one who must defend oneself in a foreign legal system should have significant weight in assessing the reasonableness of stretching the long arm of personal jurisdiction over national borders."[99] But the same opinion cautioned that "[w]hen minimum contacts have been established, often the interests of the *plaintiff* and the *forum* in the exercise of jurisdiction will justify even the serious burdens placed on the alien defendant."[100] Given that Karadzic had other contacts with the United States, that many of the Bosnian plaintiffs resided there, that the U.S. forum had strong interests in punishing the universal crimes alleged, and that no other court had yet obtained jurisdiction over Karadzic, I would argue that even if the Second Circuit had applied the *Asahi* balance of reasonableness, rather than the bright-line *Burnham* rule, the balance still would have tipped firmly in plaintiffs' favor.[101]

At this writing, the international legal acceptability of "tag jurisdiction"—in which a defendant may be served during a temporary visit to the forum jurisdiction—remains unresolved. Although drafts of the Hague Convention on the Recognition and Enforcement of Foreign Judgments initially sought to limit this form of jurisdiction, human rights advocates opposed that limitation as a threat to much of the transnational public law litigation brought against foreign human rights violators described in Chapter III.[102] The prohibition on both "long arm" and "tag" jurisdiction in the Hague Judgments Convention eventually proved fatal to the participation of the United States in that drafting exercise,[103] and so in

diction, and that a default judgment was thus entered against him pursuant to Federal Rule of Civil Procedure 55 in June 2000. After the trial court issued a default judgment against him, plaintiffs proceeded with a trial to determine the amount of damages to be awarded and after a two-week jury trial in September 2000, a jury awarded plaintiffs approximately $4.5 billion in compensatory and punitive damages. *See* Doe v. Karadzic, 2001 WL 986545 (S.D.N.Y. Aug. 28, 2001).

**99.** *Asahi*, 480 U.S. at 114.

**100.** *Id.* (emphasis added).

**101.** The Second Circuit noted that "at this stage of the litigation no party has identified a more suitable forum [than the New York federal court], and we are aware of none.... [i]t seems evident that the courts of the former

Yugoslavia, either in Serbia or war-torn Bosnia, are not now available to entertain plaintiffs' claims, even if circumstances concerning the location of witnesses and documents were presented that were sufficient to overcome the plaintiffs' preference for a United States forum." *Kadic*, 70 F.3d at 232, 250–51.

**102.** Draft Hague Convention, art. 18(f), *available at* http://www.hcch.net/index_en.php?act=conventions.publications&dtid=35&cid=98.

**103.** *See generally* Thomas E. Vanderbloemen, *Assessing the Potential Impact of the Proposed Hague Jurisdiction and Judgments Convention on Human Rights Litigation in the United States*, 50 DUKE L.J. 917 (2000); Jeffrey Talpis and Nick Krnjevic, *The Hague Convention on Choice of Court Agreements of*

the end, no prohibition against this form of jurisdiction was included in the much narrower Hague Convention on Choice of Court Agreements, which was designed primarily to promote international business-to-business agreements.[104]

*June 30, 2005: The Elephant That Gave Birth to a Mouse*, 13 Sw. J.L. & Trade Am. 1, 3 (2006); Letter from Jeffrey D. Kovar, U.S. Dept. of State, Assistant Legal Advisor for Private Int'l Law, to J.H.A. van Loon, Sec'y Gen., Hague Conference on Private Int'l Law 2 (Feb. 22, 2000), *available at* http://www.cptech.org/ecom/hague/kovar2loon22022

000.pdf, at 9 ("A generally-acceptable provision that exempts existing civil suits to redress human rights violations from prohibition under Article 18 is necessary or there will be intense opposition to this convention in the United States.").

**104.** *See* Chapter XII, infra.

# CHAPTER VIII

# VENUE

## A. General Principles

To complete any discussion of Choice of Forum, one must address not just jurisdiction, but also venue. Although often discussed and confused with jurisdictional doctrines, venue is not jurisdictional in nature. Venue is primarily a matter of *convenience* for litigants, witnesses, and the courts, a pragmatic effort to place a suit in the forum that most plausibly constitutes its center of gravity.

At the outset, two distinctions should be drawn, between types of motions and types of cases. First, "initiation moves," which the plaintiff usually makes by "laying initial venue" in the forum she most prefers, should be distinguished from "post-initiation venue moves," which the defendant usually makes in seeking subsequently to "shift venue" to her preferred location. In U.S law, 28 U.S.C. § 1391 states the core rules of initiating venue. The basic post-initiation moves are set forth in 28 U.S.C. §§ 1404 (statutory transfer), 1407 (multi-district transfer), 1441 (state-federal removal) and in the common-law doctrine of *forum non conveniens*, which is increasingly used by defendants in transnational tort litigation to send unwanted cases abroad.

Second, we should distinguish among those suits in which venue doctrines are invoked between strangers—usually tort cases—and those in which the litigants have previously met and agreed, and contractually selected a forum in the event of disagreement—usually contract cases. This distinction raises two questions: If parties are strangers, under what circumstance can the suit be dismissed from a jurisdictionally competent forum on grounds of *forum non conveniens*? And if the parties have signed a forum-selection clause, how much deference should the court accord it?

Both sets of distinctions are revealed by *Piper Aircraft Co. v. Reyno*,[1] the Supreme Court's leading decision on *forum non conveniens*. In *Piper*, a twin-engine Piper Aztec airplane, built in Pennsylvania by Piper Aircraft Co. and flying with a propeller made in Ohio by Hartzell Propeller, Inc., crashed into the Scottish high-

---

1.  454 U.S. 235 (1981).

153

lands.[2] The pilot and five passengers, all Scottish citizens and residents, died instantly. It remains unclear whether the proximate cause of the crash was mechanical failure or human error.[3] A California probate court appointed Reyno, a California citizen unrelated to any of the decedents, as personal representative for the estates of all five passengers. Reyno then brought separate wrongful death actions alleging strict liability and negligence against Piper and Hartzell, laying initial venue in California state court.[4]

Defendants then played three successive *post-initiation* venue moves. They first removed the case vertically from California state to federal court under 28 U.S.C. § 1441, which permits defendants to remove a case one-way from a state court to a federal court in the district in which the case could have initially been brought. Second, defendants moved to transfer the case horizontally from the California federal court to the Middle District of Pennsylvania under 28 U.S.C. § 1404 (a), which authorizes one federal judge to transfer a case from one federal district court to another, so long as the interests of justice permit. Having reached Pennsylvania, defendants thirdly moved for common law *forum non conveniens*, now asking that the case be dismissed to Scotland, where the accident occurred.[5]

Both the plaintiffs and defendants in *Piper* were undeniably forum-shopping. By so doing, both sides were really shopping for

**2.** After manufacturing the aircraft, Piper sold it to an Ohio dealer, who in turn sold it to a British air chartering corporation based in Blackpool. After one of its regular shuttle planes malfunctioned on the outbound leg of a Perth–Blackpool round trip, a Scottish air taxi service chartered the Piper plane for the return flight. But the Piper Aztec never reached Perth, ending its odyssey in Tulla, near the town of Moffat.

**3.** A British Department of Trade investigator's preliminary report concluded that mechanical failure in the plane or propeller had caused the accident. After a three-member Review Board held a nine-day adversary hearing attended by all interested parties, the Board modified the report, reidentifying the accident's probable cause as loss of control following attempted shutdown of the port engine. The Board further suggested that the twenty-two-year-old pilot's inexperience and error were at least partly responsible for the loss of control and subsequent crash.

**4.** Avco Lycoming, the engine manufacturer, was subsequently dismissed

from the suit by stipulation. Reyno sued neither the plane's British owner, nor the Scottish air taxi service, presumably because both lacked minimum contacts with the United States.

**5.** Under 28 U.S.C. § 1404(a), sometimes called "statutory *forum non conveniens*," a district court may transfer any civil action to any other district where it might have been brought "for the convenience of parties and witnesses [and] in the interests of justice." Defendants usually file Section 1404(a) motions when proposing to transfer cases to other federal courts and common law *forum non conveniens motions* when proposing foreign countries as the alternate forum. Because a common law *forum non conveniens* motion, unlike a statutory *forum non conveniens* motion, entails dismissal rather than transfer, the defendant generally carries a heavier burden of proof on a common law motion to dismiss. *See, e.g.*, Norwood v. Kirkpatrick, 349 U.S. 29, 32 (1955).

procedural and substantive law. The plaintiffs deliberately lay venue in California seeking the advantages of the American jury system, which is capable of awarding huge punitive damages. The availability of contingent fees and a specialized and aggressive personal injury bar plainly reduced the barriers to their bringing the case. As the Court pointed out, plaintiff Reyno was herself a legal secretary of the law firm that represented plaintiffs, who acted as a cat's paw to enable the lawsuit to be brought.[6] Once the case had been lodged in American courts, liberal discovery, pleading, and joinder rules made it far easier for plaintiffs to prove their product liability claims.

If, on the other hand, the case had been brought in Scotland, Reyno would have been doubly barred from bringing one wrongful death action for the estates of five strangers. Scottish law generally recognizes wrongful death actions only when brought by a decedent's relatives and further bars survivors of several decedents killed in the same incident from amalgamating their actions. Nor did Scottish law, unlike more than forty of the United States, recognize strict liability in tort. Thus, even if permitted to sue in Scotland, Reyno could not have established liability without proving defendants' negligence. Furthermore, even surviving relatives in Scotland may bring wrongful death actions only for "loss of support and society," thus imposing a ceiling on any potential recovery.[7]

In policing this battle between forum-shoppers, *forum non conveniens* has emerged as a critical judicial tool. The doctrine functions, as one commentator has noted, as

> a discretionary adjunct to the rules regulating place of trial. The parties may have legitimate differences as to the appropriate place to try the lawsuit, differences which cannot always be satisfactorily resolved by rules of jurisdiction, venue, and service of process. *It may be better to have them resolved under the discretion of an impartial judge than by the unfettered option of either party.*[8]

Trial judges applying the doctrine of *forum non conveniens* must therefore walk a fine line to avoid implicitly sanctioning forum-shopping by either litigant at the other's expense. While defendants have traditionally carried a burden of establishing that plaintiffs'

---

**6.** *Piper*, 454 U.S. at 239.

**7.** In addition, many countries (for example, Norway) lack a collateral source rule. Thus, tort recovery under Norwegian law is typically reduced by the amount of any insurance, pension, or social security payments received by the plaintiffs. *See, e.g.*, Pain v. United Technologies Corp., 637 F.2d 775, 794 n.103 (D.C. Cir. 1980), *cert. denied*, 454 U.S. 1128 (1981).

**8.** Robert Braucher, *The Inconvenient Federal Forum*, 60 HARV. L. REV. 908, 931 (1947) (emphasis added).

choice of forum is inappropriate, plaintiffs who choose to sue in an improbable forum "should be required to show some reasonable justification for his institution of the action in the forum state rather than in a state with which the defendant or the res, act or event in suit is more significantly connected."[9]

A final point concerns the litigants' procedural options. If the aircraft crash had been a mass tort, rather than a single accident, plaintiffs could have filed actions in many different federal courts, all possessing jurisdiction. In that event, the defendants could have invoked the fourth available post-initiation move, by petitioning the Judicial Panel on Multi–District Litigation ("JPML") under 28 U.S.C. § 1407[10] to consolidate the similar cases before a single federal district judge for the coordinated management of pretrial proceedings. Two prominent international business episodes applying this complex management device have been the Iranian letter of credit litigation during the Iranian Hostages Crisis of 1979–80, and the litigation following the Bhopal gas disaster of 1984.

Both episodes well illustrate the intertwining of public and private in the transnational legal process on which I have remarked throughout this volume. In the Iranian episode, following the overthrow of the Shah and the Iranian revolution, scores of American contractors were contingently liable to the Iranian government, then controlled by the Ayatollah Khomeini, for millions of dollars in guarantee letters of credit contingently payable to the Government of Iran. When multiple litigation ensued across the United States, most of these cases were transferred by the JPML to New York

---

**9.** *See* Ruth Bader Ginsburg, *The Competent Court in Private International law: Some observations on Current Views in the United States*, 20 RUTGERS L. REV. 89, 100 (1965).

**10.** Section 1407, which was enacted by Congress in 1968, authorizes the JPML, a standing panel of seven court of appeals and district judges, to temporarily transfer civil actions involving one or more common questions of fact pending in different districts to a single district for purposes of coordinated or consolidated pretrial proceedings, after which time the actions are usually settled. Multi-district transfers are intended to serve the convenience of parties and witnesses and to promote the just and efficient conduct of consolidated ac-

tions by coordinating the treatment of complex cases, avoiding conflict and duplication in discovery, and promoting a more efficient allocation of judicial resources. The statute specifies that "[e]ach action so transferred shall be remanded by the panel at or before the conclusion of the pretrial proceedings to the district from which it was transferred unless it shall have been previously terminated." Yet, in fact, most cases are settled by the transferee judge and only a tiny fraction are ever tried. Virtually no such cases are returned to the transferor court, which has recently given rise to Supreme Court litigation. *See* Lexecon, Inc. v. Milberg Weiss, Bershad, Hynes and Lerach, 523 U.S. 26, 118 S.Ct. 956 (1998), (successfully chal-

federal courts for consolidated pretrial proceedings.[11] Similarly, the Bhopal litigation, which arose out of the December 1984 leak of highly toxic methyl isocyanate gas from a pesticide factory located in Bhopal, India, triggered scores of suits by the Union of India and private plaintiffs against Union Carbide in American courts.[12] Like the Iranian letter of credit litigation, these cases were transferred under 28 U.S.C. § 1407, and consolidated before a Manhattan federal court, which ultimately dismissed them to India, applying the *forum non conveniens* rule enunciated in *Piper* itself.[13]

## B. *Forum Non Conveniens*

Against this background, *Piper*'s significance can now be understood. Before the Pennsylvania federal district court, both defendants moved for dismissal under common law *forum non conveniens*, contending the case should be heard in Scotland. The trial judge granted those motions, applying the Supreme Court's 1947 decision in *Gulf Oil Corp. v. Gilbert*.[14] *Gilbert* and its companion decision, *Koster v. Lumbermens Mutual Casualty Co.*,[15] had together extended the doctrine of *forum non conveniens* for the first time beyond its historical Anglo–American roots in admiralty and equity.[16] Upholding a *forum non conveniens* dismissal in both cases,

---

lenging the practice of extended retention by the § 1407 transferee judge.)

**11.** For a discussion of these cases, see Note, *Fraud in the Transaction: Enjoining Letters of Credit During the Iranian Revolution*, 93 HARV. L. REV. 992 (1980).

**12.** For an early description of the facts and legal issues raised by the tragedy, see generally *Symposium, The Bhopal Tragedy*, 20 TEX. INT'L L.J. 267 (1985); Harold Hongju Koh, *The Responsibility of the Importer State*, in TRANSFERRING HAZARDOUS TECHNOLOGIES AND SUBSTANCES: THE INTERNATIONAL LEGAL CHALLENGE 171 (G. Handl and R. Lutz, eds., 1989).

**13.** *See* In re Union Carbide Corp. Gas Plant Disaster at Bhopal, India in December, 1984, 634 F.Supp. 842 (S.D.N.Y. 1986), *aff'd in part*, 809 F.2d 195 (2d Cir. 1987).

**14.** 330 U.S. 501 (1947).

**15.** 330 U.S. 518 (1947). *Koster*, decided together with *Gilbert*, was a shareholder's derivative action brought in the Eastern District of New York by a New York resident against three Illinois defendants. As in *Gilbert*, the Court upheld

dismissal of the case on *forum non conveniens* grounds. In reaching this conclusion, Justice Jackson observed that:

> Where there are only two parties to a dispute, there is good reason why it should be tried in the plaintiff's home forum if that has been his choice. He should not be deprived of the presumed advantages of his home jurisdiction except upon a clear showing of facts which either (1) establish such oppressiveness and vexation to a defendant as to be out of all proportion to plaintiff's convenience, which may be shown to be slight or nonexistent, or (2) make trial in the chosen forum inappropriate because of considerations affecting the court's own administrative and legal problems.

**16.** For a discussion of the history and evolution of the doctrine of *forum non conveniens*, see generally Alexander Bickel, *The Doctrine of* Forum Non Conveniens *As Applied in the Federal Courts in Matters of Admiralty*, 35 CORNELL L. Q. 12 (1949); Edward Barrett, *The Doctrine of Forum Non Conveniens*, 35 CAL. L. REV. 380 (1947).

Justice Jackson articulated the general principle "that a court may resist imposition upon its jurisdiction even when jurisdiction is authorized."[17]

He then enumerated two lists of factors to guide trial court discretion, one of "private interest factors" affecting the convenience of the *litigants*, and another of "public interest factors" affecting the convenience of the *forum*. Under private interest factors, he directed, a trial court must determine the "relative advantages and obstacles to fair trial" in plaintiff's chosen forum:

(1) relative ease of access to sources of proof;

(2) availability of compulsory process for attendance of unwilling, and the cost of obtaining attendance of willing, witnesses;

(3) possibility of viewing of premises, if ... appropriate;

(4) enforceability of a judgment if one is obtained; and

(5) all other practical problems that make trial of a case easy, expeditious and inexpensive.[18]

By public interest factors, Justice Jackson referred to

(1) the [a]dministrative difficulties resulting if litigation is piled up on congested centers instead of being handled at its origin;

(2) the burden of jury duty for people who live in a community without relation to the litigation;

(3) the desirability of holding trial in a central location when a case touch[es] the affairs of many persons;

(4) the local interest in having localized controversies decided at home; and

(5) the appropriateness of having a diversity case tried in a forum at home with the state law that must govern the case, rather than problems in conflict of laws, and in law foreign to itself.[19]

Applying this test in *Piper*, the district judge ruled that application of Scottish law would confuse a local jury and unduly burden the court. He chose to accord little weight to California, Piper's original forum choice, citing decisions holding that less deference is due to the forum choice of a foreign plaintiff seeking the benefit from liberal American tort rules,[20] He further found that *Gilbert's*

---

**17.** *Gilbert*, 330 U.S. at 507.

**18.** *Id.* at 508.

**19.** *Id.* at 508–9.

**20.** *See, e.g.*, Olympic Corp. v. Societe Generale, 462 F.2d 376, 378 (2d Cir. 1972); Fitzgerald v. Texaco, Inc., 521 F.2d 448, 451 (2d Cir. 1975) (for-

private interest factors "overwhelmingly" favored dismissal to Scotland. All witnesses and evidence on both the liability and damages issues—including the crash site, the wreckage, official investigators, mechanics, heirs and next-of-kin—were available only in the British Isles. Furthermore, all of those witnesses as well as two necessary parties, the British owner and the Scottish charterer, lay beyond the compulsory process of the court.

The Court of Appeals for the Third Circuit reversed, holding that the district court's allocation of burdens and weighing of factors constituted an abuse of discretion.[21] Ruling that American law should govern the suit, the Court held dismissal unjustified, because it would change the applicable law and bar plaintiff's strict liability claim. The appeals court further decided that the district judge had improperly denigrated plaintiffs' forum choice simply because the "real" plaintiffs were foreigners suing away from home. Examining the trial judge's weighing of the *Gilbert* factors virtually *de novo*, the appellate court then held that defendants had failed to prove that those factors favored dismissal. Because American and not Scottish law should apply, the *Gilbert* public interest factors also mitigated against dismissal.

The Supreme Court reversed yet again, holding that the plaintiffs may not defeat a *forum non conveniens* motion merely by showing that the substantive law that would be applied in the United States would be more favorable to them than the law that would be applied abroad. The Court implied that an unfavorable change in law would often follow dismissal, and thus, that that factor alone should not be dispositive. Instead, the Court directed that a district judge's *forum non conveniens* inquiry should proceed in five steps.[22] First, the court must establish that an adequate alternative forum exists which possesses jurisdiction over the whole case. Second, the trial judge must apply a strong presumption against disturbing plaintiffs' initial forum choice, although no such presumption need be given to a foreign plaintiff, or an American citizen like Reyno, who was a nominal representative of foreign parties. Third, the court must weigh all relevant *private* interest factors. Fourth, the trial judge must weigh *Gilbert*'s *public* interest factors, to determine whether they tip the balance in favor of a trial in a foreign forum. If so, the court may dismiss to the foreign forum, so long as it has ensured that plaintiffs can reinstate their

eigner suing); Fitzgerald v. Westland Marine Corp., 369 F.2d 499, 502 (2d Cir. 1966) (American plaintiff suing on behalf of foreign real parties in interest).

**21.** 630 F.2d 149 (3d Cir. 1980).

**22.** *See Piper*, 454 U.S. at 255–61. Remarkably, a computer-assisted search reveals that *Piper* has been cited more than 1200 times since the decision came down.

suit in the alternative forum without undue inconvenience or prejudice. Fifth and finally, the Supreme Court advised, all of these determinations should be subjected to deferential appellate review under an abuse-of-discretion standard.

The Court clearly reached the correct result in *Piper*. The real issue was whether the center of gravity of the lawsuit was in Scotland or the United States. In fact, *Piper* was in all respects a Scottish lawsuit, involving six Scottish decedents, injured in Scottish territory in a Scottish-owned, maintained and operated place, and with litigation already underway in the U.K. relating to the accident.[23] Given this reality, *Piper* properly affirmed a federal court's discretion to balance the *Gilbert* factors on a *forum non conveniens* motion and to award dismissal where the balance of public and private factors favored that result.[24]

In hindsight, *Piper* marked a tremendously important turning point in transnational business litigation. First, the case sharpened a long-standing split between Anglo–American and civil law jurisdictions. As noted above, civil law jurisdictions generally disfavor the notion that a court has discretion to divest itself of jurisdiction in unwanted cases. Common law jurisdictions, by contrast, have long recognized the need for trial judges to resist plaintiffs' "temptation to resort to a strategy of forcing the trial at a most inconvenient place for an adversary, even at some inconvenience to himself."[25] The Court's task was to cut a solomonic compromise between the common law and civil law approaches, which arguably gave too much and too little freedom, respectively, to the plaintiff's forum choice.[26]

---

**23.** *See* 479 F.Supp. 727, 730 (M.D. Pa. 1979) ("[A]t least one action is pending before the Courts in the United Kingdom against the present Defendants and other involved parties.").

**24.** Justices White, Brennan and Stevens all pointedly refused to join Part III of the Court's opinion, which *in dicta* gave what has since proven to be necessary and valuable guidance to lower court judges seeking to apply the Court's test.

**25.** *Gilbert*, 330 U.S. at 507.

**26.** As Professor Bickel put it:

The problem of *forum non conveniens* is really an obvious one. It is this: How much freedom is a plaintiff to have in choosing the place where he wishes to bring suit. He once had next to none. In modern times he has been largely freed of rigid venue restrictions, and been given an area of discretion so wide that, in the judgment of many commentators, he is able to abuse it. He may bring suit in the forum in which, for various reasons, it is most cumbersome and expensive for the defendant to present his case. . . . Plaintiff may sue in that part of the country in which juries are least likely to be startled by and most likely to grant a large verdict. . . . In the process of thus getting the full advantage of their positions, plaintiffs often overcrowd the dockets of a small number of popular courts, and burden judges with unnecessary and difficult decisions on points of conflict of laws and . . . the laws of another jurisdiction.

Bickel, *supra* note 16, at 14–15.

Second, *Piper* starkly revealed the realities of modern international products liability litigation, and the interaction between the doctrines of venue and personal jurisdiction. As *Helicopteros* had showed, aircraft and helicopter manufacturers around the world have increasingly been subjected to American lawsuits arising out of foreign accidents. These suits are normally brought by foreign claimants, sometimes sought out by American tort lawyers seeking contingent fees. The critical evidence as to liability and damages is usually located abroad. Moreover, the foreign companies who maintain, operate and control the destroyed aircraft often lack the minimum contacts with the United States necessary to be sued domestically. After *Asahi*, such foreign operators may be broadly exempt from U.S. state-court suit, or may deliberately avoid visiting the U.S. forum to forestall tag jurisdiction under *Burnham*. Thus, absent dismissal based on *forum non conveniens*, American manufacturers are most likely to bear the costs of these suits in America, where they may be exposed to full liability for accidents resulting from operator error or improper maintenance.

The other side of the coin, of course, is that the defendant manufacturers are also "reverse forum shopping" for foreign fora. American manufacturers disseminate their products worldwide, sometimes at product standards below those they must meet in the United States. If defendants could invariably employ *forum non conveniens* to override the forum choice of an American plaintiff injured by their products, the defendant could escape responsibility for competent and careful manufacturing practices. Forcing under-resourced plaintiffs into undesired and undesirable fora arguably precludes them from bringing causes of action to which they are rightfully entitled.

By the time *Piper* arose, these factors had begun to provoke a repeated tactical struggle in transnational products liability cases. A foreign plaintiff would find an American attorney to bring a products liability tort suit against the product manufacturer in a U.S. state court. The manufacturers sued by foreigners for alleged product defects then adopted a standard, responsive practice. They would move to dismiss based on *forum non conveniens* to a foreign forum that would award a small recovery, and that did not have products liability jurisdiction. To promote dismissal, the manufacturer would agree to submit to that foreign court's jurisdiction with the goal of avoiding a U.S. court's ruling that their products are inherently defective, a ruling which could be used to devastating effect via *collateral estoppel* in other proceedings.[27]

---

**27.** Indeed, this is what happened in *Piper* itself. Defendants were trying to avoid plaintiffs' offensive non-mutual use of collateral estoppel on the issue of

The broader import of the *Piper* ruling became apparent during the Bhopal litigation, which arose more than a decade later. In that case, in the wake of the Bhopal tragedy, the Government of India sued Union Carbide in United States and Indian courts, alleging nearly $6 billion in damages.[28] In resisting the defendants' motion to dismiss on *forum non conveniens* grounds, the Indian government made the remarkable argument that it could not give adequate civil relief to its own citizen in its own courts. Applying *Piper*, a United States district judge dismissed the suits on grounds of *forum non conveniens*, subject to certain conditions and the circuit court affirmed.[29] In September, 1986, India and the State of Madhya Pradesh then sued Union Carbide in a Bhopal district court. After several more years of inconclusive litigation, Union Carbide paid $470 million to the Indian government pursuant to a settlement promoted by a five-judge bench of the Indian Supreme Court.[30] The motion for *forum non conveniens* proved to be the linchpin of the case, for it dropped its settlement value from six billion dollars to less than half a billion dollars in one fell swoop. Bhopal alone demonstrated the value of *forum con conveniens* as a weapon not just for litigation, but also for settlement, in international commercial litigation.

*Piper* also promoted greater uniformity of judge-made venue rules. With regard to *forum non conveniens*, a court must address a lurking question: under the doctrine of *Erie R.R. Co. v. Tompkins*,[31] must a federal court sitting in diversity jurisdiction apply state or federal *forum non conveniens* law on a common law motion to dismiss? The Court has previously chosen not to decide that question on several occasions.[32] Furthermore, a majority of lower courts

the plane's design defects. *See* Parklane Hosiery v. Shore, 439 U.S. 322 (1979) (permitting offensive nonmutual use of collateral estoppel in carefully circumscribed circumstances). To forestall that possibility, Piper and Hartzell agreed to submit to the jurisdiction of the Scottish courts and to waive any statute of limitations defense that might have been available. *See Piper*, 454 U.S. at 242. Thus, while the defendants' motive in seeking to litigate abroad was less than noble, neither was it entirely cost-free.

**28.** *See* Koh, Importer State Responsibility, *supra* note 12. The Bhopal gas release apparently killed more than 2,000 Indian citizens and injuring at least 200,000 others.

**29.** *See* In re Union Carbide Corp. Gas Plant Disaster at Bhopal, India in December, 1984, 634 F.Supp. 842 (S.D.N.Y. 1986), *aff'd in part*, 809 F.2d 195 (2d Cir. 1987).

**30.** Most of that money has gone into Indian government bonds, with less than $5 million actually reaching individual Indian beneficiaries. Beneficiaries have petitioned for reopening of the case, with little success. *See* Jeremy Main, Where Bhopal's Money Went, *Fortune*, June 3, 1991, at 17.

**31.** 304 U.S. 64 (1938).

**32.** *See Gilbert*, 330 U.S., at 509; *id.* at 529; Williams v. Green Bay and Western R.R., 326 U.S. 549, 551, 558–59 (1946).

have held that federal law governs all aspects of *forum non conveniens* in the federal courts in all federal cases.[33] Most courts have declined to deal with the question because they have found state *forum non conveniens* law to be virtually identical to federal law. Although the Supreme Court has not yet addressed the question, when it does, I believe that the Court should hold that a transnational *forum non conveniens* ruling—like the act of state rule in *Sabbatino*—is in fact a procedural ruling based on federal common law.[34] The foreign commerce implications of the *Piper* doctrine and the protection of a federal court's docket from impositions on its jurisdiction in transnational cases strike me as uniquely federal interests that warrant treating *forum non conveniens* as a federal common law rule of procedure.[35]

Bhopal confirmed a third and final trend: toward expansion of transnational public law litigation beyond individual plaintiffs to state plaintiffs. Following an environmental disaster, the importing state chose to sue a private multinational entity in domestic, rather than international, courts, making complex claims based on transnational law.[36] India sued as *parens patriae* for its citizens, claiming

---

**33.** Royal Bed and Spring Co. v. Famossul Industria e Comercio de Moveis, Ltda., 906 F.2d 45, 50 (1st Cir. 1990); Sibaja v. Dow Chemical Co., 757 F.2d 1215, 1219 (11th Cir. 1985), *cert. denied*, 474 U.S. 948 (1985); In re Air Crash Disaster Near New Orleans, 821 F.2d 1147 (5th Cir. 1987), *reinstated in part*, 883 F.2d 17 (5th Cir. 1989). *See* 15 C. A. MILLER WRIGHT AND E. COOPER, FEDERAL PRACTICE AND PROCEDURE: CIVIL § 3828 (1976); Note, Erie, Forum Non Conveniens *and Choice of Law in Diversity Cases*, 53 VA. L. REV. 380, 395–99 (1967).

**34.** In *Dow Chemical Co. v. Castro Alfaro*, 786 S.W.2d 674 (Tex. 1990), *cert. denied*, 498 U.S. 1024, this issue arose before the Texas Supreme Court, which held, by a vote of 5–4, that the Texas state legislature had statutorily abolished *forum non conveniens* with respect to certain suits by foreign plaintiffs. The case raised the issue whether the rule in *Piper* represents a federal common law procedural principle that preempts contrary state law. The federal issue was not presented in the parties' petition for *certiorari*, however, and so the United States Supreme Court refused to grant review.

**35.** In *Koster*, Justice Jackson noted that *forum non conveniens* is a doctrine "concerned . . . with the autonomous administration of the federal courts in the discharge of their own judicial duties, subject of course to the control of Congress." 330 U.S. at 520 n. 1. A recent Supreme Court decision, American Dredging v. Miller, 510 U.S. 443, 453 (1994), treats *forum non conveniens* as a doctrine of procedure, not substance, which suggests that *Erie* would authorize a federal court sitting in diversity jurisdiction to apply *Piper* as a rule of federal procedural law in transnational cases.

**36.** In the United States, and India, the plaintiffs offered a novel theory of "multinational enterprise liability." They claimed that, notwithstanding traditional notions of limited shareholder liability, a parent multinational corporation that controls a majority interest in a foreign subsidiary that in turn runs a hazardous production facility has a nondelegable duty to assure that the activity causes no harm. *See* Union of India's Complaint, *reprinted in* MASS DISASTERS AND MULTINATIONAL LIABILITY: THE BHOPAL CASE 1 (U. Baxi and T. Paul, eds. 1986). Although plaintiffs attempted to use this

to seek judicial reparations for their injuries, but its apparent motive in turning to American courts was not so much to win enforceable relief, as to obtain a judicial declaration of Union Carbide's liability for the disaster. By filing suit in the U.S., India apparently hoped to use such a declaration to provoke a political settlement that would bind Union Carbide, India, the United States, as well as the private Indian plaintiffs. Thus, the Bhopal case is yet another graphic example of the intertwining of public and private that we have witnessed in international business litigation throughout this volume.

The Supreme Court returned to the *forum non conveniens* issue, and clarified the goals of the doctrine in 2007. In *Sinochem Int'l Co. v. Malaysia International Shipping Corp.*,[37] a Malaysian shipping company carrying steel coils for a Chinese chemical company filed suit in a Pennsylvania federal district court, accusing Sinochem of fraudulent misrepresentation. Sinochem replied that the U.S. court had no personal jurisdiction over the Chinese company, but the District Court declined to rule on the issue, dismissing instead on *forum non conveniens*, so that the case might be tried instead in Chinese Admiralty Court. In an opinion by Justice Ginsburg, the Court's civil procedure expert,[38] the Supreme Court unanimously ruled that "a district court has discretion to respond at once to a defendant's *forum non conveniens* plea, and need not take up first any other threshold objection. In particular, a court need not resolve whether it has authority to adjudicate the cause— *i.e.*, subject-matter jurisdiction—or personal jurisdiction over the defendant, if it determines that, in any event, a foreign tribunal is plainly the more suitable arbiter of the merits of the case."[39] The ruling made clear that if a case would plainly be tried more conveniently in a foreign court, a court should immediately dismiss for *forum non conveniens* rather than undergo a burdensome and unnecessary task of determining jurisdiction before dismissing the case anyway. The Court found that the purpose of the *forum non conveniens* doctrine is to spare the court from dealing with inconvenient cases; it would therefore defeat that purpose to force the court to wrestle with difficult jurisdictional issues when it has

theory as a novel way to pierce the corporate veil under domestic law, they also suggested that such a theory could be justified by international law, such as international codes of conduct directed at guiding the conduct of multinational enterprises. *See* Jay Westbrook, *Theories of Parent Company Liability and the Prospects for International Settlement,* 20 Tex. Int'l L.J. 321, 326–27 (1985).

**37.** ___ U.S. ___, 127 S.Ct. 1184 (2007).

**38.** Justice Ruth Bader Ginsburg did her early academic work on Swedish civil procedure, and for many years taught Civil Procedure as a professor at Columbia Law School.

**39.** 127 S.Ct. at 1188.

discretion to decide and dispose of the case on venue grounds, without conducting that vexing inquiry.

## C. Forum–Selection Clauses

We now arrive at the final venue question: if the parties to the litigation are not strangers, but have previously signed a forum-selection clause, how much deference should the court pay to that clause? Again, this is an issue that has historically divided common law and civil law jurisdictions. In civil law jurisdictions, the words *prorogatio fori* derived from the term used in Roman canon law to signify that the parties were themselves stipulating a forum.[40] Some "prorogation" clauses purported to confer jurisdiction on one court, while others (sometimes called "derogation" clauses) went further and purported to oust other courts of jurisdiction to hear a dispute.[41] Thereafter, the civil law jurisdictions have been virtually unanimous in enforcing such forum-selection clauses, with only minor exceptions.[42] In more recent times, however, this rule of near-total deference to party autonomy has had the effect of subjecting weaker contracting parties to adhesion contracts, which the courts have then enforced almost blindly. In response, more progressive civil law authorities, such as France and Germany, have recently enacted laws providing that forum-selection clauses are invalid unless all parties to the contract are merchants.[43] Following this trend, Articles 12 and 15 of the Brussels Convention invalidated most jurisdictional clauses in insurance policies and consumer contracts which grossly favor the stronger bargaining power (the insurer and the creditor, respectively).

American courts came at the issue from virtually the opposite direction, yet have now arrived at almost the same place. Early American cases began by holding that the parties have no power to oust another court of jurisdiction by agreement, and indeed that such clauses violated public policy.[44] Beginning in the mid–1950s,

---

**40.** *See* RUDOLF SCHLESINGER, HANS BAADE, MIRJAN DAMASKA & PETER HERZOG, COMPARATIVE LAW: CASES, TEXT, MATERIALS 386 (5th ed. 1988).

**41.** *See generally* 1 Georges Delaume, *Transnational Contracts—Applicable Law and Settlement of Disputes* (2d ed. 1986).

**42.** *See* SCHLESINGER, *supra* note 40, at 387 (noting, for example, the exception for title to land located in another country).

**43.** Zivilprozessordnung (German Code of Civil Procedure), § 38, par. 2, as amended in 1986; French Code of Civil Procedure, art. 48.

**44.** *See, e.g.*, Carbon Black Export, Inc. v. The Monrosa, 254 F.2d 297, 300–01 (5th Cir. 1958); United Fuel Gas Co. v. Columbian Fuel Corp., 165 2d. 746, 749 (4th Cir. 1948). *See generally* Michael Karayanni, *The Public Policy Exception to the Enforcement of Forum Selection Clauses*, 34 DUQ. L. REV. 1009 (1996).

however, U.S. courts began to modify that view, giving effect to the forum-selection clause if it was deemed fair and reasonable.[45]

In *M/S Bremen v. Zapata Offshore Co.*,[46] the Supreme Court took up the question and reversed the presumption to favor such clauses. In that case, Zapata, a Houston-based corporation, contracted that Unterweser, a German corporation, would tow an ocean-going drilling rig from Louisiana to Italy. The contract between the two parties stated simply that any dispute arising between the two parties must be treated before the London Court of Justice. As Unterweser was hauling the rig, it became damaged in a storm off the coast of Florida and was towed to Tampa. Zapata then filed an *in personam* suit in Florida federal district court against Unterweser and an *in rem* action against Unterweser's ship, the *M/S Bremen*, for negligence and breach of contract. Unterweser responded by filing a motion for specific performance of the forum-selection clause, for dismissal on *forum non conveniens*, and for a stay of the action pending litigation in London, the contractually selected forum. Unterweser simultaneously started an action in the London court as the contract provided. Thus, *Bremen* shows us two ways in which the validity of a forum-selection clause can be judicially tested: first, by one party to the contract starting an action in the non-selected forum, and the other party moving to dismiss on *forum non conveniens*. The second option is for the party seeking to enforce the clause to file affirmative litigation in the selected forum, here London, seeking specific performance and a stay of the other forum's action.

Here the first option was invoked, leaving it to the non-selected forum to decide whether or not to relinquish jurisdiction over the case by enforcing the forum-selection clause[47] The district court chose to retain jurisdiction, reasoning that the plaintiff Zapata's forum choice should not be disturbed unless the balance of conveniences strongly favored the defendant. A closely divided *en banc* court of appeals affirmed. In an opinion by Chief Justice Burger, the Supreme Court reversed and remanded with orders to enforce the forum-selection clause. In the process the court issued a ringing endorsement of party autonomy in international business transactions.

**45.** *See, e.g.*, Wm. H. Muller and Co. v. Swedish American Line Ltd., 224 F.2d 806 (2d Cir. 1955), *cert. denied*, 350 U.S. 903 (1955).

**46.** 407 U.S. 1 (1972).

**47.** Because the Florida court had admiralty jurisdiction over the ship, both the British and the American courts had subject matter and personal jurisdiction over the defendants. The sole issue was thus venue, not jurisdiction.

For at least two decades we have witnessed an expansion of overseas commercial activities by business enterprises based in the United States. The barrier of distance that once tended to confine a business concern to a modest territory no longer does so. Here we see an American company with special expertise contracting with a foreign company to tow a complex machine thousands of miles across seas and oceans. The expansion of American business and industry will hardly be encouraged if, notwithstanding solemn contracts, we insist on a parochial concept that all disputes must be resolved under our laws and in our courts. . . . We cannot have trade and commerce in world markets and international waters exclusively on our terms, governed by our laws, and resolved in our courts.[48]

The Court went on to hold that forum-selection clauses are "prima facie valid and should be enforced unless enforcement is shown by the resisting party to be 'unreasonable' under the circumstances."[49]

In so holding, the Court gave heavy weight to four factors. First, the Court stressed deference to *party autonomy* as an engine for promoting U.S. business ventures abroad. A presumption in favor of forum-selection clauses, the Court found, "accords with ancient concepts of freedom of contract and reflects an appreciation of the expanding horizons of American contracts who seek business in all parts of the world."[50] When a choice of forum is freely "made in an arm's-length negotiation by experienced and sophisticated businessmen," the Court suggested, "absent some compelling and countervailing reason it should be honored by the parties and enforced by the courts."[51]

At the same time, however, the Court placed unusual weight on *comity* toward other nations and their judicial systems. The Court decided that the prejudice against forum-selection clauses "reflects something of a provincial attitude regarding the fairness of other tribunals,"[52] which failed to recognize the value of London courts as "a neutral forum with expertise in the subject matter" that plainly "meet the standards of neutrality and long experience in admiralty litigation."[53]

---

**48.** *Bremen*, 407 U.S. at 8–9.

**49.** *Id.* at 10. Although the Court's holding strictly applied only to federal district courts sitting in admiralty jurisdiction, the *Bremen* presumption has since been applied to all forum-selection clauses. *See* Young Lee, *Forum Selection Clauses: Problems of Enforcement in Di-* *versity Cases and State Courts*, 35 Co-LUM. J. TRANSNAT'L L. 663, 668 n. 22 (1997) (collecting cases).

**50.** *Id.* at 11.

**51.** *Id.* at 12.

**52.** *Id.* at 12.

**53.** *Id.* at 12.

Third, the Court stressed the need of business people "to obtain *certainty* as to the applicable substantive law" in the modern international business environment.[54] "The elimination of all such uncertainties by agreeing in advance on a forum acceptable to both parties is an indispensable element in international trade, commerce, and contracting."[55] In a world in which "business once essentially local now operate in world markets,"[56] the Court suggested, this need for business certainty had fueled the emerging international consensus in support of forum-selection clauses.[57]

A fourth and overlooked factor was the American courts' own crowded dockets, a particular concern of Chief Justice Burger. The presumption against forum-selection clauses, the Court said, "appears to rest at core on historical judicial resistance to any attempt to reduce the power and business of a particular court and has little place in an era *when all courts are overloaded.*"[58] As we shall see below, this impulse to relieve perceived overcrowding of the federal courts has undergirded the Burger Court's and now the Rehnquist Court's support of case-diversion efforts that include not just forum-selection clauses, but also alternative dispute-resolution in domestic courts and domestic and international commercial arbitration.

These factors help explain why the *Bremen* Court held that the forum-selection clauses should be enforced absent "compelling and countervailing reason[s]." These include claims that the contract was unreasonable, unjust, invalid for fraud, overreaching or overweening influence, or otherwise in violation of public policy.[59] As a practical matter, *Bremen* interacts with the doctrine of *forum non conveniens* to strongly shift the burden of demonstrating an inconvenient venue. Absent a forum-selection clause, *Piper* places the burden on the *defendant* to overcome the presumption in favor of the plaintiff's selected forum by showing that private and public interest factors favor dismissal. But if the parties have previously concluded a forum-selection clause, and the plaintiff sues in a non-selected forum, *Bremen* shifts the burden to the *plaintiff* of showing why the forum-selection clause should not presumptively enforced. Under *Bremen*, the plaintiff cannot overcome that presumption

---

**54.** *Id.* at 14 (emphasis added).

**55.** *Id.* at 14.

**56.** *Id.* at 12.

**57.** *Id.* at 11 (noting that the Court's "approach is substantially that followed in other common-law countries including England"); *id.* at 13 ("Manifestly much uncertainty and possibly great in-

convenience to both parties could arise if a suit could be maintained in any jurisdiction in which an accident might occur . . .").

**58.** *Id.* at 13 (emphasis added).

**59.** As in *Piper*, the Court chose, after declaring its holding, to give extensive guidance to the lower courts as to how to apply its test. *See id.* at 15–20.

merely by showing that the contractually selected forum has become inconvenient. "[I]t should be incumbent on the party seeking to escape his contract to show that trial in the contractual forum will be so gravely difficult and inconvenient that he will for all practical purposes be deprived of his day in court."[60] Alternatively, the plaintiff must show that the clause by which he agreed to the forum did not represent a true exercise of personal autonomy, because it was obtained by fraud, undue influence, or is otherwise unreasonable or unjust.

On its face, *Bremen* seems correct. As in the foreign sovereign immunity area, the U.S. was slowly catching up with evolving trends in international law. As the Court noted, a presumption favoring rather than disfavoring prior forum-selection is far better suited to "present-day commercial realities and expanding international trade."[61] Like the plaintiffs in *Piper*, Zapata chose to sue in Tampa because it was forum-shopping for a more favorable body of law.[62] To allow it to escape its prior agreement would have stripped Unterweser of the benefit of its bargain. *Bremen* thus struck a balance between judicial deference and examination of the underlying power relationship between contracting parties. On the one hand, deferring to contractual provisions seems consistent both with the notion of sanctity of contract and with the traditional functions of the doctrine of venue. As a personal privilege, venue—unlike subject matter jurisdiction—can always be waived by the defendant. Unlike the jurisdiction of the federal courts—a grant of authority by the legislature that is beyond the litigants' power to stipulate—the place *where* the judicial authority is exercised relates to the convenience of the litigants and hence has always been more subject to their contractual disposition. On the other hand, the exception to enforceability for fraud and overweening influence supports party autonomy, by giving courts discretion to decline enforcement of clauses that violate a forum's public policy, or that reflect one party's unfair bargaining power.

The Supreme Court's latest encounter with forum-selection clauses, *Carnival Cruise Lines v. Shute*,[63] has arguably tipped the balance too far toward deference to contract. There, the Court sustained a domestic forum-selection clause giving jurisdiction over a suit arising out of a holiday cruise to the courts of Florida, where the shipowner was headquartered. The Court so ruled despite the

**60.** *Id.* at 18.

**61.** *Id.* at 15.

**62.** As Justice Douglas noted in dissent, the contract contained two clauses purporting to exculpate Unterweser, which were not enforceable under U.S. law, but would have been under UK law. *See id.* at 23 (Douglas, J., dissenting).

**63.** 499 U.S. 585 (1991).

fact that the forum-selection clause was contained only on the passenger's cruise ticket.[64] In *Bremen*, the Court had emphasized that "we are concerned with a far from routine transaction between companies of two different nations contemplating the tow of a extremely costly piece of equipment from Louisiana across the Gulf of Mexico and the Atlantic Ocean, through the Mediterranean Sea." The Court further recognized that the choice of forum had been "made in an arm's-length negotiation by experienced and sophisticated businessmen." In *Carnival Cruise Lines*, by contrast, the Court deferred broadly to what appeared to be an adhesion contract between a sophisticated seller and an ordinary consumer. Its deference was so broad that it appears to grant virtually unlimited forum choice to the contract's drafter. While the Court's opinion strengthens even more the uniformity of the pro-forum selection rule, it does so at the expense of party autonomy and international commercial realities.

As the common and civil law views on forum-selection clauses have converged, the possibilities have increased for addressing the question by international treaty or other uniform rule. Before appraising those treaty efforts,[65] we must first examine how the U.S. courts have construed parallel, existing multilateral conventions regarding service of process, taking of evidence and the enforcement of foreign arbitral awards.

---

**64.** 407 U.S. 1 (1972).

**65.** *See* Chapter XI, *infra*. *See generally* Kurt Nadelmann, *The Hague Conference on Private International Law and the Validity of Forum Selecting Clauses*, 13 AM. J. COMP. L. 157 (1964). For commentary on the Hague Judgments Convention drafting exercise, see Arthur T. von Mehren, *Recognition and Enforcement of Foreign Judgments: A new Approach for the Hague Conference?*, 57 LAW & CONTEMP. PROBS. 271 (1994). For a prescient proposal for a multilateral treaty to secure uniform enforcement of forum-selection clauses, see Nicolas Fernandez, *Enforcement of Forum–Selection Clauses in Transnational Contracts—Is Agreement Possible Between the United States and the European Economic Community?*, 3 FLA. INT'L L.J. 264, 297–300 (1988).

# Chapter IX

## SERVICE OF PROCESS

I have described how *de facto* Federal Rules of Transnational Civil Procedure have evolved in the courts of the United States to govern international business lawsuits, particularly with respect to the doctrines that govern choice of forum: jurisdiction to adjudicate and venue. This Chapter examines how American courts have viewed the related doctrines of transnational service of process and taking of evidence abroad. Again, my attention will focus on the leading Supreme Court decisions: with respect to service of process, *Volkswagenwerk Aktiengesellschaft v. Schlunk*,[1] and with respect to the taking of evidence, *Societe Nationale Industrielle Aerospatiale v. United States District Court*.[2]

Each of these decisions has reflected the same interplay among the core judicial concerns identified earlier: the Supreme Court's desire to promote uniformity of procedural rules and deference to party autonomy in transnational business decisions, often at the expense of national sovereignty and comity. In the choice-of-forum doctrine reviewed in the last chapter, the Court's main challenge has been to adapt existing common law rules regarding personal jurisdiction and venue to the transnational setting. Yet with respect to the three doctrines at issue here, the Court's primary task has been to interpret the relationship between the Federal Rules of Civil Procedure and two multilateral treaties, the Hague Service and Evidence Conventions.

These treaties grew out of a movement toward coordinated international judicial assistance that built momentum in the 1950s. Shortly after its founding, the Hague Conference on Private International Law produced a Convention on Civil Procedure in 1896, which dealt with international judicial cooperation, with respect not only to service of documents but also the taking of evidence abroad.[3] Under this convention, to which primarily European par-

**1.** 486 U.S. 694 (1988).

**2.** 482 U.S. 522 (1987).

**3.** Organized in 1893 by the Netherlands Government at the initiative of Nobel Prize-winner T.M.C. Asser, the Hague Conference has been critical in the negotiation and drafting of private international law treaties. *See generally* Peter Pfund, *The Progressive Development of Private International Law: The International Process and the United States Approach*, 249 RECUEIL DES COURS 21 (1994); Georges Droz, *A Comment on the Role of the Hague Conference on Private International Law*, 57 LAW & CONTEMP. PROBS. 3 (1994).

ties adhered, transmissions of requests for service were handled exclusively by diplomats, and were abysmally slow. In the early 1950s, the Convention was redrafted to add Japan, the United States and the United Kingdom (among others) and to add English as an official language along with French. Part I of the resulting 1954 Civil Procedure Convention covered service of process, while Part II covered the taking of evidence abroad. By the mid–1960s, these two conventions took separate life. Part I became the 1965 Hague Convention on the Service Abroad of Judicial and Extrajudicial Documents in Civil and Commercial Matters (commonly known as the "Hague Service Convention.")[4] A few years later, Part II became the 1969 Hague Convention on the Taking of Evidence Abroad in Civil or Commercial Matters (commonly known as the "Hague Evidence Convention.").[5] Both Hague Conventions enable litigants to seek assistance from a Central Authority in their sending state to forward a request for service or evidence to a designated central authority in the receiving state, which then passes the request along in a manner consistent with the internal law of the recipient country. These convention processes bring comity and party autonomy into conflict with one another, for while their use is designed to ensure that comity is paid to another nation's sovereignty, that respect comes at a cost to litigants' individual freedom to serve process and to acquire evidence in the manner to which they are accustomed under their national law.

This background helps give context to the particular controversies that have arisen in U.S. courts surrounding each of these treaties, and helps us to assess the correctness of the Supreme Court decisions construing them. Moreover, this background helps explain how state law, the Federal Rules, due process, international law, and comity concerns have all come to intersect in these procedural areas. As in other doctrinal areas, I will argue, the courts have begun to interpret the governing treaties in these procedural areas in deference to private autonomy and separation of powers, but too often at the expense of comity.

## A.  Service

### 1.  *Transnational Service Under the Federal Rules*

At first blush, service seems deceptively simple. The mundane logistical question is how one should deliver court papers, and ensure that others know that it has been done. On examination,

---

4.  20 U.S.T. 361, T.I.A.S. No. 6638.     5.  23 U.S.T. 2555, T.I.A.S. No. 7444.

however, the service issue proves remarkably multi-faceted. To see this point, we must first distinguish between two functions of service. Do the court documents simply give *notice* of the pendency of a lawsuit, or do they represent the delivery of compulsory *process* to an unwilling recipient? When a plaintiff serves a defendant with notice of the pendency of an action, he simply supplies the recipient with information upon which to base a decision whether or not to answer and defend. But when a party serves compulsory process upon an opposing party or third-party witness, he effectively *compels* that witness to do something and threatens him with immediate sanctions should he not comply. If a defendant does not answer a complaint, eventually he may be liable, but only after a default has been pursued and granted, which could take months or even years. But if a witness refuses to comply with compulsory process— for example, an investigatory subpoena—the full enforcement power of the federal courts may immediately be brought to bear upon him.[6]

The Federal Rules of Civil Procedure illustrate this distinction. Federal Rule 4, which governs service of process in the U.S. federal courts, is primarily concerned with bringing *notice* of the commencement of an action to the attention of both the defendant and the court. To that end, the rule provides for a wide range of alternative methods of service. Traditionally, process consists of a copy of the plaintiff's complaint, together with a summons directing the defendant to answer. As in the *Burnham* case, discussed in Chapter VII, process was traditionally served by personal delivery of both documents upon the defendant. But with the rise of long-arm statutes and national commerce, other techniques of service, including mail, came to assume greater prominence. To address the need for greater flexibility, while still ensuring the defendant's receipt of actual notice of the pendency of the action, the service provisions of Federal Rules of Civil Procedure were twice significantly amended, once in 1983, and again in 1993. The 1983 revisions prescribed a host of methods in Federal Rule 4 for serving individuals, corporations, partnerships, other associations, as well as broadly authorizing litigants to use in federal courts the service procedures applied by the courts of the state in which the federal district sits.[7] These revisions allowed various forms of service, including by various forms of mail. By contrast, Federal Rule 45(b), governing subpoena service, does not permit mail service, nor does

---

**6.** *See* Fed. R. Civ. P. 45(e) ("Failure by any person without adequate excuse to obey a subpoena served upon that person may be deemed a contempt of the court from which the subpoena is issued.").

**7.** *See* Fed. R. Civ. P. 4(e).

it allow service of the subpoena merely by delivery to a witness' dwelling. Thus, under the Federal Rules, compulsory process may be served upon an unwilling witness only in person, even within the United States, and even upon a United States citizen.

To evaluate fully the legality of service, it is not sufficient to ask simply whether the plaintiff has followed the service procedures specified by state, federal, statutory or treaty law. In addition to these Federal Rule requirements, any technique of service—whether specified in state, federal, statutory, or treaty law—must also satisfy the U.S. Constitution. In *Pennoyer v. Neff*, the Supreme Court made clear that service of process raises a due process inquiry into whether a plaintiff has properly perfected personal jurisdiction over the defendant by properly serving him with notification of the lawsuit, giving him a reasonable opportunity to be heard.[8] Thus, in addition to satisfying the Federal Rules, any technique of service—whether specified in state, federal, statutory or treaty law—must also meet due process standards. As stated in the Supreme Court's leading decision, *Mullane v. Central Hanover Bank and Trust Co.,*[9] due process mandates that defendant has received "notice reasonably calculated, under all the circumstances, to apprise interested parties of the pendency of the action and afford [him] an opportunity to present [his] objections.... But when notice is a person's due, process which is a mere gesture is not due process. The means employed must be such as one desirous of actually informing the absentee might reasonably adopt to accomplish it."[10]

## a. SERVICE ABROAD

When a party attempts service on an individual residing abroad, both treaty and foreign law enter the picture. After extensive discussions, Federal Rule 4 was finally amended in 1993 to deal with transnational variations in service-of-process law. The most significant changes may be found in the Federal Rules of Civil Procedure 4(f) and 4 (k)(2).

Federal Rule 4(f) provides for six alternative methods by which a party may serve individuals in a foreign country.[11] These meth-

---

**8.** 95 U.S. (5 Otto) 714 (1877).

**9.** 339 U.S. 306 (1950).

**10.** 339 U.S. at 314–15. *See also id.* ("The notice must be of such nature as reasonably to convey the required information, ... and it must afford a reasonable time for those interested to make their appearance.... But if with due regard for the practicalities and peculiarities of the case these conditions are reasonably met the constitutional requirements are satisfied.").

**11.** Rule 4(f) provides that foreign service may be made:

ods, which are followed closely by the service provision for foreign sovereigns in the FSIA,[12] were prompted by a dual concern: to avoid violating the sovereignty of other countries by committing "official" acts within their borders, and thereby to maximize the likelihood that the judgment rendered in the U.S. action could be recognized and enforced abroad.[13]

Federal Rule 4(f)(1) specifies as the first method of serving process abroad "any internationally agreed means reasonably calculated to give notice, such as the Hague Convention on Service Abroad of Judicial and Extrajudicial Documents." The Hague Service Convention, and the Inter–American Convention on Letters Rogatory that is modeled upon it,[14] create an intergovernmentally

(1) by any internationally agreed means reasonably calculated to give notice, such as those means authorized by the Hague Convention on the Service Abroad of Judicial and Extrajudicial Documents; or

(2) if there is no internationally agreed means of service or the applicable international agreement allows other means of service, provided that service is reasonably calculated to give notice:

   (a) in the manner prescribed by the law of the foreign country for service in that country in an action in any of its courts of general jurisdiction; or

   (b) as directed by the foreign authority in response to a letter rogatory or letter of request; or

   (c) unless prohibited by the law of the foreign country, by

      (i) delivery to the individual personally of a copy of the summons and the complaint; or

      (ii) any form of mail requiring a signed receipt, to be addressed and dispatched by the clerk of the court to the party to be served; or

(3) by other means not prohibited by international agreement as may be directed by the court.

**12.** Fed. R. Civ. P. 4(j)(1) directs that "[s]ervice upon a foreign state or a political subdivision, agency or instrumentality thereof shall be effected pursuant to 28 U.S.C. § 1608," the service-of-process provision of the Foreign Sovereign Immunities Act. 28 U.S.C. § 1608 specifies a precise sequence to be followed for suing foreign states and their entities, starting by delivery of summons and complaint in accordance with any special arrangement between the parties, or in accordance with an applicable service convention like the Hague Service Convention, or by any form of mail from clerk of the court to the foreign ministry, or by the clerk of the court to the U.S. Secretary of State. When serving an agency or instrumentality of a foreign state, § 1608 specifies that this be done by special arrangement, or by roughly the same sequence found in Federal Rule 4(f).

**13.** The Reporter to the Advisory Committee on the Civil Rules when the predecessor provision to Rule 4(f) was adopted later verified that concern for the territorial sovereignty of foreign countries had helped spur adoption of the rule. *See* Benjamin Kaplan, *Amendments of the Federal Rules of Civil Procedure, 1961–1963(I)*, 77 Harv. L. Rev. 601, 635–36 (1964).

**14.** *See* Inter–American Convention on Letters Rogatory, Jan. 30, 1975, *reprinted in* 14 Int'l Leg. Mats. 339 (1975); Additional Protocol to the Inter–American Convention on Letters Rogatory, May 8, 1979, *reprinted in* 18 Int'l Leg. Mats. 1238 (1979). *See also* Pizzabiocche v. Vinelli, 772 F.Supp. 1245 (M.D. Fla. 1991) (holding that Inter–American Convention was not intended to be mandatory or exclusive means of serving process among signatory nations).

approved method for serving documents abroad in a signatory state by enabling litigants to use their own State's Central Authority to forward to a designated Central Authority in the receiving state a request to serve process on the defendant. Article 1 states that the Convention "shall apply in all cases, in civil or commercial matters where there is occasion to transmit a judicial or extrajudicial document for service abroad." Thus, service through the Convention is available only in civil or commercial, not criminal, matters and may be used to send any judicial or extrajudicial document, including subpoenas (if the host government does not object). The Convention authorizes service in the manner prescribed by the internal law of the country where service is made, by any particular method requested by the applicant which is not incompatible with the internal law, or any other means not incompatible with local law if as the recipient voluntarily accepts it.[15]

If one does not resort to Convention service, a second method permitted by Rule 4(f)(2)(a) is service "reasonably calculated to give notice ... in the manner prescribed by the law of the foreign country for service in that country in an action in any of its courts of general jurisdiction." The advantage of serving as permitted by internal law is that plaintiff is less likely to encounter objections from the foreign government, thereby avoiding the need to involve the Central Authority of the country of service. Particularly if the assets against which enforcement is likely to be sought are located within that jurisdiction, it makes sense for the plaintiff to follow local standards to the extent feasible. The countervailing danger is that a U.S. court might later find the foreign method of service "not reasonably calculated to give notice" as due process requires, thus rendering the judgment null and void in an American court.[16]

Third, a litigant may attempt service "as directed by the foreign authority in response to a letter rogatory or letter of request."[17] A letter rogatory is a formal court-to-court letter of request from a U.S. court invoking the aid of the foreign court in helping to serve process. The transmittal of letters rogatory is governed by statute and federal regulations, which authorize the U.S. State Department to receive, forward, and return after execu-

---

**15.** Hague Convention on the Service Abroad of Judicial and Extra–Judicial Documents in Civil or Commercial Matters, art. 5, Nov. 15, 1965, 20 U.S.T. 361, 658 U.N.T.S. 163.

**16.** If process is not served under one of the methods sanctioned by Federal Rule 4, the defendant not only has a defense for insufficiency of service of process under Fed. R. Civ. P. 12(b)(5), but can also move that any later judgment be vacated under Fed. R. Civ. Pro. 60(b)(4) (motion for relief from judgment).

**17.** Fed. R. Civ. P. 4(f)(2)(B).

tion, letters rogatory requesting service of process abroad.[18] Those provisions do not preclude transmittal of letters rogatory directly from the issuing court to the addressee court, nor their return in similar fashion, if the foreign country so permits. The usual procedure is to apply to the U.S. court for a letter rogatory, with an affidavit, two copies of the documents to be served, certified translations, and a "request for international judicial assistance." The court will sign, seal, and send the request to the U.S. Department of State special consular services with a check, and the papers will be delivered by the U.S. Embassy to the receiving country's Ministry of Foreign Affairs with a request to transmit to through appropriate channels. The service return then comes back through the same channels.[19] The principal advantage of letters rogatory is that some countries—notably Switzerland—permit no other form of service.[20] But the disadvantage, as the above description makes evident, is that the procedure is time-consuming, cumbersome, and often requires the expensive assistance of foreign counsel. Moreover, letters rogatory may become delayed or quashed if chilly relations prevail between the U.S. and the country of whom service is requested, or if the foreign authorities refuse to serve process for certain types of actions. As a result, litigants tend to avoid using letters rogatory, unless no other method of local service is available and enforcement of the judgment is expected to be sought in the foreign country.

Rule 4(f)(2)(C) specifies the fourth and fifth service methods— personal service and service by "any form of mail requiring a signed receipt—so long as neither of these methods is "prohibited by the law of the foreign country."[21] This proviso was added in

---

**18.** *See* 28 U.S.C. § 1781 (1994) (authorizing U.S. Department of State both to receive letters rogatory from foreign courts and to transmit them to American courts and to receive letters rogatory from American courts and to transmit them to foreign courts). The State Department's controlling regulations may be found at 22 C.F.R. § 92.54 (1995). *See also* 28 U.S.C. § 1696 (governing incoming service).

**19.** Certain bilateral treaties (for example France–Belgium), and Latin American countries (for example Colombia), for example, have in the past permitted direct court-to-court communication. Otherwise, the papers are sent either directly to U.S. Embassy in the country of service or to the Office of Special Consular Services of the De-

partment of State in Washington, D.C., which it turn forwards the request to the foreign Ministry of Foreign Affairs.

**20.** *See* Swiss Penal Code, art. 271 ("whoever, without authorization, executes acts in Swiss territory which are attributed to an administrative or government authority, on behalf of a foreign state ... and whoever executes such acts on behalf of a foreign person or another foreign organization ... will be punished with prison, and in severe cases with penitentiary.").

**21.** Some countries, for example Japan, require that service be made as an official act by an officer of the court. *See, e.g.*, Chin Kim and Eliseo Sisneros, *Comparative Overview of Service of Process: United States, Japan, and Attempts at*

response to several U.S. court decisions permitting use of these alternative service methods in the prior version of Rule 4, even if they violated the law of the country in which service is effected.[22] Given *Burnham*, personal in-hand service, usually by foreign counsel, appears most likely to satisfy American standards of due process, and most likely to give actual notice, but may violate local law.[23] The fifth method, return receipt mail, has the advantage of being inexpensive and fairly quick, as well as requiring no activity from foreign authorities higher than the postal service. But service by mail does not permit enforcement of a U.S. judgment in those countries that require personal service and is considered offensive by such countries as Switzerland and the Federal Republic of Germany.[24] As a last resort, Rule 4(f)(3) finally permits service by "any other means not prohibited by international agreement as may be directed by the court." This umbrella provision has the advantage of allowing a court to tailor the method to a particular circumstance, particularly when all other methods have been tried and failed.[25]

In choosing from among these available service modes, a plaintiff's attorney should first ask a practical question: "Where are defendant's assets?" If those assets are in the country where defendant is being served, it seems most sensible to serve according to that country's internal law, while paying heed that due process requirements in the U.S. are also satisfied. If those assets are in a third country, serving in a manner consistent with the third country's internal law similarly maximizes the chance of rendering

*International Unity*, 23 VAND. J. TRANSNAT'L L. 299, 306 (1990); *see also id.* at 309 ("Failure to follow the explicit requirements of the Japanese courts may result in a subsequent judgment's having no effect.").

**22.** *See, e.g.*, SEC v. International Swiss Investments Corp., 895 F.2d 1272 (9th Cir. 1990); Bersch v. Drexel Firestone, Inc., 389 F.Supp. 446 (S.D.N.Y. 1974), *modified*, 519 F.2d 974 (2d Cir. 1975), *cert. denied*, 423 U.S. 1018 (1975).

**23.** *See* note 20, *supra*. Swiss authorities have been known to arrest process servers trying to serve foreign process in Switzerland. *See* Kenneth Riesenfeld, *Service of Process Abroad*, 24 INT'L LAW. 55, 59 n.14 (1990).

**24.** *See, e.g.*, Atlantic Steamers Supply Co. v. International Maritime Supplies Co., 268 F.Supp. 1009 (S.D.N.Y.

1967) (Switzerland lodges diplomatic protests with the U.S. Department of State in response to service of process within its territory by both mail and personal service); Low v. Bayerische Motoren Werke, A.G., 88 A.D.2d 504, 449 N.Y.S.2d 733 (1982) (holding mail service to West Germany invalid). Even if mail service is permitted under local law, a practical difficulty arises in proving receipt of mail service based on foreign postal markings, without more concrete proof that the addressee has actually received the documents.

**25.** In the well-publicized case of fugitive financier Robert Vesco, the court apparently authorized service under the predecessor to this provision by allowing the plaintiff's attorney to throw the papers onto the grounds of Vesco's residence, while fleeing from pursuing bodyguards.

service a non-issue in any ultimate enforcement effort there. But if defendant's assets are in the U.S., the pragmatic question becomes: "What is the quickest and most inexpensive method of service that is still likely to give actual notice?" The most reasonable sequence would appear to be: first, receipted mail; second, personal delivery in the receiving country by foreign co-counsel or a process-server (if that country permits); third, any other method permitted in the foreign country that seems consistent with Rule 4(f); fourth, court-ordered ordinary mail under Fed. Rule 4(f)(3); and only in the last resort, service by Hague Service Convention and letters rogatory.[26] The broader point is that, despite the Rule drafters' best efforts to make the Hague Service Convention the service mode of first resort, over time, the practical incentives that transnational litigators face have pushed Convention service far down the preferred list of service options.

## b. NATIONAL CONTACTS AND TRANSIENT JURISDICTION

The 1993 amendments to Federal Rule 4 also addressed two lingering issues of personal jurisdiction discussed in Chapter VII national contacts and transient jurisdiction.[27] The first issue was twice raised and ducked by the Supreme Court: how to subject foreign defendants in federal question cases to the personal jurisdiction of federal courts, based upon their national contacts with the United States?[28] After studying that question, the Advisory Committee for the Federal Rules found a gap in the enforcement of federal law. If a corporate defendant residing outside the United States had sufficient contacts with the U.S. as a whole to justify the application of United States law under the "effects doctrine," but lacked minimum contacts with any single state to support jurisdiction under that state's long-arm law, no American court in the

---

**26.** *See* Riesenfeld, *supra* note 23, at 76.

**27.** For a thorough discussion of these issues, see Gary Born and Andrew Vollmer, *The Effect of the Revised Federal Rules of Civil Procedure on Personal Jurisdiction, Service, and Discovery in International Cases*, 150 F.R.D. 221 (1993).

**28.** See Omni Capital Int'l, Ltd. v. Rudolf Wolff and Co., 484 U.S. 97, 102 n. 5 (1987); Asahi Metal Indus. Co. v. Superior Court, 480 U.S. 102, 113 n. *

(1987). Lower federal courts had regularly upheld the constitutionality of federal court assertions of personal jurisdiction based on national contacts, at least in federal question cases. *See, e.g.*, Go–Video, Inc. v. Akai Electric Co., 885 F.2d 1406 (9th Cir. 1989); Trans–Asiatic Oil, Ltd. v. Apex Oil Co., 743 F.2d 956, 959 (1st Cir. 1984); FTC v. Jim Walter Corp., 651 F.2d 251, 256 (5th Cir. 1981); Mariash v. Morrill, 496 F.2d 1138 (2d Cir. 1974). *See generally* Robert Casad, *Personal Jurisdiction in Federal Question Cases*, 70 Tex. L. Rev. 1589 (1992).

United States could hear a valid civil claim under the statute against that defendant. To address that lacuna, in 1993 the Supreme Court finally added Federal Rule of Civil Procedure 4(k)(2), which provides:

> If the exercise of jurisdiction is consistent with the Constitution and laws of the United States, serving a summons ... is also effective, with respect to claims arising under federal law, to establish personal jurisdiction over the person of any defendant who is not subject to the jurisdiction of the courts of general jurisdiction of any state.

In combination, new Federal Rules 4(k)(2) and 4(f) come close to authorizing world-wide service of process in federal question cases.[29] But ironically, this revision may not prove to be nearly as great a boon for American plaintiffs as one might first think. As Born and Vollmer note, since this provision only applies to a "defendant who is not subject to the jurisdiction of the courts of general jurisdiction of any state," a plaintiff will not be able to invoke Rule 4(k)(2)'s "national contacts" test "unless it identifies all the states in which the defendant has some contacts, analyzes the long-arm statute of each of those states, researches the judicial decisions applying the statutes, and properly concludes that none of the statutes would permit the state to exercise personal jurisdiction over the defendant."[30]

Conversely, if Rule 4(k)(2) does end up significantly expanding federal court personal jurisdiction, that may sound its death knell. For as noted above, the federal rulemakers lack power under the Rules Enabling Act "to abridge, enlarge or modify any substantive right."[31] If, in fact, Rule 4(k)(2) has granted to federal courts an authority to exercise personal jurisdiction that they did not earlier possess, then arguably that provision lies beyond the scope of the

---

**29.** Federal Rule 4 does *not* provide an independent basis for extraterritorial assertion of personal jurisdiction, which must be found in the relevant federal or state statute. Until now, express statutory provisions for service abroad pursuant to court order have been scattered throughout the U.S. Code. *See, e.g.,* 35 U.S.C. §§ 146, 293 (1952) (patents); 38 U.S.C. § 784(a) (1958) (veterans' insurance); 38 U.S.C. § 1292 (*as amended* 1965) (marine war risk insurance). Section 12 of the Clayton Act, 15 U.S.C. § 12 *et seq.* (1976), for example, permits service of process on corporations in judicial districts where the corporation is an "inhabitant," or "wherever it may be found"—thereby establishing personal jurisdiction over the corporation in the forum district. In addition, U.S. courts have found valid extraterritorial service by mail pursuant to various statutes that do not specify the manner of service. *See* Zurini v. United States, 189 F.2d 722 (8th Cir. 1951) (8 U.S.C. § 1451 (1976), immigration law); SEC v. Briggs, 234 F.Supp. 618 (N.D. Ohio 1964) (1933 and 1934 Securities Acts, 15 U.S.C. § 77 *et seq.*) (1976 and Supp. II 1978).

**30.** Born & Vollmer, *supra* note 27, at 226.

**31.** 28 U.S.C. § 2072 (1994).

Supreme Court's formal rule-making authority. As a red flag to the Supreme Court, the Committee on Rules of Practice and Procedure of the Judicial Conference even added a "Special Note" to its report "call[ing] the attention of the Supreme Court and Congress to new subdivision (k)(2)," with the clear aim of triggering further Supreme Court or legislative study of this question.[32]

Although the Federal Rules Advisory Committee stated during its deliberations that it "does not recommend language to deal with th[e] problem" of transient jurisdiction, the final language of Rule 4(k)(2) also seems to cover that issue.[33] By stating that service establishes personal jurisdiction when "the exercise of jurisdiction is consistent with the Constitution and laws of the United States," under the *Burnham* rule discussed in Chapter VII, Rule 4(k)(2) would appear to allow a federal court to assert transient jurisdiction over a person temporarily in the United States on a federal claim, even if he has almost no contacts with any state of the United States. If federal courts apply the rule to assert tag jurisdiction over European defendants, we may soon expect a clash between this new federal rule and the "exorbitant jurisdiction" provisions of the Brussels Convention. A further result could also be to reverse, in a future case, the result in the *Helicopteros Nacionales* case discussed in Chapter VII. For it would appear that a federal court could henceforth assert jurisdiction over a foreign company based solely on service made upon its corporate representative who is temporarily passing through the district.[34] It would remain to be seen whether such a result would trigger a foreign outcry and perhaps even retaliatory legislation in foreign countries, aimed at American corporate executives who may happen to pass temporarily through those jurisdictions.

## c.  TREATIES, COMITY, AND CUSTOMARY INTERNATIONAL LAW

When service in a U.S. civil action is attempted upon a foreign subject on foreign soil, international law enters the analysis in two ways. First, the party attempting service must ask whether the

---

**32.** Advisory Committee on Civil Rules of the Committee on Rules of Practice and Procedure of the Judicial Conference, *Committee Notes*, 146 F.R.D. 401, 557 (1993).

**33.** *See* Letter from John F. Grady, Chair, Advisory Committee on Civil Rules to Hon. Joseph F. Weis, Jr., Chair, Standing Committee on Rules of Practice and Procedure, at 14 (June 19,

1990) *quoted* in Born & Vollmer, *supra* note 27, at 228.

**34.** *See, e.g.*, Aluminal Indus., Inc. v. Newtown Commercial Assocs., 89 F.R.D. 326 (S.D.N.Y. 1980); *Cf. Burnham*, 495 U.S. at 610 n.1 (Scalia, J.) (finding that "regular service of summons upon [the corporation's] president while he was in [the forum State] acting in that capacity" was sufficient to support general jurisdiction over his company).

procedure employed comports with comity and customary international law, and if not, whether the rules be construed in a way that avoids conflict with those international law standards. Second, the party must ask whether the mode of service applied comports with the Hague Service Convention or any other relevant treaty. The first issue was raised most prominently in the D.C. Circuit's 1980 opinion in *FTC v. Compagnie De Saint–Gobain–Pont–A–Mousson (SGPM)*;[35] the second in the U.S. Supreme Court's 1988 decision in *Volkswagenwerk Aktiengesellschaft v. Schlunk*.[36]

### i. Service in Accordance with Customary International Law

In *SGPM*, the U.S. Federal Trade Commission sought to serve an investigatory subpoena by registered mail to Paris upon a French company that was being investigated for possible unfair trade practices. When the company and the French government protested, the FTC successfully petitioned a Washington D.C. federal district judge for orders enforcing the subpoena. The district court found that Congress "intended" the FTC to deliver its compulsory processes solely with the aid of foreign postal authorities, but the U.S. Court of Appeals for the D.C. Circuit reversed. Writing for the court, Judge Wilkey (the author of the *Laker* decision discussed in Chapter IV) found that the FTC's authorizing statute was silent on the question whether Congress had authorized extraterritorial service of investigatory subpoenas by registered mail. After a detailed examination of international law, however, the court concluded that international law principles "disfavor methods of extraterritorial subpoena service circumventing official channels of judicial assistance, oppose judicial enforcement of investigatory subpoenas abroad, and prohibit the particular method of service employed here."[37] In particular, Judge Wilkey noted, the FTC's mailing of an investigatory subpoena into French territory constituted an extraterritorial act of enforcement jurisdiction undertaken before any court had determined that the FTC possessed prescriptive jurisdiction over SGPM's acts under the effects doctrine. This, he concluded, violated the Permanent Court of International Justice's directive in *S.S. "Lotus"* that "the first and foremost restriction imposed by international law upon a State is that failing the existence of a permissive rule to the contrary it may not

---

**35.** 636 F.2d 1300 (D.C. Cir. 1980).

**36.** 486 U.S. 694 (1988).

**37.** *SGPM*, 636 F.2d at 1310.

exercise its powers in any form in the territory of another State."[38] Applying the *Charming Betsy* presumption that ambiguous statutes must be construed, wherever possible, consistently with international law, the court vacated the enforcement orders on the ground that Congress had not intended to authorize the FTC to serve investigatory subpoenas directly on citizens of other countries by regular mail.

*SGPM* recognized that the distinction between the service of notice and the service of compulsory process takes on greater significance in the event of extraterritorial service. For when notice in the form of summons and complaint is served overseas, the informational nature of that process renders the act of service relatively benign. When compulsory process is served, however, the very act of service may constitute an exercise of U.S. sovereignty within the territory of another sovereign.[39]

This led Judge Wilkey to note a curiosity about service by mail:

Given its informational nature, service of process from the United States into a foreign country by registered mail may thus be viewed as the least intrusive means of service, i. e., the device which minimizes the imposition upon the local authorities caused by official U.S. government action within the boundaries of the local state. Given the compulsory nature of a subpoena, however, subpoena service by direct mail upon a foreign citizen on foreign soil, without warning to the officials of the local state and without initial request for or prior resort to established channels of international judicial assistance, is perhaps maximally intrusive. Not only does it represent a deliberate bypassing of the official authorities of the local state, it allows the full range of judicial sanctions for noncompliance with an agency subpoena to be triggered merely by a foreign citizen's unwillingness to comply with directives contained in an ordinary registered letter.[40]

**38.** *Id.* at 1313 n.67, citing *Case of The S.S. "Lotus,"* (1927) P.C.I.J., Ser. A., No. 10 at 18.

**39.** Thus, the Swiss, for example, traditionally distinguished between "legal documents issued in connection with the proceedings before a foreign tribunal that are of an informational nature, such as papers notifying the recipient of a tax deficiency or of probate matters, [which] may be served privately in Switzerland without the assistance or intervention of the federal or cantonal authorities" and documents relating to any phase of civil litigation that attempt to command the addressee to appear or perform an act, which may not be served privately. Arthur R. Miller, *International Cooperation in Litigation Between the United States and Switzerland: Unilateral Procedural Accommodation in a Test Tube,* 49 MINN. L. REV. 1069, 1075 (1965) (emphasis added).

**40.** *SGPM,* 630 F.2d at 1313–14. *See also* Hans Smit, *International Aspects of Federal Civil Procedure,* 61 COLUM. L. REV. 1031, 1042 n.58 (1961) ("[S]ince service [of process] by mail requires ac-

Congress provided the FTC with the missing authority in a statute enacted shortly after the issuance of the subpoena disputed in the SGPM case.[41] But more recently, the foreign sovereignty issue arose again with respect to another 1993 amendment to Federal Rule 4(d)(2), concerning so-called "waivers" of service. That provision authorizes plaintiffs to send process to defendants, with a request that they "waive" formal service of process. If a "defendant located within the United States" fails to comply and refuses to waive service, he may be penalized by an award of fees and costs, but foreign defendants who similarly refuse suffer no parallel financial penalty.[42] The limitation of the cost-shifting provision to U.S. residents resulted from forceful objections raised by foreign governments to the original amendment, which drew no distinctions between American and foreign resident defendants. The proposal not only triggered negative reactions from several foreign countries, but also the U.S. State and Justice Department.[43] Following this critical commentary, the Supreme Court took the virtually unprecedented step of returning the proposed amendment to the Judicial Conference for further examination, which eventually led to its revised language. In an oddly diffident statement, the Committee Notes suggested the hope "that, since transmission of the notice and waiver forms is a private nonjudicial act, does not purport to effect service, and is not accompanied by any summons or directive from a court, use of the procedure will not offend foreign sovereignties. . . ."[44]

tivity only on the part of a foreign country's postal authorities, it is one of the forms of service least likely to be prohibited.").

**41.** *See* 636 F.2d at 1325 n. 140.

**42.** The rule provides: "If a defendant located within the United States fails to comply with a request for waiver made by a plaintiff located in the United States, the court shall impose the costs subsequently incurred in effecting service on the defendant unless good cause for the failure be shown." For fuller discussion of the issue, see Born & Vollmer, *supra* note 27, at 229–35.

**43.** *See, e.g.,* U.K. Embassy Note No. 63 (20 February 1991) attached to Letter from Edwin D. Williamson, The Legal Adviser of the U.S. Department of State to the Honorable William H.

Rehnquist, The Chief Justice of the United States (Apr. 19, 1991), *reprinted in* Born & Vollmer, *supra* note 27, at 231–32 ("The waiver system would conflict with the Hague Service Convention, and it would be oppressive, since agreement would be elicited under the threat of the proposed sanction in costs. . . . We believe that the waiver provision would be objectionable to many other foreign governments as well.")

**44.** Committee Notes, *supra* note 32, at 562. The same concern for foreign sovereignty led the Committee to render the waiver-of-service provisions inapplicable to persons subject to service under Fed. R. Civ. P. 4(j)(1), namely, foreign states or political subdivisions or foreign state agencies and instrumentalities, such as corporations owned by foreign countries.

## ii.  Service in Accordance with Treaty

Given that direct service of American documents abroad, particularly in the form of compulsory subpoenas, would likely offend foreign sovereignty, two obvious solutions appear. First, a nation may *specifically* consent to a particular request for service, specifying an appropriate special arrangement to minimize the infringement to its own sovereignty.[45] A more flexible and global solution, however, would be for trading nations to consent generally to service of compulsory process upon their nationals by another nation's government agencies by signing an international convention. It was precisely for this reason that the Hague Service Convention was drafted and concluded, with the signatories taking pains to recognize a signatory's right to refuse to honor any particular foreign request for service of judicial documents "if it deems that compliance would infringe its sovereignty or security."[46] For this general solution to be effective in ensuring comity and protecting sovereignty, however, the Convention should ideally apply to all cases in which service is being made abroad.

In *Volkswagenwerk Aktiengesellschaft v. Schlunk*,[47] the Supreme Court rejected that possibility and dramatically narrowed the scope of the Hague Service Convention. The plaintiff brought a wrongful death action in Illinois state court against a German corporation, Volkswagen AG. But rather than serving the lead defendant in Germany under the Convention, the plaintiff instead served its wholly-owned U.S. subsidiary, VW of America, in Illinois. The Illinois courts ruled, as a matter of state law, that the subsidiary acted as an alter ego of the German parent, and hence an involuntary agent for service of process. Given that service could be made in the United States this way, service on the German parent via the Convention was not required.

The Supreme Court, in an opinion by Justice O'Connor, affirmed. Her discussion turned on the text of Article 1, which as we have earlier noted, states that the Convention *"shall apply* in all cases, in civil or commercial matters *where there is occasion to transmit* a judicial or extrajudicial document *for service abroad*." The Court acknowledged that the words "shall apply" meant that

---

**45.** *See, e.g.*, U.S. Department of State, MS file 711.33 1/11–1661, 28 Nov. 1961, *reprinted in* Practice Note, *Contemporary Practice of the United States Relating to International Law*, 56 Am. J. Int'l L. 793, 794 (1962) (recounting November 1961 incident in which Swiss aide-memoire protested service by mail of judicial documents on Swiss residents by a U.S. government agency, and instead requested that "documents destined for Switzerland should be transmitted by the U.S. Embassy in Berne to the Federal Division of Police.").

**46.** *See* Hague Service Convention, art. XIII.

**47.** 486 U.S. 694 (1988).

compliance with the Convention was mandatory, but only when "there is occasion" to transmit a document for service abroad. Whether there is an "occasion" for "service abroad," she said, must be determined by the internal law of the forum, here Illinois. The Court acknowledged that one prime objective of the Convention was that "documents to be served abroad shall be brought to the notice of the addressee in sufficient time."[48] But "we do not think," she said, that "any other country, will draft its internal laws so as to circumvent the Convention in cases in which it would be appropriate to transmit judicial documents for service abroad."[49]

The Court's analysis seems remarkably naive and blind to the very international realities that Chief Justice Burger had stressed so strongly in *Bremen* (discussed in Chapter VIII). While recognizing the mandatory language in Article I, the Court nevertheless treated the Convention as a kind of optional protocol for facilitating service abroad, but only in a very narrow class of cases. If, as the Court suggests, it is up to each forum's internal law to determine when there is "occasion for service abroad," each jurisdiction could gut the Convention's mandatory language simply by deciding under its local law never to require "service abroad." Moreover, as Justice Brennan pointed out in his opinion concurring in the judgment, the negotiating history amply showed that this is exactly what the drafters sought to prevent.[50] The Hague Conference spent much time discussing elimination of *notification au parquet*, a device by which process could be served on a foreign defendant simply by depositing the documents with a designated local official. But as Justice Brennan observed, the Court's solution now leaves contracting nations free entirely to ignore the Convention's terms:

> Under the Court's analysis ... a forum nation could prescribe direct mail service to any foreigner and deem service effective upon deposit in the mailbox, or could arbitrarily designate a domestic agent for any foreign defendant and deem service complete upon receipt domestically by the agent even though there is little likelihood that service would ever reach the defendant [overseas]. In fact, so far as I can tell, the Court's interpretation permits any contracting nation to revive *notification au parquet* so long as the nation's internal law deems

---

**48.**  *Id.* at 703.

**49.**  *Id.* at 705.

**50.**  "Even assuming any quantum of evidence from the negotiating history would suffice to support an interpretation so fundamentally at odds with the Convention's primary purpose, the evidence the Court amasses in support of its reading—two interim comments by the reporter on initial drafts of the Convention suggesting that the forum's internal law would dictate whether a particular form of service implicates the Convention—falls far short." *Id.* at 711.

service complete domestically, ... even though, as the Court concedes, "such methods of service are the least likely to provide a defendant with actual notice," and even though "[t]here is no question but that the Conference wanted to eliminate *notification au parquet*."[51]

Moreover, the concurrence noted, the Court bizarrely clung to a strained reading of the treaty language, even if this interpretation "does not necessarily advance the primary purpose that the Convention itself announces, ... [and] notwithstanding its duty to read the Convention with a view to effecting the objects and purposes of the States thereby contracting."[52]

After *Schlunk*, American plaintiffs have strong incentives to serve a foreign defendant by serving a U. S. subsidiary, by demanding waiver of service, or by simply mailing the process to the defendant. The Court created almost no occasion for such plaintiffs to avoid potential conflict with other jurisdictions by using the painstakingly negotiated Service Convention. The opinion left open several questions: whether service by mail should be permitted under the Convention in the future, and how Convention interacts with Rule 4's new waiver-of-service provisions.[53] But the decision's broader import rests in its blindness to the very international commercial realities that had bulked so large in the Court's earlier opinion in *Bremen*. *Schlunk*'s nominal focus seemed to be autonomy: giving private American litigants maximum freedom to sue foreign defendants at home by deeming their local subsidiaries to be involuntary agents for service of process. But as a matter of separation of powers, the opinion is once again remarkably deferential to the U.S. government's *amicus curiae* brief, and oblivious to international system concerns, which cut strongly in favor of Justice Brennan's view.

---

**51.** *Id.* at 710–11 (Brennan, J.) (citations and quotation marks omitted).

**52.** *Id.* (Brennan, J.) (citations omitted).

**53.** After *Schlunk*, a number of courts have held that service abroad by direct mail is not authorized by Article 10(a) of the Service Convention, which provides only that "the present Convention shall not interfere with ... the freedom to send judicial documents, by postal channels, directly to persons abroad." *See, e.g.,* Bankston v. Toyota Motor Corp., 889 F.2d 172 (8th Cir. 1989). Justice Brennan suggested that the Convention did not authorize service by mail on a defendant residing in another state party, an assertion that seems plainly correct given the "non-interference" language of Article 10. With the promulgation of the new waiver-of-service rules in Federal Rule 4, the Hague Service Convention may become even less important over time. For if the *Schlunk* Court is correct that the Convention applies only when there is an "occasion for service abroad," then an agreement to waive service will not be such an occasion, thereby taking more and more cases outside the ambit of the Convention.

Despite the Court's apparent desire to maximize the perceived freedom for American plaintiffs in the international business environment, its decision, ironically, will likely have the opposite result. For as Justice Brennan noted in his separate opinion, foreign defendants being sued in United States courts are "persons" for purposes of the Due Process clauses, and thus are entitled under the *Mullane* standard to receive reasonable notice under all the circumstances. There is thus little likelihood that alien defendants in the United States will be accorded substantially inferior notice to that awarded to American defendants. But other nations need not apply a due process rule to notice, and are free to deem service complete against a U.S. national based on someone placing the papers, for example, in a local mailbox held in the name of the U.S. national's local subsidiary. If the U.S. national goes into the foreign court to complain about local methods of service, it seems highly unlikely that the foreign court will see any need to grant her relief based upon the Convention.[54] So ironically, the Court's opinion may end up hurting American businesses far more than it hurts America's competitors.

Two factors that were dramatically under-considered in *Schlunk* were uniformity and comity. How, first, should litigants deal with the problem that fifty different states may now adopt their own rules to determine when there is an "occasion" for service abroad under the service convention? If litigants need a uniform federal rule, one should be created by either treaty, federal common law, Federal Rule, or statute. The treaty interpretation selected by the Court clearly will not suffice, and the Court has been reluctant to decide these matters by federal common law, which leaves an amended Federal Rule as the prime alternative. Two commentators have suggested, for example, that courts may resolve an issue left open by *Schlunk*—whether a plaintiff may use the alternative methods in Rule 4(f)(2) if an international agreement such as the Hague Service Convention permits the use of several different methods of service—by holding that a plaintiff "may use any method of service authorized or approved under the terms of the Convention.... If Convention mechanisms are available, the plaintiff may not use the alternative methods in Rule

---

**54.** As Justice Brennan pointed out, "while other nations are not bound by the Court's pronouncement that the Convention lacks obligatory force, after today's decision their courts will surely sympathize little with any United States national pleading that a judgment violates the Convention because (notwithstanding any local characterization) service was abroad." *Id.* at 716.

4(f)(2) unless those alternatives also happen to be authorized by the Convention itself."[55]

Second, it is still possible for a forum to alleviate the harsh result of *Schlunk* by applying comity on a case-by-case basis. As we shall see in our discussion of *Aerospatiale* later in this Chapter, comity permits a court to engage in particularized analysis. U.S. courts could apply such analyses to develop a particular construction of the Service Convention. Courts could balance the interests of foreign states regarding service of process upon their own nationals, against the plaintiff's countervailing burden of complying with the Convention's non-onerous procedures, and require resort to the Convention as a matter of comity.

With the advent of the internet, these issues regarding the Service Convention may soon simply be overtaken by technology. For at this writing, there is much new discussion of the prospect of enabling service upon foreign defendants by e-mail, an issue that clearly demands a negotiated international approach.[56]

In the end, *Schlunk* is striking in its willingness to ignore not just customary law, but also painstakingly negotiated positive international law. Far from being an isolated misreading, the Court's decision in *Schlunk* fits within a broad recent pattern of treaty misconstruction by the U.S. Supreme Court. Over the past two decades, the Court has generally followed the U.S. executive branch in sanctioning the non-exclusivity of the procedures specified in a range of treaties. In our earlier discussion of human rights cases, we saw this pattern unfold in two areas. First, with regard to criminal judicial assistance, with the Court's decision sanctioning the extraterritorial kidnapping of a criminal suspect notwithstanding the presence of a bilateral extradition treaty.[57] Second, we reviewed its decision in the Haitian refugee case, sanctioning the return (*refouler*) of refugees taken on the high seas notwithstanding the 1951 Refugee Convention's guarantee of *nonrefoulement*, or nonreturn.[58] In both of these cases, at the U.S. Government's urging, the Court applied a three-part technique, which led it to

---

**55.** Born & Vollmer, *supra* note 27, at 238 (emphasis in original).

**56.** For a thoughtful exploration, see generally David P. Stewart and Anna Conley, *E-mail Service on Foreign Defendants: Time for an International Approach*, 38 GEO. J. INT'L LAW 755 (2007)

**57.** United States v. Alvarez–Machain, 504 U.S. 655 (1992). I should disclose that I filed an *amicus curiae* brief in support of Alvarez–Machain in this case.

**58.** Sale v. Haitian Centers Council, 509 U.S. 155 (193).

sanction essentially the opposite result from the one the treaty had been drafted to ensure.

First, in each case, the Court read unambiguous treaty language to be ambiguous. In *Alvarez–Machain*, the treaty's mandatory language demonstrated the parties' intent to provide mandatory procedures governing the extradition of persons in all cases not involving consensual rendition. Yet at the Government's urging, the Court effectively wrote a new, implied term into the treaty permitting forcible, unconsented governmental kidnapping. Similarly, in *Haitian Centers Council*, both a statute (the Immigration and Nationality Act) and a treaty provision (Article 33 of the 1951 Refugee Convention) categorically mandated the mutually reinforcing requirement that the United States not return or *"refouler"* "any alien" to his persecutors. In ruling for the Government, the Court implied a territorial limit upon that requirement, thus freeing the Executive to return Haitian refugees interdicted on the high seas.

Second, in each case the Court declined to construe the contested language in light of the treaty's object and purpose. Article 31 of the Vienna Convention on the Law of Treaties directs that treaties first be construed according to both their ordinary meaning and their object and purpose.[59] But in these recent Supreme Court decisions, the Court construed language in treaties whose aim was to make the treaty's procedures the normal and presumptive mode for dealing with a problem so as to *offend*, not support, the spirit of the treaty. Thus, in *Alvarez–Machain*, the Court construed an extradition treaty that was silent with regard to governmental kidnapping of criminal suspects to permit that result. Justice Stevens vigorously dissented, reasoning that unconsented kidnapping was precisely the result that the treaty had been drafted to forbid.[60] Similarly, in *Haitian Centers Council*, Justice Stevens, now writing for the Court, oddly construed Article 33 of the Refugee Convention as permitting a nation to "gather fleeing refugees and return them to the one country they had desperately sought to escape," even while recognizing that "such actions may even violate the spirit of Article 33."[61]

---

**59.** Vienna Convention on the Law of Treaties, art. 31, May 23, 1969, 1155 U.N.T.S. 331, T.S. No. 58 (entered into force Jan. 27, 1980).

**60.** United States v. Alvarez–Machain, 504 U.S. at 677 (Stevens, J., dissenting).

**61.** *Haitian Centers Council*, 509 U.S. at 183. As Justice Blackmun recalled in his forceful dissent, the refugee treaty's purpose was to prevent a replay of the forced return of Jewish refugees to Europe by extending international protections to those who, having fled persecution in their own country, could no longer invoke that government's legal protection. Yet the Court construed the treaty to permit that result, so long as those refugees were taken on the high seas. *Id.* at 207–08 (Blackmun, J., dissenting).

Third, the Vienna Convention on Treaties directs that reliance on a treaty's negotiating history be the alternative of last, not first, resort in treaty interpretation. Article 32 permits use of the negotiating history in treaty construction only as a last resort, and even then only if a plain language analysis "leaves the meaning ambiguous or obscure" or leads to a "manifestly absurd or unreasonable result."[62] In one recent treaty case, Justice Scalia pointedly argued that if "the Treaty's language resolves the issue presented, there is no necessity of looking further to discover 'the intent of the parties.' "[63] Yet in both *Alvarez* and the *Haitian* case, the Court subordinated the treaty's text to the negotiating history, thereby elevating snippets of negotiating history into definitive interpretive guides.[64]

Although this pattern of treaty misinterpretation has been particularly glaring in the international human rights cases, they seem equally to have influenced the Court's reading of the Hague Service Convention. For in *Schlunk*, the Court relied on the Solicitor General's *amicus curiae* brief to hold that U.S. plaintiffs are free to serve foreign defendants by serving their U.S. agents by non-treaty means—a substantial narrowing of the treaty—because such cases present no "occasion to transmit a judicial or extrajudicial document for service abroad." As in the human rights cases, the Court reached its conclusion by twisting clear treaty language, ignoring the treaty's object and purpose, and unduly relying upon snippets of legislative history. As we shall see shortly, these same factors have equally distorted the Court's jurisprudence on the taking of evidence abroad.

---

**62.** Article 31 instructs courts to rely primarily on a treaty's language and purpose. Article 32 permits use of the negotiating history in treaty construction only as a last resort, and even then only if a plain language analysis "leaves the meaning ambiguous or obscure" or leads to a "manifestly absurd or unreasonable result."

**63.** United States v. Stuart, 489 U.S. 353, 371 (1989) (Scalia, J., concurring).

**64.** In the *Haitian* case, for example, the Court reversed a decades-old interpretation of a multilateral treaty, by relying on statements of two foreign delegates that were never commented or voted upon by the United States, that were never presented to or considered by the Senate during its ratification of the 1968 Refugee Protocol, and that were explicitly rebutted by a sworn affidavit submitted by the U.S. government official who negotiated the treaty. *See* Affidavit of Professor Louis Henkin, appendix to Brief for Respondent, Sale v. Haitian Centers Council, 509 U.S. 155 (1993), *reprinted in* 35 Harv. Int'l L.J., 44–47 (1994).

# CHAPTER X

## Taking of Evidence

## A. Transnational Discovery and Foreign Sovereign Compulsion

Although much ink has been spilled over the taking of evidence abroad,[1] the basic issues are remarkably straightforward. The three core questions are: first, in what ways does the American notion of "pretrial discovery" really differ from other countries' notion of "taking of evidence?" Second, what information is properly subject to American-style discovery, and what checks exist on discovery abuse? And third, what should a domestic court do if a party subject to its discovery orders becomes subject to competing nondisclosure demands of another legal system?

At base, the controversy centers around the historic American attachment to a right to take not just evidence, but pretrial "discovery." The Federal Rules define "discovery" as information that "need not be admissible at the trial if the information sought appears reasonably calculated to lead to the *discovery* of admissible evidence."[2] In writing America's discovery rules, the drafters of the Federal Rules of Civil Procedure sought to execute Justice Jackson's directive in *Hickman v. Taylor*[3] that "[m]utual knowledge of all the relevant facts gathered by both parties is essential to proper litigation."[4] The drafters' twin goals were to escape the "sporting theory" of justice, under which attorneys could withhold key evidence until the day of trial, and to promote settlements by giving parties a basis on which to assess both their case and their adversaries.

---

**1.** For some of the better writing, see Lawrence Collins, *The Hague Evidence Convention and Discovery: A Serious Understanding?*, 35 INT'L AND COMP. L. 765 (1986); Gary B. Born and Scott Hoing, *Comity and the Lower Courts: Post–Aerospatiale Applications of the Hague Evidence Convention*, 24 INT'L LAW. 393 (1990); Gary B. Born, *The Hague Evidence Revisited: Reflections on Its Role in U.S. Civil Procedure*, 57 LAW & CONTEMP. PROBS. 77 (1994); Symposium, *Compelling Discovery in Transnational Litigation*, 16 N.Y.U. J. INT'L L. & POL. 957 (1984) (including bibliography).

**2.** The key language of Fed. R. Civ. P. 26(b)(1), the scope-of-discovery provision of the Federal Rules, reads: "Parties may obtain discovery regarding any matter, not privileged, which is relevant to the subject matter involved in the pending action. The information sought need not be admissible at the trial if the information sought appears reasonably calculated to lead to the discovery of admissible evidence."

**3.** 329 U.S. 495 (1947).

**4.** *Id.* at 507.

Thus, the only restraints placed by the drafters upon pretrial discovery were that matters be relevant, not privileged, and reasonably calculated to lead to the discovery of admissible evidence. The drafters contemplated that discovery would reach both parties and non-parties to the litigation. The Rules then afforded the litigants an array of discovery devices: written interrogatories to parties, requests for admissions and production of documents, oral depositions and depositions upon written questions, and requests for court orders for physical and mental examinations of parties (for good cause shown) in cases where the party's mental and physical condition are in controversy.[5]

Although the drafters envisioned that discovery would be managed by the parties, not the court, they gave the judge a significant, and expandable, role in the process. If need be, a court was empowered to compel discovery,[6] overrule objections to discovery, hold witnesses in contempt for failing to respond to discovery, grant protective orders to persons being harassed,[7] and impose a wide range of sanctions for failures to comply with orders, ranging from orders taking the contested matters as established, restricting the disobedient party's freedom to challenge claims, striking pleadings, dismissing actions, granting default judgments, or even "requir[ing] the party failing to obey the order or the attorney advising that party or both to pay the reasonable expenses, including attorney's fees, caused by the failure...."[8] In wielding these considerable powers, the judge has wide latitude to engage in what has become known in America as "managerial judging."[9] Moreover, under Federal Rules 16 and 26(f), the judge is empowered to hold meetings to control discovery, and following the British model, to use extrajudicial personnel to help process disputes.[10]

European civil and common lawyers who are appalled by the transnational abuses of the American discovery process often fail to appreciate four features of it. First, in the U.S., discovery is conducted before the trial, not before the lawsuit. To file a suit and enter the discovery phase, the plaintiff must first survive a motion to dismiss, and can be sanctioned for failing to have a reasonable basis for bringing a claim. Yet it was in good measure a misconception by many signatories to the Hague Evidence Convention that

---

**5.** *See* Fed. R. Civ. P. 27–36 (describing these devices).

**6.** Fed. R. Civ. P. 37(a).

**7.** Fed. R. Civ. P. 26(c).

**8.** Fed. R. Civ. P. 37(b).

**9.** Judith Resnik, *Managerial Judges*, 96 HARV. L. REV. 374 (1982).

**10.** *See* Fed. R. Civ. P. 53, 72–76; Linda Silberman, *Masters and Magistrates, Part I: The English Model*, 50 N.Y.U. L. REV. 1070 (1975); Linda Silberman, *Masters and Magistrates, Part II: The American Analogue*, 50 N.Y.U. L. REV. 1297 (1975).

"pretrial discovery" meant a right to secure evidence *before the complaint was even filed* that led them to declare under the Convention's most famous article—Article 23—that they "will not execute Letters of Request issued for the purpose of obtaining pretrial discovery of documents as known in Common Law countries."[11] Second, although discovery is theoretically a stage en route to trial, remarkably few American lawsuits actually ever reach the trial stage today. Most cases are settled, with discovery, summary judgment,[12] and pretrial judicial management being the key stages on route to that result. As the trial has slipped in importance, the pretrial phase has become the main event of U.S. litigation.

Third, in distinguishing among civil procedure systems, we must remember the key ways in which common law and civil law systems differ. In pathbreaking work, Mirjan Damaška rejected the traditional dyad of comparative procedure, which equates common law with adversarial process and civil law with inquisitorial process.[13] Instead, Damaška suggested a more nuanced descriptive framework, organized along two different axes. The first is a "hierarchical–coordinate" axis, which reflects the way a state has organized its judicial officials, with hierarchic states structuring their judicial branches with stratified authority and rigid role definition, in contrast to coordinate states, who organize their judges loosely, with overlapping spheres of authority and concentrated, informal decision-making processes. Damaška's second, "state activism" axis labeled as "activist" those states who seek to implement substantive values through many vehicles, including the judicial process, while reactive states endorse no specific substantive vision of the good life, with their judiciary playing the role of neutral arbiter of private disputes, enforcing contestants' bargains, and deferring to party autonomy.

Viewed in this light, the classic Anglo–American trial is coordinate/reactive, while the classic continental approach is hierarchic/activist. Within these frameworks, procedural rules evolve to carry out the work that they are doing, and reflect an organizational structure that captures the society's preferred view of the state, and complex sociopolitical attitudes and choices about the social ends trials are designed to achieve. By viewing procedural rules as components of larger legal systems, this approach shifts the explanatory weight from narrow policies designed to explain particular

---

**11.** Convention on Taking of Evidence Abroad in Civil or Commercial Matter, art. 23, Mar. 18, 1970, 23 U.S.T. 2555, T.I.A.S. No. 7444 [hereinafter Hague Evidence Convention].

**12.** Fed. R. Civ. P. 56.

**13.** *See* Mirjan Damaška, The Faces of Justice and State Authority: A Comparative Approach to the Legal Process 208–10 (1986).

rules toward broader cultural attitudes in civil and common law countries toward governance and state authority.[14]

This difference emerges in the divergent roles played by the common law and the civil judge in developing the evidence and legal concepts that govern the decision. As John Langbein has argued, the civil-law "advantage" in civil procedure derives in part from the incentive structures of the career judiciary and the appellate safeguards for litigants, which facilitate a judicially-dominated discovery and fact-finding process.[15] But to focus inordinately on the divide between civil and common-law procedure tends to overlook the ways in which the American system differs from *both* civil and common law systems alike. The American system seems procedurally remarkable in not just one respect, but five: first, with respect to discovery, second, in America's embrace of a politically chosen, as opposed to professional, judiciary; third, in the availability of a jury trial as of right in American federal civil cases under the Seventh Amendment to the Constitution; fourth, in an adversary system that affords lawyers far greater latitude in presentation than exists in other systems; and fifth, in having a fees and costs system in which each party generally bears his own expenses, rather than having the loser pay.

Fourth and finally, we must note that the Supreme Court is no stranger to transnational discovery. Indeed, it was a 1958 transnational discovery case, *Societe Internationale Pour Participations Industrielles Et Commerciales, S.A. v. Rogers* (the *Interhandel*

---

**14.** Under Damaška's two-by-two matrix, for example, the distrust of hearsay in Anglo–American procedure (as opposed to the relative tolerance of hearsay by civil law procedure) does not simply reflect distrust of the cognitive limitations of lay juries. More fundamentally, the more restrictive hearsay rule in common law countries is a functional antidote to the nonhierarchical, coordinate structure of decisionmaking in those countries, a structure that increases the risk that derivative evidence will be entered in error. *See* Mirjan Damaška, *Of Hearsay and Its Analogues*, 76 MINN. L. REV. 425, 427–29 (1992). Damaška notes that Anglo–American courts typically have juries deliberating *in camera*, left to their own devices outside the judge's earshot, while continental courts allow factfinders to sit side by side with professional judges. Civil law

trials are only one stage in an ongoing sequence of hearings; thus, if a witness reproduces an out-of-court statement in a civil law trial, the factfinder can usually find the original declarant in time to secure his testimony in court during the next phase in proceedings. Thus, the unhurried pace of the civil law system, made possible by the *hierarchical* organization of its judicial system—permits hearsay to be vetted more easily and hence entered into evidence with less risk of error.

**15.** *See* John Langbein, *The German Advantage in Civil Procedure*, 52 U. CHI. L. REV. 823 (1985). *But see* John Reitz, *Why We Probably Cannot Adopt the German Advantage in Civil Procedure*, 75 IOWA L. REV. 987 (1990); Samuel Gross, *The American Advantage: The Value of Inefficient Litigation*, 85 MICH. L. REV. 734, 756 (1987).

case),[16] which helped established the American rules on discovery sanctions in the first place. The *Interhandel* case illustrates yet again the percolation and transformation from private to public and back again that I have spoken of throughout these lectures. During World War II, the U.S. government vested the assets of a German corporation pursuant to the Trading With the Enemy Act. When the war ended, a Swiss company, Interhandel, claimed that it had owned the assets at the time of the vesting and was entitled to return of the property. When Interhandel sued the Attorney General in U.S. court, the U.S. government moved for an order requiring Interhandel to make available large number of Swiss bank records that were relevant to its claim of title. Interhandel refused to comply, asserting that disclosure would violate various provisions of the Swiss banking and penal codes. The district court dismissed Interhandel's complaint and the court of appeals affirmed, but the Supreme Court granted certiorari and unanimously reversed. While this domestic litigation proceeded, Switzerland brought suit against the United States before the International Court of Justice. When the U.S. Supreme Court agreed to review the discovery dispute, the World Court held the Swiss Application inadmissible, finding that Switzerland had still to exhaust its domestic remedies.[17] The Supreme Court went on to hold that Interhandel appeared to be the target of *bona fide* foreign sovereign compulsion.[18] The Court remanded with instructions that the district court continue the inquiry, requiring the non-disclosing party to make a good faith effort to secure permission to disclose the documents covered by the foreign secrecy law. "It may be that in the absence of complete disclosure by petitioner, the District Court would be justified in drawing inferences unfavorable to petitioner ... as to particular events," the Court said, but concluded that the ultimate sanction of dismissal was too harsh in light of the conflicting orders Interhandel faced.[19]

*Interhandel* again illustrates the marvels of transnational legal process: how an ostensibly private dispute could bubble up to both the U.S. Supreme Court and the International Court of Justice at the same time.[20] As in the *Fruehauf* and *Soviet Pipeline* cases

---

**16.** 357 U.S. 197 (1958).

**17.** *Interhandel Case (Switzerland v. United States)*, (Preliminary Objections), [1959] I.C.J. Rep. 6.

**18.** 357 U.S. at 211 ("petitioner's failure to satisfy fully the requirements of this production order was due to inability fostered neither by its own conduct nor by circumstances within its control. It is hardly debatable that fear of criminal prosecution constitutes a weighty excuse for nonproduction, and this excused is not weakened because the laws preventing compliance are those of a foreign sovereign.").

**19.** *Id.* at 212–13.

**20.** The Iranian Hostages Crisis, discussed in Chapter II, and the *Medellin* case, in Chapter XIII *infra*, are two oth-

discussed in Chapter IV, a hard conflict precipitated as the private entity (Interhandel) became subject to conflicting orders and claimed a form of the foreign sovereign compulsion defense. The domestic and international judicial proceedings then briefly intersected and resolved separately, creating two new rules of transnational law which have subsequently been internalized into our dualistic legal system: a public international law rule governing exhaustion of domestic remedies in international adjudication and a private domestic discovery rule of *Interhandel*, now set forth in the *Restatement (Third) of Foreign Relations Law*.[21]

Moreover, *Interhandel* reveals the differences between the foreign sovereign compulsion defense in substantive law, discussed in Chapter V, and the defense of foreign compulsion as an explanation for nondisclosure in transnational discovery. While the traditional foreign sovereign compulsion defense holds that a defendant should be completely absolved of his liability because of a direct foreign government command, the courts have perceived a procedural conflict over discovery as a somehow "softer," more reconcilable conflict, of the type discussed in Chapter IV. Thus, the U.S. Supreme Court has concluded that persons to whom discovery orders are addressed who face conflicting orders from foreign blocking statutes should not, on the one hand, be punished by dismissal, but should, on the other hand, be obliged to make "good faith efforts" to secure permission to comply with the American discovery order. The *Restatement (Third)*'s jurisdictional reasoning is that "when a state has jurisdiction to prescribe and its courts have jurisdiction to adjudicate, adjudication should take place on the basis of the best information available, and that [foreign blocking] statutes that frustrate this goal need not be given the same

---

er American examples of this phenomenon.

**21.** *See* RESTATEMENT (THIRD) OF THE FOREIGN RELATIONS LAW OF THE UNITED STATES § 442(2):

If disclosure of information located outside the United States is prohibited by a law, regulation or order of a court or other authority of the state in which the information or prospective witness is located, or of the state of which a prospective witness is a national,

(a) a court or agency in the United States may require the person to whom the order is directed to make a good faith effort to secure permission from the foreign authorities to make the information available;

(b) a court or agency should not ordinarily impose sanctions of contempt, dismissal, or default on a party that has failed to comply with the order for production, except in cases of deliberate concealment or removal of information or of failure to make a good faith effort in accordance with paragraph (a);

(c) a court or agency may, in appropriate cases make findings of fact adverse to a party that has failed to comply with the order for production, even if that party has made a good faith effort to secure permission from the foreign authorities to make the information available and that effort has been unsuccessful.

deference by courts of the United States as differences in substantive rules of law."[22]

On reflection, this analysis bears a family resemblance to the majority's reasoning in *Hartford Fire Insurance*, discussed at the close of Chapter IV. For there, as you will recall, the majority found that the U.S. had jurisdiction to prescribe under the effects doctrine of the antitrust laws and then asked what weight to give a claim of inconsistency with foreign law. The Court decided that comity did not require dismissal on this factor unless the regulated company could demonstrate that there was a true conflict that prevented it from complying with both country's laws.[23] If this statement of the issue resonates, it is no accident. For in developing that test for the *Hartford Fire Insurance* Court, Justice Souter expressly relied on Justice Blackmun's partial concurrence in the leading case on transnational discovery, *Societe Nationale Industrielle Aerospatiale v. United States District Court*.[24]

## B. *Aerospatiale* and the Federal Rules

*Aerospatiale*, like *Helicopteros* and *Piper*, arose out of an air crash disaster. A plane designed, manufactured and marketed by Aerospatiale (an entity wholly owned by the French government) and by its wholly-owned French subsidiary, crashed in Iowa, injuring the pilot and passenger. When plaintiffs sued both French companies in Iowa federal court, the defendants did not challenge the court's personal jurisdiction or venue, probably due to the extensive advertising and marketing of the plane in the U.S. and the location of the crash in Iowa. But a discovery battle ensued before a magistrate when plaintiffs sought production of documents under the Federal Rules, which they claimed required discovery in France. Defendants reasoned that exclusive resort had to be made to the procedures of the Hague Evidence Convention, to which both the United States and France are parties. In essence, the Evidence Convention requires that in civil or commercial matters, courts of one contracting state "may, in accordance with the provisions of the law of that State," send letters rogatory through the Central Authority of the other State requesting and obtaining evidence from the courts of another contracting party.[25]

---

**22.** *Id.* at § 442 reporter's note 5.

**23.** *Hartford Fire Insurance*, 509 U.S. at 798 (the court need not dismiss the antitrust claim on international comity unless there is a "true conflict between domestic and foreign law").

**24.** 482 U.S. 522 (1987); *see also Hartford Fire Insurance*, 509 U.S. at 798 (quoting Justice Blackmun's partial concurrence in *Aerospatiale*, 482 U.S. at 555), discussed in Chapter IV, *supra*.

**25.** Hague Evidence Convention, art. 1. For a cogent description of how the

By seeking discovery in France, plaintiffs were invoking the very *raison d'etre* for the Evidence Convention: to obtain evidence from persons or witnesses who were outside the scope of an American court's jurisdictional power. Defendants sought a protective order against plaintiff's discovery requests, arguing first, that by ratifying the Convention, the two countries had assumed an exclusive treaty obligation to honor foreign evidence requests in an instance covered by the Convention; and second, that as in *Interhandel*, they were barred by foreign penal law[26] from responding to discovery requests that did not comply with the Convention. The magistrate rejected both of defendants' claims, suggesting that the Convention could not displace the normal operation of the federal discovery rules, finding the French penal statute potentially inapplicable and probable interests outweighed by the plaintiffs' interests in disclosure. The defendants unsuccessfully sought a writ of mandamus before the Eighth Circuit, and the Supreme Court granted review.

By the time the case reached the Court, it had mutated from a private tort dispute into an inter-governmental *cause celebre*. *Amicus curiae* briefs were filed not just by the United States government, but also by France, West Germany, Switzerland, and the United Kingdom. Writing for five Justices, Justice Stevens reviewed four possible roles the treaty might play in extraterritorial discovery. I will call these four approaches: (1) exclusive use; (2) first (but not exclusive) use; (3) presumptive resort; and (4) optional means. The first option, exclusive use, would have read the treaty's language to require that the Convention be used "to the exclusion of any other discovery procedures whenever evidence located abroad is sought for use in an American court."[27] This reading the Court rejected, noting that Article 1 says only that a judicial authority in one contracting state "may" and not "must" forward a letter of request for purposes of obtaining evidence.[28] Option Two, which the Court also rejected, was the notion that the Convention "might be

---

Convention functions, see Collins, *supra* note 1.

**26.** In making this form of foreign sovereign compulsion defense, defendants cited the same French blocking statute invoked by Compagnie de Saint–Gobain Pont-a-Mousson in resisting the FTC's investigatory subpoena in the *SGPM* case, discussed in the previous chapter. The Eighth Circuit later found the magistrate's ruling on the *Interhandel* issue premature.

**27.** *Aerospatiale*, 482 U.S. at 533.

**28.** *Id.* at 535. This is in contrast to the mandatory language of article 1 of the Hague Service Convention. In rejecting the exclusive use position, Justice Stevens was joined by the four partially dissenting Justices, thus making the Court unanimous on this point. *See id.* at 548 (Blackmun, J.) ("The Court also correctly rejects the ... position that the Convention provides the exclusive means for discovery involving signatory countries.").

required to require first, but not exclusive, use of its procedures."[29] Requiring American litigants to make first resort to the expensive and time-consuming letter rogatory process, the Court suggested, would be inconsistent with the Federal Rules' objectives: to promote the "just, speedy, and inexpensive determination of litigation in our courts."[30]

Justice Blackmun, writing for four Justices, argued that the Court should have opted for the third option: requiring presumptive resort to Convention procedures as a general rule in furtherance of comity.[31] But, Justice Stevens rejected this third possibility, reasoning that:

> [T]he concept of international comity requires in this context *a more particularized analysis of the respective interests of the foreign nation and the requesting nation* than petitioners' proposed general rule would generate. We therefore decline to hold as a blanket matter, that comity requires resort to Hague Evidence Convention procedures *without prior scrutiny in each case of the particular facts, sovereign interests, and likelihood that resort to those procedures will prove effective.*[32]

Instead, the majority adopted the fourth and final option: that the Convention is an optional means to facilitate discovery "to which an American court should resort when it deems that course of action appropriate, after considering the situations of the parties before it as well as the interests of the concerned foreign state."[33] While contemplating that comity might at times require resort to the Convention, the Court seemed to prescribe deliberate vagueness with regard to the precise weight to be given sovereignty and comity. The Court almost defiantly announced: "[w]e do not articulate specific rules to guide this delicate task of adjudication."[34]

The result in *Aerospatiale* entirely foreshadowed the result the following term in *Schlunk*. As we saw, the *Schlunk* Court relied on the Solicitor General's *amicus curiae* brief to hold that U.S. plain-

---

**29.** *Id.* at 542–43.

**30.** *Id.* at 543 (quoting Fed. R. Civ. P. 1).

**31.** *See id.* at 548–49 (Blackmun, J.) ("I ... would apply a general presumption that, in most cases, courts should resort first to the Convention procedures. An individualized analysis of the circumstances of a particular case is appropriate only when it appears that it would be futile to employ the Convention or when its procedures prove to be unhelpful.").

**32.** *Id.* at 543–44 (emphasis added).

**33.** *Id.* at 533.

**34.** *Id.* at 546. At the same time, however, the Court affirmed that American courts should exercise "special vigilance" to balance costs and curb discovery abuse, should give "careful consideration" to objections, and should "take care to demonstrate the respect for any special problem confronted by the foreign litigant ... and for any sovereign interest." *Id.*

tiffs are free to serve foreign defendants by non-treaty means through an oddly constricted reading of the Hague Service Convention, despite substantial evidence that the signatories had expected the Convention to provide the default channel for transborder service. In *Aerospatiale*, decided one term earlier, the Court similarly read the Hague Evidence Convention to leave U.S. plaintiffs free to seek discovery from foreign defendants by non-treaty means without any presumption in favor of resort to that treaty, again despite substantial evidence that the signatories had expected the Convention to provide the normal channels for transborder discovery. As in *Schlunk*, the majority's opinion rested almost entirely on deference to the *autonomy of American litigants*. From the American litigant's perspective, the Court said, the real problem with the presumptive resort option was that the "Letter of Request procedure authorized by the Convention would be unduly time consuming and expensive, as well as less certain to produce needed evidence than direct use of the Federal Rules." In other cases, however, "the *calculations of the litigant* will naturally lead to a first-use strategy."[35] Although the Court paid lip service to balancing "sovereign interests," its prime concern was the "likelihood that resort to those procedures will prove effective" for individual litigants.[36]

Justice Blackmun's concurring opinion, by contrast, emphasized the other values we have stressed here: the greater uniformity and predictability of a comity-based rule,[37] separation of powers,[38] and the sovereign interests, of both the foreign states and the United States.[39] Perhaps more than any opinion since *Bremen*,[40] Justice Blackmun also emphasized the broader needs of the international commercial system. He urged judges to look beyond paro-

---

**35.** *Id.* at 542–43 and n.26 (emphasis added).

**36.** *Id.* at 544.

**37.** After analyzing the way in which comity analysis has been applied with respect to choice of forum, maritime law, and sovereign immunity, Justice Blackmun decided that "[t]he principle of comity leads to more definite rules than the ad hoc approach endorsed by the majority." *See id.* at 550 and nn.7–9 (Blackmun, J.).

**38.** *See id.* at 552 (Blackmun, J.).("The Convention embodies the result of the best efforts of the Executive Branch, in negotiating the treaty, and the Legislative Branch, in ratifying it, to balance competing national interests. As such, the Convention represents a political determination—one that, *consistent with the principle of separation of powers*, courts should not attempt to second-guess.") (emphasis added).

**39.** The sovereign interests of the foreign state and of the United States were the first two factors Justice Blackmun weighed in his comity test. See *id.* at 556–67 (Blackmun, J.)

**40.** A possible exception is Justice Blackmun's own opinion in Mitsubishi Motors Corp. v. Soler Chrysler–Plymouth, Inc., 473 U.S. 614 (1985) (enforcement of foreign arbitration clause), discussed in Chapter XII *infra*.

chial private interests and the self-interest of sovereigns, to more broadly

> consider if there is a course that furthers, rather than impedes, the development of an ordered international system. *A functioning system for solving disputes across borders serves many values, among them predictability, fairness, ease of commercial interactions, and "stability through satisfaction of mutual expectations."* ... These interests are common to all nations, including the United States.[41]

In the years since, *Aerospatiale* has proven triply memorable: for what it says about transborder discovery and the Federal Rules; for what Justice Blackmun said about comity; and for what the result says about the value of future multilateral judicial assistance treaties. Let me address its first two legacies here, and leave the last to next two Chapters' discussion of the recognition and enforcement of foreign judgments, decrees, and arbitral awards.

In 1989, the Federal Rules Advisory Committee proposed, as part of its proposed amendments to the federal discovery rules, language that would, effectively, have codified Justice Blackmun's concurring opinion in *Aerospatiale*. The Committee proposed to add to the language of Rule 26(a) a presumptive first-resort rule.[42] Not surprisingly, a proposal to enshrine a Supreme Court *minority* position into Federal Rule quickly attracted criticism, forcing the Advisory Committee to withdraw it. The Committee then suggested a new amendment that would have granted district courts discretion to determine that treaty-based discovery "methods are inadequate or inequitable and [to] authoriz[e] other discovery methods not prohibited by the treaty." This proposal issued along with a Committee Note saying that "[t]he rule of comity stated in this rule does not apply to discovery ... from parties who are subject to the court's personal jurisdiction and who may be required to produce ... materials at the place of trial"[43] When the Judicial Conference submitted this new version to the Supreme Court in November 1990, the United Kingdom sent a vigorous diplomatic protest

---

**41.** *Id.* at 567 (Blackmun, J.).

**42.** *See* 127 F.R.D. 318:

If an applicable treaty or convention provides for discovery in another country, the discovery methods agreed to in such treaty or convention shall be employed; but if discovery conducted by such methods is inadequate or inequitable and additional discovery is not prohibited by the treaty or convention, a party may employ the methods here provided in addition to those provided by such convention or treaty....

The Committee Note openly acknowledge that the amendment was "to reflect the policy of accommodation to internationally agreed methods of discovery expressed" in Justice Blackmun's minority opinion in *Aerospatiale*. *Id.* at 320.

**43.** Gary Born & Andrew Vollmer, *The Effect of the Revised Federal Rules of Civil Procedure on Personal Jurisdiction, Service, and Discovery in International Cases*, 150 F.R.D. 221, 243 (1993).

through the State Department to the Supreme Court.[44] The Supreme Court withheld approval from the proposed amendment and returned it to the Advisory Committee for further study, at the same time as it withheld approval of the Rule 4 waiver-of-service provision discussed earlier. When the Advisory Committee retained the language, the United Kingdom, Switzerland, and the U.S. Department of State all filed objections, charging that the proposed rule changes "will adversely affect international judicial cooperation, weaken United States treaty relationships under the Hague Conventions on Service and the Taking of Evidence Abroad, and unnecessarily create difficulties with our major trading partners on issues of territorial sovereignty."[45] The Judicial Conference's Committee on Rules of Practice and Procedure then refused to recommend the amendment.[46] As a result, unlike Rule 4, Fed. R. Civ. P. 26 went unamended, and remains unaltered today. As one might have predicted from comparable interest-balancing in the extraterritoriality area, lower courts applying the Court's particularized case-by-case comity analysis have generally concluded that American litigants' interests in faster, wide-ranging discovery should prevail over foreign interests in narrower, slower judicially-supervised discovery[47] At this writing, it remains unclear when and how the next, transnational version of Rule 26 might develop.

The issue of blocking statutes was not directly before the Court in *Aerospatiale*, but seems almost certain to rise again. A lengthy footnote in Justice Stevens' majority opinion loosely endorsed the *Restatement (Third)*'s position and concluded that "the [French] blocking statute thus is relevant to the court's particularized comity analysis *only to the extent that its terms and its enforcement identify the nature of the sovereign interests in nondisclosure of specific kinds of material.*"[48]

**44.** *Id.*

**45.** Letter from Edwin D. Williamson, The Legal Adviser of the U.S. Department of State, to Joseph F. Spaniol, Jr., Secretary, Committee on Rules of Practice and Procedure of the Judicial Conference at 1, 2 (June 12, 1992), excerpted in Born & Vollmer, *supra* note 43, at 244.

**46.** 146 F.R.D. 515 n.1.

**47.** For a recounting of recent decisions see Born & Hoing, *supra* note 1. This result is hardly surprising, given Judge Wilkey's observation regarding interest-balancing in the *Laker* case: "A pragmatic assessment of those decisions adopting an interest balancing approach indicates none where United States jurisdiction was declined when there was more than a de minimis United States interest." Laker Airways v. Sabena, Belgian World Airlines, 731 F.2d 909, 950–51 (D.C. Cir. 1984).

**48.** 482 U.S. at 544 n.29 (emphasis added). *See also id.*:

It is clear that American courts are not required to adhere blindly to the directives of such a statute. Indeed, the language of the statute, if taken literally, would appear to represent an extraordinary exercise of legislative jurisdiction by the Republic of France over a United States district judge,

It thus seems likely that the federal rulemakers will await another Supreme Court decision before making their next run at amending Rule 26. American litigators will continue to avoid using the Evidence Convention, and the courts will defer to their choice by conducting pro-American interest-balancing on a "case-by-case basis". The next case to come before the Court may well involve a foreign blocking statute, perhaps in the context of litigation brought under legislation similar to the Helms–Burton or Iran–Libya sanctions bills discussed in Chapter IV.[49] In such a case, the Court would have new opportunity to test both footnote 29 in *Aerospatiale* and its ruling in *Hartford Fire Insurance*.[50] My own prediction is that the Court would find, as it did in *Interhandel* and *Hartford Fire Insurance*, that the foreign blocking statute did not present a true, hard conflict requiring the Court to grant comity out of a sense of foreign sovereign compulsion. The *Restatement (Third)*'s approach, which the Court cited in *Aerospatiale*, frees American judges to grant less deference to foreign blocking statutes than to other kinds of foreign, substantive regulation. Should the Court apply the particularized comity analysis from *Aerospatiale* in a blocking statute case, I would be surprised if the American litigant still did not get his discovery. For when American courts undertake interest-balancing, a clear pattern has emerged. In Judge Wilkey's prescient words from *Laker*: "When push comes to shove, the domestic forum is rarely unseated."[51]

forbidding him or her to order any discovery from a party of French nationality, even simple requests for admissions or interrogatories that the party could respond to on the basis of personal knowledge. It would be particularly incongruous to recognize such a preference for corporations that are wholly owned by the enacting nation. Extraterritorial assertions of jurisdiction are not one-sided. While the District Court's discovery orders arguably have some impact in France, the French blocking statute asserts similar authority over acts to take place in this country.

Justice Blackmun's opinion for four Justices noted only the barrier that the blocking statute would pose to discovery, suggesting that this was all the more reason why comity required first resort to Convention procedures. *See id.* at 565 (Blackmun, J.).

**49.** *See* Chapter IV, *infra*.

**50.** *See id.* at 567 (Blackmun, J.) ("the threshold question in a comity analysis is whether there is in fact a true conflict between domestic and foreign law. When there is a conflict, a court should seek a reasonable accommodation that reconciles the central concerns of both sets of laws. In doing so, it should perform a tripartite analysis that considers the foreign interests, the interests of the United States, and the mutual interests of all nations in a smoothly functioning international legal regime.").

**51.** Laker Airways v. Sabena, Belgian World Airlines, 731 F.2d 909, 950–51 (D.C. Cir. 1984).

# CHAPTER XI

## RECOGNITION AND ENFORCEMENT OF FOREIGN JUDGMENTS AND DECREES

The last two chapters explained how judicial interpretation of the Hague Service and Evidence Conventions has brought comity into conflict with party autonomy. For by seeking to ensure that comity is paid to another nation's sovereignty, such conventions limit the freedom of individual litigants to serve process and acquire evidence in the manner to which they are accustomed under national law. This chapter, by contrast, discusses two treaties that attempt to place sovereignty in service of party autonomy.

The first, the Convention on the Recognition and Enforcement of Foreign Arbitral Awards of 1958 (commonly known as the "New York Convention") facilitates the enforcement of foreign arbitral awards.[1] To do so, the treaty obligation cuts across national borders to support transnational enforcement of awards achieved by arbitration, a party-chosen method of dispute resolution.

The second treaty was originally intended to be a new Hague Convention on Jurisdiction and Foreign Judgments, but in October 1999 and June 2001, preliminary drafts of that document failed to gain widespread support. Instead, a much more limited treaty, the Hague Convention on Choice of Court Agreements, was finally adopted by the Hague Conference on Private International Law in June 2005.[2] The original goal of a Judgments Convention was to

---

**1.** June, 10, 1958, 21 U.S.T. 2517, T.I.A.S. No. 6997. At this writing the New York Convention has over 104 party countries. For text and negotiating history, see GARY BORN, INTERNATIONAL COMMERCIAL ARBITRATION IN THE UNITED STATES: COMMENTARY AND MATERIALS 18–20, 875–80 (1994).

**2.** All of the preliminary documents leading to the treaty may be viewed at http://www.hcch.net/index_en.php?act= conventions.publications&dtid=35&cid =98 and the text of the final treaty at http://www.hcch.net/index_en.php?act= conventions.text&cid=98. For earlier discussions of the the issues that faced the drafters of the Judgments Convention, see, for example, Catherine Kessedjian, International Jurisdiction and For- eign Judgments in Civil and Commercial Matters, Hague Conference on Private International law, Enforcement of Judgments (Preliminary Document No. 7) (Apr. 1997); Catherine Kessedjian, Synthesis of the Work of the Special Commission of June 1997 on International Jurisdiction and the Effects of Foreign Judgments in Civil and Commercial Matters, Hague Conference on Private International law, Enforcement of Judgments (Preliminary Document No. 8) (Nov. 1997); Arthur T. von Mehren, *Recognition and Enforcement of Foreign Judgments: A New Approach for the Hague Conference*, 57 LAW & CONTEMP. PROBS. 271 (1994); Andreas Lowenfeld, *Thoughts About a Multinational Judgments Convention: A Reaction to the von*

link sovereign states in a reciprocal transborder effort to enforce foreign judgments, which are themselves the products of private litigant activity and public judicial interpretation. Hence these various multilateral exercises have sought to increase by treaty obligation the uniformity and predictability of judicial enforcement. These treaties also ask national courts to effectuate political policies favoring the recognition and enforcement of foreign acts. Thus, these final chapters again reveal the complex link between the private and public in international business dispute-resolution as well as the continuing competition for ascendancy among the jurisprudential principles of comity, private autonomy, national sovereignty, uniformity, and separation of powers.

## A. Domestic Enforcement of Foreign Judgments: The *Hilton v. Guyot Standard*

The lodestar for all transnational enforcement doctrines in the U.S. is the Supreme Court's 1895 opinion in *Hilton v. Guyot*.[3] In *Hilton*, the liquidator and surviving members of a French firm sued two U.S. citizens in a U.S. court, seeking to enforce an unpaid judgment from a French court. Had the judgment been from another state of the United States, the local court would have been constitutionally required to grant it "full faith and credit." For within the United States, the Full Faith and Credit Clause of the Constitution (and its accompanying federal legislation) obligates both state and federal courts to recognize and enforce acts, orders, and decisions of sister-state courts.[4] These provisions have helped to "weld the independent states [of the union] into a nation by giving judgments within the jurisdiction of the rendering state the same full faith and credit in sister states as they have in the state of the original forum."[5] In English common law, foreign judgments were not traditionally afforded full faith and credit, but rather, were regarded solely as *prima facie* evidence of the matter adjudi-

*Mehren Report*, 57 LAW & CONTEMP. PROBS. 289 (1994).

**3.** 159 U.S. 113 (1895). For an absorbing account of the story behind *Hilton*, see Louise Ellen Teitz, *The Story of* Hilton: *From Gloves to Globalization, in* KEVIN CLERMONT ED., CIVIL PROCEDURE STORIES 445 (2d ed. 2008).

**4.** 4 U.S. CONST. art IV, § 1 ("Full Faith and Credit shall be given in each state to the public Acts, Records, and judicial Proceedings of every other State."). In 1790, Congress commanded, in the same language used in the Constitution itself, that "[a]cts, records and judicial proceedings or copies there of, so authenticated, shall have the same full faith and credit in every court within the United States and its Territories and Possessions as they have by law or usage in the courts of such State, Territory or Possession from which they are taken." 28 U.S.C. § 1738 (2000).

**5.** Johnson v. Muelberger, 340 U.S. 581, 584 (1951).

cated and hence, not given conclusive effect.[6] Thus, the question presented in *Hilton* was when the United States should "recognize" the foreign state's judgment—in the sense of treating it as valid and preclusive of relitigation of the matter—and "enforce" that judgment—in the sense of affirmatively authorizing the plaintiff to enlist an American court's coercive judicial processes to vindicate the foreign judgment?

To answer that question, the Court surveyed a rich historical blend of common law, comparative law, and international law.[7] In an opinion by Justice Gray, the author of the *Paquete Habana*,[8] the Court declared that "[t]he extent to which the law of one nation, as put in force within its territory, whether by executive order, by legislative act, or by judicial decree, shall be allowed to operate within the dominion of another nation, depends upon ... the comity of nations."[9] As noted in Chapter I, the Court adopted the term from Justice Joseph Story's *Commentaries on the Conflict of Laws*, which had in turn derived it from the Roman law concept of *comitas*, as refined by the Dutch scholar, Huber, and the British common-law courts.[10] Justice Gray declared that:

> "Comity," in the legal sense, is neither a matter of absolute obligation, on the one hand, nor of mere courtesy and good will upon the other, ... [but] the recognition which one nation allows within its territory to the legislative, executive or judicial acts of another nation, having due regard both to international duty and convenience, and to the rights of its own citizens or of other persons who are under the protection of its laws....[11]

Justice Gray then concluded that comity required that "the merits of the case should not, in an action brought in this country upon the judgment, be tried afresh, as on a new trial or on appeal, upon

---

**6.** *See, e.g.*, Walker v. Witter, 99 Eng. Rep. 1 (K.B. 1778).

**7.** The Court conducted a detailed survey of the law of "civilized nations," including England, Russia, France, Holland, Belgium, the United States, Denmark, Germany, Switzerland, Poland, Romania, Bulgaria, Austria, Italy, Monaco, Spain, Portugal, Greece, Egypt, Cuba, Puerto Rico, Mexico, Peru, Chile, Brazil, Argentina, and Norway. *Id.* at 206–27.

**8.** 175 U.S. 677 (1900). Justice Gray's earlier decision offers the now-canonical statement "International law

is part of our law, and must be ascertained and administered by the courts of justice of appropriate jurisdiction as often as questions of right depending upon it are duly presented for their determination." *Id.* at 700.

**9.** *Id.* at 164.

**10.** *See generally* Harold G. Maier, *Extraterritorial Jurisdiction at a Crossroads: The Intersection Between Public and Private International Law*, 76 Am. J. Int'l L. 280, 281–82 & n.4 (1982).

**11.** Hilton v. Guyot, 159 U.S. 113, 164 (1895).

the mere assertion of the party that the judgment was erroneous in law or in fact . . ." so long as ten key conditions obtained:

> When an action is brought in a court of this country, by a citizen of a foreign country against one of our own citizens, to recover a sum of money adjudged by a court of that country to be due from the defendant to the plaintiff, and [1] the foreign judgment appears to have been rendered by a competent court, having [2] jurisdiction of the cause [*subject matter jurisdiction*] and [3] of the parties [*personal jurisdiction*], and [4] upon due allegations and proofs, and opportunity to defend against them [*notice and opportunity to be heard*], and [5] its proceedings are according to the course of a civilized jurisprudence [*impartial judicial system with proceedings under due process of law*], and are stated in a clear and formal record, the judgment is *prima facie* evidence, at least, of the truth of the matter adjudged; and it should be held conclusive upon the merits tried in the foreign court; unless [6] some *special ground* is shown for impeaching the judgment, as by showing that it was affected by [7] *fraud* or [8] *prejudice* or that [9] by the principles of *international law, and* [10] *by the comity* of our own country, it should not be given full credit and effect.[12]

When *Hilton* came down, the *New York Times* reported that "[t]he final disposition of this question will be received with much satisfaction by the lawyers of this country, who have not been able to determine from the many conflicting decisions by lower courts just what force a foreign judgment against a citizen of the United States had in the United States. The financial interests involved are said to amount in the aggregate, to many millions of dollars."[13] As elaborated in subsequent case law, the conditions enumerated in *Hilton*[14] effectively established the framework of available grounds

---

**12.** *Id.* at 205–06. Elsewhere in the opinion, Justice Gray repeated the standard in much the same way:

[W]e are satisfied that where there has been opportunity for a full and fair trial abroad before a court of competent jurisdiction, conducting the trial upon regular proceedings, after due citation or voluntary appearance of the defendant, and under a system of jurisprudence likely to secure an impartial administration of justice between the citizens of its own country and those of other countries, and there is nothing to show either prejudice in the court, or in the system of laws under which it was sitting, or

fraud in procuring the judgment, or any other special reason why the comity of this nation should not allow it full effect, the merits of the case should not in any action brought in this country upon the judgment, be tried afresh . . .

*Id.* at 202–03.

**13.** *Foreign Judgment Cases*, N.Y. Times, June 4, 1895, quoted in Teitz, *supra* note 3, at 463.

**14.** *Hilton* also established the principle of "reciprocity." That principle requires a judgment rendered in a foreign nation to be reexamined on the merits by the federal courts in this country if

for non-enforcement of a foreign judgment in U.S. courts.[15] As is evident from the numbered text quoted from *Hilton* itself, the Court's stated requirements for enforcing a judgment are that the judgment be rendered by a

(1) impartial and competent court with

(2) subject matter jurisdiction,

(3) personal jurisdiction, and

(4) notice and an opportunity to be heard, in an

(5) impartial judicial system, under proceedings conducted under due process of law

(6) without some special ground shown for impeaching the judgment, such as

(7) fraud,

(8) prejudice,

(9) violation of the principles of international law or

(10) violation of the principles of comity.

Translated into modern terms, *Hilton*'s requirements can be clearly seen in section 482 of the *Restatement (Third) of the Foreign Relations Law* of the United States, which enumerates the third and fifth *Hilton* conditions—lack of personal jurisdiction and absence of impartial tribunals or procedures compatible with due process of law—as mandatory "grounds for nonrecognition of foreign judgments."[16] The same section lists as discretionary grounds for nonenforcement most of the remaining *Hilton* factors: lack of subject matter jurisdiction, notice, fraud, and repugnance to public policy.[17] Finally, the *Restatement (Third)* also authorizes discretionary nonenforcement in any case where the "judgment conflicts with another final judgment that is entitled to recognition" or when "the proceeding in the foreign court was contrary to an agreement between the parties to submit the controversy on which the judg-

---

an American judgment would be given similar treatment in the foreign nation involved. It is now doubtful, however, whether that doctrine remains viable. *See* Tahan v. Hodgson, 662 F.2d 862, 867–68 (D.C. Cir. 1981); RESTATEMENT (THIRD) OF THE FOREIGN RELATIONS LAW OF THE UNITED STATES § 481 cmt. d.

**15.** For a discussion of this extensive case law, see generally Willis Reese, *The Status in This Country of Judgments Rendered Abroad*, 50 COLUM. L. REV. 783,

796–98 (1950); RONALD BRAND ED., ENFORCING FOREIGN JUDGMENTS IN THE UNITED STATES AND UNITED STATES JUDGMENTS ABROAD (American Bar Association 1992). For comparative analysis, see Friedrich Juenger, *The Recognition of Money Judgments in Civil and Commercial Matters*, 36 AM. J. COMP. L. 1 (1988).

**16.** *See* RESTATEMENT (THIRD) § 482(1)(a)–(b).

**17.** *See id.* § 482(2)(a)–(d).

ment is based to another forum."[18] The commentary to the *Restatement (Third)* makes clear that this latter ground is broad enough to embrace both traditional forum-selection clauses that choose particular national courts, of the kind seen in the *Bremen* case discussed in Chapter VIII, as well as arbitration clauses of the kind at issue in the *Mitsubishi* case, to be discussed in Chapter XII.[19]

Although the *Restatement (Third)* has brought some clarity to this area, the search continues in the U.S. for a controlling uniform standard. To this day, Congress has enacted no federal statute to governs the enforcement of foreign judgments in the United States. Moreover, following *Erie R.R. Co. v. Tompkins*,[20] federal courts have generally held that state law governs the recognition and enforcement of judgments in diversity actions, thus requiring federal courts to engage in sometimes obscure determinations of what the applicable state law might be to decide whether a foreign judgment should be enforced (potentially leading the federal court into examinations of not one, but two bodies of unfamiliar law). In an effort to achieve uniformity within this framework, the National Conference on Commissioners on Uniform State Law and the American Bar Association in 1962 prepared the Uniform Foreign Money–Judgments Recognition Act (UFMJRA), for adoption by the several states.[21] By and large, the Uniform Act has been built on the principles of *Hilton* and its progeny. It provides that a foreign judgment is "final and conclusive and enforceable where rendered even though an appeal therefrom is pending or it is subject to appeal," at which point it becomes "conclusive between the parties to the extent that it grants or denies recovery of a sum of money," so long as certain grounds for non-recognition do not exist.[22] At the end of the twentieth century, yet another statutory drafting exercise began in connection with the treatymaking exercise described below. The American Law Institute's project on Recognition and Enforcement of Foreign Judgments, which was concluded in 2006 under the direction of reporters Andreas Lowenfeld and Linda Silberman of New York University Law School, included both an analysis and a proposed federal statute, a "Foreign Judgments

**18.** *See id.* § 482(2)(e)–(f).

**19.** *See id.* § 482(a)(f) cmt. h and reporter's note 5.

**20.** 304 U.S. 64 (1938) (absent federal statute, treaty or other basis for federal jurisdiction federal courts sitting in diversity jurisdiction must apply state law as rules of decision on substantive matters).

**21.** The Act, 13 (pt. II) U.L.A. (Supp. 2005), which is reproduced as Appendix M of Gary Born, International Civil Litigation in United States Courts (3d ed. 1996), has been followed, in various forms, by some twenty states. *See id.* at 941 n.40.

**22.** UFJMA, §§ 2–3.

Recognition and Enforcement Act,'' which would federalize the treatment of most foreign judgments.[23] That project sought both to minimize forum shopping and to give foreign courts faced with the question whether to enforce an American judgment a clearer sense of U.S. practice.[24]

## B. Treatymaking Exercises

The United States is yet to become party to a full-fledged international agreement governing the recognition and enforcement of judgments. In 1925, the Hague Conference on Private International Law first attempted to create such a convention, but the draft failed to gain acceptance and was instead used primarily as a model for regional treaties.[25] In 1971, a second attempt was made, with the first Hague Convention on Recognition and Enforcement of Foreign Judgments in Civil and Commercial Matters, but this attempt also failed, so that as of 2005, only four countries, and none of the major superpowers, had ratified the treaty.[26]

Indeed, the very question of what kind of Judgments Convention to ratify has itself posed a major issue for U.S. public policy. In the early 1970s the U.S. began efforts to negotiate a bilateral treaty on the reciprocal recognition and enforcement of judgment in civil matters with the United Kingdom.[27] One would have thought that before attempting to reach a broader rapprochement with the civil law countries, the United States would have been best off by first obtaining an accord with its leading common-law ally. But eventually, negotiations broke down over a number of issues related to the unique characteristics of the American system of civil wrongs discussed above, particularly, British concerns over punitive damages and the American law of products liability.[28] Consequently, the United States has largely remained outside treaty arrangements, leaving parties that have won judgments in American courts facing difficulties in enforcing their judgments abroad and vice versa.

**23.** AMERICAN LAW INSTITUTE, RECOGNITION AND ENFORCEMENT OF FOREIGN JUDGMENTS: ANALYSIS AND PROPOSED FEDERAL STATUTE (2006).

**24.** *See generally* Linda J. Silberman & Andreas F. Lowenfeld, *A Different Challenge for the ALI: Herein of Foreign Country Judgments, an International Treaty, and an American Statute*, 75 IND. L.J. 635 (2000)

**25.** Actes de la Cinquieme session de la Conference de La Haye de Droit International Prive 332 (1925).

**26.** *See generally* Adair Dyer, *Synthesis of the Recognition and Enforcement of Judgments under the Hague Conventions and the EEC Convention*, 7(i) INT'L LEGAL PRAC. 23 (1982). The four ratifying states include Cyprus (1976), the Netherlands (1979), Portugal (1983), and Kuwait (2002).

**27.** For an *ad referendum* text, which was initialed, but never concluded, see 16 INT'L LEG. MATS. 71 (1976).

**28.** For a discussion of the failure of the bilateral negotiations, see von Mehren, *supra* note 2, at 273–74.

The absence of a multilateral judgments convention has also hastened a flight toward international commercial arbitration as a means of transnational dispute resolution, given that New York Convention now has more than one hundred contracting parties. This situation has created the anomaly that foreign arbitral awards—the products of private-ordering—are more likely to be enforced in a transnational setting than are official judgments of national courts, even though the latter have been concluded under the auspices of official authority and with formal institutional guarantees of due process.

By eschewing treaty frameworks, the United States stands in contrast to a large number of its trading partners. As we have seen in Chapter VII, the European countries, by their accession to the Brussels and Lugano Conventions, have developed a uniform, integrated scheme to govern both jurisdictional rules and reciprocal recognition and enforcement of foreign judgments. The European conventions are archetypes of what are sometimes called a *convention double*. Such enforcement treaties rest on the notion that a double set of rules—uniform rules on judicial jurisdiction and uniform rules on recognition and enforcement of judgments—will facilitate each other's operation. A significant number of the members of the Organization of American States have similarly become parties to the Montevideo Convention of May 8, 1979, which governs the extraterritorial validity of foreign judgments and arbitral awards. Unlike the Brussels Convention, the Montevideo treaty is a simple Convention (*convention simple*), which deals only with recognition and enforcement without addressing issues of judicial jurisdiction, a result that achieves far less clarity and predictability than a *convention double*, by leaving many more questions to be addressed by the internal law of the individual member states.[29]

The United States' problems in this area have been compounded by the comparative generosity of the United States' *Hilton* standard toward enforcement. Thus, the U.S. faces a higher risk that it will enforce judgments from foreign countries who may not reciprocate under their local law.[30] Moreover, the Supreme Court's

---

**29.** Inter-American Convention on General Rules of Private International Law, May 8, 1979, 1457 U.N.T.S. 6, 18 I.L.M. 1236. The Convention is currently in force between Argentina, Brazil, Colombia, Ecuador, Mexico, Paraguay, Peru, Uruguay and Venezuela. To remedy problems, the Montevideo Convention was complemented in 1984 by the La Paz Convention, 50 U.N.T.S. OEA/Ser. A/28, which addresses international jurisdiction for the extraterritorial validity of foreign judgments. Though widely signed, that Convention has been ratified only by Mexico and thus has not entered into force.

**30.** *Cf.* Kevin M. Clermont, *Jurisdictional Salvation and the Hague Treaty*, 85 CORNELL L. REV. 89, 89 (1999) (stating "the United States eagerly gives appropriate respect to foreign judgments, despite sometimes getting no respect in return").

decision in the *Schlunk* case discussed in Chapter IX has also exacerbated the problem. For given that parties who comply with the Hague Service Convention generally find it easier to enforce their own judgments abroad,[31] the Court's decision narrowing the "occasions for service abroad" under the Convention has limited the number of U.S. cases initiated under the Service Convention, and hence, reduced the number of cases in which the mode of notice-giving is unassailable in any subsequent enforcement effort.

Following the collapse of the U.S.–U.K. bilateral negotiations, the United States government began to reexamine its treaty negotiation strategy in the judgments field.[32] The U.S.–U.K. episode revealed the weakness of a series of bilateral treaties, each of which could founder on particular issues, as the U.S.–U.K. treaty had done. Moreover, the U.S. Government recognized that a series of bilateral treaties would require a much large commitment of human and financial resources than a multilateral effort, and that separately negotiated texts could vary, creating confusion, lacunae, and questions of disuniformity. Subtle differences among treaties could be exploited by other countries during negotiations and by attorneys after ratification. Worst of all, each treaty would need to be separately ratified by the U.S. Senate, leaving the possibility that they would be rejected for reasons peculiar to particular Senators or held hostage to other unrelated foreign policy agenda items.

The U.S. considered engaging in multilateral negotiations with the EU Member States of the Brussels Convention and the EFTA members of the Lugano Convention, but the U.S. feared that the project would thereby exclude many states (other than those of Western Europe in which those conventions are in force). A further American fear was that a Judgments Convention modeled too closely on the Brussels and Lugano Conventions might then have its interpretation effectively governed by rulings of the European Court of Justice construing those conventions. For these and other reasons, the United States eventually chose to turn to the Hague Conference on Private International Law, under whose auspices a number of other private international law treaties have been negotiated.[33] The Hague Conference's membership extends beyond EU members, to Mexico and the Latin American states, as well as to

---

**31.** *See* David Westin, *Enforcing Foreign Commercial Judgments and Arbitral Awards in the United States, West Germany, and England*, 19 LAW AND POLICY INT'L BUS. 325, 340–341 (1987).

**32.** I am grateful to Peter H. Pfund, formerly Special Adviser for Private In-

ternational Law, U.S. Department of State for much of the information that follows regarding the U.S. government's position regarding the Convention.

**33.** *See* Chapter VII, *supra*.

China, Japan, Australia, several Eastern European countries, Israel, Morocco and Egypt. As important, the Hague Conference's extensive experience with such treaty drafting had allowed it to develop an apparently manageable four-year timetable for treaty preparation, running from preparatory study to the adoption of the final convention text.

Acting upon many of these concerns, in May 1992, the United States finally proposed that the Hague Conference on Private International Law draft a new multilateral convention to address the reciprocal recognition and enforcement of civil and commercial judgments.[34] As noted earlier, the Hague Conference on Private International Law is an inter-governmental organization with sixty member states representing all continents, the purpose of which is "to work for the progressive unification of the rules of private international law."[35] To investigate the possibility of negotiating a new treaty, a Working Group consisting of experts from Argentina, the People's Republic of China, Finland, France, Hungary, the United Kingdom, and the United States was convened in 1993, which concluded that the Hague Conference should negotiate a global judgments convention.[36] Learning from the mistakes of the earlier Hague Judgments Convention, however, the Working Group decided that any convention needed to address jurisdiction in addition to enforcement of judgments for the project to be successful.[37] Based on the recommendations of the Working Group, the Hague Conference convened a Special Commission, which met in June 1997 and October 1999.[38] After several meetings to consider the matter, the Hague Conference formally took up the challenge in the October 1996.[39]

**34.** *See* Letter from Edwin D. Williamson, Legal Adviser, U.S. Department of State to Georges Droz, Secretary General, Hague Conference on Private International Law, May 5, 1992, enclosure to Hague Conference document L.C. O.N. No. 15 (92).

**35.** Statute of the Hague Conference on Private International Law, July 15, 1955, art. 1, 220 U.N.T.S. 121. The Hague Conference has adopted thirty-six International Conventions on private international law since 1951. *See* Overview of Hague Conference on Private International Law, http://www.hcch.net/index_en.php?act=text.display&tid=4.

**36.** SAMUEL BAUMGARTNER, THE PROPOSED HAGUE CONVENTION ON JURISDICTION AND FOREIGN JUDGMENTS 1 (2003). *See also* Gregoire Andrieux, *Declining Jurisdic-*

*tion in a Future International Convention on Jurisdiction and Judgments— How Can We Benefit from Past Experiences in Conciliating the Two Doctrines of Forum Non Conveniens and Lis Pendens?*, 27 Loy. L.A. INT'L & COMP. L. REV. 323, 326–27 (2005).

**37.** Hague Conference, Preliminary Document 19, at 3 (2002); Hague Conference, Preliminary Document 7, at 4 (1996).

**38.** Hague Conference, Preliminary Document 11, at 25 (2000) (Nygh & Pocar Report).

**39.** Hague Conference on Private International Law, Final Act, Eighteenth Session, Final Edition, Part B, item 1. The chair of the special commission for the Judgments Convention was T.B. Smith of Ottawa, Canada, who chaired

From the outset of negotiations, the meetings were plagued by a series of battles between the United States and European countries, with other countries feeling marginalized in the process.[40] While the United States pushed for a convention that more closely resembled its own conception of jurisdiction, the European delegations pushed for the new convention to model the successful Brussels and Lugano Conventions on jurisdiction and enforcement of judgments.[41] The European delegations also sought to limit the jurisdictional reach of the U.S. courts, which they viewed as both exorbitant and unjust.[42] That the Brussels and Lugano Conventions already existed, and that foreign judgments were already liberally accepted by U.S. courts even without a treaty, gave the European delegations little incentive to negotiate. Meanwhile, the United States, on its side, felt constrained by what it saw as constitutional constraints.[43] At the close of its October 1999 session, the Special Commission adopted a draft convention entitled the Preliminary Draft Hague Convention on Jurisdiction and Foreign Judgments in Civil and Commercial Matters, a document that wholly satisfied none of the drafters.[44]

In the ensuing months, the Draft Convention sustained heavy criticism. Shortly thereafter, the Head of the U.S. Delegation wrote to the Secretary General of the Hague Conference proposing "a stock-taking session when delegations can discuss in a frank, informal, and serious way whether there is the desire and political will

---

the special commission that produced the Hague Intercountry Adoption Convention in 1993, and the U.S. member was Professor Arthur von Mehren, the noted conflicts of law expert from Harvard Law School.

**40.** BAUMGARTNER, *supra* note 36 at 4–5.

**41.** Brussels Convention on Jurisdiction and Enforcement of Judgments in Civil and Commercial Matters, Sept. 27, 1968, 1972 O.J. (L 299) 32, *reprinted in* 8 I.L.M. 229 (1969), *as amended by* 1990 O.J. (L 189) 1, *reprinted as amended in* 29 I.L.M. 1413 (1990) [hereinafter Brussels Convention]; Lugano Convention on Jurisdiction and Enforcement of Judgments in Civil and Commercial Matters, Sept. 16, 1998 O.J. (L 319) 9, *reprinted in* 28 I.L.M. 620 (1989) [hereinafter Lugano Convention].

**42.** BAUMGARTNER, *supra* note 36, at 4.

**43.** *See generally* Arthur T. Von Mehren, *Drafting a Convention on International Jurisdiction and the Effects of Foreign Judgments Acceptable Worldwide: Can the Hague Conference Project Succeed?*, 49 AM. J. COMP. L. 191, 194–95 (2001); Linda Silberman, *Comparative Jurisdiction in the International Context: Will the Proposed Hague Judgments Convention Be Stalled?*, 52 DEPAUL L. REV. 319, 321–22 (2002).

**44.** BAUMGARTNER, *supra* note 36, at 5. The Draft Convention applied to civil and commercial matters but excluded various listed matters such as status and legal capacity of natural persons, domestic relations, wills and succession, insolvency, administrative law, taxation, customs, social security, arbitration and proceedings related thereto, and admiralty or maritime matters. 1999 Draft Hague Convention, art. 1.

to depart from the current text and seek new avenues for agreement."[45] He said, bluntly:

> The project as currently embodied in the October 1999 preliminary draft convention stands no chance of being accepted in the United States. Moreover, our assessment is that the negotiating process so far demonstrates no foreseeable possibility for correcting what for us are fatal defects in the approach, structure, and details of the text. In our view there has not been adequate progress toward creation of a draft convention that would represent a worldwide compromise among extremely different legal systems. . . .[46]

In response, the Special Commission submitted a second draft in June 2001, which included multiple alternate versions of some articles, but again there was very little consensus. When negotiations again stalled in 2001, the delegates finally agreed that the draft Convention stood no chance of being adopted by the Hague Conference and should be abandoned.[47] Instead, the Hague Conference turned to the much more limited task of drafting a convention on which there had always been relatively broad consensus: a much narrower treaty to govern international choice of court agreements.[48]

After working through the next two years, the informal working group submitted a draft that to the Commission on General Affairs and Policy of the Hague Conference in April 2003. That Commission in turn met to produce a Preliminary Draft Convention, and, after further deliberations, convened a diplomatic session in June 2005 that unanimously adopted the Hague Convention on Choice of Court Agreements.[49] At this writing, the United States has signed, but not ratified the Convention, and only Mexico has acceded to the Convention.[50] Before describing the key features of the Hague Choice-of-Court Convention, let me review the policy

---

**45.** *See* Letter from Jeffrey D. Kovar, U.S. Dept. of State, Assistant Legal Advisor for Private Int'l Law, to J.H.A. van Loon, Sec'y Gen., Hague Conference on Private Int'l Law 2 (Feb. 22, 2000), *available at* http://www.cptech.org/ecom/hague/kovar2loon22022000.pdf [hereinafter "State Department Letter"].

**46.** *Id.*

**47.** Jeffrey Talpis and Nick Krnjevic, *The Hague Convention on Choice of Court Agreements of June 30, 2005: The Elephant That Gave Birth to a Mouse*, 13 Sw. J.L. & Trade Am. 1 (2006); Hague Conference, Preliminary Document 26, at 7 (2004) ("As work proceeded on

drafting . . . it became apparent that it would not be possible to draw up a satisfactory text for a 'mixed' convention within a reasonable period of time.").

**48.** Ved P. Nanda, *The Landmark 2005 Hague Convention on Choice of Court Agreements*, 42 Tex. Int'l L.J. 773, 776 (2007).

**49.** Hague Convention, Preliminary Document 30 (2005).

**50.** Status Table, Hague Convention on Choice of Court Agreements, http://www.hcch.net/index_en.php?act=conventions.status&cid=98.

differences between the common and civil law systems that led to the demise of a global Jurisdiction and Foreign Judgments Convention.

## C. Points of Contention in Drafting a Global Judgments Convention

The common law-civil law struggle that doomed the Judgments Convention devolved into a dispute between the Americans, who desired greater flexibility in the recognition and enforcement of judgments, and the civil law countries that desired greater predictability.[51] I review some of the most contentious issues below.

### 1. *Convention Mixte vs. Convention Double*

The primary issue facing the drafters of the Judgments Convention was whether to adopt a convention based on predictability or flexibility. Those favoring predictability argued for either a convention devoted to recognition and enforcement (a *convention simple* like the Montevideo Convention) or a *convention double*, like the Brussels and Lugano Convention, which would address both recognition and enforcement and broader issues regarding permissible bases for jurisdiction to adjudicate. Although a *convention double* solution would clearly have been broader, inter-country differences on points of procedural law had always made such a treaty far more difficult to negotiate. The unsuccessful 1925 and 1971 Hague Conventions had been *conventions simples*, insofar as they did not contain any prohibited grounds of jurisdiction and concerned only the enforcement of foreign judgments.[52] Thus, the Convention negotiations in 1992 began with the ambitious goal of establishing a universal regime for jurisdiction, based on a prerequisite of fairness and impartiality of adjudicatory process in the rendering court.[53]

To achieve this goal, the European delegations favored a *convention double*, similar to the Brussels Convention, under which all permitted jurisdictional bases were categorized on a "white list" of mandatory bases of jurisdiction and all prohibited bases are listed

---

**51.** *See generally* Gregoire Andrieux, *Declining Jurisdiction in a Future International Convention on Jurisdiction and Judgments—How Can We Benefit from Past Experiences in Conciliating the Two Doctrines of Forum Non Conveniens and Lis Pendens?*, 27 Loy. L.A. Int'l & Comp. L. Rev. 323 (2005).

**52.** Baumgartner, *supra* note 36, at 4.

**53.** Stephen B. Burbank, *Jurisdictional Equilibration, the Proposed Hague Convention and Progress in National Law*, 49 Am. J. Comp. L. 203, 204 (2001).

on a "black list" of "exorbitant jurisdiction."[54] The "white list" provisions were to detail all of the bases on which jurisdiction might validly be based, with all judgments resulting from such assumptions of jurisdiction automatically satisfying the Judgments Convention's jurisdictional requirements. At the same time, the Europeans envisioned a "black list," parallel to the list of exorbitant jurisdictions in Article 3 of the Brussels Convention (discussed in Chapter VII), which would be automatically deemed unenforceable.

Against this model, the United States proposed to the Special Commission a hybrid version—dubbed a *convention mixte*—which would incorporate elements of simple and double conventions, and thereby perhaps mediate between diverse legal systems.[55] For the sake of flexibility and compromise, the mixed convention model would have accepted a broader "grey zone" of ambiguous enforcement options, or in Professor Lowenfeld's colorful phrase, "green, red and yellow lights for jurisdiction."[56] Such a mixed convention would have achieved some of the advantages of a double convention, while offering greater flexibility than the more predictable, but also more rigid, Brussels/Lugano structure.

In 1997, the Permanent Bureau of the Hague Conference distributed two reports pulling together the major issues and suggestions for their possible resolution.[57] The list of grounds for refusal to recognize and enforce foreign judgments largely tracked the *Hilton* list, as updated in the *Restatement (Third)*, and extended to such grounds as the independence and impartiality of the court of origin, fraud, fairness of proceedings, public policy, conflicting judgments, and the like. Although the United States advocated forcefully for a *convention mixte*, the 1999 Draft Convention was modeled heavily on the Brussels Convention at the insistence of the European delegations.[58] The report from the Special Commission in 1995 confirmed that it "favoured the preparation of a double Convention limiting itself, as do the Conventions of Brussels and Lugano, to bases for assuming jurisdiction which are accepted and those which are rejected."[59]

---

**54.** *Id.* at 204–05.

**55.** *See* von Mehren, *supra* note 2, at 282–87.

**56.** *See* Lowenfeld, *supra* note 2, at 289.

**57.** *See* Kessedjian papers, *supra* note 2. These papers, and other documents relating to the Convention, may for now be examined on the web site of the Private International Law data base of the Legal Adviser's Office at the United States Department of State, which may be accessed at http://www.state.gov/s/l/c3452.htm.

**58.** *Id.* at 194.

**59.** Hague Convention, Preliminary Document 2, at 13 (1995).

After years of negotiation, however, the conflict between the flexible common law tradition and the European civil law tradition favoring clearly delineated and predictable rules, could not be simply papered over.[60] While the Brussels model worked well on a regional level, the much greater diversity of legal systems led the *Convention double* model to fail at a global level. Only four days before the October 1999 Draft Convention was adopted, the Special Commission finally accepted the concept of a *convention mixte*, but when the "black" and "white" lists were finalized, they proved so extensive that some considered it, in effect, a *convention double* masquerading as a *convention mixte*.[61] As one participant recalled, an intractable "problem in the negotiations at the Hague was reaching a consensus on jurisdictional grounds appropriate for the 'gray area.' The gray areas [we]re not easy to find, due partially to the two hundred footnotes and close to one hundred passages in square brackets that appear in the June 2001 Draft."[62] Calling for a halt to the Convention, the U.S. State Department opined that "[d]espite nearly eight years of discussion of the fundamental importance and need for a mixed convention, and agreement by vote that the Special Commission would work to that end, what we see in the present text is for all intents and purposes a narrow double convention."[63] Thus, until the fundamental conflict between the *convention double* and the *convention mixte* approaches can be resolved, there would seem to be little prospect for a revived Judgments Convention anytime in the near future.[64]

## 2. *Permitted Jurisdictional Bases*

A further source of conflict concerned the jurisdictional bases themselves, particularly with respect to the "hard cases" that I have discussed with respect to jurisdiction in Chapter VII. Problems for negotiation included the problems of minimum contacts and long-arm jurisdiction over foreign tortfeasors in products liability cases (the *Asahi* problem); the *Burnham* problem of transient jurisdiction; and nonenforcement in cases of forum-selection clauses. In particular, the U.S. and European delegations diverged over whether suits against multiple defendants could proceed even if not

**60.**  Arthur T. Von Mehren, *Drafting a Convention on International Jurisdiction and the Effects of Foreign Judgments Acceptable World-wide: Can the Hague Conference Project Succeed?*, 49 Am. J. Comp. L. 191, 197–200 (2001).

**61.**  *Id.* at 199.

**62.**  Silberman, *supra* note 43, at 325.

**63.**  State Department Letter, *supra* note 45, at 4–5.

**64.**  Ved P. Nanda, *The Landmark 2005 Hague Convention on Choice of Court Agreements*, 42 Tex. Int'l L.J. 773, 776 (2007).

all defendants satisfied the jurisdictional requirements. The Brussels Convention allowed jurisdiction over a person "where he is one of a number of defendants, in the courts for the place where any one of them is domiciled," but allowing jurisdiction over one defendant based on the domicile of another would violate the personal jurisdiction rule in the United States, which require an individualized determination, based on the due process rights of the particular defendant in question.[65] Although the 1999 Draft Convention allowed such suits against multiple defendants, the 2001 Draft Convention removed this provision, instead placing it in the "gray area" of permissible but not mandatory jurisdiction.[66]

More intractable was the dispute over jurisdiction based on the location of injury. Regardless of whether the defendant had sufficient minimum contacts to sustain personal jurisdiction in the U.S. context, the 1999 Draft Convention nevertheless required courts to exercise jurisdiction if they were from contracting states "in which the act or omission that caused injury occurred" or "in which the injury arose, unless the defendant establishes that the person claimed to be responsible could not reasonably have foreseen that the act or omission could result in an injury of the same nature in that State."[67] The United States identified the broad scope of jurisdiction for defendants as one of the main reasons it recommended that the 1999 Draft Convention be abandoned.[68] Although the 2001 Draft Convention attempted to assuage U.S. reservations by allowing contracting states to take a reservation if a required ground of jurisdiction would violate its own constitutional norms, the inevitable conflict between this provision and U.S. personal jurisdiction law was one of the main grounds that drove the ultimate U.S. recommendation that the 2001 Draft Convention be abandoned as well.[69]

Additional conflicts arose over several other jurisdictional bases in the civil law tradition that the United States found unacceptable,

**65.** Brussels Convention, art. 6(1).

**66.** Compare Draft Hague Convention, art. 14 (2001) with Draft Hague Convention, art. 14 (1999), which states that

1. A plaintiff bringing an action against a defendant in a court of the State in which that defendant is habitually resident may also proceed in that court against other defendants not habitually resident in that State if—

a) the claims against the defendant habitually resident in that State and the other defendants are so closely connected that they should be adjudicated together to avoid a serious risk of inconsistent judgments, and b) as to each defendant not habitually resident in that State, there is a substantial connection between that State and the dispute involving that defendant.

**67.** Draft Hague Convention, art. 10 (1999).

**68.** State Department Letter, *supra* note 45, at 7.

**69.** Draft Hague Convention, art. 10 (2001).

including jurisdiction based purely on the nationality of the plaintiff (based on French law) and based purely on the existence of real property in the forum state (based on German law).[70] As we saw in Chapter VIII, the plaintiff's nationality may be a basis for a presumption again *forum non conveniens* dismissal, but not a factor that conclusively establishes personal jurisdiction. And in *Shaffer v. Heitner*,[71] the U.S. Supreme Court made clear that the relevant test for asserting jurisdiction was no longer the *Pennoyer v. Neff* standard of "territorial presence of property within the jurisdiction," but rather, the "minimum contacts" test of *International Shoe Co. v. Washington*.[72] After the U.S. delegation resisted, in a major compromise, European delegations allowed both jurisdictional bases to be entered on the "black list" in the 1999 Draft Convention.[73]

But if the 1999 Draft Convention provided for more jurisdiction over defendants than the United States felt comfortable accepting, it also prohibited jurisdiction on two grounds that the United States felt essential. First, the 1999 Draft Convention prohibited jurisdiction based upon "business activity" unrelated to the dispute, directly conflicting with the U.S. "long arm" statutes and caselaw relying upon the notion, discussed in Chapter VII, that a defendant with sufficient contacts with a forum may be sued under "general jurisdiction," even upon causes of action unrelated to the underlying contacts between the defendant and the forum.[74] Such jurisdictional bases were prohibited under civil law and made the European delegations profoundly uncomfortable. The compromise reached in the 1999 Draft Convention was to allow jurisdiction based on a defendant's primary place of business, but to prohibit jurisdiction based on "the carrying on of commercial or other activities by the defendant in that State, except where the dispute is directly related to those activities."[75]

**70.** Linda Silberman, *Can the Hague Judgments Project Be Saved?: A Perspective from the United States*, in A GLOBAL LAW OF JURISDICTION AND JUDGMENTS: LESSONS FROM THE HAGUE 159–89 (John J. Barcelo III & Kevin Clermont eds., 2002); Von Mehren, *supra* note 43, at 195–96.

**71.** 433 U.S. 186 (1977).

**72.** See Chapter VII, *supra*.

**73.** Draft Hague Convention, art. 18(a)–(c) (1999); Von Mehren, *supra* note 43, at 195.

**74.** *See* Chapter VII, *supra* (discussing *Perkins v. Benguet* and *Helicopteros Nacionales v. Hall*). *Compare* Draft Hague Convention, art. 18(e) (1999),

*with* BAUMGARTNER, *supra* note 36 at 128–145.

**75.** The 1996 Nygh–Pocar Report explained that the hesitation to accept jurisdiction based on "business activity" was based in part on the "significant margin of uncertainty" as to when a general jurisdiction basis such as "doing business" applies because of "the difficulty of determining the quality and quantity of activity which is needed in order to found jurisdiction." Hague Conference, Preliminary Document 11, at 75 (2000); Draft Hague Convention, art. 18(e) (1999).

Second, the Draft Convention prohibited transient or "tag jurisdiction," of the type used in the *Burnham* or *Karadzic* cases discussed in Chapter VII, in which a defendant otherwise lacking significant conduct with the forum may be served personally during a temporary visit to the forum jurisdiction.[76] This prohibition particularly worried human rights advocates, who saw it as a threat to much of the transnational public law litigation brought against foreign defendants under the Alien Tort Claims Act and the Torture Victim Protection Act.[77] These prohibitions on both "long arm" and "tag" jurisdiction eventually proved fatal to the participation of the United States.[78]

## 3. Punitive Damages

Yet another point of contention between the U.S. and European delegations was the treatment of punitive (or exemplary) damage awards, which are common in the U.S. context but are considered excessive in the European context (and the related issue of American civil jury trials). It has long been settled enforcement law that comity principles do not require domestic courts "to recognize and enforce judgments for the collection of taxes, fines, or penalties rendered by the courts of other states."[79] The rationale for the rule has been two-fold. On one hand, like the act of state doctrine, the bar against penal enforcement reflects the reluctance of courts to subject a foreign public law to judicial scrutiny; on the other hand, like the restrictive rules regarding extradition, the rule reflects the particular skepticism and distrust of most national courts toward foreign criminal procedures. The question thus arose whether foreign courts would agree under any Judgments Convention to enforce U.S. decisions awarding large punitive and exemplary damages in tort and product liability cases, particularly in cases where the multiplication of damages has been mandated by statute and the judgment is based on a distinctively American jury verdict following a civil jury trial. The problem of perception was particularly severe with regard to awards rendered in certain states of the Union, such as Texas, which are perceived by Europeans not just as

---

**76.** *Id.* art. 18(f).

**77.** *See generally* Chapter III *supra*; Thomas E. Vanderbloemen, *Assessing the Potential Impact of the Proposed Hague Jurisdiction and Judgments Convention on Human Rights Litigation in the United States*, 50 DUKE L.J. 917 (2000); State Department Letter, *supra* note 45, at 9 ("A generally-acceptable provision that exempts existing civil suits to redress human rights violations from prohibition under Article 18 is necessary or there will be intense opposition to this convention in the United States.").

**78.** Talpis & Krnjevic, *supra* note 47, at 3.

**79.** *See* RESTATEMENT (THIRD) § 483.

special magnets for such personal injury and products liability litigation, but also as awards that are relatively immune from appellate review.

In fact, these were precisely the issues on which the U.S.–U.K. bilateral negotiations in the mid–1970s had previously foundered.[80] Despite U.S. efforts to allay U.K. concerns, the negotiations failed because U.K. manufacturers and insurers held deep concerns about these issues and lobbied against the treaty on that ground.[81] Moreover, the German courts have held, as a general rule, that punitive damages cannot be enforced in Germany, because such judgments amount to criminal sanctions and because German public policy does not permit the civil imposition of criminal sanctions.[82] A Japanese court has similarly refused to enforce a California judgment, not because such damages are criminal in nature, but because the findings of fact in the judgment were deemed unreasonably insufficient to justify an award punitive damages.[83] The Drafters faced at least three options: first, to deem such awards to be punitive, and hence place them outside the scope of the definition of the "civil and commercial matters" to which the Convention would apply; second to develop a clause similar to the one proposed in 1978 to break the U.S.–U.K. deadlock, which would have permitted an enforcing court to recognize and enforce an exemplary judgment in a lesser dollar amount,[84] or third, to draft a provision similar to Article 23 of the Evidence Convention (permitting reservations to pretrial discovery under the Convention), whereby countries could reserve to the Convention obligation with respect to punitive or exemplary awards issued pursuant to civil jury trials.[85]

In the end, the 1999 Draft Convention went in a fourth direction. In a concession to the United States, the drafters allowed forum states to refuse to enforce punitive damage awards only in certain circumstances.[86] But at the same time, the European delega-

---

**80.** *See* von Mehren, *supra* note 2, at 273–74.

**81.** *See* Peter North, The Draft U.K./ U.S. Judgments Convention: A British Viewpoint, 1 Nw. J. Int'l L. and Bus. 219, 223, 238 (1979) (discussing these concerns).

**82.** Judgment of June 4, 1972, BGH Sen X., *reprinted in* 1992 Zeitschrift fur Wirtschaftsrecht und Insolvenzpraxis (ZIP) 1256 (F.R.G) (German Federal Court) (*Bundesgerichtshof*). For discussion, see Joachim Zekoll, *The Enforceability of American Money Judgments*

*Abroad: A Landmark Decision by the German Federal Court of Justice*, 30 Colum. J. Transnat'l L. 641 (1992).

**83.** Judgment of Tokyo District Court of 18 Feb. 1991, *in* 35 Jap. Annual Int'l L. 177 (1992).

**84.** *See* von Mehren, *supra* note 2, at 274 (citing Article 8A of the draft U.S.– U.K. Convention).

**85.** *Cf.* Chapter X, *supra*.

**86.** Draft Hague Convention, art. 33(1) (1999) ("In so far as a judgment awards non-compensatory, including ex-

tions compromised by allowing a downward adjustment of damages to account for differences in costs and attorney's fees.[87] That the two sides were able to reach a tentative accord suggests that an impasse on this topic has now been broken and that this issue need not be an intractable source of division between the U.S. and Europe in any future negotiations.

## 4. *Lis Pendens vs. Forum Non Conveniens: Declining Jurisdiction*

A similar controversy arose over the issue of declining jurisdiction, with the American delegation preferring a flexible approach modeled on the *forum non conveniens* doctrine, which gives courts broad discretion to decline jurisdiction when they find a more appropriate alternate forum, while the European delegations preferred the continental *lis pendens* approach, in which a court may decline jurisdiction only in situations in which a suit in another forum is actually pending.[88]

As we saw in Chapter VIII, *forum non conveniens* was born as an Anglo–American doctrine of venue, largely unknown to the civil law countries. The Europeans have long feared that the doctrine might be used in a discriminatory fashion to prevent foreigners from having free access to national courts.[89] They also have expressed concern that *forum non conveniens* may be applied more broadly in circumstances in which the alternative forum would be a noncontracting state.

Over the objections of the United States, the Special Commission rejected a pure *forum non conveniens* approach in favor of a more limited, clearly delineated scheme.[90] The 1999 Draft Convention represented an attempt at compromise, modeled on the *lis pendens* approach, requiring that courts decline jurisdiction when a

emplary or punitive, damages, it shall be recognised at least to the extent that similar or comparable damages could have been awarded in the State addressed.").

**87.** *Id.* art. 33(2).

**88.** This controversy consumed much discussion early in the negotiations. *See* Martine Stückelberg, *Lis Pendens and Forum Non Conveniens at the Hague Conference*, 26 BROOKLYN J. INT'L L. 949 (2001); *See, e.g.*, Hague Conference, Preliminary Document 9, at 42 (1998); Michael Traynor, *An Introducto-*

*ry Framework for Analyzing the Proposed Hague Convention on Jurisdiction and Foreign Judgments in Civil and Commercial Matters: U.S. and European Perspectives*, 6 ANN. SURV. INT'L & COMP. L. 1, 9 (2000).

**89.** This fear may well be exacerbated by the ruling in *Piper* that a court need give no presumption in favor of a plaintiff's forum choice if that plaintiff is a foreign citizen or a nominal representative of foreign real parties in interest. *See* Chapter VIII, *supra*.

**90.** Hague Conference, Preliminary Document 3, at 4 (1996).

suit is pending in another forum.[91] However, the 1999 Draft Convention also contained a safety valve drawn from the common law tradition, allowing courts to exercise jurisdiction "if the court first seised, on application by a party, determines that the court second seised is clearly more appropriate to resolve the dispute, under the conditions specified in Article 22."[92] Article 22 provided exceptional circumstances for declining jurisdiction and imported into the test many of the interest-balancing factors present in the *forum non conveniens* doctrine, as described in Chapter VIII. Article 22 also outlined a non-exhaustive list of exceptional circumstances, which provided the flexibility for declining jurisdiction that had been sought by the United States.

Whether this approach would have worked as a long-term compromise remains unclear. The Draft Convention authorized a tribunal with jurisdiction over a dispute unilaterally to declare itself not to have jurisdiction, if it were established that the court would be inappropriate to handle the litigation. The problem, as we have seen from our prior discussions of *Laker* (in Chapter IV) and *Aerospatiale* (in Chapter X), is that national courts have not proven themselves adept at divesting themselves of jurisdiction through discretionary doctrines such as interest-balancing or comity. Thus, even if accepted, such an exception might have created a practical asymmetry, in which Anglo–American courts familiar with the *forum non conveniens* doctrine would have been more inclined to dismiss cases than foreign courts, to whom a divestment option would be initially novel and unfamiliar.

Despite the attempt to accommodate both doctrines in the 1999 Draft Convention, the dispute over *forum non conveniens* became a major point of concern for the United States. The State Department's Letter declared that "The lis pendens and forum non conveniens provisions in articles 21 and 22 represent good faith attempts to create novel provisions to bridge legal traditions that do not know one or the other practice. Nevertheless, controversy over them could pose a substantial risk to the wide acceptability of the convention."[93] In the end, this dispute was never resolved; instead, Hague Conference chose to address the choice of forum issue not *ex post*, by authorizing a global variant of *forum non conveniens*

---

**91.** Draft Hague Convention, art. 21(1) (1999) ("When the same parties are engaged in proceedings in courts of different Contracting States and when such proceedings are based on the same causes of action, irrespective of the relief sought, the court second seised shall suspend the proceedings if the court first seised has jurisdiction."). *See generally* Burbank, *supra* note 53 at 219–20.

**92.** *Id.* art. 21(7).

**93.** State Department Letter, *supra* note 45, at 9.

dismissal, but *ex ante*, by permitting instead enforcement of judgments arising under approved choice of court agreements.[94]

## 5.  *Internet Commerce and Intellectual Property*

Much of the negotiations that took place between 1999 and 2001 centered on the issues of e-commerce and intellectual property.[95] The resulting draft contained many alternative articles that reflected a lack of consensus on the part of the Special Commission regarding these issues.[96] Indeed, the 1999 and 2001 Draft Conventions, which began in the early days of the internet, never adequately addressed the special concerns that arise in e-commerce.[97] Negotiations had begun before the advent or acceleration of the Internet and many participants saw the Draft Convention as outdated even while it was being drafted.[98] In particular, Article 7, which governed consumer contracts, was seen as significantly expanding the liability of U.S. companies engaged in e-commerce in foreign courts.[99] Furthermore, U.S. companies feared that the Draft Convention would leave them overly vulnerable to defamation suits in jurisdictions with less robust free speech protections.[100]

The 1999 Draft Convention also sparked robust debate over intellectual property rights.[101] In particular, the 1999 Draft Convention never resolved the question whether copyright infringement would be a basis for exclusive jurisdiction, a matter of great importance to the United States, where copyright protections have traditionally fallen within the exclusive jurisdiction of the federal courts.[102] Nor was agreement ever fully reached on the scope of

**94.** Silberman, *supra* note 43, at 346.

**95.** Ronald A. Brand, *Intellectual Property, Electronic Commerce and the Preliminary Draft Hague Jurisdiction and Judgments Convention*, 62 U. PITT. L. REV. 581, 598 (2001).

**96.** Draft Hague Convention, art. 12 (2001).

**97.** Talpis & Krnjevic, *supra* note 47 at 4.

**98.** *See* State Department Letter, *supra* note 45, at 4 (identifying "crucial concerns related to electronic commerce"); Von Mehren, *supra* note 43, at 194 ("[I]n the last decade the rapid development and spread of commerce and new technologies have raised difficult and still unresolved economic, political, and legal issues in such fields as intellectual property and electronic commerce.").

**99.** Brand, *supra* note 95 at 597; Timothy P. Lester, *Globalized Automatic Choice of Forum: Where Do Internet Consumers Sue?: Proposed Article 7 of the Hague Convention on International Jurisdiction and Foreign Judgments in Civil and Commercial Matters and its Possible Effects on e-Commerce*, 9 NEW ENG. J. INT'L & COMP. L. 431 (2003).

**100.** Lester, *supra* note 99, at 433.

**101.** Ronald A. Brand, *Community Competence for Matters of Judicial Cooperation at the Hague Conference on Private International Law: A View from the United States*, 21 J.L. & COM. 191, 198 (2002).

**102.** The Draft Convention provided, bracketed language, that:

In proceedings which have as their object the registration, validity, [or]

exclusive jurisdiction for other kinds of intellectual property disputes under Article 12.

## 6.   *Consumer and Employer Protection*

Finally, the U.S. and European delegations also disagreed on choice-of-court agreements and jurisdiction for suits brought by consumers and employers.[103] Under the 1999 Draft Convention, consumers could bring suit in the jurisdiction of their habitual residence, so long as the consumer accepted the terms of the contract in that State or if the defendant solicited the consumer's business in that State.[104] Jurisdictional bases for disputes over employment contracts were likewise more expansive than for other types of disputes.

The 1999 Draft Convention rendered choice-of-court agreements invalid if they conflicted with Articles 7 and 8 of the Draft Convention, which provided these special jurisdictional bases for consumer and employee suits.[105] Under Article 8, only choice-of-court agreements in employment contracts made after a dispute arose were valid, which effectively prohibited most choice-of-court agreements in employment contracts.[106]

The 2001 Draft Convention reflected the dispute between the U.S. and European delegations over choice-of-court agreements. Through the drafting process, this section remained bracketed, with a footnote stating that "[t]he relationship between the choice of forum provisions and consumer transactions and employment contracts still has to be resolved."[107] Articles 7 and 8 underwent significant revisions between the 1999 and 2001 Draft Conventions.[108] The final draft contained several alternate versions of each article, representing the persistent disagreement between the U.S. and European delegations on this issue, and in the end, no compromise was struck before the treaty negotiations terminated.[109]

nullity[, or revocation or infringement,] of patents, trade marks, designs or other similar rights required to be deposited or registered, the courts of the Contracting State in which the deposit or registration has been applied for, has taken place or, under the terms of an international convention, is deemed to have taken place, have exclusive jurisdiction.

Draft Hague Convention, art. 12(4) (1999).

**103.**   *Id.* at 325–26.

**104.**   Draft Hague Convention, art. 7 (1999).

**105.**   *Id.* art. 4(3).

**106.**   *Id.* art. 8.

**107.**   *Id.* at n.29.

**108.**   Silberman, *supra* note 43, at 325.

**109.**   *See* Hague Convention, arts. 7, 8 (2001); Talpis & Krnjevic, *supra* note 47, at 3–4 (identifying as one of the main points of contention that led to its failure, "an impasse on the effectiveness

## D. The Hague Convention on Choice of Court Agreements

Following the demise of the Judgments Convention, the much-narrower Hague Convention on Choice of Court Agreements, signed on June 30, 2005, came into existence, mainly to promote enforceability of business-to-business forum-selection clauses. The new Hague Convention may be thought of as a litigation analogue to the New York Arbitration Convention, inasmuch as it was likewise designed to promote predictability of international business arrangements by establishing rules for enforcing the outcome of a particular kind of international dispute resolution device: namely forum-selection clauses and the recognition and enforcement of judgments rendered by the selected forum.

To accomplish this, the Convention set out four simple forum-selection rules: that

1) the court chosen by the parties in an exclusive choice-of-court agreement has jurisdiction;

2) if an exclusive choice-of-court agreement exists, a court not chosen by the parties does not have jurisdiction, and must decline to hear the case;

3) a judgment resulting from jurisdiction exercised in accordance with an exclusive choice-of-court agreement must be recognized and enforced in the courts of other Contracting States; and[110]

4) by optional declaration, Contracting States may announce that their courts will recognize and enforce judgments given by courts of other Contracting States that they have deemed acceptable and designated in a non-exclusive choice of court agreement. This last provision increases the mobility of a judgment by permitting Contracting States (and the industries inside them) to exercise this declaration option, in conjunction

---

of choice of court agreements involving consumers and employees—specifically, although the notion that a consumer should not be able to sign away his right to select a forum is readily accepted in Europe, South America, and Quebec, it is directly contrary to U.S. practice and the American business lobby was unwilling to compromise on this issue"). *See also* State Department Letter, *supra* note 54, at 7 ("This article, which is derived from the Brussels Convention, seems to us to be out of touch with

modern employment practice, good economic policy, and evolving practices. It does not permit even sophisticated employees (e.g., senior and middle management of major multinationals from all Conference member states) to agree to a choice of forum.").

**110.** Ronald A. Brand, *The New Hague Convention on Choice of Court Agreements*, ASIL INSIGHTS (2005), *available at* http://www.asil.org/insights/2005/07/insights050726.html.

with non-exclusive choice-of-court clauses, to expand the range of recognition and enforcement options available through the Convention.

By its own terms, the Choice of Court Agreements Convention applies to

1) exclusive choice-of-court agreements[111]

2) in an international setting,[112]

3) and excluding from its scope sources of conflict in the earlier treaty-drafting exercise, namely, intellectual property disputes,[113] contracts that include consumers as a party, employment relationships, family law matters, insolvency proceedings, nuclear damage and personal injury cases.[114]

In essence, the Hague Conference solved most of the disputes simply by writing them out of the Convention.[115] Following the reasoning of the Supreme Court's decision in *Bremen v. Zapata*, discussed in Chapter VIII, its primary objective was "ensur[ing] that choice of court agreements will be as effective as possible in international business transactions."[116] The very narrowness of the Convention has already permitted it to gain widespread acceptance.[117]

Because the treaty does not suspend traditional rules found in national and regional law, following *Hilton*, recognition or enforcement of a judgment may be refused if it "would be manifestly incompatible with the public policy of the requested State."[118] Thus, Article 11 of the Convention allows refusal of recognition and enforcement of a judgment "if, and only to the extent that, the judgment awards damages, including exemplary or punitive damages, that do not compensate a party for actual loss or harm suffered," and recognizes existing practice in the use of public policy defenses to refuse recognition and enforcement of such punitive damage awards.

---

**111.** *Id.* art. 1(1).

**112.** A case is international unless the parties are residing in the same Contracting State and all relevant elements except the location of the chosen court are connected only with that State. Hague Convention on Choice of Court Agreements, art. 1(2), June 30, 2005, 44 I.L.M. 1294, *available at* http://www.hcch.net/index_en.php?act=conventions.text&cid=98 [hereinafter Hague Convention].

**113.** *Id.* art. 2(2).

**114.** *Id.* art. 2(1).

**115.** For this reason, some authors described the treaty as "The Elephant That Gave Birth to a Mouse." Talpis & Krnjevic, *supra* note 47, at 1.

**116.** Talpis & Krnjevic, *supra* note 47, at 7.

**117.** Nanda, *supra* note 48, at 787.

**118.** Hague Convention, art. 9(e).

The Convention's text similarly reflects the past controversies over the Judgments Convention in the area of intellectual property rights. Because many international business transactions include the transfer of some form of intellectual property rights in some manner, the Hague Convention on Choice of Court Agreement excludes most issues of validity and infringement of intellectual property rights (other than copyright and related rights), but not when those issues arise only as preliminary matters in reaching the main object of the proceedings.[119] If fully ratified, the new Hague Convention on Choice of Court Agreements could restore the current imbalance between litigation and arbitration by doing what the New York Convention has done for arbitration, namely placing the two forms of dispute resolution on equal footing in global commerce by allowing business parties to select in advance the form of dispute resolution that best serves their transaction.

# E. Transnational Enforcement of Injunctions and Equity Decrees

This chapter's final topic—enforcement of foreign injunctions and equity decrees—encompasses not just enforcement questions, but also the difficult issues of provisional relief, antisuit injunctions, parallel proceedings, and *lis alibi pendens* (stay of parallel proceedings), all of which are subjects of a detailed and growing literature.[120]

While this is not the place for a comprehensive treatment of this subject, a few basic observations should be made. Recognition and enforcement of a foreign equity decree plainly differs from the complex question whether and when national court may enforce its *own* injunction transnationally. In such cases, U.S. courts have sometimes weighed foreign affairs, national security, and political question considerations to withhold judicial relief in certain circumstances.[121] Some prominent judicial critics of the equitable discre-

---

**119.** Hague Convention, arts. 2(2) (n)–(o), 2(3) and 10.

**120.** *See* Gary B. Born, *supra* note 19, at 459–90; George Bermann, *The Use of Antisuit Injunctions in International Litigation*, 28 Colum. J. Transnat'l L. 589 (1990); George Bermann, *Provisional Relief in Transnational Litigation*, 35 Colum. J. Transnat'l L. 553 (1997); Willis Reese, *Full Faith and Credit to Foreign Equity Decrees*, 42 Iowa L. Rev. 183 (1957).

**121.** *See, e.g.*, Crockett v. Reagan, 720 F.2d 1355, 1357 (D.C. Cir. 1983),

*cert. denied*, 467 U.S. 1251 (1984) (withholding relief in case where twenty-nine members of Congress charged that continuing military assistance to El Salvador violated the Foreign Assistance Act of 1961). For a collection of cases on the Equitable Discretion Doctrine, see generally Thomas M. Franck, Michael J. Glennon & Sean D. Murphy, Foreign Relations and National Security Law: Cases, Materials, and Simulations 1062–65 (3d ed. 2008).

tion doctrine have suggested that the separation-of-powers considerations that animate its use should be injected instead into the inquiry into whether the plaintiffs, sometimes legislators, have standing to seek the relief being sought.[122] In one famous transnational public law lawsuit, *Ramirez de Arellano v. Weinberger*, an en banc U.S. Court of Appeals for the D.C. Circuit addressed the case of a U.S. citizen, living in Honduras, who sought declarative and injunctive relief against officials of the United States government to abate the alleged occupation and destruction of his Honduran property for use as a regional military center without legal authority and for taking his use and enjoyment of that property without due process of law.[123] The district court dismissed the complaint without discovery or factfinding, ruling that the dispute constituted a nonjusticiable political question. But the D.C. Circuit, sitting en banc, reversed the dismissal of the complaint as "precipitous," holding that

> the doctrine of equitable discretion might permit the district court to grant some form of injunctive relief for the stated claims. ... The duty of the trial court is to decree relief that corrects the condition offending the Constitution or U.S. laws. In exercising its broad equitable powers, a trial court must balance the nature of the proved violation against the affected public and private interests. An equitable remedy is proper (1) when the plaintiff lacks an adequate remedy at law and (2) when a balancing of the rights and interests involved as well as other prudential considerations permit injunctive or declaratory relief. Plaintiffs' complaint shows that their stated claims

---

**122.** *See, e.g.,* Vander Jagt v. O'Neill, 699 F.2d 1166 (D.C. Cir. 1982) (Bork, J., concurring); Moore v. United States House of Representatives, 733 F.2d 946, 958–59 (D.C. Cir. 1984) (Scalia, J., concurring), *cert. denied*, 469 U.S. 1106 (1985).

**123.** 745 F.2d 1500 (DC Cir. 1984) (en banc) (Wilkey, J.), vacated and remanded in light of subsequent legislation, 471 U.S. 1113 (1985). After the en banc ruling in *Ramirez*, Congress went on to enact the 1985 Foreign Assistance and Related Programs Appropriations Act, which authorized the use of funds for the contested military training center in Honduras, but subject to specified conditions more protective of the plaintiff's legal interests. After failing to reach agreement with the Honduran Government regarding how to operate the military center in light of the Act's requirements, the United States Government discontinued its participation in the center and withdrew its military personnel from Ramirez's land. Accordingly, the Supreme Court subsequently granted the Government's petition for a writ of certiorari, vacated the *en banc* court's judgment and remanded the case for reconsideration in light of the intervening foreign assistance statute. On remand, the D.C. Circuit, again sitting en banc, dismissed the case in light of the undisputed fact that all U.S. military personnel had departed from the land in question. *See* Ramirez de Arellano v. Weinberger, 788 F.2d 762, 763 (D.C. Cir. 1986) (en banc).

may be irremediable at law and that a balancing of the equities may favor relief.[124]

The *Ramirez* court found that "[w]here, as here, the court adjudicating the controversy has personal jurisdiction over the defendants, the extraterritorial nature of the property involved in the litigation is no bar to equitable relief. Under such circumstances, courts in equity do not hesitate to order the defendants, who are present before the court, to do or refrain from doing something directly involving foreign property."[125] The court further noted that "[a]n equitable decree would not challenge the sovereignty of Honduras because it would only adjudicate the rights of plaintiffs under United States law vis-à-vis the United States officials named as defendants."[126] Dismissing as "wild speculation" the claim that injunctive relief would oblige the court to engage in unmanageable extraterritorial judicial monitoring, the D.C. Circuit declared: "It must be presumed that the defendants, all officials of the United States government present in Washington, D.C., will obey an order of the district court. ... If a dispute arises over compliance with any remedial decree, the parties can introduce evidence in the district court to establish whether a violation in fact has occurred. This is the only method to determine a violation of a decree of which we are aware; it is a method universally used no matter where any acts occur or property is located."[127]

At the same time, national courts have been generally hostile to using their own equitable powers to enforce injunctions issued by foreign courts. Some of the problems with extraterritorial enforcement of equity decrees were graphically revealed in the case of *United States v. Imperial Chem. Industries.*[128] There, the U.S. government alleged a worldwide cartel by ICI to control production and distribution of nylon, a product covered by both U.S. and foreign patents. ICI claimed that it was simply exercising its patent rights in the U.K., in a manner consistent with U.K. law. Nevertheless, the U.S. judge concluded that the effect of ICI's conduct on American commerce was so adverse as to warrant an injunction ordering ICI to cease and desist. Although the U.S. district court ordered ICI to reconvey its foreign patent, the British court then refused to give effect to the U.S. decree because the patent was English in character and beyond the jurisdiction of U.S. courts.[129]

---

**124.** 745 F.2d at 1522.
**125.** *Id.* at 1529.
**126.** *Id.* at 1530.
**127.** *Id.* at 1531–32.
**128.** 105 F.Supp. 215 (S.D.N.Y. 1952). The full episode is recounted in

ANDREAS F. LOWENFELD, INTERNATIONAL LITIGATION AND ARBITRATION 50–68 (1993).

**129.** *See* British Nylon Spinners Ltd. v. Imperial Chemical Industries, Ltd., 1952 All E.R. 780.

The *ICI* case reveals why courts hesitate to enforce other court's injunctions. Such injunctions are perceived as requiring continuing judicial supervision, and are thus not easily transferred from state to state. The court from whom enforcement is requested may perceive that it is being asked to make complex determinations under foreign law, just to determine whether the decree is being violated. Those problems are magnified by the question of which forum's law has primary claim to govern the dispute in the first place. Moreover, courts asked to enforce foreign equity decrees are loath to grant any form of relief that is not available under their own law. They may feel uncomfortable, as well, exercising the formidable power of contempt on behalf of a decree that originated in a foreign court's decision. Particularly when a court entering an equity decree seeks to require a defendant to perform certain acts in a foreign country, it may well lack the power to make the extraterritorial aspects of its decree effective. As in the *SGPM* case discussed in Chapter IX, an injunction in such circumstances would constitute an extraterritorial exercise of the court's enforcement jurisdiction within another nation's sovereign territory, and hence, could trigger a blocking statute or even a diplomatic protest. Finally, foreign money judgments can generally be reduced to a dollar sum, which can in turn be translated into local currency. But a court enforcing a foreign equity decree must enter a judgment of its own, mimicking the relief that had been granted abroad. This is made even more difficult because injunctions are often interlocutory and subject to modification, and hence do not fit easily into the definition of a final judgment.[130]

All of this having been said, there are still good arguments why, if a global Judgments Convention were ever considered again, injunctions should be included in some way as part of the convention.[131] As Professor Lowenfeld has noted, when a party has been ordered by a court in one state not to dispose of his assets wherever they may be located, such as under a *Mareva*-type injunction,[132] for example, it may be appropriate to give courts of other states a

**130.** *See, e.g.,* Pilkington Bros. P.L.C. v. AFG Indus., Inc., 581 F.Supp. 1039 (D. Del. 1984) (concluding that *Hilton* standard should not be limited to money judgments and applying comity principles in refusing to issue requested preliminary injunction against disclosure of technology in violation of licensing agreement).

**131.** *Cf.* ALAN DASHWOOD, RICHARD HACON AND ROBIN WHITE, A GUIDE TO THE CIVIL JURISDICTION AND JUDGMENTS CONVENTION 36, 145 (1987) (Brussels Convention defines judgments to include "order," thus suggesting that Convention applies to "provisional decisions" by participating courts, although provisional rulings based on *ex parte* applications will not be recognized).

**132.** *See* Mareva Compania Naviera S.A. v. International BulkCarriers S.A., [1975] 2 Lloyd's L. Rep. 509 (C.A.) (Eng.).

treaty obligation to cooperate.[133] The argument would be that at least permanent injunctions in the nature of restraining orders ought to be recognized and enforced like other final judgments.[134] The argument would be particularly powerful with respect to a case like the *Karadzic* litigation in New York, discussed in Chapter III, in which the defendant is being sued civilly in a domestic court for universal crimes. Although the case law on this issue is still undeveloped, some U.S. courts have used comity to enforce foreign decrees in similar situations.[135]

Given that the U.S. standard of enforcement of foreign judgments, stated in *Hilton*, is more generous than that of many of its allies, the U.S. potentially has far more to gain from a global judgments convention than do those countries who are already parties to the Brussels, Lugano, or Montevideo Conventions. Despite the claim that common law and civil law systems of procedure exhibit irreconcilable differences, the recently completed ALI/UNIDROIT Principles of Transnational Civil Procedure, adopted in 2004, demonstrate that a single unified set of rules that bridges the two procedural systems is indeed possible.[136] The ALI/UNIDROIT Principles make the simple, compelling point that "[t]he fundamental similarities among procedural systems" dominate the differences and "can be summarized as follows:

- Standards governing assertion of personal jurisdiction and subject-matter jurisdiction

**133.** *See, e.g.*, Lawrence Collins, *The Territorial Reach of Mareva Injunctions*, 105 L.Q. Rev. 262 (1989) (discussing cases in which English courts have restrained parties over whom they have jurisdiction from dealing with any of their assets worldwide).

**134.** Professor Lowenfeld uses as his example the case of an injunction brought in the course of a divorce action by a wife in one country against a husband with assets in the U.S., but domiciled in a third country. *See* Andreas Lowenfeld, *Injunctions Across National Frontiers: A Tale of Two Cities*, 3 Am. Rev. Int'l Arb. 3 (1992).

**135.** *See, e.g.,* Clarkson Co. v. Shaheen, 544 F.2d 624 (2d Cir. 1976) (recognizing order of foreign bankruptcy trustee regarding preservation of documents); Wolff v. Wolff, 389 A.2d 413 (Md. App. 1978), *aff'd mem.*, 401 A.2d 479 (Md. 1979) (enforcing English alimony decree). *See generally* Note, *U.S.*

*Recognition and Enforcement of Foreign Country Injunctive and Specific Performance Decrees*, 20 Cal. W. Int'l L.J. 91 (1990); Lowenfeld, *supra* note 2, at 301 (arguing that contracting states should agree to "consider conditions under which orders of courts of other contracting states enjoining the transfer of funds or the bringing of claims against bankrupt estates shall be recognized in other contracting states").

**136.** *See generally* ALI/UNIDROIT Principles of Transnational Civil Procedure (2004). The task of driving this Herculean project to conclusion was carried out with brilliant skill and determination by the Reporters, the former ALI Director and Yale Law Professor Geoffrey C. Hazard, Jr. and Professor Michele Taruffo of the University of Pavia Faculty of Law, and Associate Reporter Antonio Gidi of Salvador, Brazil. I should disclose that I served as one of the U.S. Advisers for this ALI Project.

- Specifications for a neutral adjudicator
- Procedure for notice to defendant
- Rules for formulation of claims
- Explication of applicable substantive law
- Establishment of facts through proof
- Provision for expert testimony
- Rules for deliberation, decision, and appellate review [and]
- Rules of finality of judgments."[137]

Given these transsystemic commonalities, the idea of a global judgments convention may not be dead, but only in abeyance for the time being. The question is whether the U.S. Government will use its political leverage to reconvene the global conversation, and whether its position with respect to particular provisions will help to determine the Convention's ultimate shape. That position will in turn depend in part on how the private bar and industry choose to lobby on the question, both in the United States and in the EU.

Thus, once again, the issue of reciprocal enforcement of judgments and decrees illustrates the broader phenomenon of percolation and transformation of international business disputes from the public to the private and back again. The question of how to enforce an ostensibly "private" judgment across borders, once writ large, percolates up to the intergovernmental level and leads to negotiation of one or more multilateral treaties that will be in turn be internalized into national law to shape the future of private and public transnational litigation alike. When the new Hague Choice of

---

**137.** *Id.* at 5. The Principles also go on to clarify the key systemic differences, stating:

Of these, the rules of jurisdiction, notice, and recognition of judgments are sufficiently similar from one country to another that they have been susceptible to substantial resolution through international practice and formal conventions. Concerning jurisdiction, the United States is aberrant in that it has an expansive concept of "long-arm" jurisdiction, although this difference is one of degree rather than one of kind, and in that U.S. law governing authority of its constituent states perpetuates jurisdiction based on simple presence of the person

("tag" jurisdiction). Specification of a neutral adjudicator begins with realization that all legal systems have rules to assure that a judge or other adjudicator should be disinterested. Accordingly, in transnational litigation reliance generally can be placed on the local rules expressing that principle. Similarly, an adjudicative system requires a principle of finality. Therefore, the concept of "final" judgment is also generally recognized, although some legal systems permit the reopening of a determination more liberally than other systems do. The corollary concept of mutual recognition of judgments is also universally accepted. *Id.*

Court Agreements Convention comes before U.S. courts for interpretation, the same interpretive issue raised with respect to the Hague Service and Evidence Conventions will likely arise: namely, to what extent should U.S. courts defer to separation of powers and comity principles to further the creation of uniform procedural rules that are likely to affect the autonomy of private litigants?

# CHAPTER XII

## RECOGNITION AND ENFORCEMENT OF FOREIGN ARBITRAL AGREEMENTS AND AWARDS

Chapters IX and X explained how judicial interpretation of the Hague Service and Evidence Conventions has brought comity into conflict with party autonomy. For by seeking to ensure that comity is paid to another nation's sovereignty, such conventions limit the freedom of individual litigants to serve process and acquire evidence in the manner to which they are accustomed under national law. This chapter, by contrast, discusses a final treaty that, like the newly minted Hague Convention on Choice of Court Agreements described in the last chapter, attempts to place sovereignty in service of party autonomy. The New York Convention on the Recognition and Enforcement of Foreign Arbitral Awards of 1958 (commonly known as the "New York Convention") facilitates the enforcement of foreign arbitral awards by creating an international obligation to support transnational enforcement of awards achieved by arbitration.[1] The New York Convention, ratified by over 135 nations, now includes virtually every significant trading nation.[2] Unlike the conventions governing service, taking of evidence, and choice of court agreements, that Convention was negotiated not at the Hague Conference of Private International Law, but under the auspices of the United Nations Conference on Commercial Arbitration in New York. The United States, which was not a signatory to any prior multilateral agreement on enforcement of arbitral awards, initially declined to sign, but ratified the Convention twelve years later,[3] in the process implementing its accession with an amendment to existing Federal Arbitration Act.[4]

1. June, 10, 1958, 21 U.S.T. 2517, T.I.A.S. No. 6997 [hereinafter New York Convention]. At this writing the New York Convention has over 104 party countries. For text and negotiating history, see GARY BORN, INTERNATIONAL COMMERCIAL ARBITRATION IN THE UNITED STATES: COMMENTARY AND MATERIALS 18–20, 875–80 (1994).

2. GARY B. BORN & PETER B. ROUTLEDGE, INTERNATIONAL CIVIL LITIGATION IN UNITED STATES COURTS 1987 (2007). The Convention is itself now the subject of a massive commentary. For standard ref-

erence texts, see generally A. VAN DEN BERG, THE NEW YORK ARBITRATION CONVENTION OF 1958 (1981); G. GAJA, THE NEW YORK CONVENTION (1978–80); GARY BORN, supra note 1.

3. (1970) 3 U.S.T. 2517, T.I.A.S. No. 6997.

4. The Federal Arbitration Act provides in pertinent part:

A party aggrieved by the alleged failure, neglect, or refusal of another to arbitrate under a written agreement for arbitration may petition any United States district court which, save for

As the Supreme Court noted in *Scherk v. Alberto–Culver Co.*,[5] the principal purpose of the Convention "was to encourage the recognition and enforcement of commercial arbitration agreements in international contracts and to unify the standards by which agreements to arbitrate are observed and arbitral awards are enforced in the signatory countries."[6] A predecessor convention, the Geneva Convention of 1927,[7] had placed the burden of proof on the party seeking enforcement of a foreign arbitral award and had nowhere clearly circumscribed the range of available defenses to those enumerated in the convention. The 1958 Convention clearly shifted the burden of proof to the party defending against enforcement: Article II(3), the core provision, provides that the court of a Contracting State, "when seized of an action in a matter in respect of which the parties have made an agreement within the meaning of this article, shall, at the request of one of the parties, refer the parties to arbitration."

At the same time, the Convention limited defenses to arbitration to a specified number of grounds set forth in Article V (and a few others dispersed throughout the treaty), which basically mirror the exceptions to enforcement of judgments outlined in the discussion of *Hilton* above. Valid grounds for refusal under the Convention to enforce an award under the convention thus include:

(1) if the agreement was invalid under the applicable law or otherwise "null and void, inoperative or incapable of being performed,"[8] because, for example, the parties lacked capacity to enter the agreement (*validity of agreement issues*);

(2) if the dispute does not concern "a subject matter capable of settlement by arbitration,"[9] or deals with matters beyond the scope of the submission to arbitration (*subject matter jurisdiction defects*);

(3) if the party against whom the award was rendered did not receive proper notice and opportunity to be heard (*notice and opportunity to be heard issues*);

such agreement, would have jurisdiction ... for an order directing that such arbitration proceed in the manner provided for in such agreement....

9 U.S.C. § 4 (2000); 9 U.S.C. §§ 201–08, which was added by the 1970 implementing legislation, provides that "The Convention on the Recognition and Enforcement of Foreign Arbitral Awards of June 10, 1958, shall be enforced in United States courts in accordance with this chapter." *Id.* § 201.

**5.** 417 U.S. 506 (1974).

**6.** *Id.* at 520 n.15.

**7.** 92 L. N. T. S. 302n.

**8.** New York Convention, art. II(3).

**9.** *Id.* art. II(1).

(4) if the award was rendered by an improperly composed tribunal applying procedures that did not meet due process (*tribunal and due process* issues);

(5) if the award is not yet binding or has been suspended or set aside (*finality of award issues*), or

(6) is otherwise in violation of public policy, for example, because the agreement or the award was secured by fraud, mistake, duress, or any other problems of procedural fairness and feasibility (*public policy issues*).[10]

In U.S. courts, perhaps the two most litigated issues under the Convention have been those cases regarding the scope of the public policy exception and those addressing the question of arbitrability. On both points, the U.S. courts have taken an extremely strong stand in favor of arbitrability. In the leading public policy case, *Parsons and Whittemore Overseas Co. v. Societe Generale de L'Industrie du Papier (RAKTA)*,[11] the Second Circuit declared that "[e]nforcement of foreign arbitral awards may be denied on this basis only where enforcement would violate the forum state's most basic notions of morality and justice."[12] In so saying, the court relied on the Convention's general pro-enforcement bias and "considerations of reciprocity," which "counsel courts to invoke the public policy defense with caution lest foreign courts frequently accept it as a defense to enforcement of arbitral awards rendered in the United States."[13]

On two important occasions, the Supreme Court has addressed the issue of transnational arbitrability, and in both cases concluded that compliance with international commercial arbitral regimes is a critical tool for resolving transnational commercial disputes. In both cases, the Court addressed the question not upon reviewing the enforcement of an arbitral award, but in deciding *ex ante* whether a dispute arguably falling within the scope of a contractual arbitration clause was a non-arbitrable subject matter. In both cases, the issue arose procedurally because an agreement to arbitrate is judicially enforceable in much the same way as a forum-selection clause of the kind discussed in *Bremen*.[14] Thus, if a controversy regarding an agreement to arbitrate comes before the

---

**10.** *Id.* art. V. The Convention makes clear that this is meant to be an exclusive list of defenses. The *Restatement (Third)* enumerates essentially the same list of grounds for non-recognition in § 488.

**11.** 508 F.2d 969 (2d Cir. 1974).

**12.** *Id.* at 974.

**13.** *Id.* at 973–74. *See generally* Hakan Berglin, *The Application in United States Courts of the Public Policy Provision of the Convention on the Recognition and Enforcement of Foreign Arbitral Awards*, 4 Dickinson J. Int'l L. 167 (1986).

**14.** *See* Chapter VIII, *supra.*

court, the court must stay or dismiss the judicial action, pending arbitration, and specifically enforce the arbitration clause, thereby directing the parties to proceed to the contractually agreed arbitration.[15] But an agreement to arbitrate is in turn judicially enforceable only if it concerns a controversy capable of arbitration according to the law of the state where the agreement is sought to be enforced.[16]

In *Scherk v. Alberto–Culver Co.*,[17] the Court held an international arbitration clause extending to certain claims under the Securities and Exchange Act of 1934 to be arbitrable. In so doing, the Court was forced to distinguish an earlier case, *Wilko v. Swan*,[18] in which the Court had declined to compel arbitration of a dispute arising out of alleged violations of the Securities Act of 1933, as required by the standard form contract between the parties. The *Scherk* Court distinguished *Wilko* by saying that the agreement now *sub judice* was "truly international" in the sense that a contract between an American corporation and a German entity, negotiated in Europe and concerning the sale of European entities "involves considerations and policies significantly different from those found controlling in *Wilko*."[19] To invalidate an arbitration agreement in an international transaction "would surely damage the fabric of international commerce and trade and imperil the willingness and ability of businessmen to enter into commercial agreements."[20] Like *Bremen*, *Scherk* emphasized international commercial realities, the need for contractual certainty, deference to party autonomy, and a distaste for parochialism on the part of American courts.[21] By focusing on the international character of the

**15.** RESTATEMENT (THIRD) § 487 cmt. e.

**16.** Such disputes also involve an issue of treaty interpretation, for under Article II(1) of the Convention, "[e]ach Contracting State shall recognize an agreement in writing under which the parties undertake to submit to arbitration all or any differences which have arisen or which may arise between them in respect of a defined legal relationship, whether contractual or not, *concerning a subject matter capable of settlement by arbitration*" *See* New York Convention, 21 U.S.T. at 2519 (emphasis added).

**17.** 417 U.S. 506 (1974).

**18.** 346 U.S. 427 (1953).

**19.** *Scherk*, 417 U.S. at 515. The Court found that the arbitration agreement between Scherk and Alberto–Culver, unlike the contract in *Wilko*, was expressly designed to eliminate both the uncertainty generated by the different substantive law and conflict-of-law rules of the countries affected by the contract, and the danger that the dispute would be handled by a forum hostile to the interests of one of the parties. *Id.* at 516–17.

**20.** *Id.* at 517.

**21.** *See id.* at 516–17 ("A contractual provision specifying in advance the forum in which disputes shall be litigated and the law to be applied is ... an almost indispensable precondition to achievement of the orderliness and predictability essential to any international business transaction.... A parochial refusal by the courts of one country to enforce an international arbitration agreement would not only frustrate these purposes, but would invite un-

underlying transaction, the *Scherk* Court deftly bifurcated the arbitrability of Securities and Exchange Act claims. On the one hand, it permitted international claims to proceed to arbitration, while leaving undisturbed (for the time being) the line of authority holding non-arbitrable similar claims arising out of domestic transactions.

*Scherk* reflected two powerful trends affecting the Supreme Court in the early 1970s. The first, reflected in both *Scherk* and in *Bremen* (discussed in Chapter VIII), which was decided only two years earlier, was the Court's desire to promote business certainty through deference to private-ordering arrangements in a rapidly changing international commercial context. At the same time, however, the Court also saw arbitration, and the pro-arbitration policy of the Federal Arbitration Act, as a way to ameliorate the overcrowding of the U.S. federal courts. In three famous cases known as the *Steelworkers Trilogy*,[22] the Court had enforced arbitration clauses in collective bargaining agreements, thereby shifting the emphasis in the American industrial relations community from strikes and lockouts toward presumptive reliance on arbitration as the preferred means of resolving disputes arising during the terms of a collective-bargaining agreement. Following that same vein in a string of cases under the Federal Arbitration Act, the Court shifted from the distrust for arbitration expressed in *Wilko* in the early 1950s to a strong presumption favoring arbitration as a sound and acceptable mode of alternative dispute resolution conducted outside the courts.[23] Indeed, one of these cases specifically overruled *Wilko v. Swan*, thirty-six years later, as "inconsistent with the prevailing uniform construction of other federal statutes governing arbitration agreements in the setting of business transactions."[24]

This led in 1985 to the leading Supreme Court decision with regard to arbitration agreements in *international* business transactions, *Mitsubishi Motors Corp. v. Soler Chrysler–Plymouth, Inc.*[25] In *Mitsubishi*, the question was not strictly whether to enforce an arbitral award under the New York Convention, but whether to

seemly and mutually destructive jockeying by the parties to secure tactical litigation advantages...").

**22.** United Steelworkers of America v. American Mfg. Co., 363 U.S. 564 (1960); United Steelworkers of America v. Warrior and Gulf Navigation Co., 363 U.S. 574 (1960); United Steelworkers of America v. Enterprise Wheel and Car Corp., 363 U.S. 593 (1960).

**23.** *See, e.g.*, Southland Corp. v. Keating, 465 U.S. 1 (1984); Shear-

son/American Express, Inc. v. McMahon, 482 U.S. 220 (1987); Rodriguez de Quijas v. Shearson/American Express, 490 U.S. 477 (1989); Gilmer v. Interstate/Johnson Lane Corp., 500 U.S. 20 (1991); Allied–Bruce Terminix Co. v. Dobson, 513 U.S. 265 (1995).

**24.** *See Rodriguez de Quijas*, 490 U.S. at 484.

**25.** 473 U.S. 614 (1985).

enforce a general arbitration clause in an international sales agreement which would have compelled arbitration of an alleged violation under the Sherman Act. When new car sales dropped, Soler, a Puerto Rican auto dealer, canceled orders from Mitsubishi, its Japanese manufacturer. Mitsubishi brought suit under both the Federal Arbitration Act and the New York Convention to compel arbitration under a clause in their agreement which provided for arbitration before the Japanese Chamber of Commerce. Soler counterclaimed, alleging Sherman Act violations, perhaps as a gambit to oust the dispute from arbitration. Under the so-called *American Safety* doctrine, a number of lower courts had deemed federal antitrust claims to be non-arbitrable, focusing upon the unique federal interests expressed in the Sherman Act.[26]

Endorsing the *American Safety* doctrine, the U.S. Court of Appeals for the First Circuit refused to send Soler's antitrust claim to arbitration. But by a 5–3 vote, the Supreme Court reversed.[27] Justice Blackmun, writing for the Court, at first noted the Federal Arbitration Act's liberal federal policy favoring any kinds of arbitration agreements—domestic or international. Noting that the Act had been passed to overcome an "anachronistic judicial hostility" to agreements to arbitrate, he declared, "[w]e are well past the time when judicial suspicion of the desirability of arbitration and of the competence of arbitral tribunals inhibited the development of arbitration as an alternative means of dispute resolution."[28] Then turning to the *American Safety* doctrine, the Court found that it had no function in the international environment. In a ringing endorsement of international commercial arbitration, Justice Blackmun declared:

> "we conclude that concerns of international comity, respect for the capacities of foreign and transnational tribunals, and sensitivity to the need of the international commercial system for predictability in the resolution of disputes require that we enforce the parties' agreement, *even assuming that a contrary result would be forthcoming in a domestic context.*"[29]

By so ruling, the Court rested on two decisions: its opinion upholding transnational judicial forum-selection clauses in *Bremen*, discussed in Chapter VIII, and its decision in *Scherk* upholding arbi-

---

**26.** The doctrine was named after American Safety Equipment Corp. v. J.P. Maguire and Co., 391 F.2d 821 (2d Cir. 1968), which had held that rights conferred by the federal antitrust laws are inappropriate for enforcement by arbitration.

**27.** Justice Powell did not participate in the decision.

**28.** *Id.* at 627.

**29.** *Id.* at 629 (emphasis added).

tration in the international securities context. These two cases, Justice Blackmun decided, "establish a strong presumption in favor of enforcement of freely negotiated contractual choice-of-forum provisions . . . reinforced by the emphatic federal policy in favor of arbitral dispute resolution [which] since this Nation's accession in 1970 to the [New York] Convention . . . applies with special force in the field of international commerce."[30]

The result in *Mitsubishi* demonstrated that the Court's support for international commercial arbitration overwhelmed even its traditional solicitude for the federal antitrust laws. After all, federal antitrust claims may only be brought within the exclusive jurisdiction of the federal courts.[31] Thus, the Court saw fit to send to a group of arbitrators impaneled by the Japanese Chamber of Commerce a claim that Congress had decreed that even a state court in the United States could not hear. Moreover, *Mitsubishi* is one of the very few international business cases in the last two decades in which the U.S. Supreme Court squarely rejected the U.S. government's position. In his stinging dissent, Justice Stevens, himself a former antitrust attorney, argued that neither comity concerns nor deference to the Executive required compelling arbitration in this case.[32]

While some have been critical of *Mitsubishi*, with the passage of time, it seems to have been correctly decided.[33] In permitting the arbitration to go forward, the Court did not abdicate its duty to supervise the development of federal antitrust law. To the contrary, it made clear that having let the arbitration go forward, the national courts of the United States would have a second opportunity at the award-*enforcement* stage to ensure that the nation's interest in the enforcement of the antitrust laws has been ad-

---

**30.** *Id.* at 636–37.

**31.** *See* 28 U.S.C. § 1337 (1994).

**32.** As Justice Stevens noted, the United States government had advised the Court that the Convention contemplated that signatory nations would enforce domestic laws prohibiting the arbitration of certain subject matters. "[T]he branch of Government entrusted with the conduct of political relations with foreign governments has informed us that the United States' determination that federal antitrust claims are nonarbitrable under the Convention . . . is not likely to result in either surprise or recrimination on the part of other signatories to the Convention." *Id.* at 659 (Stevens, J., dissenting).

**33.** I say so with the benefit of hindsight, having helped at the time as an attorney at the U.S. Department of Justice to prepare the Solicitor General's *amicus curiae* brief in the case, which the Court rejected. For critical commentary, see, for example, Thomas Carbonneau, Mitsubishi: *the Folly of Quixotic Internationalism*, 2 ARB. INT'L 116 (1986); Sharon Cloud, Mitsubishi *and the Arbitrability of Antitrust Claims: Did the Supreme Court Throw the Baby Out with the Bathwater?*, 18 L. & POL'Y INT'L BUS. 341 (1986). For favorable commentary, see, for example, Andreas Lowenfeld, *The* Mitsubishi *Case: Another View*, 2 ARB. INT'L 178 (1986).

dressed.[34] Moreover, by "declin[ing] to indulge the presumption that the parties and arbitral body conducting [an international] proceeding will be unable or unwilling to retain competent, conscientious, and impartial arbitrators,"[35] the Court cast a vote for the competence of sophisticated arbitrators to interpret the law and manage the difficult discovery, choice-of-law, and damages questions that modern antitrust litigation entails. As impressive, the Court itself conducted a detailed investigation of both the rules of international commercial arbitration, the practical realities of arbitration, and various bodies of foreign law to conclude that the "obstacles confronted by the arbitration panel in this case ... should be no greater than those confronted by any judicial or arbitral tribunal required to determine foreign law."[36] In the end, Justice Blackmun suggested, national courts have little choice but to shed parochialism and trust global arbitrators to do diligent work:[37]

> As international trade has expanded in recent decades, so too has the use of international arbitration to resolve disputes arising in the course of that trade. The controversies that international arbitral institutions are called upon to resolve have increased in diversity as well as in complexity. Yet the potential of these tribunals for efficient disposition of legal disagreements arising from commercial relations has not yet been tested. If they are to take a central place in the international legal order, national courts will need to 'shake off the old judicial hostility to arbitration,' ... and also their customary and understandable unwillingness to cede jurisdiction of a claim arising under domestic law to a foreign or transnational tribunal. To this extent, at least, it will be necessary for national courts to subordinate domestic notions of arbitrability to the international policy favoring commercial arbitration.[38]

Since *Mitsubishi*, the Supreme Court has returned to the subject of arbitration on numerous occasions, usually in a domestic setting. In *First Options of Chicago, Inc. v. Kaplan*,[39] the Court considered an issue frequently recurring in international arbitration, namely, the so-called *Kompetenz–Kompetenz* question. In asking who has competence to determine arbitral competence, the question becomes who should decide a challenge to an arbitral tribunal's jurisdiction, the arbitral tribunal itself, or a national

**34.** *Id.* at 637–38.
**35.** *Id.* at 634.
**36.** *Id.*
**37.** *See id.* at 639 n.21 ("The utility of the Convention in promoting the process of international commercial arbitra-

tion depends upon the willingness of national courts to let go of matters they normally would think of as their own.").
**38.** *Id.* at 638–39.
**39.** 514 U.S. 938 (1995).

court resolving disputes over the interpretation and enforceabilility of an arbitration agreement? The Court essentially answered that question by deference to party autonomy, stating that "the question 'who has the primary power to decide arbitrability' turns upon what the parties agreed about that matter. Did the parties agree to submit the arbitrability question itself to arbitration?"[40] In adopting this "contractual" answer, the Court essentially followed it own prior view in *Mitsubishi*, where Justice Blackmun noted that "[n]othing ... prevents a party from excluding statutory claims from the scope of an agreement to arbitrate."[41] Thus, the contract selecting arbitration as the desired mode of dispute resolution must expressly delegate to the arbitrators the authority to pass on jurisdictional challenges. As the Court said:

> Courts should not assume that the parties agreed to arbitrate arbitrability unless there is "clea[r] and unmistakabl[e]" evidence that they did so. In this manner the law treats silence or ambiguity about the question "who (primarily) should decide arbitrability" differently from the way it treats silence or ambiguity about the question "whether a particular merits-related dispute is arbitrable because it is within the scope of a valid arbitration agreement"—for in respect to this latter question the law reverses the presumption.[42]

In other words, unless the parties have plainly agreed to arbitrate jurisdictional disputes before the arbitral tribunal, the issue of deciding challenges to a tribunal's competence falls to the national court asked to enforce the judgment. At the same time, *First Options* makes clear that in assessing whether a particular dispute falls within the scope of a valid arbitration agreement, "any doubts concerning the scope of arbitrable issues should be resolved in favor of arbitration."[43] Although this decision was made in a domestic arbitration setting, subsequent lower court decisions have not hesitated to apply the *First Options* analysis to transnational settings.[44]

Thus, like so many other areas of transnational procedure, the subject matter area of recognition of foreign arbitration awards and agreements fundamentally turns on the relationship between party autonomy and judicial competence. As in the forum-selection clause

---

**40.** *Id.* at 943.

**41.** *Mitsubishi*, 437 U.S. at 628.

**42.** 514 U.S. at 944–45.

**43.** *Id.* at 945.

**44.** *See, e.g.*, Sarhank Group v. Oracle Corp., 404 F.3d 657, 661 (2d Cir. 2005) (international contract dispute between Egyptian and Delaware corporations); Menorah Ins. Co. v. INX Reinsurance Corp., 72 F.3d 218, 222 (1st Cir. 1995).

and choice-of-court agreements setting, the courts trust knowledgeable transnational business actors to make the contractual decisions regarding dispute resolution that best serve their anticipated needs. Once such a decision is clearly made, the primary job of a court acting later in time is to reinforce that decision by giving deference to the arbitrators' authority to make the decision that the parties intended them to make.

# PART FOUR
## THE FUTURE OF TRANSNATIONAL LITIGATION
## CHAPTER XIII
### THE SUPREME COURT'S EMERGING JURISPRUDENCE OF TRANSNATIONAL LITIGATION

When Justice Harry Blackmun retired from the Supreme Court in 1994, his influence upon the law of transnational litigation in U.S. courts went virtually unnoticed. But in a series of opinions over more than two decades, he had helped to chart the emerging law on judicial jurisdiction,[1] forum-selection clauses,[2] transnational discovery,[3] and enforcement of agreements to arbitrate.[4] Indeed, in retrospect, two of his international business opinions—for the Court in *Mitsubishi*[5] and for four concurring Justices in *Aerospatiale*[6]—represent as much wisdom as the Supreme Court has mustered in the last part of the Twentieth Century on how U.S. national courts should construe rules that affect transnational litigation. Through opinions like these, during nearly a quarter-century on the Supreme Court, Justice Blackmun emerged as the Court's leading exponent of an outward-looking, "transnationalist" jurisprudence."[7]

On closer examination, it seems clear that Justice Blackmun's "transnationalist" approach represents only one of two distinct

---

**1.** Helicopteros Nacionales de Colombia, S. A. v. Hall, 466 U.S. 408 (1984) (developing rules of *in personam* jurisdiction in transnational business setting).

**2.** Carnival Cruise Lines v. Shute, 499 U.S. 585 (1991) (upholding forum-selection clauses).

**3.** Societe Nationale Industrielle Aerospatiale v. United States District Court, 482 U.S. 522, 548 (1987) (opinion of Blackmun, J.).

**4.** Mitsubishi Motors Corp. v. Soler Chrysler–Plymouth, Inc., 473 U.S. 614, 629 (1985) (upholding international arbitration clause of agreement in light of

the "need of the international commercial system for predictability in the resolution of disputes")

**5.** 473 U.S. 614 (1985) (upholding international arbitrability of antitrust claim).

**6.** 482 U.S. 522 (1987) (opinion of Blackmun, J.), discussed in Chapter X, *supra*.

**7.** For discussion of Justice Blackmun's international experience, both on and off the bench, see Harold Hongju Koh, *Justice Blackmun and the "World Out There,"* 104 YALE L.J. 23, 28–31 (1994).

jurisprudential approaches that have emerged within the U.S. Supreme Court regarding America's role in the world. In hindsight, America's "transnationalist jurisprudence" has a venerable lineage, which began with early Chief Justices John Jay and John Marshall, was carried forward by Justice Gray in the *The Paquete Habana* case,[8] was advanced during the Warren Court by Justices Brennan, Douglas[9] and White[10] and during the Burger Court in the opinions of Justice Blackmun cited above.[11] In the new millennium, the transnationalist banner is now being carried forward by Justices Stephen Breyer and Ruth Bader Ginsburg.[12] But a second, competing strand is the Court's emerging "nationalist jurisprudence," exemplified by opinions by Justices Antonin Scalia, Clarence Thomas, and, since he came to the Court in 2005, Chief Justice John Roberts, Jr. The nationalist approach is characterized by commitments to territoriality, national politics, deference to executive power, and resistance to comity or international law as meaningful constraints on national prerogative.

## A.    The Court's Transnationalist Jurisprudence

Upon examination, the Court's "transnational" jurisprudence has had five core premises. First, it has accepted the collapse of the traditional distinctions between private and public, domestic and international law in favor of a transnational vision of law that percolates from the realm of the public into the public sphere and generates rules that can be internalized into domestic legal systems. By so doing, the transnational vision recognizes that "international law is part of U.S. law," not just in the public realm, but also in the private realm, which in both domains, U.S. courts have a duty to consult.

This insight is an ancient, not a modern, one. For as Justice Blackmun reminded the American Society of International Law

**8.**  175 U.S. 677, 700 (1900) ("International law is part of our law.... ").

**9.**  *See generally* Harold Hongju Koh, *The Liberal Constitutional Internationalism of Justice Douglas, in* "HE SHALL NOT PASS THIS WAY AGAIN": THE LEGACY OF JUSTICE WILLIAM O. DOUGLAS 297 (Stephen Wasby ed., 1990).

**10.**  *See, e.g.,* Banco Nacional de Cuba v. Sabbatino, 376 U.S. 398, 439 (1964) (White, J., dissenting), discussed in Chapter V, *supra.*

**11.**  *See* Koh, *supra* note 7, at 28–31 (collecting cases).

**12.**  Justice Breyer has cogently argued in favor of using foreign and international law precedent to inform U.S. constitutional interpretation. *See, e.g.,* Stephen Breyer, *Keynote Address,* 97 ASIL PROC. 265 (2003), *available at* http://www.supremecourtus.gov/publicinfo/speeches/sp_04–04–03.html. *See also* Ruth Bader Ginsburg & Deborah Jones Merritt, *Affirmative Action: An International Human Rights Dialogue, Fifty–First Cardozo Memorial Lecture (Feb. 11, 1999),* 21 CARDOZO L. REV. 253, 282 (1999).

shortly after his retirement, the Declaration of Independence itself obligated the early architects of the United States to pay "a decent Respect to the Opinions of Mankind."[13] In *Chisolm v. Georgia,* Chief Justice John Jay acknowledged that the United States "had, by taking its place among the nations of the earth, become amenable to the law of nations."[14] It was against that backdrop that the Court declared, in the *Charming Betsy* case that "an act of congress ought never to be construed to violate the law of nations if any other possible construction remains."[15] Unlike modern U.S. judges, who lack "the diplomatic expertise of early Justices such as John Jay and John Marshall," the early U.S. judges "were familiar with the law of nations and comfortable navigating by it."[16] Nor did those judges rigidly separate questions of public from questions of private international law. For the maxim "international law is part of our law, and must be ascertained and administered by the courts of justice of appropriate jurisdiction as often as questions of right depending upon it are duly presented for their determination"[17] was not first articulated by the Supreme Court in a public international law case, *The Paquete Habana,* but rather, in *Hilton v. Guyot,*[18] which as we have seen was a *private* international law case about the enforcement of foreign judgments. Justice Gray, who wrote for the Court in both cases declared in *Hilton* that:

> International law, in its widest and most comprehensive sense—including not only questions of right between nations, governed by what has been appropriately called the law of nations, *but also questions arising under what is usually called private international law, or the conflict of laws,* and concerning the rights of persons within the territory and dominion of one nation, by reason of acts, private or public, done within the dominions of another nation—is part of our law, and must be ascertained and administered by the courts of justice, as often as such questions are presented in litigation between man and man, duly submitted to their determination.[19]

**13.** *See* Harry Blackmun, *The Supreme Court and the Law of Nations,* 104 YALE L.J. 39, 39 (1994) (speech to American Society of International Law on the occasion of Blackmun's retirement) (citing U.S. Declaration of Independence).

**14.** 2 U.S. (2 Dall.) 419, 474 (1793).

**15.** 6 U.S. (2 Cranch) 64, 118 (1804).

**16.** Blackmun, *supra* note 13, at 49.

**17.** 175 U.S. 677, 700 (1900).

**18.** 159 U.S. 113 (1895).

**19.** *Id.* at 163 (emphasis added). While conceding that treaties or statutes provided American courts with "[t]he most certain guide ... for the decision of such questions," when "there is no written law upon the subject," Justice Gray repeated, "the duty still rests upon the judicial tribunals of ascertaining and declaring what the law is, whenever it becomes necessary to do so, in order to determine the rights of parties to suits regularly brought before them." *Id.*

Second, as *Hilton* itself suggest, the core concept undergirding this transnationalist vision is *comity*. As Justice Blackmun wrote in *Aerospatiale*,[20] comity is "not just a vague political concern favoring international cooperation when it is in our interest to do so. Rather it is a principle under which judicial decisions reflect the systemic value of reciprocal tolerance and good will."[21] Under this perspective, when courts construe statutes, they should do so with three propositions in mind. The first, the *Charming Betsy* presumption, assures that regulatory legislation will not be assumed to come into conflict with international rules. The second, a *non-presumption* about extraterritoriality, makes no assumption (as the current presumption against extraterritoriality does) that Congress generally legislates solely with domestic concerns in minds. Rather, a court should construe these legislative decisions on a case-by-case basis, finding statutes to have an extraterritorial effect when it would be reasonable to do so. In effect, this is what the *Restatement (Third) of the Foreign Relations Law* directs in stating the rules of "reasonableness" with regard to jurisdiction to prescribe. Under the *Restatement*'s principles, the reasonableness of a nation's extraterritorial exercise of jurisdiction depends, in part, on the importance of the regulation to the international system and the extent to which the regulation is consistent with the international system's traditions.[22]

Third, when confronted with a conflict between a U.S. law and a foreign sovereign act, judges should conduct a comity balancing that weighs foreign interests, U.S. interests and the needs of an ordered international system.[23] In so doing, the courts must look beyond the United States' immediate interests to the

> mutual interests of all nations in a smoothly functioning international legal regime, urging judges to consider if there is a course that furthers, rather than impedes, the development of an ordered international system. A functioning system for solving disputes across borders serves many values, among them predictability, fairness, ease of commercial interactions, and stability through satisfaction of mutual expectations.... These interests are common to all nations, including the United States.[24]

**20.** 482 U.S. 522, 548 (1987) (opinion of Blackmun, J.).

**21.** *Aerospatiale*, 482 U.S. at 555.

**22.** *See* RESTATEMENT (THIRD) OF THE FOREIGN RELATIONS LAW OF THE UNITED STATES § 403(e) & (f) (1987).

**23.** *See id.* at 556–67.

**24.** *Aerospatiale*, 482 U.S. at 555, 567 (Blackmun, J.) (citation and quotation marks omitted).

Third, a transnationalist vision of law's role in the global order focuses upon the notion of *economic interdependence*.[25] In a world in which "regular commercial and legal channels loom ever more crucial,"[26] political and economic stability depends on regimes of law, as manifested in well-functioning international institutions and treaties that are construed in a fashion consistent with their clear meaning and object and purpose. Accepting this interdependence, transnationalist judges tend to believe that U.S. courts should use their interpretive powers to help develop a global legal system, as Justice Blackmun's statement in *Aerospatiale* specifically envisioned. Nationalist judges, by contrast, tend to believe that domestic courts should focus solely on the development of a national legal system.[27]

But as the Court held in *Mitsubishi*, "concerns of international comity [and] respect for the capacities of foreign and transnational tribunals," foster "sensitivity to the need of the international commercial system for predictability in the resolution of disputes." As Justice Blackmun wrote:

> As international trade has expanded in recent decades, so too has the use of international arbitration to resolved disputes arising in the course of that trade.... If [international tribunals] are to take a central place in the international legal order, ... it will be necessary for national courts to subordinate domestic notions of arbitrability to the international policy favoring commercial arbitration.[28]

Respecting economic interdependence requires that U.S. judges to value three factors. First, they should respect *private autonomy*: i.e., sanctity of contract and private-ordering in transnational business arrangements.[29] Second, they should accept *dispute-resolution by other fora*, whether by *forum non conveniens*, forum-selection clauses, choice of court agreements, agreements to arbitrate, or the like. As the Court put it in *Mitsubishi*, if international commercial

---

**25.** *Cf.* Harry Blackmun, *Address at the 69th Annual Dinner of the American Law Institute* (May 14, 1992), in AMERICAN LAW INSTITUTE, REMARKS AND ADDRESSES AT THE 69TH ANNUAL MEETING 47, 59 (1992) ("We are all in this together, and how vulnerable we all are as we see the turmoil and the struggle all over the world, including our own country.").

**26.** *Aerospatiale*, 482 U.S. at 548 (Blackmun, J., dissenting).

**27.** For a striking example of such a nationalist ruling, see Chief Justice John Roberts's opinion for the Court in *Medellin v. Texas*, 128 S.Ct. 1346 (2008), which declared a judgment of the International Court of Justice is not self-executing in U.S. law, and that "a 'non-self-executing' treaty does not by itself give rise to domestically enforceable federal law. Whether such a treaty has domestic effect depends upon implementing legislation passed by Congress." *Id.* at 1346 n.2.

**28.** 473 U.S. at 638–39.

**29.** 473 U.S. at 628.

tribunals are to promote the "efficient disposition of legal disagreements arising from commercial relations" and "take a central place in the international legal order, national courts will need to" shed "their customary and understandable unwillingness to cede jurisdiction of a claim arising under domestic law to a foreign or transnational tribunal."[30] National courts need to try using multilateral procedural channels, which have the benefit of promoting uniformity and potentially greater efficiency in the resolution of legal disputes. Third, as interdependence grows, *uniformity* and harmonization of both procedural and substantive regulatory norms become an increasingly important values, both as a way of promoting predictability and mitigating conflict among competing sovereignties. Intergovernmentally negotiated treaties and international regimes (such as the various multilateral conventions on transnational procedure described in the chapters above) have the greatest potential for promoting this uniformity, but so too, does executive willingness to seek negotiated solutions in cases such as the Soviet Pipeline or Helms–Burton incidents, and legislative willingness to bring U.S. law into line with that of other nations (as in the foreign sovereign immunity and forum-selection clause areas). Within these regimes, the United States is not the only power, and all U.S. officials—executive, legislative and judicial alike— should act by reference to shared, not simply local, norms.[31] Moreover, as the American Law Institute's *Restatement (Third)* and the ALI/UNIDROIT project on the Transnational Rules of Civil Procedure illustrate, nongovernmental organizations have a critical role to play in promoting transnational uniformity.[32]

Fourth, *separation of powers* plays an important role in this "transnationalist vision." The basic judicial approach (demonstrated by the Court's treatment of the executive position in *Mitsubishi*) has been one of *respectful, but not blind, deference* to executive power. Obviously, the political branches of the government are the most expert branches in dealing with international business matters that touch on foreign affairs, but that should not consign the national courts, in Justice Douglas' famous phrase, to act as "mere errand boy which may choose to pick some people's chestnuts from

---

**30.** 473 U.S. at 639.

**31.** Blackmun, *supra* note 13, at 31 n.65 ("If the substance of the Eighth Amendment is to turn on the 'evolving standards of decency' of the civilized world, there can be no justification for limiting judicial inquiry to the opinions of the United States").

**32.** See discussion of ALI/UNIDROIT Transnational Rules project in

the Foreword and Chapter XI *supra. See also* Harold Hongju Koh, *Why Do Nations Obey International Law?*, 106 YALE L.J. 2599, 2656 (1997) (discussing the constructive role of nongovernmental organizations in transnational legal process and internalizing international rules into domestic legal systems).

the fire, but not others."[33] Particularly when the Executive Branch has embodied its view in a ratified treaty, it is the job of the courts to enforce the treaty consistently with its object and purpose.[34] Thus, although the Court may properly defer to the U.S. Government's expertise on foreign policy matters, it should do so mindful that issues of foreign sovereign immunity, the act of state doctrine, and treaty interpretation are fundamentally legal questions on which courts, not politicians, have the final say.

A key element of transnationalist jurisprudence has been the notion that domestic courts, and not just the political branches alone, have a critical role to play in internalizing international norms into domestic law. As the foregoing chapters have demonstrated, in the transnational litigation area, courts have enunciated federal common law rules for such doctrines as the act of state, *Timberlane* interest-balancing, foreign sovereign compulsion, and *forum non conveniens.* Some nationalist legal scholars have challenged this notion, arguing against the idea that "unelected federal judges [should] apply customary international law made by the world community at the expense of state prerogatives [in which] the interests of the states are neither formally nor effectively represented in the lawmaking process."[35] But as Professor Neuman has noted, none of this is new: because federal courts have applied customary international law since the beginning of the Republic, "one might think it was rather late to claim that judicial application of customary international law was in principle inconsistent with the American understanding of democracy."[36] Moreover, the notion that unelected judges apply law that was made elsewhere is hardly an indictment, but rather, a *description* of the traditional process of common law judging. For every court in the United States—including the state courts that Bradley and Goldsmith champion—applies law that was not made by its own polity whenever the court's own choice-of-law principles so direct. Nor is there anything undemocratic about judges applying norms of customary

---

**33.** First National City Bank v. Banco Nacional de Cuba, 406 U.S. 759, 771 (1972) (Douglas, J., concurring) (citing National City Bank v. Republic of China, 348 U.S. 356, 361–62 (1955)).

**34.** *See Aerospatiale,* 482 U.S. at 552 (Blackmun, J) ("The Convention embodies the result of the best efforts of the Executive Branch, in negotiating the treaty, and the Legislative Branch, in ratifying it, to balance competing national interests. As such, the Convention represents a political determination—one that, *consistent with the principle of*

*separation of powers,* courts should not attempt to second-guess.") (emphasis added).

**35.** Curtis A. Bradley & Jack L. Goldsmith, *Customary International Law as Federal Common Law: A Critique of the Modern Position,* 110 HARV. L. REV. 815, 868 (1997).

**36.** Gerald L. Neuman, *Sense and Nonsense About Customary International Law: A Response to Professors Bradley and Goldsmith,* 66 FORDHAM L. REV. 371, 383 (1997).

law that were made outside the United States, which American judges have done since the beginning of the Republic, whenever they declared rules of customary international law to be part of "general common law."[37] In its seventy-year jurisprudence of "new" federal common law, the Supreme Court has never treated the decisions of unelected federal judges as constitutionally illegitimate, so long as the case involved " 'uniquely federal interests' [which were] so committed by the Constitution and laws of the United States to federal control that state law is pre-empted and replaced . . . by federal law of a content prescribed by the courts."[38]

When construing customary international law, federal courts do not offend the separation of powers, because they arguably exercise less judicial discretion than when making other kinds of federal common law. Their task is not to create rules willy-nilly, but rather, to discern rules of decision from an existing corpus of customary international law rules.[39] Insofar as customary international law rules arise from traditional State practice, the United States has been, for most of this century, the world's primary maker of and participant in this practice. And the United States is also the leading actor in the multilateral treaty drafting processes and fora such as the United Nations, regional fora, standing and ad hoc intergovernmental organizations, and diplomatic conferences, which have become the driving forces in the creation and shaping of contemporary international law.

Perhaps most important, for separation of powers purposes, these federal common law rules of customary international law are perennially subject to a democratic check: supervision, revision, and endorsement by the federal political branches. Take, for example, the federal common law rule of comity in international antitrust cases, discussed in Chapter IV above. As we saw, international comity represents a principle with roots in both common law and international law, which now may be evolving into a rule of customary international law. The rule was first articulated as a

**37.** See id. at 389 ("State judges must have been behaving undemocratically through all the years since 1776 when they were applying international law, whether as 'general common law' or as anything else.").

**38.** Boyle v. United Techs. Corp., 487 U.S. 500, 504 (1988) (quoting Texas Indus., Inc. v. Radcliff Materials, Inc., 451 U.S. 630, 640 (1981)). For a discussion of the legitimacy of federal common lawmaking, see, for example, Stephen B. Burbank, *Federal Judgments Law:*

*Sources of Authority and Sources of Rules*, 70 Tex. L. Rev. 1551, 1571–87 (1992).

**39.** See Louis Henkin, *International Law as Law in the United States*, 82 Mich. L. Rev. 1555, 1561–62 (1984) ("In a real sense federal courts find international law rather than make it, . . . as is clearly not the case when federal judges make federal common law pursuant to constitutional or legislative delegation.").

principle of general common law, which then-Professor Kingman Brewster redefined in his international antitrust treatise as a so-called "jurisdictional rule of reason." In the *Timberlane* case, the Ninth Circuit applied Brewster's analysis to permit U.S. regulation of extraterritorial conduct through an interest-balancing test, which other federal courts then applied as a judicial "brake" on the extraterritorial exercise of U.S. prescriptive jurisdiction.[40] And in time, the American Law Institute's *Restatement (Third) of Foreign Relations Law* adapted *Timberlane*'s interest-balancing test to aid determination of when a nation's exercise of prescriptive jurisdiction is or is not "reasonable," and the United States and foreign governments have begun to follow suit. This story illustrates that federal common law rulemaking in international affairs remains a critical element of the process of transnational legal rulemaking, which I have called in Chapter I, "transnational legal process." In this process, there is no separation of powers problem involved in treating international comity—whether viewed as a rule of statutory construction or justiciability, or a principle of reasonableness—as a doctrine of federal law, generated by all three branches of the federal government, and capable of revision by Congress, the executive branch, or the federal courts, as circumstances demand.

Fifth and finally, with respect to *national sovereignty*, U.S. courts should be mindful of the concept's changing meaning in an interdependent world. In the words of Abram and Antonia Chayes, we live in an era of "The New Sovereignty," in which the key variable is no longer territorial control nor governmental authority, but "status—the vindication of the state's existence as a member of the international system" through its participation in the operation of transnational legal regimes.[41] As the Court's rulings in the sovereignty area show over the past few decades, the Court has treated sovereignty with respectful, but not blind deference. The Court must now be aware that if its rulings are insufficiently respectful of national sovereignty, those rulings "are not necessarily the final word on questions of international law."[42] Thus, U.S. Supreme Court rulings can be subsequently analyzed in other national courts, as well as subjected to review before World Trade Organization panels (as in the Helms–Burton Affair), challenged before an array of international fora, and otherwise tested for their correctness under international law.[43]

---

**40.** Timberlane Lumber Co. v. Bank of America, 549 F.2d 597 (9th Cir. 1976), discussed in Chapter IV, *supra*.

**41.** ABRAM CHAYES & ANTONIA CHAYES, THE NEW SOVEREIGNTY 27 (1995).

**42.** *See* Blackmun, *supra* note 13, at 42.

**43.** *See generally* Koh, *supra* note 7 (describing a number of cases in which such review has been promoted by transnational legal process).

## B.  The Court's Nationalist Jurisprudence

If these are the core tenets of a "transnationalist jurisprudence" of international business transactions, what is the alternative? As I have noted, Justice Blackmun's vision of a jurisprudence mindful of stable and predictable commercial relations, and well-functioning transnational dispute-resolution systems has only partially taken hold in the current Court. With the departure of Justice Blackmun, Justice Scalia, the author of *Weltover, Kirkpatrick*, and the dissent in *Hartford Fire Insurance* emerged as the Court's new expert on international business transactions.[44] At the same time, since his elevation, the new Chief Justice, John Roberts, has taken the lead as the Supreme Court has begun to examine the degree of deference that it owes to the parallel rulings of international judicial bodies.

Although far from coherent, five themes increasingly run through the current Court's "nationalist jurisprudence." First, as I have noted throughout this book, the Court has broadly deferred to executive power to deal with perceived exigencies, largely unchecked by individual rights, framework statutes, or judicial oversight.[45] Second, the Justices have rarely treated treaty or customary international law rules as meaningful restraints upon U.S. action, usually construing them out of context to permit U.S. actions that plainly offend the underlying purpose of the international-law norm.[46] Third, the Court has paid lip service at best to international comity as a reason unilaterally to restrict the scope of U.S. regulation.[47] Fourth, the Court has largely refused to look beyond parochial United States' interests to the needs of an ordered international system when assessing the legality of extraterritorial action. While the Court has sometimes recognized party-autonomy and uniformi-

---

**44.** Although Justice Scalia is now perhaps the leading voice on the Court, he is not the only one. Justice Stevens, who authored lengthy opinions in the Haitian case, *Aerospatiale*, and the dissent in *Mitsubishi* and *Alvarez-Machain*, has strong views in the area, as does Justice Ruth Bader Ginsburg, who came to the bench with prior academic experience in private international law. Justice Souter, a relative neophyte in international law before joining the Court, has gone on to write the important majority opinions in *Nelson v. Saudi Arabia, Hartford Fire Insurance,* and *Sosa v. Alvarez-Machain.*

**45.** *See generally* HAROLD HONGJU KOH, THE NATIONAL SECURITY CONSTITUTION: SHARING POWER AFTER THE IRAN-CONTRA AFFAIR 117–49 (1990) (reviewing cases).

**46.** Harold Hongju Koh, *The "Haiti Paradigm" in United States Human Rights Policy*, 103 YALE L.J. 2391, 2413–23 (1994).

**47.** *See, e.g.,* Hartford Fire Insurance Co. v. California, 509 U.S. 764 (1993) (holding that principle of international comity did not bar district court from exercising Sherman Act jurisdiction over foreign reinsurance claims); *see generally* Harold Hongju Koh, *Transnational Public Law Litigation*, 100 YALE L.J. 2347, 2392 (1991) (reviewing "discernible decline in the American deference to foreign sovereignty").

256

ty and predictability as values, it has exhibited no consistent consciousness about the need to promote thus values. Moreover, Justice Scalia's proclivity toward historical and conflict-of-laws approaches has privileged an abiding commitment to territoriality, not transnationalism, as the driving jurisprudential value. Fifth and finally, the Court has shown only minimal deference to the rulings of international tribunals on parallel issues of law, and far less deference than it shows to the judgments of foreign courts. In *Sanchez–Llamas v. Oregon*, Chief Justice Roberts declared that an International Court of Justice ruling regarding the Vienna Convention on Consular Relations was entitled to "respectful consideration."[48] But in *Medellin v. Texas,* decided the following term, the Court took the additional step of saying that final judgments of the International Court of Justice are not self-executing and do not constitute binding federal law.[49]

Taken together, these tenets of the Court's "territorialist" or "nationalist" jurisprudence have empowered the executive branch to act unilaterally in the international realm, at times based upon subjective and myopic assessments of our national interests. In so acting, U.S. officials have generally consulted local rules, customs and cultures, while ignoring extraterritorial impacts, and giving far too little weight to foreign laws or sensibilities. Congress, our treaty partners, and other affected nations and nationals have found few meaningful avenues of protest, as the courts have construed ambiguities in previously negotiated accords—whether inter-branch or intergovernmental—to permit the executive action. Nor have injured private individuals had much recourse, being deemed to lack standing or even rights to challenge arbitrary executive action.

The result: a realist world in which an American judicial focus on national self-interest has too often trumped human rights (of citizens, and especially aliens), democratic decisions, and the settled expectations that flow from negotiated agreements and shared norms.[50] Under this vision, concerns about conflict of laws, separation of powers, national sovereignty, and party autonomy have overridden concerns about comity, international law, and the development of uniform substantive and procedural rules. One might well ask whether our law wouldn't be better served by prudent

**48.** 548 U.S. 331, 126 S.Ct. 2669, 2685 (2006). For an analysis of the decision and its precedents, see generally Steven Arrigg Koh, *"Respectful Consideration" After* Sanchez–Llamas v. Oregon: *Why the Supreme Court Owes More to the International Court of Justice*, 93 CORNELL L. REV. 243 (2007).

**49.** 128 S.Ct. 1346 (2008).

**50.** *See* Koh, *supra* note 46, at 2391, 2409–34 (tracing this pattern in the context of the Haitian refugee crisis of the 1990s).

application of Justice Blackmun's "transnationalist canon" in the *Aerospatiale* case, the notion that courts "must look beyond U.S. interests to the 'mutual interests' of all nations in a smoothly functioning international legal regime" and "consider if there is a course that furthers, rather than impedes, the development of an ordered international system."[51]

In the last decade, the transnationalist/nationalist divide within our own Supreme Court's jurisprudence has evolved into a contentious public debate over whether and when U.S. courts may cite or follow foreign or international law in constitutional interpretation.[52] The nationalist/transnationalist debate now consumes much of the recent scholarship on international law in U.S. courts. And significantly, whatever their rhetoric may be, nearly every member of the current Court has, at one time or another, looked to foreign or international practice or precedent to illuminate interpretations of the U.S. Constitution.[53] Chief Justice Rehnquist, a

**51.** Societe Nationale Industrielle Aerospatiale v. United States Dist. Court, 482 U.S. 522, 555, 567 (1987) (Blackmun, J., concurring in part)

**52.** For discussions of this debate, see generally Harold Hongju Koh, *The Ninth Annual John W. Hager Lecture, The 2004 Term: The Supreme Court Meets International Law*, 12 Tulsa J. Comp. & Int'l L. 1 (2004); Harold Hongju Koh, *International Law as Part of Our Law*, 98 Am. J. Int'l L. 43 (2004).

**53.** In footnote 10 of his recent opinion in Medellin v. Texas, 128 S.Ct. 1346 n.10 (2008), Chief Justice Roberts, an outspoken opponent of citing foreign and international law by "looking out over a crowd and picking our your friends," cited Moroccan and Belgian cases to demonstrate that World Court judgments are not binding as a matter of municipal law, but omitted mention, for example, of a contrary decision of the German Constitutional Court of Sept. 19, 2006 on the effect of ICJ decisions in the domestic law of the Germany. *See also* Planned Parenthood v. Casey, 505 U.S. 833, 945 n.1 (1992) (Rehnquist, C.J., concurring in part and dissenting in part) (citing abortion decisions by West German Constitutional Court and Canadian Supreme Court); Thompson v. Oklahoma, 487 U.S. 815, 830, 851 (1988) (Stevens, J.) (finding that execution of juveniles violates norms shared "by other nations that share our Anglo–American heritage, and by the leading members of the Western European community"); *id.* at 851 (O'Connor, J., concurring) (noting that U.S. had agreed by ratifying Article 68 of the Geneva Convention to set a minimum age of 18 for capital punishment in certain circumstances); Enmund v. Florida, 458 U.S. 782, 796–97 n.22 (1982) (O'Connor, J.) (noting elimination or restriction of felony murder in England, India, Canada, and a "number of other Commonwealth countries"); United States v. Stanley, 483 U.S. 669, 710 (1987) (O'Connor, J., concurring in part and dissenting in part) (relying on Nuremberg Military Tribunals in arguing against nonconsensual medical experimentation on humans); McIntyre v. Ohio Elections Comm'n, 514 U.S. 334, 381 (1995) (Scalia, J., dissenting) (arguing that Australian, Canadian, and English legislation banning anonymous campaign speech suggest that such bans need not impair democracy); Zadvydas v. Davis, 533 U.S. 678, 721 (2001) (Kennedy, J., dissenting) (stating that particular detention of aliens "accords with international views" and referencing Report of U.N. Working Group on Arbitrary Detention & U.N. High Comm'r for Refugees, *Guidelines on Detention of Asylum–Seekers*); Washington v. Glucksberg, 521 U.S. at 785–87 (Souter, J., concurring) (examining Dutch constitutional

leading Nationalist on the Court that bore his name, announced that "now that constitutional law is solidly grounded in so many [foreign] countries, *it is time that the United States courts begin looking to the decisions of other constitutional courts to aid in their own deliberative process.*"[54] Important Supreme Court decisions in such diverse areas as international business, cyberspace, the death penalty, immigration, gay and lesbian rights, as well as post–9/11 controversies, have divided along transnationalist/nationalist lines.[55] As in other areas of the Court's jurisprudence, the swing Justice is Anthony Kennedy, who has not yet firmly committed himself to one side or another of the debate.[56]

I began this book by asking, "Does the U.S. Supreme Court have a discernable jurisprudence of transnational civil litigation?" I close with my answer: that upon inspection, it has not one, but two.

practice on physician-assisted suicide); Holder v. Hall, 512 U.S. 874, 906 n.14 (1994) (Thomas, J., concurring) (mentioning voting systems of Belgium, Cyprus, Lebanon, New Zealand, West Germany, and Zimbabwe in assessing race consciousness in U.S. voting system); Nixon v. Shrink Mo. Gov't PAC, 528 U.S. 377, 403 (2000) (Breyer, J., concurring) (finding Court's First Amendment jurisprudence consistent with decisions of European Court of Human Rights and Canadian Supreme Court); Knight v. Florida, 528 U.S. 990, 995–98 (Breyer, J., dissenting from denial of certiorari) (finding instructive decisions of Privy Council, Supreme Court of India, Supreme Court of Zimbabwe, European Court of Human Rights, Canadian Supreme Court, and U.N. Human Rights Committee on whether lengthy delay in execution renders it inhumane).

**54.** William H. Rehnquist, *Constitutional Court—Comparative Remarks (1989), reprinted in* GERMANY AND ITS BASIC LAW: PAST, PRESENT AND FUTURE—A GERMAN-AMERICAN SYMPOSIUM 411, 412 (Paul Kirchhof & Donald P. Kommers eds., 1993) (emphasis added). As the Chief Justice explained:

> For nearly a century and a half, courts in the United States exercising the power of judicial review had no precedents to look to save their own, because our courts alone exercised this sort of authority. When many new constitutional courts were created after the Second World War, these

courts naturally looked to decisions of the Supreme Court of the United States, among other sources, for developing their own law. But now that constitutional law is solidly grounded in so many countries, it is time that the United States courts begin looking to the decisions of other constitutional courts to aid in their own deliberative process.

*Id.*; *see also* Raines v. Byrd, 521 U.S. 811, 828 (1997) (Rehnquist, C.J.) (noting European law on legislative standing but declining to find it in U.S. constitutional regime); Washington v. Glucksberg, 521 U.S. 702, 710, 718 n.16, 785–87 (1997) (Rehnquist, C.J.) (declaring that "in almost every State—indeed, in almost every western democracy—it is a crime to assist a suicide" and noting that "other countries are embroiled in similar debates" concerning physician-assisted suicide, citing Canadian Supreme Court, British House of Lords Select Committee, New Zealand's Parliament, Australian Senate, and Colombian Constitutional Court).

**55.** See cases cited in Koh, International Law as Part of Our Law, *supra* note 52.

**56.** Thus, Justice Kennedy wrote the majority opinions in Lawrence v. Texas, 539 U.S. 558 (2003) (invalidating Texas same sex sodomy statute) and Roper v. Simmons, 543 U.S. 551 (2005) (declaring juvenile death penalty cruel and unusual punishment), but silently joined the majority in Medellin v. Texas.

The first is a nationalist jurisprudence that looks backward to territory and sovereignty and sideways toward executive power. This approach looks curiously inward at a time when our allies look outward to greater reliance on international law to facilitate international commerce, migration, and democratization. The other is a "transnational jurisprudence," which looks forward toward political and economic dependence and outward to rules of international law and comity to play their traditional functions in coordinating international system interests and promoting a well-functioning international commercial system.

The Twenty First Century is still young, and these issues are destined with time to command only a greater share of America's judicial dockets in the years ahead. Only time will tell which of these visions will ultimately prevail in shaping the jurisprudence of transnational litigation in United States Courts in the new global century.

# TABLE OF CASES

Principal cases are in bold type. Non-principal cases
are in roman type. References are to Pages.

*

# INDEX

**References are to Pages.**

269

✝